1991
The Supreme Court Review

1991
The

"Judges as persons, or courts as institutions, are entitled to
no greater immunity from criticism than other persons
or institutions . . . [J]udges must be kept mindful of their limitations and
of their ultimate public responsibility by a vigorous
stream of criticism expressed with candor however blunt."
—*Felix Frankfurter*

". . . while it is proper that people should find fault when
their judges fail, it is only reasonable that they should recognize the
difficulties. . . . Let them be severely brought to book,
when they go wrong, but by those who will take the trouble
to understand them."
—*Learned Hand*

THE LAW SCHOOL

THE UNIVERSITY OF CHICAGO

Supreme Court Review

EDITED BY

DENNIS J. HUTCHINSON

DAVID A. STRAUSS

AND GEOFFREY R. STONE

THE UNIVERSITY OF CHICAGO PRESS

CHICAGO AND LONDON

INTERNATIONAL STANDARD BOOK NUMBER: 0-226-09574-6

LIBRARY OF CONGRESS CATALOG CARD NUMBER: 60-14353

THE UNIVERSITY OF CHICAGO PRESS, CHICAGO 60637

THE UNIVERSITY OF CHICAGO PRESS, LTD., LONDON

© 1992 BY THE UNIVERSITY OF CHICAGO, ALL RIGHTS RESERVED, PUBLISHED 1992

PRINTED IN THE UNITED STATES OF AMERICA

The paper used in this publication meets the minimum requirements of American National Standard for Information Sciences—Permanence of Paper for Printed Library Materials, ANSI Z39.48-1984. ∞

TO THE UNIVERSITY OF CHICAGO

on the occasion of its Centennial

"[U]niversities exist for the long run. They are the custodians not only of the many cultures of man, but of the rational process itself. Universities are not neutral. They do exist for the propagation of a special point of view: namely, the worthwhileness of the intellectual pursuit of truth. . . ."

—Edward H. Levi (1968)

CONTENTS

LEE C. BOLLINGER

THE END OF NEW YORK TIMES
v SULLIVAN:
REFLECTIONS ON MASSON
v NEW YORKER MAGAZINE

Virtually every year since *New York Times v Sullivan*,[1] the Supreme Court has decided at least one or two First Amendment cases involving the press. This now seemingly permanent, annual pageant of media cases undoubtedly has significance for the development of both constitutional law and the character of American journalism, though oddly that significance has been little explored in the scholarly literature. This past year the Court had two cases, both of which received an unusual amount of discussion within the press. It is, of course, understandable, even if not wholly defensible, for the press to give disproportionate coverage to the press cases before the Court, but these two received even more than the usual share of publicity.[2] To say that the press did not look very good in either

Lee C. Bollinger is Dean and Professor, University of Michigan Law School.

AUTHOR'S NOTE: I want to thank the following individuals for comments and advice on earlier drafts of this article: Vincent A. Blasi, Robert A. Burt, Larry Kramer, Richard H. Pildes, James B. White, and Yoichiro Yamakawa. I would also like to acknowledge the valuable research assistance I received from Teresa Snider.

[1] 376 US 254 (1964).

[2] E.g., *Libel Law; Don't Quote Me*, The Economist, Jan. 19, 1991, at 27:

> The first amendment guarantees America the world's freest press; also, ironically, its most defensive and self-important one. Criticism[s], no matter how niggling, are often met with pages of pompous lecturing about "journalistic ethics" and the indispensability of reporters (even those on television) to the "democratic dialogue." More serious charges—such as those made in big libel cases—get the same treatment, only the ink is spilt by the barrel rather than by the bucket.

one would be an understatement. The reputation of journalism was blemished.

The Court decided both cases within a week of each other, in its usual last-minute rush to finish the Term.[3] The first was *Cohen v Cowles Media Co.*,[4] in which a reporter promised a source that his identity would not be revealed and then the editors overruled the reporter and published the source's identity. When the source sued for breach of contract, the press raised the First Amendment as a bar to recovery of damages.

In the other decision, *Masson v New Yorker Magazine*,[5] the Court was confronted with a libel action brought by an individual (Masson) who claimed that the defendants had published an article in which he was quoted as saying things he never in fact said. As the case was presented to the Supreme Court, the reporter (Janet Malcolm) and the press (*The New Yorker Magazine* and Knopf) conceded for purposes of their motion for summary judgment that some quotations had, indeed, been deliberately "fabricated," but also asserted the First Amendment protected their right to do so.[6]

Needless to say, the right to break promises and the right to fabricate quotes do not seem like promising cases for expanding First Amendment protection for the press. And many within the press waited anxiously for the Court's responses, and probably even with some ambivalence about which way they hoped the Court would come out. It is, understandably, against a journalist's nature to wish to lose a case before the Supreme Court, but here the reasons for harboring at least a secret wish were fairly strong. While losses in these cases could induce an avalanche of cases against the press for broken promises and misquotes,[7] the freedom to break promises of confidentiality or to fabricate quotes might well significantly reduce the willingness of people to be informants or interviewees. Laws restricting the press sometimes help the press too. A victory for the press might also turn pyrrhic very

---

[3] David A. Kaplan & Bob Cohn, *The Annual Rush to Judgment*, Newsweek, July 1, 1991, at 67.

[4] 111 S Ct 2513 (1991).

[5] *Masson v New Yorker Magazine, Inc.*, 111 S Ct 2419 (1991).

[6] Id.

[7] Linda Greenhouse, *Justices Refuse to Open a Gate for Libel Cases*, NY Times, June 21, 1991, at A1; Albert Scardino, *Ethics, Reporters and The New Yorker*, NY Times, Mar. 21, 1989, at C20.

quickly, becoming a stimulus for public resentment toward an arrogant press with unreasonable rights.[8] Whether it achieved a victory or suffered a defeat in each of these cases, however, the press no doubt also dreaded a judicial lecture about the general sins of modern journalism, which might in itself create an inhospitable climate in the lower courts for years to come and stimulate an already negative climate of public opinion about the press, which sometimes manifests itself in legal results (juries, after all, decide libel cases).[9]

It was, therefore, seemingly with some relief that the press watched its compatriots lose in both cases without many of the ill consequences the press feared from an unfriendly, or possibly even hostile, Court.[10] The Court sent both cases back for further proceedings, holding that states can force the press to live up to their promises just like anyone else and that the press can be sued for libel if they make up quotes that "materially" depart from the "substance" of what the plaintiff actually said.[11] A tone of sensibleness, of wholesome reasonableness, seemed to pervade both decisions; the middle course appeared to have been taken.

In this article I want to examine one of these decisions—the *Masson* case—closely, and at two levels. The *Masson* decision raises extremely interesting and important issues about the dimensions

---

[8] See, e.g., Joan Beck, *Court Strikes Just the Right Balance in Ruling on Quotations*, Chi Trib, June 24, 1991, Sec 1, at 11 ("To ask the Supreme Court to rule that the 1st Amendment protects even deliberately falsified quotes seemed arrogant and dangerous. Too much of the public already distrusts the media. Such a decision would further erode our credibility and raise new questions about 1st Amendment rights."); Doug Ramsey, *A Free Press Can Take the Heat*, LA Times, Mar. 26, 1988, Part 2, at 8:

> With a persistent current feeling in the United States that somehow the press should be given its comeuppance, there is a clear and present danger to the venerable and cherished notion that only with a free press can a free people receive the uncensored information it needs to make its choices. Journalists need to closely examine their professional behavior; that is essential.

[9] See Lee C. Bollinger, *Images of a Free Press* 40–61 (1991); Ramsey at 8 (cited in note 8) ("In the last decade, Americans' dissatisfaction with newspeople seems to have grown. . . .").

[10] See, e.g., *A Controversy Over Quotations . . .* , Wash Post, June 23, 1991, at B6 ("Thursday's opinion strikes us as a balanced one that puts no unreasonable burden on the press."); Paul Gray, *Justice Comes in Quotes*, Time, July 1, 1991, at 68 ("[T]he reaction from most reporters, though hardly unanimous, tended toward a collective sigh of relief that the decision showed a subtle sensitivity to their craft."); *Reporters: Get It Right or Get Out of the Business*, Newsday, July 1, 1991, at 32 ("This is a decision every responsible journalist should be able to live with.")

[11] *Cohen v Cowles Media Co.*, 111 S Ct 2513 (1991); *Masson v New Yorker Magazine, Inc.*, 111 S Ct 2419 (1991).

of the constitutional exception for defamation law. We have not by any means seen the end of the problems raised by *Masson*. Moreover, *Masson* is significant for what it reveals about the phenomenon of an annual stream of decisions involving the press, which I noted at the outset.

I begin with a close look at the facts of *Masson* and then turn to the constitutional problems presented to, and decided by, the Court.

I. MASSON: THE CONSTITUTIONAL CONTEXT AND THE COURT'S DECISION

In *Masson*, the Court was confronted with a strikingly complicated problem. Indeed, the case is so analytically puzzling that it is easy to become mildly obsessed with trying to unravel its complexities—a fact that, as we shall see, may itself contain an important lesson for the press about its future litigation strategy.

In thinking about the First Amendment, libel, and fabricated quotes, one must begin with the fountainhead of *New York Times v Sullivan*. We know from that decision and its sequels several things relevant to this case: Since Masson concedes he is a public figure, he bears the burden of establishing that the fabricated quotes, or defamatory statements, were published with "actual malice," that is, with knowledge or reckless disregard of their falsity. He must show this with "clear and convincing" evidence. And there must be some proof of actual harm brought about by the publication.[12] This adds up to a trinity of basic requirements: A (1) knowing (or reckless) (2) falsehood (3) causing reputational injury.

Most of the Court's time in the libel area over the past nearly three decades has been devoted to defining who are "public officials" and "public figures" for purposes of the Constitution.[13] In

---

[12] In *Gertz*, the Court found that the "state interest extends no further than compensation for actual injury." *Gertz v Robert Welch, Inc.*, 418 US 323, 349 (1974). Therefore, it held that in defamation suits by private individuals, "the States may not permit recovery of presumed or punitive damages, at least when liability is not based on a showing of knowledge of falsity or reckless disregard for the truth." Id. Although the court declined to define "actual injury," it did go on to say that "the more customary types of actual harm inflicted by defamatory falsehood include impairment of reputation and standing in the community, personal humiliation, and mental anguish and suffering." Id at 350.

[13] See, e.g., *Philadelphia Newspapers, Inc. v Hepps*, 475 US 767 (1986); *Gertz v Robert Welch*, 418 US 323 (1974); *Curtis Publishing Co. v Butts* and *Associated Press v Walker*, 388 US 130 (1967).

comparison very little attention has been paid to exploring what
can be taken, constitutionally, as a "libelous" or "defamatory" statement. In the Court's most recent case in the libel area, however,
Milkovich v Lorain Journal Co.,[14] the Court did confront that question to some extent, with a press claim that any statement of "opinion" is constitutionally protected. The Court refused to "create a
wholesale defamation exception" for statements of "opinion," saying that as long as the challenged statement, whether explicitly or
implicitly, communicated or was understood as communicating a
statement of fact it was properly actionable under the Constitution.[15]

In severely trimming back the common law action for defamation, *New York Times v Sullivan* developed a now-famous theoretical
foundation for approaching not only the constitutionally permissible scope for libel law but also for thinking about virtually all
First Amendment issues. According to *Sullivan*, the fundamental
purpose of the First Amendment is to establish and preserve a
system of wide-open discussion in order to serve a democratic form
of government.[16] The principle of freedom of speech and press is
premised on a deep distrust of the government, whose anti-
democratic instincts are volcanic in both power and unpredictabil-
ity, characteristics infamously memorialized by the Sedition Act
of 1798.[17] To achieve an authentic and vigorous system of self-
government, therefore, one must be overly generous to speech,
especially because the average citizen is easily discouraged from
participating in public affairs. The prospect of libel judgments is
daunting to most, and the legal system is imperfect at separating
good from bad defamation claims. Therefore, the line of constitutional protection must be moved considerably beyond the ideal
line. Though libelous statements may not be of positive value to
the society, the interests of the First Amendment command that
they must be endured. We need to favor bad discussion so as not
to unduly discourage good discussion. The essence of *Sullivan*,
therefore, is a celebration of the constitutional commitment to a
world in which debate on public issues is "uninhibited, robust, and
wide-open."[18]

---

[14] 110 S Ct 2695 (1990).

[15] Id at 2705–06.

[16] *New York Times v Sullivan*, 376 US 254, 269–70 (1964).

[17] Sedition Act of 1798, 1 Stat 596 (expired by its own terms in 1801).

[18] 376 US at 270.

Sullivan and its successors are exceedingly important to defining both basic First Amendment theory and the constitutional space left for state libel law. Yet there are absolutely vital matters on which the decision (and its sequels) is strangely silent. The first and perhaps most notable omission from the Court's libel decisions is any justifications for why there should be *any* exception at all for libel actions. After all, under the First Amendment the press can lie, misrepresent, distort, be viscious and unfair about many matters, all with the impunity that comes with full protection of the First Amendment. Only if the press lies about a particular *individual* in a way that injures his or her reputation may the press be held legally accountable. That is what *New York Times v Sullivan* did. It severely cut back the traditional common law action for libel, but it did not take it down root and branch (as Justices Douglas and Black recommended [19]). Therefore, libel law remains today one of the few exceptions to First Amendment protection of the press. It is, needless to say, somewhat ironic that *Sullivan* provided a basic theory for the First Amendment but did not provide a theory for why the particular regulation of speech it upheld was justified when other forms of regulation are not. [20]

The second major omission in the *New York Times v Sullivan* analysis is any consideration of how libelous remarks can damage public discourse and undermine the very values that animated the Court to protect them (absent actual malice) in the first place. Falsehoods, of course, may not only injure an individual's reputation but mislead the public as well. Moreover, sensitive individuals, those who place a high value on their reputations within the community, may choose to forego politics altogether rather than put their reputations at risk. *Sullivan*'s passionate defense of freedom

---

[19] Id at 297 (Black, J, and Douglas, J, concurring).

[20] In 1942, in *Chaplinsky v New Hampshire*, 315 US 568 (1942), the Supreme Court first identified libel, among other areas of speech, as excluded from first amendment protection. "[S]uch utterances," the Court reasoned, "are no essential part of any exposition of ideas, and are of such slight social value as a step to truth that any benefit that may be derived from them is clearly outweighed by the social interest in order and morality." 315 US at 572. This is as close as the Court has come to giving a reason why there should be an exception for libel, but it is not very close. It is simply unclear why false statements of fact injurious to the reputations of individuals are less "part of any exposition of ideas" or of "such slight social value as a step to truth" than other forms of misrepresentations that regularly occur (including about groups of individuals) with the full protection of the First Amendment. For an argument that speech having "slight social value" can still have value from a First Amendment standpoint, see Lee C. Bollinger, *The Tolerant Society* 179–86 (1986).

of speech and press ignores the costs of liberty to the character and quality of the public debate it purports to regard as the ultimate value and the foundation of its decision.

A

Masson v New Yorker Magazine [21] is a case that invites artistic exploration and leaves the legal analyst feeling inadequate. Apart from its analytical complexity, it is a wellspring of ironies. It is also built upon layers of allegations of betrayal.

Jeffrey Masson is the central figure in this drama. Everything emanates from Masson's appointment as Projects Director of the Sigmund Freud Archives, which are located near London and contain the writings and other personal documents of Sigmund Freud. Masson had come to this position through meeting two famous psychoanalysts, Dr. Kurt Eissler and Dr. Anna Freud, Sigmund Freud's daughter. He himself had undergone psychoanalytic training, while pursuing a career as a Sanskrit scholar. [22]

Masson's charm for Eissler and Anna Freud, however, soon dissipated. The year after his appointment he delivered a lecture at the Western New England Psychoanalytical Society in New Haven, Connecticut, at which he introduced the theme that would ultimately lead to his dismissal as Director of the Freud Archives. His claim was that Sigmund Freud had abandoned the so-called "seduction" theory of neurosis, under which all neurotic behavior was believed traceable to actual incidents of incestuous seduction or abuse of the patient, for a theory that identifies neurosis with the patient's early fantasy life of Oedipal love and fear of abuse. Masson charged Freud with having changed his theory knowing that it was false in order to enhance his reputation. Not one to shy away from controversy, Masson closed his lecture with a declaration of the "sterility of psychoanalysis throughout the world." [23]

In 1982, Janet Malcolm conducted a series of interviews with Masson for articles she eventually wrote for *The New Yorker* magazine. [24] These were subsequently combined and became a book enti-

---

[21] 111 S Ct 2419 (1991).

[22] Id at 2424.

[23] See id at 2424, 2427.

[24] Janet Malcolm, *Annals of Scholarship: Trouble in the Archives* (pts. 1 & 2), New Yorker, Dec. 5, 1983, at 59, New Yorker, Dec. 12, 1983, at 60.

tled *In the Freud Archives* (published by Knopf).[25] As noted in the Court's opinion, "[o]ne of Malcolm's narrative devices consists of enclosing lengthy passages in quotation marks, reporting statements of Masson, Eissler, and her other subjects."[26] The articles in *The New Yorker* appeared in late 1983. The book appeared in the following year.

Malcolm recounted the events surrounding Masson's appointment as Projects Director of the Freud Archives and his eventual dismissal from that position. The overall effect of the book, with its voluminous quotations mixed with Malcolm's commentary, is to portray Masson's character as one few readers would admire unreservedly. One contemporaneous review of *In the Freud Archives* (quoted by the Supreme Court) describes Malcolm's story and technique and their devastating consequences for Masson's image: "Masson, the promising psychoanalytic scholar, emerges gradually, as a grandiose egotist—mean-spirited, self-serving, full of braggadocio, impossibly arrogant and, in the end, a self-destructive fool. But it is not Janet Malcolm who calls him such: His own words reveal this psychological profile—a self-portrait offered to us through the efforts of an observer and listener who is, surely, as wise as any in the psychoanalytic profession."[27] Undoubtedly, this is one glowing review Malcolm now feels she could have done without.

In 1984 Masson sued for libel in the United States District Court. Since Malcolm had tape recorded approximately forty hours of interviews with Masson, Masson's litigating strategy was simply to compare the transcripts of the taped interviews with the actual quotations in the book. Eventually the alleged discrepancies were narrowed to six instances.[28] Since this is not a case to play with paraphrase, and since it is extremely important to see how the Court conceived of the issue to be decided, what follows is the Court's description of Masson's claims of fabrication:

> (a) *"Intellectual Gigolo."* Malcolm quoted a description by [Masson] of his relationship with Eissler and Anna Freud as follows:

[25] Janet Malcolm, *In the Freud Archives* (1984).

[26] 111 S Ct at 2424.

[27] Robert Coles, *Freudianism Confronts Its Malcontents*, Boston Globe, May 27, 1984, at 58, 60, quoted in *Masson*, 111 S Ct at 2425.

[28] 111 S Ct at 2425.

" 'Then I met a rather attractive older graduate student and I had an affair with her. One day, she took me to some art event, and she was sorry afterward. She said, "Well, it is very nice sleeping with you in your room, but you're the kind of person who should never leave the room—you're just a social embarrassment anywhere else, though you do fine in your own room." And you know, in their way, if not in so many words, Eissler and Anna Freud told me the same thing. They like me well enough "in my own room." They loved to hear from me what creeps and dolts analysts are. I was like an intellectual gigolo—you get your pleasure from him, but you don't take him out in public. . . .' "

The tape recordings contain the substance of [Masson's] reference to his graduate student friend, but no suggestion that Eissler or Anna Freud considered him, or that he considered himself, an " 'intellectual gigolo.' " Instead, [Masson] said:

"They felt, in a sense, I was a private asset but a public liability. . . . They liked me when I was alone in their living room, and I could talk and chat and tell them the truth about things and they would tell me. But that I was, in a sense, much too junior with the hierarchy of analysis, for these important training analysts to be caught dead with me."

(b) *"Sex, Women, Fun."* Malcolm quoted [Masson] as describing his plans for Maresfield Gardens, which he had hoped to occupy after Anna Freud's death:

" 'It was a beautiful house, but it was dark and sombre and dead. Nothing ever went on there. I was the only person who ever came. I would have renovated it, opened it up, brought it to life. Maresfield Gardens would have been a center of scholarship, but it would also have been a place of sex, women, fun. It would have been like the change in *The Wizard of Oz*, from black-and-white into color.' "

The tape recordings contain a similar statement, but in place of the reference to "sex, women, fun," and *The Wizard of Oz*, [Masson] commented:

"[I]t is an incredible storehouse. I mean, the library, Freud's library alone is priceless in terms of what it contains: all his books with his annotations in them; the Schreber case annotated, that kind of thing. It's fascinating."

[Masson] did talk, earlier in the interview, of his meeting with a London analyst:

"I like him. So, and we got on very well. That was the first time we ever met and you know, it was buddy-buddy, and we were to stay with each other and [laughs] we were

going to pass wommen on to each other, and we were
going to have a great time together when I lived in the
Freud house. We'd have great parties there and we were
[laughs]—

. . .

". . . going to really, we were going to live it up."

(c) "*It Sounded Better.*" [Masson] spoke with Malcolm about
the history of his family, including the reasons his grandfather
changed the family name from Moussaieff to Masson, and why
[Masson] adopted the abandoned family name as his middle
name. The article contains the passage:

" 'My father is a gem merchant who doesn't like to stay in
any one place too long. His father was a gem merchant,
too—a Bessarabian gem merchant, named Moussaieff,
who went to Paris in the twenties and adopted the name
Masson. My parents named me Jeffrey Lloyd Masson, but
in 1975 I decided to change my middle name to
Moussaieff—it sounded better.' "

In the most similar tape recorded statement, Masson explained at considerable length that his grandfather had changed
the family name from Moussaieff to Masson when living in
France, "[j]ust to hide his Jewishness." [Masson] had changed
his last name back to Moussaieff, but his then-wife Terry ob-
jected that "nobody could pronounce it and nobody knew how
to spell it, and it wasn't the name that she knew me by." [Mas-
son] had changed his name to Moussaieff because he "just liked
it." "[I]t was sort of part of analysis: a return to the roots, and
your family tradition and so on." In the end, he had agreed
with Terry that "it wasn't her name after all," and used Moussaieff as a middle instead of a last name.

(d) "*I Don't Know Why I Put It In.*" The article recounts part
of a conversation between Malcolm and [Masson] about the
paper [Masson] presented at his 1981 New Haven lecture:

"[I] asked him what had happened between the time of the
lecture and the present to change him from a Freudian
psychoanalyst with somewhat outre views into the bitter
and belligerent anti-Freudian he had become.

"Masson sidestepped my question. 'You're right, there
was nothing disrespectful of analysis in that paper,' he
said. 'That remark about the sterility of psychoanalysis
was something I tacked on at the last minute, and it was
totally gratuitous. I don't know why I put it in.' "

The tape recordings instead contain the following discussion
of the New Haven lecture:

Masson: "So they really couldn't judge the material. And,
in fact, until the last sentence I think they were quite
fascinated. I think the last sentence was an in, [sic] possi-

bly, gratuitously offensive way to end a paper to a group of analysts. Uh,—"

Malcolm: "What were the circumstances under which you put it [in]? . . ."

Masson: "That it was, was true.

. . . . .

". . . I really believe it. I didn't believe anybody would agree with me.

. . . . .

". . . But I felt I should say something because the paper's still well within the analytic tradition in a sense.

. . . . .

". . . It's really not a deep criticism of Freud. It contains all the material that would allow one to criticize Freud but I didn't really do it. And then I thought, I really must say one thing that I really believe, that's not going to appeal to anybody and that was the very last sentence. Because I really do believe psychoanalysis is entirely sterile . . . ."

(e) "*Greatest Analyst Who Ever Lived.*" The article contains the following self-explanatory passage:

"A few days after my return to New York, Masson, in a state of elation, telephoned me to say that Farrar, Straus & Giroux has taken *The Assault on Truth* [Masson's book]. 'Wait till it reaches the best-seller list, and watch how the analysts will crawl,' he crowed. 'They move whichever way the wind blows. They will want me back, they will say that Masson is a great scholar, a major analyst—after Freud, he's the greatest analyst who ever lived. Suddenly they'll be calling, begging, cajoling: "Please take back what you've said about our profession; our patients are quitting." They'll try a short smear campaign, then they'll try to buy me, and ultimately they'll have to shut up. Judgment will be passed by history. There is no possible refutation of this book. It's going to cause a revolution in psychoanalysis. Analysis stands or falls with me now.'"

This material does not appear in the tape recordings. [Masson] did make the following statements on related topics in one of the taped interviews with Malcolm:

". . . I asure you when that book comes out, which I honestly believe is an honest book, there is nothing, you know, mean-minded about it. It's the honest fruit of research and intellectual toil. And there is not an analyst in the country who will say a single word in favor of it."

"Talk to enough analysts and get them right down to these concrete issues and you watch how different it is from my position. It's utterly the opposite and that's finally what I realized, that I hold a position that no other analyst holds, including, alas, Freud. At first I thought: Okay, it's me and Freud against the rest of the analytic world, or me and Freud and Anna Freud and Kur[t] Eissler and Vic Calef and Brian Bird and Sam Lipton against the rest of the world. Not so, it's me. It's me alone."

The tape of this interview also contains the following exchange between [Masson] and Malcolm:

Masson: ". . . analysis stands or falls with me now."

Malcolm: "Well that's a very grandiose thing to say."

Masson: "Yeah, but it's got nothing to do with me. It's got to do with the things I discovered."

(f) "*He Had The Wrong Man.*" In discussing the Archives' board meeting at which [Masson's] employment was terminated, Malcolm quotes [Masson] as giving the following explanation of Eissler's attempt to extract a promise of confidentiality:

" '[Eissler] was always putting moral pressure on me. "Do you want to poison Anna Freud's last days? Have you no heart? You're going to kill the poor old woman." I said to him, "What have I done? *You're* doing it. *You're* firing me. What am I supposed to do—be grateful to you?" "You could be silent about it. You could swallow it. I know it is painful for you. But you could just live with it in silence." "Why should I do that?" "Because it is the honorable thing to do." Well, he had the wrong man.' "

From the tape recordings, on the other hand, it appears that Malcolm deleted part of [Masson's] explanation (italicized below), and [Masson] argues that the "wrong man" sentence relates to something quite different from Eissler's entreaty that silence was "the honorable thing." In the tape recording, [Masson] states:

"But it was wrong of Eissler to do that, you know. He was constantly putting various kinds of moral pressure on me and, 'Do you want to poison Anna Freud's last days? Have you no heart?' He called me: 'Have you no heart? You're going to kill the poor old woman. Have you no heart? Think of what she's done for you and you are now willing to do this to her.' I said, 'What have I, what have I done? *You* did it. You fired me. What am I supposed to do: thank you? be grateful to you?' He said, 'Well you could never talk about it. You could be silent about it. You could swallow it. I know it's painful for you but just live with it in silence.' 'Fuck you,' I said, 'Why should I do that? Why? You know, why should one do that?' 'Because it's the honorable thing to do *and you will save face. And who knows? If you never speak about it and you quietly and humbly accept our judgment, who knows that in a few years if we don't bring you back?* Well, he had the wrong man." [29]

_____
[29] Id at 2425–28 (citations omitted).

The case went through the early stages of discovery and Malcolm and *The New Yorker* then moved for summary judgment. Since Masson conceded he was a public figure, under the rule of *New York Times v Sullivan* he would lose on the summary judgment motion if the record as it stood would not "permit a reasonable finder of fact, by clear and convincing evidence, to conclude that respondents published a defamatory statement with actual malice as defined by our cases." [30] Both the District Court [31] and the Court of Appeals [32] concluded that the allegedly fabricated quotations did not warrant submission to a jury. It was assumed, for purposes of reaching this judgment, that Malcolm had deliberately changed the quotations from those on the tapes. Malcolm claimed, and continues to claim, that if the summary judgment motion fails she will present evidence that the quotes do accurately reflect what Masson said in conversations with her that were not tape recorded.

B

The Supreme Court's opinion begins with a description of California libel law. The working legal rule in that state, as in other states, is that "[l]ibel is a false and unprivileged publication by writing . . . which exposes any person to hatred, contempt, ridicule, or obloquy, or which causes him to be shunned or avoided, or which has a tendency to injure him in his occupation." [33] The Court observed that under California law it is appropriate to focus on "only part of the work" in determining whether it is "false" or "defamatory." [34] And so: " '[T]he test of libel is not quantitative; a single sentence may be the basis for an action in libel even though buried in a much longer text,' though the California courts recognize that '[w]hile a drop of poison may be lethal, weaker poisons are sometimes diluted to the point of impotency.' " [35]

Turning to the constitutional standard of *New York Times v Sullivan*, the Court repeated the usual well-known rules. One notewor-

---

[30] Id at 2428.

[31] *Masson v New Yorker Magazine, Inc.*, 686 F Supp 1396, 1407 (ND Cal 1987).

[32] *Masson v New Yorker Magazine, Inc.*, 895 F2d 1535, 1546 (9th Cir 1989).

[33] 111 S Ct at 2429.

[34] Id.

[35] Id (quoting *Washburne v Wright*, 68 Cal Rptr 224, 228 (1968)).

thy aspect of the Court's discussion, however, is its recommendation that the term "actual malice" be abandoned. The Court
described the term actual malice as simply a "shorthand" meant
only "to describe the First Amendment protections for speech injurious to reputation . . . ." [36] The Court said the term "can confuse
as well as enlighten," and since the "phrase may be an unfortunate
one," "it is better practice that jury instructions refer to publication
of a statement with knowledge of falsity or reckless disregard as to
truth or falsity." [37]

At this point the analysis begins. The Court's posture is to take
the middle course between two extreme positions. The structure
of the opinion creates and reinforces this impression. It starts with
the issue of what quotation marks "indicate to the reader." [38] Its
conclusion is simple and straightforward: "In general, quotation
marks around a passage indicate to the reader that the passage
reproduces the speaker's words verbatim." [39] The Court further
observed that a "fabricated quotation *may* injure reputation" in at
least two ways.[40] First, the false quotation may be substantively
untrue. For example, "a fabricated quotation of a public official
admitting he had been convicted of a serious crime" would be
defamatory "when in fact he had not." [41] Second, a fabricated quotation may be defamatory "because the manner of expression or
even the fact that the statement was made indicates a negative
personal trait or an attitude the speaker does not hold." [42] In a
somewhat incongruous example for a Supreme Court opinion (one
that perhaps reveals the drafting influence of younger law clerks),
the Court referred to a quotation once attributed to John Lennon
that the Beatles were "more popular than Jesus Christ now." [43]
Though the substance of that statement may be true, said the

---

[36] Id at 2430.

[37] Id.

[38] Id.

[39] Id. The Court acknowledged that quotation marks do not always indicate a verbatim
transcription to the "reasonable reader." Id. In historical fiction, for example, the reader is
not led to understand that the speaker actually said the words quoted. Id at 2430–31.

[40] Id at 2430 (emphasis added).

[41] Id.

[42] Id.

[43] Id (quoting Time, Aug. 12, 1966, at 38).

Court, it might still be defamatory because people would think less of Lennon for having said it.[44]

Having said all this, the Court reaches its conclusion about what Malcolm's quotes signify to the reasonable reader. Malcolm's work, the Court said, "provides the reader no clue that the quotations are being used as a rhetorical device or to paraphrase the speaker's actual statements. To the contrary, the work purports to be non-fiction, the result of numerous interviews."[45] Furthermore, the Court observes, Malcolm's work "contains lengthy quotations attributed to petitioner, and neither Malcolm nor her publishers indicate to the reader that the quotations are anything but the reproduction of actual conversations,"[46] and *The New Yorker* is a magazine that "seemed to enjoy a reputation for scrupulous factual accuracy," which would itself contribute to a reader taking "the quotations at face value."[47] All these factors could lead a reasonable trier of fact to find Malcolm's quotations as offering a "nearly verbatim" account of Masson's remarks.[48]

C

With this the Court felt it was ready to face the main question at hand, whether the defendants acted "with the requisite knowledge of falsity or reckless disregard as to truth or falsity."[49] To the Court that "inquiry" required a focus on the "concept of falsity."[50]

The Court's analysis proceeds by rejecting, on the one hand, a claim nobody was making, namely, that "*every*" alteration of a speaker's actual words constitutes sufficient "falsity" to satisfy the Constitution and, on the other hand, the rule applied by the lower courts in this case, that the Constitution protects any quotation that is a "rational interpretation" of what the individual actually said.[51] Against these two poles, the Court opted for a standard under which a libel plaintiff must show that there is a "material

---

[44] Id.

[45] Id at 2431.

[46] Id.

[47] Id.

[48] Id.

[49] Id.

[50] Id.

[51] Id (emphasis added).

change in the meaning" conveyed by the quotation compared to that conveyed by the actual statements.[52] The issue, according to the Court, is whether there is "substantial truth" in the reconstructed quotation.[53]

The Court's reasoning for this conclusion is neither entirely consistent nor well developed. To support the case that any change in the actual statement should not permit the states to impose liability the Court asserts simply that reporters "by necessity" alter what subjects say to "eliminate grammatical and syntactical infelicities." [54] It is not entirely clear of what this "necessity" consists, but the Court does offer the additional assertion, which it repeats at several points in the opinion, that it is standard journalistic practice to alter quotations to some extent: "If every alteration constituted the falsity required to prove actual malice, the practice of journalism, which the First Amendment standard is designed to protect, would require a radical change, one inconsistent with our precedents and First Amendment principles." [55] Perhaps it is only quibbling to ask for more, but one is moved to say that, of course, the "practice of journalism" would have to be changed and that's precisely the point. It also seems fair to ask the Court to explain why such a standard, which admittedly leaves the states considerable room to develop libel actions, is nevertheless "inconsistent with . . . precedents and First Amendment principles." [56]

In any event, Masson's position was not that extreme. Masson's claim is that journalists should be free to change "grammar or syntax" but not the actual "words" spoken by the plaintiff. Since there is "falsity" (because the plaintiff did not say these words in this fashion) so long as the journalist "knew" that "words" were added or subtracted, then the actual malice standard should be regarded as satisfied.[57] The Court describes Masson as making the obvious point that to protect more would be to allow more "falsehoods," which it is further said would contravene the First Amendment interest in creating a "well-informed public".[58]

---

[52] Id at 2433.

[53] Id.

[54] Id at 2431.

[55] Id.

[56] Id.

[57] Id.

[58] Id.

Once again the Court answers this position with the simple assertion that, at least in the case of the "interviewer who writes from
notes," journalists will "often" attempt "a reconstruction of the
speaker's statement." [59] The Court never pauses to consider
whether there is any discrepancy, and, if so, what it might mean,
between its frequent claims about it being standard journalistic
practice to alter (even reconstruct) quotations and its opening conclusion that "[i]n general, quotation marks around the passage indicate to the reader that the passage reproduces the speaker's words
verbatim." [60] If standard journalistic practice is as the Court says,
then one wonders whether readers really have a contrary expectation. And if they do, then one wonders how this gap arose and
whose understanding or practice should be respected.

The opinion continues in this vein: Even when there is a tape
recording of the interview, the Court says, it assumes that a "full
and exact statement will be reported in only rare circumstances." [61]
The Court's reasoning here is unclear. The opinion seems to claim
that journalists must make changes in quotes in order to remain
faithful to the "truth" of an interview: "The existence of both a
speaker and a reporter; the translation between two media, speech
and the printed word; the addition of punctuation; and the practical
necessity to edit to make intelligible a speaker's perhaps rambling
comments, all make it misleading to suggest that a quotation will
be reconstructed with complete accuracy." [62] Sometimes, as with
"an obvious misstatement, for example by unconscious substitution
of one name for another, a journalist might alter the speaker's
words but preserve his intended meaning." [63] On the other hand,
the Court observes, changes in punctuation alone may "distort a
speaker's meaning"; and a literal quotation "out of context" could
also be distorting. [64]

But this is a peculiar way to think about the problem raised by
Masson. Masson's claim is not, as this portion of the Court's opinion appears to assume, that a quotation with only "grammar or
syntax" corrected (or changed) is necessarily non-defamatory, but

---

[59] Id at 2432.

[60] Id at 2430.

[61] Id at 2432.

[62] Id.

[63] Id.

[64] Id.

only that this is a workable line that will minimize defamatory quotations and yet accord the press some flexibility to render actual statements readable. It is also the case that Masson's position does not depend upon a conclusion that any "word" change is necessarily defamatory. Again, the question is what degree of *constitutional* intrusion into state libel law there should be, and it is certainly arguable that the constitutional interests can be adequately served if the state has more power than it needs to implement its interest in protecting individual reputations.

The Court argues that a "grammar and syntax" test would not be "workable," saying that the only "method by which courts or juries would draw the line between cleaning up and other changes" would be "by reference to the meaning a statement conveys to a reasonable reader."[65] Besides not being a "workable" line, however, the grammar and syntax rule would be a "departure from the underlying purposes of the tort of libel as understood since the latter half of the 16th century."[66] The traditional function of tort law, according to the Court, is to "redress injury to the plaintiff's reputation by a statement that is defamatory and false."[67] This, the Court continues, is also the basis for the constitutional exception, namely recognition of the state interest in "compensation of individuals for the harm inflicted on them by defamatory falsehood."[68] By this passage alone the Court appears to embrace an "injury to reputation" requirement as part of the constitutional standard—a matter about which I will have more to say at a later point.

The Court then moves toward its holding. First it reasserts the position it took the year before in *Milkovich v Lorain Journal Co.*,[69] that the courts should avoid, as much as possible, creating a web of constitutional privileges and doctrines in the libel area.[70] Then it announces that the plaintiff may recover for libel only when, viewed from the mind of the reasonable reader, the contested statement lacks "substantial truth" or affects a "material change in the meaning" of the speaker's actual words.[71] "Put another way," the

---

[65] Id.

[66] Id.

[67] Id.

[68] Id (quoting *Gertz v Robert Welch, Inc.*, 418 US 323, 341 (1974)).

[69] 110 S Ct 2695 (1990).

[70] 111 S Ct at 2432.

[71] Id at 2433.

Court says, "the statement is not considered false unless it 'would have a different effect on the mind of the reader from that which the pleaded truth would have produced.'"[72] This, concludes the Court, is also the constitutional definition of "actual malice."[73] And so the Court states its holding: "We conclude that a deliberate alteration of the words uttered by a plaintiff does not equate with knowledge of falsity for purposes of *New York Times Co. v Sullivan* and *Gertz v Robert Welsh, Inc.*, unless the alteration results in a material change in the meaning conveyed by the statement."[74] Contrary to Masson's claim, the Court decides that deliberately fabricated quotations are not necessarily without constitutional protection; but it also decides that changes of punctuation, grammar, or syntax are not necessarily entitled to constitutional protection.[75]

D

Having now selected the relevant constitutional principle, the Court sets out to explain why it rejects the more extreme principle of protection applied by the Court of Appeals in this case. From the Supreme Court's perspective, the Court of Appeals had also applied a version of the "substantial truth" test, but it had interpreted it broadly to protect quotations that are a "rational interpretation" of the plaintiff's actual statements.

The Court begins with a self-evident observation that, while "a rational interpretation" test gives greater "interpretive license" to the press, it also creates a gap in the understanding of the average reader (that the quotation is verbatim) and the reality (that the reporter has "interpreted" the statement).[76] Of course, exactly the same could be said of the Court's own choice of a test of "substantial truth," or "a material difference in meaning," since there, too, the reader assumes (by the Court's own initial premise) a "verbatim" quote but receives an interpreted one.[77]

The opinion continues with the observation that this degree of constitutional protection would give journalists greater freedom to

---

[72] Id (quoting R. Sack, *Libel, Slander and Related Problems* 138 (1980)).

[73] Id (citations omitted).

[74] Id.

[75] Id.

[76] Id at 2434.

[77] Id at 2433.

"place statements in their subjects' mouths without fear of liability." [78] At this point, however, the Court says something quite interesting, even remarkable. It worries openly about extending constitutional protection this far because it would "diminish to a great degree the trustworthiness of the printed word, and eliminate the real meaning of quotations." [79] Additionally, the Court suggests "[n]ewsworthy figures might become more wary of journalists." [80] For the Court, the "values of the First Amendment" would be "ill serve[d]" by the "rational interpretation" test. [81] The Court, therefore, rejects the greater degree of constitutional protection afforded to the press under the Court of Appeals' standard because of a concern about the adverse effects the speech so protected would have on the *quality of public discourse.*

E

After observing that this is a case to be decided in the context of a summary judgment motion, such that all reasonable inferences must be drawn in Masson's favor, and that Masson "is [therefore] correct in denying that he made the statements attributed to him by Malcolm, and that Malcolm reported with knowledge or reckless disregard of the differences between what petitioner said and what was quoted," the Court turns to apply its test to the facts of this case. [82] First, with respect to the "intellectual gigolo" quote, the Court agreed with the dissenting opinion in the Court of Appeals that "[f]airly read, intellectual gigolo suggests someone who forsakes intellectual integrity in exchange for pecuniary or other gain." [83] A "reasonable jury," the Court concluded, could find that this constitutes a material difference in meaning from Masson's actual statement. [84]

---

[78] Id at 2434.

[79] Id. For some reason the Court seemed to think this would occur because the Court of Appeals' standard would "eliminat[e] any method of distinguishing between the statements of the subject and the interpretation of the author," when it seems fairly clear that the problem, to the extent there is a problem, is not the absence of a "method" but the degree of freedom extended under that standard.

[80] Id.

[81] Id.

[82] Id at 2435.

[83] Id (quoting 895 F2d at 1551) (Kozinski, J, dissenting).

[84] Id at 2435.

With respect to the "sex, women, fun" passage, the Court reached the same conclusion, saying that, even though Masson's other tape-recorded remarks indicated that he and another analyst planned to have great parties at the Freud house and, in a context that may not even refer to Freud house activities, "to 'pass women on to each other,'" it would be reasonable to find a material difference in meaning.[85]

On the other hand, with respect to the "it sounded better" quotation, the Court found no material difference, holding that Malcolm did "convey the gist of [Masson's] explanation: [p]etitioner took his abandoned family name as his middle name."[86] It is noteworthy that here the Court defines the "material difference in meaning" test as requiring simply that the attributed statement "convey the gist" of what a party said.[87] That seems like a fairly lenient standard. However, the Court seems unaware that the problem is not in Masson's description of what he did in fact (namely, take his family name as his middle name) but in the *reason* for doing that— which was not that "it sounded better" but that he "just liked" the name Moussaieff.[88] In other words, the difference may not be defamatory, in the sense that Masson could reasonably be regarded as harmed, but it certainly is a different reason than the quotation ascribes.

As to the "I don't know why I put it in" quotation, the Court found that a reasonable jury could believe this materially different from what Masson actually said in his lecture about the "sterility of psychoanalysis." Malcolm quoted Masson as saying that he added that to his lecture for "no particular reason," when the tape showed that Masson said he had done it because "it was true . . . I really believe it."[89] "[I]t is conceivable," the Court said, "that the alteration results in a statement that could injure a scholar's reputation."[90]

For the "greatest analyst who ever lived" quotation, the Court held that a "material difference exists" and that "a jury could find

---

[85] Id at 2436.
[86] Id.
[87] Id.
[88] Id at 2426.
[89] Id at 2437.
[90] Id.

that the difference exposed petitioner to contempt, ridicule or obloquy." [91] The Court's view of the gap is expressed in this statement:
"While petitioner did, on numerous occasions, predict that his theories would do irreparable damage to the practice of psychoanalysis, and did suggest that no other analyst shared his views, no
tape-recorded statement appears to contain the substance or the
arrogant and unprofessional tone apparent in this quotation." [92]

Finally, as to the "he had the wrong man" quotation, the Court
also concluded that "a jury might find it defamatory." [93] The opinion interprets Masson's actual statement as meaning that he was
"willing to undergo a scandal in order to shine the light of publicity
upon the actions of the Freud Archives," and Malcolm's quotation
as making Masson appear to say that he was the "wrong man" to
do "the honorable thing." [94]

II. Making the Case for Legal Control of Fabricated Quotations

The facts of the *Masson* case stir deep and strong emotions,
generating feelings that lead us to want law available to punish
and stop such behavior. It is useful to begin by exploring these
underlying emotions and the case for liability they might support.

Malcolm has said, in a book written after her encounters with
Masson, that all relationships between reporters and subjects "end
badly." [95] Indeed, anyone who is interviewed by the press hopes
for a completely uncritical story, and that hope is often fanned by
the insinuations of reporters who use pride as an ally to obtaining
revealing answers. But the wish for glorification is often unfulfilled
in life, and just because the flatteries of the reporter do not materialize in print, our understanding—but not the power of the law—is
all we should extend to the interviewee who feels cheated.

At some level, moreover, we understand that a reporter must
reconstruct and order what a person has said orally when producing a written account. As readers, we are impatient with the impre-

---

[91] Id.

[92] Id.

[93] Id.

[94] Id.

[95] Janet Malcolm, *The Journalist and the Murderer* (1990).

cision and meanderings of talk. If we ever stop to think about it, therefore, we expect some rearranging. And the longer the quotations the more that is probably going to be true. The Court, therefore, probably overstated the degree to which the average reader expects a quotation to be a "verbatim" recording of what the interviewee actually said.

On the other hand, to say that some change in what purports to be an interviewee's actual words is expected is not necessarily to concede that wholesale invention is. Nor, as in so many areas of life (including the First Amendment itself), does our inability to define exactly where the line between appropriate and inappropriate change occurs mean that no change is ever inappropriate. The line, to the extent one can articulate it, is between minor editing and "rewriting."[96] This is a line every writer knows, precisely because every writer has experienced the sense of loss of authorship from being over-edited. Certainly, if the reporter consciously distorts and plays with the record, hoping perhaps to make a more saleable, juicier story, or wishing to do the subject in, then our inclination to condemn the reporter seems wholly justified. When people (including journalists) hear what Malcolm is alleged to have done, my experience is that they feel she clearly violated the obligation of fidelity to the actual statement.[97] In a sense, she did to

---

[96] An editorial in the *Chicago Tribune* explained:

[j]ournalists do change—"edit" is a more accurate description—some of the words they use as direct quotes. They clean up grammatical errors. They delete obscenities. They sometimes condense comments to make points quickly and clearly. But they should do so with a professional obligation to avoid distortions or misrepresentations or untruths.

Telling the Truth in Quotes, Chi Trib, Mar. 17, 1991, Editorial Section, at 2.

[97] See, e.g., id at 2 ("What Malcolm is charged with doing cannot be defended. No responsible journalist can condone making up quotes, especially when they are used to put the source in an unfavorable light."); Alex S. Jones, *Just How Sacrosanct Are the Words Inside Quotation Marks?*, NY Times, Jan. 20, 1991, Sec 4, at 6 ("By journalistic standards, if Ms. Malcolm did pipe the quotes, she would be guilty of dishonesty and unprofessional behavior."). See also Brief of Amici Curiae Reporters Committee for Freedom of the Press, American Newspaper Publishers Association, the Society of Professional Journalists, and Radio-Television News Directors Association in Support of Respondents, *Masson v New Yorker Magazine, Inc.*, 895 F2d 1535 (9th Cir 1989) (No. 89-1799) ("The inaccurate or altered quote is not a goal of good journalists. . . . The first amendment does not protect only ethical journalists."); Brief of Amici Curiae the Time Inc. Magazine Company, American Society of Newspaper Editors, National Association of Broadcasters, the Authors Guild, Inc., The Point Reyes (California) Light, College Media Advisors, Inc., Student Press Law Center, American Civil Liberties Union, Newsletter Association, Edmund Morris and David McCullough, *Masson v New Yorker Magazine, Inc.*, 895 F2d 1535 (9th Cir 1989) (No. 89-1799) ("Amici disapprove of deliberate alteration of fabrication of quotes.").

Masson what she says he did to Freud and what Masson said Freud did to others. She crossed this line, and in doing so committed a serious breach of journalistic ethics.[98] She was entitled, ethically (without misrepresenting what she was doing by using quotation marks), to edit Masson's remarks into a coherent whole. But Malcolm's changes went beyond that and had an adverse effect on how Masson would be perceived by the general reader. To have him "say" that he refused to behave honorably because he was not an honorable person, when his actual statement indicates a quite different, and honorable, intention; to have him "say" that he thought himself the greatest analyst ever when his actual statement says his discovery was the greatest discovery ever; or to have him "say" that to Eissler and Anna Freud he was like an "intellectual gigolo" when his actual statement indicates a relationship far less sleazy—these are the sorts of changes in meaning that leave the realm of editing for the realm of editorial invention.

It is one of the many ironies in this very special case that Malcolm, who made her reputation in part by an extremely sensitive popular rendering of the profession of psychoanalysis,[99] should be in the position of claiming that there is not a significant difference between quoting what in the reporter's view a person essentially "meant" and what a person actually said. For it is part of the essence of psychoanalysis that particular words matter, and often matter immensely. Presumably, no respectable analyst would conduct therapy through paraphrase. This view of the importance of language—that the way in which a given person puts together words, in what patterns and forms, is extremely meaningful—is even reflected in some cases in the First Amendment jurisprudence. *Cohen v California*, for example, emphasized that California could not strike out the word "Fuck" on Cohen's jacket ("Fuck the Draft") without materially altering the meaning of Cohen's "message."[100] No other word, or words, would make the sentence mean quite the same thing.

This leads to another point, one that has to do with how we interpret what a given substituted word, or set of words, "means"

---

[98] Many feel a "reporter has a basic responsibility to play it straight and get it right." Curtis Sitomer, *The Press Must Get It Right*, Christian Sci Monitor, Oct. 5, 1989, at 13. See also supra note 97.

[99] Janet Malcolm, *Psychoanalysis: The Impossible Profession* (1981).

[100] 403 US 15, 26 (1971).

in the world. Consider again the fabricated intellectual gigolo remark. The question, as the Court rightly observes, is what impact
does this have on the reader and how is it different from the impact
the actual statement would have had. The Court's approach to this
issue, however, is quite literal. It concludes that "[f]airly read,
intellectual gigolo suggests someone who foresakes intellectual integrity in exchange for pecuniary or other gain." [101] This sounds
like a dictionary. There are echoes here of Justice Harlan's amusing
priggishness in his opinion for the Court in *Cohen v California*, when
he paraphrased Cohen's statement "Fuck the Draft" as merely a
protest to the inutility or "immorality of the draft." [102] Surely one
does not have to ask the Court to travel in literary circles to at least
understand that the impact of a given statement may transcend its
literal meaning. The intellectual gigolo quote is also harmful because of its sexual overtones, because it leaves behind images in
the mind of an eroticism in the relationship between Eissler and
Anna Freud and Masson, because it indicates that Masson sees
others as sexually obsessed with him or that he thinks in sexual
terms. It characterizes the relationship as having an element of
sexual titillation, which his actual words do not say. We need to
pay attention to the subtle impact of language.

But the evils of fabricated statements, and therefore our objections to them, go well beyond any narrow conception of reputational injury traditionally associated with libel law. There is something important to us, however elusive it is to define, in being able
to control how we present ourselves to the world, which is violated
when others falsely attribute statements to us. What is involved is
a loss of identity, which is all the more painful because it appears
to come from our own hands. The violation we feel has a resonance
with, for example, our revulsion toward legally mandated loyalty
oaths.

There is still another dimension to our sense of outrage at an
author's fabrication of quotations. Like instances of academic pla-
giarism, scientific fraud, or government corruption, this is a kind
of *intellectual* violation that undermines our trust in the entire profession of journalism. Coming from one of our most distinguished

---

[101] 111 S Ct at 2435 (quoting *Masson v New Yorker Magazine, Inc.*, 895 F2d 1535, 1551
(Kozinski, J, dissenting)).

[102] 403 US at 18.

and prestigious publications, it is only natural that people will now be more wary of journalism generally.[103] Because the integrity of public discourse relies upon the good will and faith of authors, when that is broken our trust generally must be suspended.

Furthermore, this specific breach of ethics may also be part and parcel of a general decline in the quality of public discourse. Ghost-written speeches and books, the illusions of the Congressional Record, and, indeed, judicial opinions written by law clerks—all this is troublesome or ought to be troublesome for a system of self-government that is so dependent upon the integrity of discourse.

It is, therefore, with considerable concern, for specific individuals as well as for the general quality of public discussion that we expect law to play some role as a deterrent of fabricated quotes — fully recognizing that law will perhaps be of only limited helpfulness in solving the problems of which this is a part. But without the pressure that law can bring on individuals to behave properly in this area, we must expect a greater number of incidents of falsified quotations and, as a result, either a loss of public trust in the linguistic practice of quotation, which gives us as readers a less mediated access to reality than does paraphrase, or public deceit if people continue to place naive trust in quotations. Either way we suffer a serious loss.

III. The Masson Case and the Spirit of Sullivan

Now I want to look at the problem of *Masson* from the other direction, to consider the strong pro-freedom of the press spirit of *New York Times v Sullivan* and to ask where it would lead in resolving *Masson*. My ultimate thesis is that there is a serious discrepancy between the tone, and nature, of the analysis in the Court's opinion in *Masson* and that in *Sullivan*, and I want to begin to explore that discrepancy here.

Earlier, in summarizing the analysis of *Sullivan*, we saw how the Court stressed the need to see the issue not in the narrow terms of a particular libel lawsuit but in the broadest possible terms of what

---

[103] See, e.g., *Press*, Time, Aug. 21, 1989, at 49 ("Journalists publicize any prominent reporter's willful lapse from factuality because they consider it uncommon, hence newsworthy; the irony is that the coverage prompts many readers to assume that such failings are widespread.").

degree of legal intervention into public dialogue a healthy, vital system of self-government can sustain. The image of a regime of seditious libel was utilized as a reference point for appreciating the untrustworthiness of government when it comes to regulating speech.[104] And the Court's intellectual framework for deciding what First Amendment limits must be placed on libel actions was rounded out with a candid acknowledgement of the imperfections of the legal system and a recognition of how the potential exposure to lawsuits can quickly make citizens disenchanted with the charms of participation in public debate.[105]

One would expect this to be the analytic foundation for approaching *Masson* too. Moreover, with the passage of twenty-seven years since *New York Times v Sullivan*, one would also expect the Court to assess the experience with the libel system left intact by *Sullivan*. A common complaint of the press, for example, is that juries in libel actions are often biased against the press.[106] One might, accordingly, think the Court would consider the relevance of that experience for the issue of *Masson*.

But there is a deeper insight still in *Sullivan* that is of special importance for *Masson*. The essence of *Sullivan*'s intellectual approach, in taking the analysis to what Kalven correctly saw as "very high ground indeed,"[107] is rooted in the felt need to correct for the human inclination to condemn bad speakers and to forget (or insufficiently appreciate) in the process the broader, the maybe even somewhat less intuitively self-evident, commitment and need of a democratic society for a vigorous policy of open debate. The *Sullivan* analysis implicitly warns us against the tendency to be shortsighted about achieving our interests and cautions us that a choice for self-government necessarily, if unfortunately, means bearing some costs.

What this leads to—or what might be thought of as the end of *Sullivan*—is the constitutional principle that the press can be subjected to liability *only* when the state interest recognized in *Sullivan* as sufficient to justify a special constitutional exemption is

---

[104] *Sullivan*, 376 US at 273–77.

[105] Id at 278.

[106] Bollinger at 50 (cited in note 9).

[107] Harry Kalven, Jr., *The New York Times Case: A Note on "The Central Meaning of the First Amendment*," 1964 Supreme Court Review 191, 209.

present—namely, when a knowing (or reckless) falsehood threatens serious injury to an individual's reputation.

This observation has particular relevance for *Masson*, because entangled within the facts of that case are (at least) *two* falsehoods, one of which is relevant to the *Sullivan* exception and one of which is not. Earlier I said that *Masson* is analytically very complex and confusing. There are, I believe, several consequences that arise from this fact, but one is that our thinking about the constitutional issue at stake in the case is distorted by the presence of a serious but nonetheless constitutionally irrelevant aspect of Masson's allegations about Malcolm's journalistic misbehavior. It is, as we have seen, common and natural in thinking about *Masson* to characterize the issue as that of the freedom to "fabricate quotations." And, as the argument in the preceding discussion makes clear, that claim activates in most peoples' minds a broad range of concerns about the deficiencies of modern journalism.

But the act of falsely purporting to repeat a person's nearly exact wording or statement, while certainly bad as a matter of journalistic ethics, is not necessarily *defamatory* in the traditional sense of libel law, or at least not in the sense that *Sullivan* understood. While it may well be true, as the preceding section argued, that fabricated quotes to some extent "misrepresent" a person to the world, libel law has historically been concerned with insuring only that a person's reputation or standing within a community is not seriously diminished. It would be a considerable extension of this original state interest (or redefinition of the concept of reputational harm) to now say that *any* altering of the public's understanding of "the truth" of an individual—even a positive one—can be made the basis for a damage claim or for other forms of official regulation. Of course, as the preceding section also made clear, our outrage over the fabrication of quotes is based not only in our concern for the individual subject but also with the author's deception of readers. This is, once again, a very serious matter. But, so far at least, it is not a sufficient basis for removing constitutional protection. A reporter (Janet Cooke) of the *Washington Post*, for example, once invented a story about a ghetto child on drugs.[108] It was first awarded a Pulitzer prize and then, when discovered to be wholly fabricated, universally condemned, despite her claim that there

---

[108] Janet Cooke, *Jimmy's World*, Wash Post, Sept. 28, 1980, at A1.

were real children who lived *like* this.[109] Few, presumably, would think that Cook or the *Washington Post* could constitutionally have been held legally accountable for this deceit.

To extend *Sullivan*, which was decided in the context of an asserted state interest in preserving individual reputation against falsehoods, to permit the legal cleansing of deceits and misrepresentations of all kinds from public discourse would involve a dramatic contraction of constitutional protection for the press. Constitutional adjudication would then be focused broadly on the quality of public debate, not merely on the goal of protecting individual reputation.

This is not to say that the false attribution of actual words to an individual is entirely irrelevant to the question whether a person has been defamed. Recognizing that false paraphrase as well as misquoting may cause the community to think less of a person, it is nonetheless true that a false quotation may contribute specially to a diminished reputation because readers are sometimes more inclined to believe, to accept as true, that a speaker said this than they would be if presented with a reporter's paraphrase. One must be careful, however, not to overstate the degree to which readers regard quotations as more credible assertions of what some public official actually said than authors' non-verbatim descriptions. The credibility of any characterization—whether by quotation or paraphrase—will depend upon the reputation for accuracy of the author as well as the gullibility of the reader, both of which are independent of the method of characterization used. Intelligent readers of a purportedly verbatim account should know that much of a context of the statement, which can be the real source of meaning, is missing. For this very reason appellate courts are forbidden from reviewing trial courts' findings of fact, precisely because transcripts of testimony lack important elements of communication and hence meaning.

In sum, Masson's charge against Malcolm involves two kinds of deception that must be separated. One is the claim that the use of quotation marks created the mistaken impression in the minds of readers that Masson had actually said these words (perhaps with some minor editing). The second is that the *substance* of the remarks

---

[109] Arnold B. Sawislak, *Washington News*, UPI, Apr. 15, 1981, available in LEXIS, Nexis Library, UPI File.

attributed to Masson left a false impression in the minds of readers about Masson, an *unfavorable* impression that injured his reputation or standing in the community at large. While the first charge is not wholly irrelevant to the constitutional exception recognized in *Sullivan*, it is relevant only in a subsidiary way to the main constitutional issue, which is raised by the second claim of deception.

Now, the problem of the presence of dual falsehoods in a fabricated quotation case is not simply that we must be careful that the integrity-of-public-discourse concerns are not the basis of the defamation concern or action. Rather it is that we must be careful that our outrage over the integrity-of-public-discourse concerns does not affect or influence, covertly, the evaluation of the defamation claim. To keep these two matters separate, however, will not be easy and it would be important for the Court in *Masson* to address that potential confusion, and perhaps even to create a presumption of nondefamatory meaning in order to counteract this source of potential bias in fabricated quotes cases. The Court should stress that what really matters, as far as the Constitution is concerned, is whether the statement falsely attributed to the plaintiff (not the fact of the actual words or language but the meaning) did produce a false and significantly damaging image of the plaintiff.

In fact, the best way to approach the issue of *Masson* is not by asking what First Amendment protection there should be for fabricated quotations but rather by asking what First Amendment protection there should be for vigorous public *discussion* of all kinds about what public officials and public figures say. Otherwise we are too likely to lose sight of the importance and depth of our commitment to the principle of open debate. Our free speech nerves are more on edge when the proposal is to permit lawsuits against ordinary citizens and the press for "misrepresenting," or "unfairly" reporting what public officials and figures have "said." Then it is clear that analyzing, restating, and interpreting the comments of powerful individuals is just as vital to a democratic society as describing what they did or what they are like. Imagine how constraining it would be on public discussion if the press knew that a court might ultimately decide whether what they reported a politician said was a "reasonable," or "substantially true," interpretation of his or her remarks. The task of interpreting what individual speakers really "mean" by their remarks or statements is just as difficult and open to the beneficial process of collective interpretation—both wise and obtuse—as that of translating, say, a poem of Baudelaire from French to English. Intonation and facial expression, for example, make irony and sarcasm possible and, therefore, even verbatim accounts as a single method of conveying true meaning impossible.

A fundamental problem raised by *Masson*, therefore, is that of articulating the latitude we think the Constitution should guarantee to citizens, and the press, to report on the statements of public officials and public figures. Framed in this way, we understand immediately that the inquiry into "falsity" in this context, which is essentially one of interpretation of meaning, is highly uncertain and ambiguous. For the First Amendment that means, not that an "interpretation" can never be "unfair" or cause injury to reputation, but that a legal inquiry is far less certain of yielding a correct answer as to whether it is, which means, in turn, that the costs (e.g., time and legal expenses) of litigation and the opportunity for an anti-open debate bias to covertly affect the ultimate judgment are much greater.[110] It is out of these concerns that historically defamation law has been limited to actions for false statements of *fact*. To say that someone "used cocaine" is easier, and therefore safer from a First Amendment standpoint, to litigate in a libel action than to say that someone has "no status" in his or her profession.[111]

---

[110] On the importance of a First Amendment concern with avoiding doctrines that will inhibit discussion and allow excessive anti-press bias, see, e.g., *Gertz v Robert Welch, Inc.*, 418 US 323, 349 (1974):

> The largely uncontrolled discretion of juries to award damages where there is no loss unnecessarily compounds the potential of any system of liability for defamatory falsehood to inhibit the vigorous exercise of First Amendment freedoms. Additionally, the doctrine of presumed damages invites juries to punish unpopular opinion rather than to compensate individuals for injury sustained by the publication of a false fact.

[111] *Ollman v Evans*, 750 F2d 970 (DC Cir 1984). In this case, a professor of political science, Bertell Ollman, brought suit against two newspaper columnists. Mr. Ollman claimed the journalists had defamed him in a newspaper column which resulted in his being denied a nomination for chairman of the political science department at his university. One of the allegedly defamatory statements contained in the column was a supposed quote from another political scientist that *"Ollman has no status within the profession, but is a pure and simple activist."* Id at 973. The court recognized that an "individual's interest in his or her reputation is of the highest order," id at 974, but saw the main difficulty in the case as determining whether a statement was litigable fact or constitutionally protected opinion. This process of differentiation between fact and opinion is a matter of law. Id at 978. The court listed four factors which would aid it in determining whether a reader would view a statement as fact or opinion: "common usage or meaning of the specific language of the challenged statement itself[;]" verifiability—whether the statement is "capable of being objectively characterized

Reporting on what someone "said" falls into this latter category. The degree of "factualness" is far less, and this should mean for the First Amendment, not necessarily that recovery should be completely barred, but rather that the legal system should be permitted to intervene only when the challenged report constitutes a patent misinterpretation.

We must also be careful not to place too much weight on the misbehavior involved in instances of fabricated quotes. A long and distinguished line of First Amendment cases, which includes *Sullivan*, forcefully articulates both how easily good people in public debate slip into error and how easily good people with good contributions to make are discouraged from making those contributions by the fear of being taken in some future litigation to have acted willfully.[112] Particularly with a lengthy work like Malcolm's, it can be difficult to keep track of every quotation and every reference. Though Malcolm did not face a next-day deadline, surely she did not write completely without a sense of deadline. And the size of her project, essentially a book, may have led to a less-than-complete final double checking of what she had written. (Can the Justices on the Supreme Court testify that they have always read every case and article cited in their opinions?) As writing nears its end, writers often fall prey to the wish to be done. And, as for the future use of quotations should Malcolm be held liable, we might very well expect authors to shy away from that important language device.[113] That would be unfortunate.

We should also approach *Masson* with a healthy disrespect for the capacity of law to accomplish its purposes in an area like this. To permit states to prohibit and punish all fabricated quotations on its face seems indisputably valuable as a means of preserving

---

as true or false[;]" "the full context of the statement[;]" and "the broader context or setting in which the statement apears." Id at 979. The court found that the statement above was "rhetorical hyperbole," and thus constitutionally protected as an expression of opinion (as were the other challenged statements in the article). Id at 990.

[112] *New York Times v Sullivan*, 376 US 254 (1964); *Terminiello v Chicago*, 337 US 1 (1949); *Cantwell v Connecticut*, 310 US 296 (1940).

[113] Beck at 11 (cited in note 8) ([I]f Masson won, . . . [r]eporters would not dare use a quote unless they had recorded it and could prove it was completely accurate."); Roger Cohen, *Writers Mobilizing Against Restrictions on Using Quotations*, NY Times, Feb. 20, 1991, at C11, C16 ("[M]any writers are worried that a Supreme Court finding in Mr. Masson's favor, which would send the case to trial, would have a chilling effect on the use of any quotations.").

public confidence in the acuracy of quotes. But, if the Court were
to accord journalists less protection when using quotations than
paraphrase, then quotes would become more risky and, in all probability, more avoided. Moreover, if the public relies on the absence
of a lawsuit as confirmation of a quotation's accuracy, which would
be natural, that could ironically result in greater distortion of public
debate than a system in which people understand that the marketplace is the only source of restraint on falsehood. There are many
reasons why those injured by falsehoods choose not to sue (e.g.,
litigation costs), but it is not entirely clear that those inhibitions
are understood by the general public.

Thus, given a general commitment to vigorous, wide-open debate about matters of legitimate public interest, this should be our
rule: Lawsuits against citizens, or the press, arising out of their
descriptions of what public officials and public figures have said
should be constitutionally barred unless the attributed statements
are beyond the realm of any fairly conceivable construction of what
was actually said *and* the misrepresentation produces an untrue and
injurious image of that person (as measured by relevant community
opinion). This is consistent with the spirit, even if not the holding,
of *Sullivan*. Late in that Court's opinion, as it applied its newly
fashioned constitutional rules to Sullivan's claims, the Court questioned, with pregnant meaning, whether the alleged factual discrepancies between the advertisement and the truth ((1) that the
police had been "deployed near" but had not "ringed" the campus,
(2) that the police had not "gone there in connection with the State
Capitol demonstration," and (3) that King had been arrested only
four and not seven times) "were sufficient to injure [Sullivan's]
reputation" and how that "may itself raise constitutional problems. . . ."[114] Furthermore, requiring significant reputational injury is consistent with *Sullivan's* additional conclusion that the First
Amendment interest in robust debate precluded the jury from
finding that a mere discussion of official misconduct could not be
taken as a charge of misconduct against the particular government
officials who bear responsibility for the allegedly misbehaving officials.[115] In *Gertz v Welch Inc.*, the Court continued this emphasis
on the constitutional importance of real harm by precluding states

---

[114] 376 US at 289.
[115] Id at 292.

from operating under the traditional rule of presumed damages.[116] Similarly, courts should be wary of permitting interpretations of official public statements to be actionable in the absence of misrepresentations that cause genuine harm.

There are two additional points: First, to the extent that defamation lawsuits for fabricated quotations are constitutionally permitted, we must avoid being too narrow in determining whether a given false quotation actually conveys a (constitutionally) false and defamatory factual impression of the plaintiff. The tendency will be to look only at the closest passage in a tape-recorded transcript and ask whether it deviates sufficiently from the quotation. But that can be seriously misleading. If the plaintiff's claim is that the false quotation makes him sound "arrogant," the inquiry should then be (just as with the constitutional standard for obscenity [117]) whether the statements "as a whole," not just a particular passage, would have conveyed that impression if communicated. Likewise, the defendant's published statement must also be examined in its entirety, in order to decide what impact any particular, or isolated, passage had on the general reader.

Second, there is a need for clarification about the proper role of the state of mind (or actual malice) requirement. The point is a simple one: In order to satisfy *Sullivan*, a public official or public figure ought to have to show not that an actual statement was knowingly (or recklessly) altered, even in a "material" way, but rather that the press falsely attributed a statement to the plaintiff that seriously injured his reputation and that the press did *this* knowingly (or recklessly).

Thus, it would seem that a strong *Sullivan* conception of this problem would start with articulating the grave concerns about the imperfections and biases of any system that touches on the regulation of speech, would try to understand how people in the heat of debate and dealing with public issues are inevitably going to make mistakes and even to act badly, would articulate how dangerous it is to attempt to excise that which is bad without discouraging that which is needed or good, would try to understand how easily individuals are inhibited from participating in public affairs by the prospect of legal challenges, would further speak about the harmful

[116] 418 US 323, 349 (1974).
[117] *Miller v California*, 412 US 915 (1974).

consequences for public debate generally from permitting libel actions to operate freely, and would emphasize the need for giving the benefit of the doubt—instituting a presumption of truthfulness—in deciding whether defamation actions can proceed constitutionally.

IV. Comparing Masson with Sullivan

Now I want to return once more to the Court's decision in *Masson* and to suggest more precisely how it departs from this *Sullivan*-inspired analysis and, indeed, how it blends into its opinion some of the special concerns about fabricated quotes discussed earlier.

The most significant feature of the Court's opinion lies in its refusal to deny constitutional protection to any speaker who quotes words not actually spoken by a plaintiff. From the press' point of view, this was a considerable victory. But the scope of the victory remains significantly uncertain. The Court, as we know, opted for a constitutional definition of the "concept of falsity" that focuses on a comparison between the "meaning" (or "truth") of the plaintiff's statement and the "meaning" communicated by the quotation, so that a speaker is protected even if he or she misquotes a public official or figure unless the "alteration" of the plaintiff's actual words "results in a material change in the meaning conveyed by the statement." [118] There is, however, a significant ambiguity here. The uncertainty arises from the fact that attributing a false meaning to a public official or figure is not by any means always going to be defamatory (a statement may, in terms of its affect on community opinion, reflect positively on the plaintiff; and even a falsely attributed self-reported fact that hurts the plaintiff's reputation (e.g., the statement "I once regularly used cocaine.") may in fact be true (i.e., the plaintiff did in fact once regularly use cocaine)). This is just an expansion of the point made in the preceding section about how there are really multiple (we began with two) "falsehoods" involved in a fabricated quote case, which need to be disentangled for clear analysis. Thus, it is important to know whether the Court intends the constitutional protection to end whenever the plaintiff can show a material change in meaning or whether there is the additional constitutional requirement that there also be a defama-

---

[118] 111 S Ct at 2433.

tory (or reputationally injurious) image produced as well—as was proposed in the preceding section.

The reasons for being hesitant about the scope of constitutional protection the Court intended are several. When the Court rejects Masson's proposed test, it asserts that to leave states free to make any change in a speaker's wording legally actionable would force a change in standard journalistic practice, would not for unexplained reasons be "workable" (which is, hardly, the real problem), and would not correlate with whether an author's misquotes have actually resulted in the creation of a false impression of the plaintiff (i.e., changes in "grammar or snytax" may create false impressions and changes in "wording" may not), which the Court says has been the traditional concern of libel law.[119] Similarly, when the Court states its "conclusion," that the constitutional test is whether a "material change" in "meaning" is "conveyed," it omits any statement that the Constitution also requires the alteration to be defamatory. And throughout its analysis the Court can be read as interpreting the First Amendment as concerned only with allowing redress for "false impressions," whether hurtful to reputation or not. It emphasizes that a change in a speaker's wording that does not result in a "material change in the speaker's meaning" necessarily cannot defame the speaker, but it fails to address the comparable question as to its own test—namely, whether the absence of defamatory injury precludes recovery even when there is a "material change in meaning."[120]

On the other hand, it can also be said that the Court's refusal to hold constitutional protection at the point where a change in wording occurs was motivated by a felt need to maintain a test linked to actual defamation. Just before it states its conclusion, the Court points to the historical purpose of libel law as intended to "redress injury of the plaintiff's reputation by a statement that is defamatory and false."[121] And, finally, when it comes to apply its new test to the actual facts of *Masson*, the Court seems clearly to be

---

[119] Id at 2434; see, e.g., the Court's statement that the First Amendment requirement of actual malice "relies upon this historical understanding" of tort law that a "statement is not considered false unless it 'would have a different effect on the mind of the reader from that which the pleaded truth would have produced.' R. Sack, *Libel, Slander and Related Problems* 138 (1980) . . ." Id at 2432.

[120] Id at 2432.

[121] Id.

looking for not only a "material change in meaning" but also for a potentially *defamatory* "material change in meaning." [122]

Moving beyond this "multiple falsehoods" problem in the Court's opinion in *Masson*, it is also noteworthy that the Court displayed no concern over the difficulties or dangers (from a First Amendment standpoint) involved in deciding what degree of (substantive) deviation between the actual and the reported statements is constitutionally required before the press may be held liable. As indicated in the preceding section, this involves two issues: What evidence ought we to consider in locating the "meaning(s)" of both the actual statement and the alleged misquote? And given the uncertainties involved in locating the substance or meaning in expression and the potential of an anti-press bias infecting that inquiry, what degree of restraint should be imposed on libel actions to maintain a world of "uninhibited, robust and wide-open debate"?

Without analyzing the problem, the Court seemed to approve, and to follow itself, an approach of comparing the quotation with only the most obviously related statement in the actual transcript. This would seem to be the most naive of any theory of interpretation. If one, for example, reads the "I was like an intellectual gigolo" quote in the context of the discussion surrounding it, or of the book as a whole, one senses immediately that it would have a very different impact on the reader—the reflected image of sexualized and immoral relationships emanating from the remark is both subsumed and exonerated by other nearby, related remarks of Masson. [123]

---

[122] See id at 2435–37.

[123] The "intellectual gigolo" appears in a portion of Malcolm's discussion with Masson about how "he had become involved with analysis." Malcolm at 36 (cited in note 25). Masson says "It started at Harvard in the sixties. . . . When I first went there as an undergraduate, I was an obnoxious person. I knew nothing. The only things I could do were read and sleep with women." Id. Following the "intellectual gigolo," Masson acknowledges a problem of sexual promiscuity, id at 38–39:

Erik Erikson was teaching at Harvard when I was there, and I went to him and asked if I could go into treatment with him. My main symptom was total promiscuity—sleeping with every woman I could meet. He said no, but he sent me to someone he said he had great respect for, and I was in therapy with this man for a few years. But eight years later, when I was teaching in Toronto, I still had the symptom, so I went into therapy again, and then into five-times-a-week analysis. The trouble never seemed to get any better, and I figured it must have something to do with my childhood. I didn't say to myself, 'Well, you're just a lovable guy—you just love women, and women just love you.' I knew there was something wrong. I'd slept with close to a thousand women by the time I got to

Furthermore, there is no discussion of the need to beware of how the fabricated quote in a case like *Masson* inappropriately affects our judgment as we seek to determine whether there is a defamatory material change in meaning. Indeed, the fact that the Court begins its opinion with the somewhat surprisingly firm conclusion that generally quotation marks promise a "verbatim" account of a speaker's utterances signals the Court's feeling that this question is, indeed, somehow the major issue.[124] Though what quotation marks "say" or represent about alterations is, as I have said, relevant to a claim of defamation, it is only so insofar as it makes the defamatory meaning conveyed more credible and therefore more injurious. Consequently, the prominence given to the issue by the Court reinforces rather than weakens the (constitutionally) inappropriate feeling that the press should be legally accountable for fabricating quotes alone. The Court's opinion takes an even more striking turn, however, when it confronts and rejects what is portrayed as the Charbydis of the Court of Appeals test, namely that the press is constitutionally protected so long as the quote is a "rational interpretation" of the actual statement.[125] Especially striking—and entirely novel in the Court's constitutional decisions in the libel area—are the considerations taken as relevant by the Court as it rejects that broader protection. The Court restates its belief that the "reasonable reader" understands quotations as "verbatim" accounts, not authorial "interpretation[s]."[126] Without acknowledging that its own "material change in meaning" (or "substantial truth") test allows the press to violate that general understanding without fear of legal liability too (albeit to a lesser extent than the

---

Toronto. And I'd fallen in love about five times. Not a great number. And even when I was in love with a woman it didn't stop me from sleeping with other women. So I realized there was something to look for. And when I went into therapy there were things about it that just fascinated me. The idea that there could be feelings that you're not aware of utterly fascinated me. The idea of counter-phobia fascinated me: that you could climb mountains because you were terrified of heights, that you would seek out dangers because the dangers held such fear for you. The importance of dreams: that there are feelings you can recover in dreams that you've never had in real life; that you can discover from a dream that you're in love with someone. The idea of repressed memories, of early memories—all these analytic ideas captivated me, and the more I read the more fascinated I became, and the more I read Freud the more admiring I became. But I was not doing anything historical then.

[124] 111 S Ct at 2430.

[125] Id at 2433.

[126] Id at 2434.

"rational interpretation" test), the Court proceeds to reject the latter test for the reasons that it "would give journalists the freedom to place statements in their subjects' mouths without fear of liability," "diminish to a great degree the trustworthiness of the printed word," "eliminate the real meaning of quotations" because there would no longer be "any method of distinguishing between the statements of the subject and the interpretation of the author," and make "[n]ewsworthy figures . . . more wary of journalists." [127] Here for the first time, then, the Court refuses to extend First Amendment protection to speech because in its view to do so would undermine the *character and quality of public discourse.*

It is a noteworthy feature of the Court's opinion in *New York Times v Sullivan* (as I noted in my initial discussion of the decision) that the justices there did not consider the costs to public debate of defamatory falsehoods. Instead the Court conceived of the constitutional problem before it as a conflict between the states' interest in preserving individual reputation and the values of free speech in wide-open debate about public individuals and issues. [128] The omission of that set of considerations in *Sullivan* makes its inclusion in the Court's opinion in *Masson* highly significant. We now have, in the First Amendment jurisprudence, an explicit evaluation of interests of quality public discussion that was lacking in, or omitted from, *New York Times v Sullivan*. I shall have a few comments to make on this shift in analysis in the next section.

But what was present in *New York Times v Sullivan* that is absent from *Masson* is also of immense significance. What *Sullivan* did that was so important for the advancement of First Amendment jurisprudence was to articulate so forcefully, to celebrate, the virtues of a strong system of self-government. That involved two elements: a plea for heightened sensitivity to the evils of government involvement in speech and an explanation for why the mistakes and misbehavior of speakers are less worthy of condemnation than our instincts might sugest and, in any event, are inevitable by-products of a *system* of truly open discussion that we should want more than we want to eliminate its defects. [129] So eloquent, indeed so one-sided, was *Sullivan* in its articulation of the virtues

---

[127] Id.

[128] 376 US 254 (1964).

[129] Id at 269–83 is especially pertinent.

and needs of wide-open public debate, with plenty of room for error and even harmful misbehavior (the Court has acknowledged that "the truth rarely catches up with a lie" [130]), that one is tempted to interpret the decision as motivated by an implicit purpose of stretching the principle of free speech, beyond what in its own context would seem reasonable, in order to stimulate a more aggressive press and a more active self-government. Little of this rhetorical strategy is present in the Court's opinion in *Masson*.

These problematic (or, depending on your view, innovative) aspects of the Court's analysis in *Masson* are complemented by the fact that the Court never made it clear that the actual malice (or state of mind) requirement must be related to the defamatory character of the defendant's publication and not to the mere deviation between the statement quoted and the actual statement. By defining, as it does, the issue presented as what is the constitutional meaning of the "concept of falsity," and then going on to reject the plaintiff's notion that the "requisite falsity inheres in the attribution of words to the petitioner which he did not speak," the Court ends up appearing to assume the "knowledge" (actual malice) requirement is fully satisfied.[131] It never returns to that original assumption to say that the state of mind requirement must be integrated with the *relevant* falsehood.

Thus, of the trinity of constitutional requirements (knowledge, factual falsity, and injury), the Court's opinion is unfortunately vague about the role of knowledge and injury in cases involving fabricated quotations; and, while arguably insightful in identifying what "falsity" is constitutionally relevant, it is not fully sensitive to the dangers for a free press in adjudicating that issue in the context of reports or the statement of public officials and figures. The Court also introduces the new idea of limiting constitutional protection on the ground that speech injures the quality of public discourse.

This comparison with the spirit or tone of *Sullivan* also highlights just how subdued the Court has become in its passion for "uninhibited, robust and wide-open" debate. Absent are the dark expressions of concern about the strength of the forces of inhibition and their creation of chilling effects. Where *Sullivan* makes deep as-

---

[130] *Gertz v Robert Welch, Inc.*, 418 US 323, 344 n 9 (1974).

[131] 111 S Ct at 2431.

sumptions about the democratic universe, *Masson* exists in a practical vacuum. Never is there a worried brow expressing concern
that too much discretion will offer a field day to the ever-present,
anti-press forces in society. When the Court says at the end of its
analysis that a rational interpretation test would "diminish . . . the
trustworthiness of the printed word," [132] the failure to self-critically
consider how law may not be able to shore up that trust if other
means fail, and how in so many First Amendment cases it has
been said that other means besides law must be used to achieve
"trustworthy" discourse, betrays a diminished sense of passion
for—and a felt need to try to stimulate—greater press freedom,
which is at the core of *Sullivan*'s essence. There is a different perspective animating both *Sullivan* and *Masson*.

V. Some Concluding Reflections on the Relationship between the Process of Constitutional Adjudication and the Character of American Journalism

The process by which our "tradition" of freedom of speech
and press is formed has an unmistakable element of fortuity to it.
The building blocks of that tradition are largely the cases that
now annually come before the Court. A "case," of course, is not
something planned, and, though a holding usually extends well
beyond the facts of a particular case, the actual facts are often
suspiciously influential in shaping that holding. Furthermore, the
outcome of the case, whether for or against the press, seems usually
to be taken in a far less qualified way than the facts of the case
would justify. If the press in *Pentagon Papers* [133] had bribed a government official to obtain the papers, the injunction against publication would more likely have been sustained. And there is little
doubt that the favorable outcome for the press in *Pentagon Papers*
has been generally regarded as a far more striking and uncondi-
tional victory for the press than in fact it was. [134]

The decision in *Masson* was not disastrous for the press, but it
did pose a hypothetical factual picture that no doubt has been
taken by many people as not hypothetical but actual and as an

---

[132] Id at 2434.

[133] *New York Times Co. v United States*, 403 US 713 (1971)

[134] Bollinger (cited in note 9) at 48–49.

illustration, not an isolated incident, of journalistic misbehavior.[135] If, as Malcolm claims, it turns out to be true that Masson in fact said more or less all the things Malcolm quoted him as saying (but in non-tape-recorded interviews), then, I suspect, she will have paid dearly (as will the press) in her own reputation for having tried to win the case at the summary judgment stage, with the necessary assumption that the quotations were "deliberately fabricated." Similarly, because the factual picture of journalism in *Masson* does not evoke a sympathetic response from most people, including judges, there was something of a conflict between Malcolm's natural desire to defeat the lawsuit against her and the press' interest both in preserving whatever image it had before *Masson* and in avoiding the risk of a less favorable constitutional decision than it might otherwise get with a more sympathetic case.[136] Indeed, this case has generated an interesting insight into what might be the best litigation strategy for the press in trying to preserve its constitutional position. One of the judges involved in the litigation (Judge Kozinski of the Ninth Circuit) has remarked (outside the context of the case) that *Masson* was an intellectual "picnic" for a judge and that the press ought to be wary of litigating such cases—suggesting, I think, that judges are generally starved for challenging cases and when they get one they are likely to devote a lot of time to it, with the likely result of highly refined and complex decisions, rather than simple, ringing affirmations of constitutional freedoms.[137]

What should be disturbing to the press as they ponder the Court's decision in *Masson* is not just the outcome in cases involving

---

[135] Quite a few of those who wrote about the case and Miss Malcolm mistakenly reported that she had admitted to fabricating the quotes. See, e.g., Scardino at C20 (cited in note 7) ("Miss Malcolm conceded the fabrications, but said she had acted only in an effort to get behind the facts to the truth.") (*The New York Times* printed a correction a week later, saying the article "referred imprecisely to [Malcolm's] position in a lawsuit against her." *Corrections*, NY Times, Mar. 29, 1989, at A3); Richard N. Winfield, *Altered Quotes*, Editor & Publisher, Apr. 6, 1991, at 24 ("On at least nine occasions, the author did not quote Masson directly. Instead she put words in quotation marks that summed up, or characterized, what Masson had said on tape."). See also supra note 105 and accompanying text.

[136] This was a "case that made writers cringe over the facts and possible outcome." *Justices Give Writers Some Benefit of Doubt*, Nat LJ, July 1, 1991, at 5; David Margolick, *Libel Suit Uncovers Raw Nerve: Quotations*, NY Times, Oct. 5, 1990, at B8 (Press groups "had hoped a case highlighting an embarrassing but routine journalistic practice would simply go away.").

[137] Judge Kozinski, Remarks (from the floor) at the Second Panel Session of the Federal Communications Bar Association and ABA Forum on Communications (May 2, 1991) (videotape on file with author).

fabricated quotes, which are probably somewhat marginal (or can be minimized by reducing the use of quotations), but the chance— actually the likelihood—that the "material difference in meaning" test will be applied to *all* journalistic efforts to restate what public officials or public figures say. Because the Court seems bent on avoiding creating any "special" constitutional rules in the defamation area, it would seem unlikely that what is now the *Masson* principle will be limited to cases involving fabricated quotations. Therefore, every assertion in the press that a public official or public figure said something will potentially be met with a lawsuit claiming that this was not the "substantial truth" of the official's/ figure's actual statement. That, of course, may well dampen the spirit of "uninhibited, robust, and wide-open" public debate.

On the other hand, it may be that the "substantial truth" (or "material difference in meaning") test is so vague that the outcomes will vary depending upon the facts of individual cases, so that we will in effect have, contrary to the Court's stated intentions, many discrete rules or even ad hoc decisions. Thus, the fact that *Masson* involved a plaintiff who was, at best, a fairly pale public figure (in terms of political and social power) and a story not about core political issues, with fabricated quotations purportedly drawn from *private* interviews (and therefore less able to be contradicted by other witnesses), and written with a scholar's deadline, may serve to isolate its holding in practice. *Sullivan* and *Masson*, therefore, may suggest an implicit and subtle difference is developing within the constitutional framework for defamation. The facts of *Sullivan* support or create a picture of the "government" suing the "press" (as well as civil rights–seeking minorities) for criticism of government.[138] *Masson*, on the other hand, involves more of an image of an individual suing the institutional press for character assassination. It may be, in other words, that the evolution of constitutional defamation law is giving birth to different approaches when government officials are suing and when minor public figures are suing.

Even if that turns out to be so, however, I am inclined to see

---

[138] See, e.g., the first paragaraph of Justice Brennan's opinion for the Court, 376 US at 256. ("We are required in this case to determine for the first time the extent to which the constitutional protections for speech and press limit a State's power to award damages in a libel action brought by a public official against critics of his official conduct.")

the spirit of *Sullivan* as steadily diminishing under the Court's decisions in the libel area. *Sullivan's* promise, which a case like *Masson* does not completely keep, is to maintain firm pressure on the system of libel law—always demanding, before liability can be imposed, that there be gross factual misrepresentations causing serious reputational injury, along with a stated readiness to review the factual record in every case to see whether that has indeed occurred. This country does not have the British or Japanese approach of judicial findings of defamation accompanied by nominal damage awards, which has much to recommend it.[139] Without that kind of systemic constraint on damages, however, the courts must play a more interventionary role. Perhaps the weakness of *Masson's* pressure is explained by the procedural posture of the case; but I doubt that the Court would more eagerly and actively intervene at a later stage.

Then there is the Court's explicit consideration of the effects on public discourse of the journalistic abuse of misquotes. In general, I applaud this move, though the Court's treatment of this subject was incomplete (it should have considered, for example, why quotations are valuable, what pressures within journalism lead to misquotation and other related abuses, how significant a problem it would appear to be, etc.). It would seem that, assuming our ultimate concern under the First Amendment is the achievement of good public consideration of public issues, the Court ought to entertain ideas that the protection of speech may undermine that objective. A balanced and deep analysis seems more consistent with what the First Amendment purports to seek for the society as a whole, more likely to produce better decisions, to be more persuasive over time and, in the end, to bring greater stability to the First Amendment jurisprudence. But it also permits the Court to articulate concerns about contemporary practices of journalism and

---

[139] See, e.g., *Dun & Bradstreet, Inc. v Greenmoss Builders, Inc.*, 472 US 749, 771 (White, J, concurring):

> we could have achieved our stated goal by limiting the recoverable damages to a level that would not unduly threaten the press. Punitive damages might have been scrutinized . . . or perhaps even entirely forbidden. Presumed damages to reputation might have been prohibited, or limited, as in *Gertz*. Had that course been taken and the common-law standard of liability been retained, the defamed public official upon proving falsity, could at least have a judgment to that effect. . . . In this way, both First Amendment and reputational interests would have been far better served.

their effects on public debate and decision making (or to reinforce developing standards of journalism), which on the whole seems a desirable dialogue between these two major social institutions (the judiciary and the press). This has, I believe, been going on now, at various levels, since *Sullivan*, but *Masson* brings the process into a sharper focus.[140]

In general, there would appear to be three main concerns with the Court offering critiques of media practices. First, there may be a concern that a more balanced perspective, or analysis, will enervate the passion which Harry Kalven, in his assessment of the greatness of Justice Black's contribution to the First Amendment, suggested was essential to upholding freedom of speech and press.[141] Second, a related point, by considering the negative consequences of speech the Court may end up giving too much weight to them. And, third, the Court (or courts) may be too legalistic in its expectations of what journalism should be—to expect journalism to be practiced only according to the norms of law.

These are significant concerns, but they do not seem to me persuasive. Passion and balance do not seem incompatible if you have a well-developed positive theory of what the First Amendment is trying to do. And the same is true of the other claims for one-sidedness in First Amendment adjudication.

In any event, the main point is the need to focus our attention on this phenomenon of the process of constitutional adjudication having an influence on the character of journalism. We should see that the First Amendment empowers the courts to perform two roles: one is to decide the limits of legal regulation and the other is to articulate images of the character and functions of the American press.[142] This latter role, an inevitable by-product of the constitu-

---

[140] I develop this theme at greater length in Bollinger, *Images of a Free Press* (cited in note 9).

[141] Harry Kalven, Jr., *Upon Rereading Mr. Justice Black on the First Amendment*, 14 UCLA L Rev 428, 429–30 (1967). Kalven explained:

> To begin with, he passes a major test for a great judge on free speech issues. He displays the requisite passion. The requirement is not so much a question of arguing for the preferred position thesis; it is rather that the judge respond to the fact that this is not just another rule or principle of law. Mr. Justice Black has for thirty years always risen to the occasion when a free speech issue was at stake; he has always been vigilant and concerned.

[142] Bollinger at 40–61 (cited in note 9).

tional scheme that has evolved, deserves more thought than it has received.

That this process of constitutional adjudication of freedom of speech and press has real if subtle effects on the nature of American journalism is one of the most interesting features of the *Masson* litigation. Floyd Abrams, a celebrated First Amendment lawyer, warned the press, as *Masson* (and *Cohen*) were moving toward the Supreme Court, that in order to be victorious the press was going to have to concede that fabricating quotes and breaking promises of confidentiality are ethically inexcusable.[143] This testimony from such an experienced, and highly successful, media lawyer indicates not only how to be persuasive, but reveals in that recommendation a reality in which the process of legal decisionmaking puts pressure on the press to develop journalistic standards. It may be, once again, that the prevailing judicial vision is too legalistic. Since courts may have narrow ideas about what are good journalistic standards, and since it will be lawyers (representing the media) who decide what will be a "persuasive" acknowledgment of misbehavior, it is possible not only that the legal system is strongly affecting the development of the character of the American press but doing so adversely. Still, the process is alive, and it should be understood and, I also think, used well. For *Masson* that means at least that the Court should have condemned the fabrication of quotations, even if it at the same time found it necessary to extend substantial constitutional protection to those journalists who do misquote.

If, as Meiklejohn said, *Sullivan* was "an occasion for dancing in the streets,"[144] *Masson* is a time for sober reflection on where the First Amendment has come and is going—the end, in other words, of *Sullivan*. We still have no rationale for this extraordinary exception to freedom of speech and press, though maybe we will come to find one in the need, or the desirability, of having such a discrete (and historically rooted) area that offers opportunities for continual interaction between the First Amendment, legal regulation of the press, and the character of American journalism.

---

[143] Floyd Abrams, *Battles Not Worth Fighting*, Wash Post, June 13, 1991, at A21; Floyd Abrams, Panel Discussion at the Second Panel Session of the Federal Communications Bar Association and ABA Forum on Communications (May 2, 1991) (videotape on file with author).

[144] Kalven at 221 n 125 (cited in note 107).

LOUIS MICHAEL SEIDMAN

CONFUSION AT THE BORDER:
CRUZAN, "THE RIGHT TO DIE," AND
THE PUBLIC/PRIVATE DISTINCTION

The retirements of Justice Marshall and Justice Brennan mark the
end of an era in Supreme Court history and provide an appropriate
occasion for a summing up. In this article, I identify and discuss
an anomaly in the way in which both "liberal" and "conservative"
Justices have argued about constitutional law throughout this
period.

Rather than proceeding globally, I will confine my discussion to
a single case—*Cruzan v Director, Missouri Department of Public
Health*,[1] in which the Court for the first time confronted the constitutional dimensions of the "right to die."[2] Indeed, for the most
part, I will confine myself to discussion of two of the five opinions
in the case—Justice Brennan's dissent and Justice Scalia's concurrence. I believe that these opinions usefully illustrate more general
problems in the "liberal" and "conservative" positions on constitutional interpretation, but I will not insist on this point. For readers

---

Louis Michael Seidman is Professor of Law, Georgetown University Law Center.

AUTHOR'S NOTE: I am grateful to Mark Tushnet, Steve Goldberg, Gerry Spann, Patricia
King, Cara Smith, Robin West, and participants in The University of Michigan faculty
workshop for helpful comments on an earlier draft of this article.

[1] 110 S Ct 2841 (1990).

[2] For reasons that will become apparent, I believe that this characterization of the case is
inaccurate. Properly understood, the case was about whether Ms. Cruzan had a right to
live. I use the phrase "right to die" only because this is how the Court itself posed the issue.
See, for example, 110 S Ct at 2851 ("This is the first case in which we have been squarely
presented with the issue of whether the United States Constitution grants what is in common
parlance referred to as a 'right to die.' ") .

who are skeptical of more grandiose assertions, what follows can be taken as no more than a case note on a particularly interesting and problematic set of opinions.

Briefly stated, my thesis is this: *Cruzan* presented the Court with an excruciatingly difficult problem in drawing an appropriate boundary between realms of private and public decision making— between the private domain of individual rights and the public domain of community preferences. On the one hand, most of us are drawn to the ideals of impartiality and neutrality. We believe that there is a moral duty to accord equal concern and respect for all individuals. This duty calls for placing matters in a public sphere, where decision making can proceed through democratic processes that equally weigh everyone's preference. Yet on the other hand, most of us also want to foster private values of love, friendship, and special caring—values that cannot easily be reconciled with the obligation to weigh the welfare of every individual equally. Recognition of these values calls for placing decision making in the private sphere of rights, where individuals can give special preferences to themselves and to the people they care most about.

In this article, I make no claim as to how the Court should have chosen between these competing concerns in *Cruzan*. Rather, my argument is only that the positions advanced by both sides were weakened by a curious rhetorical reversal. The claims of the public and private sphere are both powerful and could both be powerfully defended. But instead of defending these claims, one side (Justice Brennan) chose to justify public values in the name of private rights, while the other side (Justice Scalia) chose to justify private values in the name of public preference.

In the last section of the article, I will tentatively advance some more sweeping claims concerning the relationship between this anomaly and the structure of constitutional discourse throughout the modern period. I will suggest that the distortion in the rhetoric of Justices Brennan and Scalia is the product of two forces: deep-seated doubts about the legitimacy of judicial intervention, and a strong libertarian bias that persists at the core of modern constitutional law. This orientation is shared by "liberal" and "conservative" Justices alike. Both camps tend to equate freedom with the assertion of private power unencumbered by state intervention and to assume that the Court's legitimate role is limited to the protection of a private sphere. Neither is willing to entertain the possibility that freedom might be maximized by government intervention or that the Court might have a role in protecting public values.

I believe that this orientation has confused constitutional discourse and weakened the arguments on both sides of the issues that divide the Court. It creates obvious problems for liberals like Justice Brennan. In order to make his position plausible in a world where judicial intervention is permitted only to protect private rights, he must somehow translate his arguments for the public good into the unfriendly rhetoric of individualism.

Less obviously, it also creates difficulties for conservatives like Justice Scalia. In order to prevent the Court from meddling with state laws that (from his perspective) properly protect private rights, he must denigrate those rights by pretending that they are not rights at all, but rather merely the expression of discretionary public preferences.

I will argue that both sides would benefit if they ended their obsessive preoccupation with the legitimacy of judicial intervention and focussed on what is really at stake: the mapping and defense of a contested boundary between mutually threatening public and private spheres.

I

In *Cruzan*, the Court faced for the first time the recurring problem posed by patients in a "persistent vegetative state." These patients have suffered severe brain damage that leaves them with motor reflexes but no cognitive functions.[3]

Ms. Cruzan, the victim of an automobile accident, was in such a state. For years, she had been attached to feeding and hydration tubes, first inserted with the consent of her then husband when

---

[3] The Court adopted the following definition of a "persistent vegetative state," which it attributed to Dr. Fred Blum, whom it identified as a "renowned expert on the subject":

> Vegetative state describes a body which is functioning entirely in terms of its internal controls. It maintains temperature. It maintains heart beat and pulmonary ventilation. It maintains digestive activity. It maintains reflex activity of muscles and nerves for low level conditioned responses. But there is no behavioral evidence of either self-awareness or awareness of the surroundings in a learned manner.

Cruzan, 110 S Ct at 2845, quoting from *In re Jobes*, 108 NJ 394, 403, 529 A2d 434, 438 (1987).

there was still some hope of recovery.[4] The state trial court found that she suffered from anoxia of the brain, and that this condition left her entirely oblivious to her environment, spastic and quadriplegic.[5] Although there was no possibility that her condition would improve, she could be kept "alive" in her current state for as long as thirty years through artificial feeding and hydration.

After the hospital refused to comply with their wishes, Ms. Cruzan's parents sought a judicial order mandating removal of the feeding and hydration tubes—a step that would have resulted in her death. The trial judge entered such an order, but the State Supreme Court reversed.[6] The United States Supreme Court, in an opinion written for a five-Justice majority by Chief Justice Rehnquist, affirmed, rejecting the Cruzans' contention that Nancy Cruzan's constitutional liberty interest required removal of the tubes.

Chief Justice Rehnquist's opinion clearly exhibits strain from the effort to keep the slim and diverse five-Justice majority together.[7] On the one hand, the opinion had to satisfy Justice O'Connor, who wrote separately to state her view that there is a constitutionally protected liberty interest in the refusal of artificially delivered food and water[8] and to suggest that the state was constitutionally obligated to vindicate that interest by allowing a surrogate decision maker, appointed through a durable power of attorney or a "living will," to order termination of treatment.[9] On the other hand, the opinion also had to satisfy Justice Scalia, who wrote separately to express his view that the Constitution simply did not speak to these issues and that the state could therefore force Ms. Cruzan

---

[4] See *Cruzan*, 110 S Ct at 2845.

[5] These findings were adopted by the Missouri Supreme Court. See *Cruzan v Harmon*, 760 SW2d 408, 411 (Mo 1988).

[6] Id at 408.

[7] Chief Justice Rehnquist's opinion was joined by Justices White, O'Connor, Scalia, and Kennedy. Justices O'Connor and Scalia wrote concurring opinions. Justice Brennan filed a dissenting opinion, which was joined by Justices Marshall and Blackmun. Justice Stevens also filed a dissenting opinion.

[8] See *Cruzan*, 110 S Ct at 2856 (O'Connor concurring).

[9]

> I . . . write separately to emphasize that the Court does not today decide the issue whether a State must also give effect to the decisions of a surrogate decisionmaker. . . . In my view, such a duty may well be constitutionally required to protect the patient's liberty interest in refusing medical treatment.

Cruzan, 110 S Ct at 2857 (O'Connor concurring).

to undergo lifesaving treatment even if she had clearly and unambiguously expressed a desire to forgo it.[10]

Since the votes of both Justices Scalia and O'Connor were necessary to the majority status of his opinion, Chief Justice Rehnquist faced an unenviable task in reconciling these seemingly irreconcilable views. He attempted to do so by writing both cautiously and cryptically.

After a lengthy discussion of the common law of informed consent and of lower court decisions concerning termination of treatment,[11] the Court implied, without quite holding, that a competent person would have the constitutional right to refuse lifesaving hydration and nutrition.[12] It did not follow, however, that such treatment should be terminated for an *incompetent* person. Because Cruzan's incompetence prevented her from making an informed and voluntary choice regarding treatment, her "right," if it was to be exercised at all, had to be exercised by a surrogate. Under Missouri law, the surrogate could exercise this right only upon a showing of clear and convincing evidence that the patient, while competent, expressed a wish to have treatment terminated—a standard that petitioners had failed to meet.[13]

Thus, for the Court, the ultimate issue boiled down to whether there was a state interest sufficient to justify the imposition of this burden of proof. Chief Justice Rehnquist identified two such

---

[10] See id at 2859 (Scalia concurring).

[11] See id at 2846–51.

[12] Chief Justice Rehnquist acknowledged that "[t]he principle that a competent person has a constitutionally protected liberty interest in refusing unwanted medical treatment may be inferred from our prior decisions." Id at 2851. A few paragraphs later, however, he carefully qualified this acknowledgement (id at 2852):

> Although we think the logic of [prior] cases . . . would embrace such a liberty interest, the dramatic consequences involved in refusal of such treatment would inform the inquiry as to whether the deprivation of that interest is constitutionally permissible. But for purposes of this case, we assume that the United States Constitution would grant a competent person a constitutionally protected right to refuse lifesaving hydration and nutrition.

Justice O'Connor's concurring opinion contained none of these qualifications. She squarely asserted that "the liberty guaranteed by the Due Process Clause must protect, if it protects anything, an individual's deeply personal decision to reject medical treatment, including the artificial delivery of food and water." 110 S Ct at 2857. Since the four dissenting Justices also embraced a right of competent persons to reject lifesaving medical treatment, there appears to have been a majority of the Court for this position.

[13] See *Cruzan v Harmon*, 760 SW2d at 424.

interests. First, Missouri had an interest in the preservation and protection of all human life.[14]

> As a general matter, the States—indeed, all civilized nations— demonstrate their commitment to life by treating homicide as serious crime. Moreover, the majority of States in this country have laws imposing criminal penalties on one who assists another to commit suicide. We do not think a State is required to remain neutral in the face of an informed and voluntary decision by a physically able adult to starve to death.

Second, apart from the interest in protecting life, there was also a state interest in the protection of "the personal element of choice" regarding medical treatment.[15] According to the Court, the state's "clear and convincing" standard of proof could be justified as vindicating this interest by avoiding the potential for abuse by surrogates motivated by their own concerns, rather than those of the patient.[16]

Unfortunately, Chief Justice Rehnquist's efforts to navigate between the Scalia and O'Connor positions left him vulnerable to attack from both sides. The opinion seems to explicitly endorse Justice Scalia's view that the state's interest in the preservation of life justifies the prohibition against even "an informed and voluntary decision by a physically able adult to starve to death."[17] Yet this endorsement flatly contradicts the Court's assumption only a

---

[14] *Cruzan*, 110 S Ct at 2852.

[15] Id at 2853. Although Chief Justice Rehnquist treated the state law as advancing this interest and devoted much of his opinion to a defense of it, it is far from clear that Missouri itself actually asserted an interest in protecting individual choice. The Missouri Supreme Court, in its opinion refusing to allow the removal of life support equipment, wrote that "In this case, *only* the state's interest in the preservation of life is implicated." *Cruzan v Harmon*, 760 SW2d 408, 419 (Mo 1989) (emphasis added). As the state court noted, see id at 419–20, Missouri's "living will" statute carefully modified the Uniform Rights of the Terminally Ill Act so as to make clear that "death-prolonging procedures" that could be controlled by living wills did not include "the performance of any procedure to provide nutrition or hydration." Mo Rev Stat § 459.010(3) (1986). This modification seems to reflect a state policy against individual choice regarding the provision of lifesaving nutrition and hydration.

There was no claim that Ms. Cruzan had executed a living will and, in any event, the living will statute had not yet gone into effect at the time of her accident. The statute was therefore not directly relevant to the *Cruzan* case. Nonetheless, the state court treated the statute as bearing upon the issue before it because the statute was "an expression of the policy of this State with regard to the sanctity of life." *Cruzan v Harmon*, 760 SW2d at 420. The state court also held that the trial judge had erred in finding its provisions unconstitutional. Id.

[16] *Cruzan*, 110 S Ct at 2853.

[17] Id at 2852.

few paragraphs earlier (presumably offered for Justice O'Connor's benefit) that "the United States Constitution would grant a competent person a constitutionally protected right to refuse lifesaving hydration and nutrition."[18]

The Court is similarly unsuccessful in turning the case into a narrow dispute about burdens of proof that can be resolved without addressing the underlying debate that divided Justices Scalia and O'Connor. To the extent that the Court agrees with Justice Scalia that Missouri's decision vindicated its legitimate interest in the preservation of life *simpliciter*, the Court cannot logically rely upon a state interest in the preservation of individual choice. One cannot both believe that Missouri is rightfully keeping people alive against their will and that it is vindicating the right of individual choice regarding death. The Court's endorsement of the state interest in preservation of life therefore renders its lengthy defense of the "clear and convincing evidence" standard entirely beside the point. As Chief Justice Rehnquist himself obliquely acknowledged by endorsing laws prohibiting suicide by fully competent adults,[19] a preservation of life rationale would support Missouri's decision even if there were overwhelmingly convincing evidence that Ms. Cruzan wished to die.

To the extent that the Court instead endorsed the state interest in the protection of individual choice regarding medical treatment, its discussion of the "clear and convincing evidence" standard was at least relevant. But on this hypothesis, the Court's defense of that standard is quite unpersuasive. As Justice Brennan convincingly argued in his dissent, this skewing of the evidentiary burden serves to defeat, rather than enhance, individual choice.[20]

Of course, even if the state used a preponderance of the evidence standard, individual choice would occasionally be frustrated by inevitable errors in determining the facts. But by artificially biasing decisions in one direction, the state necessarily increases the number of such errors. This increase might be justified if one started with the assumption that one type of error was more serious than

---

[18] Id.

[19] See id at 2852 ("[The] majority of States in this country have laws imposing criminal penalties on one who assists another to commit suicide. We do not think a State is required to remain neutral in the face of an informed and voluntary decision by a physically able adult to starve to death.").

[20] See id at 2876.

the other. But such an assumption must itself be premised on a
constitutionally adequate state interest.

Chief Justice Rehnquist's opinion advances several such interests. The Court notes that

> the possibility of subsequent development such as advanc[e]-
> ments in medical science, the discovery of new evidence regard-
> ing the patient's intent, changes in the law, or simply the un-
> expected death of the patient despite the administration of
> life-sustaining treatment at least create the potential that a
> wrong decision [to continue treatment] will eventually be cor-
> rected or its impact mitigated.[21]

But none of these possibilities provides an adequate explanation
for why the burden of proof should be tilted toward continuing
treatment. The possibility that new medical discoveries might bear
on the issue is vanishingly small in light of the fact, noted in Justice
Brennan's dissent, that only a brain transplant could lead to an
improvement in Ms. Cruzan's condition.[22] It is true that subsequent discovery of new evidence about Ms. Cruzan's intent,
changes in the law, or Ms. Cruzan's death might cause one to regret
a decision to terminate treatment. But all of these possibilities cut
both ways. The discovery of new evidence that Ms. Cruzan wished
to die, changes in the law that facilitated treatment termination,
and the unexpected prolongation of her life all might cause us to
regret *not* terminating treatment.

For reasons that are nowhere articulated, the Court seems to
assume that termination decisions are irrevocable, while nontermination decisions are not. But the additional period of time that a
person wrongly remains alive because of nontermination can no
more be recaptured than the period of life lost for a person who
wrongly dies because of termination. At bottom, the nonreciprocal
treatment of these possibilities must rest on a belief that life is
better than death and that the state can force individuals to act on
this belief even when they do not share it. The Court nowhere
explains how this position can be reconciled with the assumption,
with which it begins its analysis, that competent individuals have
a constitutional right to refuse life-saving medical treatment. Nor
does it explain how it can support the burden of proof standard on

---

[21] Id at 2854.
[22] Id at 2874 n 18 (Brennan dissenting).

this ground while also maintaining that the standard vindicates a state interest in the protection of individual choice regarding questions of life and death.

Read most charitably, Chief Justice Rehnquist's opinion represents an uneasy compromise between the positions of Justices Scalia and O'Connor. The Court suggests that freedom of choice between life and death is constitutionally compelled, but also suggests that the state may bias the choice in favor of life. Perhaps such a compromise is the best that can be done, given the problems inherent in forging a majority at the end of the Term in a close and difficult case. Chief Justice Rehnquist can hardly be blamed for being caught between two firmly held and fervently asserted views. It is more disappointing that the advocates of both those views fail to pose the hard questions in a fashion that reveals what is actually at stake.

II

One such view is that the ability to choose between life and death constitutes a liberty that is not only constitutionally protected, but also fundamental. Under prevailing doctrine, it follows that the Supreme Court should play an active role in keeping exercise of this liberty in a private sphere. The Court must assess the validity of state interests advanced as justifications for curtailing that liberty and invalidate government actions not supported by a compelling interest. Although versions of this view lie at the core of Justice O'Connor's concurrence and Justice Stevens's dissent, it is most forcefully advocated in Justice Brennan's long and eloquent dissenting opinion written for himself and Justices Blackmun and Marshall.

Unfortunately, however, Justice Brennan's opinion is dominated by a single, puzzling analytic failure. His analysis is organized around the assertion that Ms. Cruzan is a person who has a right to die and that the decision should therefore be located in the private sphere. Yet most of his argument supports the claim that she is a person who has no right to live and that public decision making is therefore appropriate. This odd reversal infects the opinion from beginning to end and, I believe, reflects a deep confusion about the status of individual rights on the one hand and the public good on the other.

A

One indication that there is something awry is the disjunction between the particular facts described in the Brennan dissent and the more abstract right that the opinion advocates. Consider, first, the graphic and moving statement of Ms. Cruzan's predicament with which the opinion begins:[23]

> [Nancy Cruzan] is oblivious to her surroundings and will remain so. Her body twitches only reflexively, without consciousness. The areas of her brain that once thought, felt, and experienced sensations have degenerated badly and are continuing to do so. . . . "Nancy will never interact meaningfully with her environment again. She will remain in a persistent vegetative state until her death."

Now consider the right that the opinion defends:[24]

> The right to be free from unwanted medical attention is a right to evaluate the potential benefit of treatment and its possible consequences according to one's own values and to make a personal decision whether to subject oneself to the intrusion.

This juxtaposition poses an obvious problem for the dissent. How does Justice Brennan suppose that Ms. Cruzan, unconscious and "oblivious to her surroundings," is going to "evaluate the potential benefit of treatment" and make a "personal decision" in accord with her "own values"?

These quotations are not aberrational. The opinion repeatedly emphasizes that patients like Ms. Cruzan "are devoid of thought, emotion and sensation; they are permanently and completely unconscious."[25] Yet the opinion is also full of the rhetoric of "choosing," "wanting," and "evaluating"—sometimes within the very same paragraph that speaks of "unconsciousness" and of "persistent vegetative states."[26]

Occasionally, as if to acknowledge the incompatibility of these two discourses, the opinion retreats to a counterfactual voice.

---

[23] Id at 2863 (Brennan dissenting) (quoting *Cruzan v Harmon*, 760 SW2d 408, 422 (Mo 1988)).

[24] *Cruzan*, 110 S Ct at 2867–68.

[25] Id at 2868.

[26] See id at 2867–68.

Thus, "[there] are affirmative reasons why someone like Nancy *might choose to* forego artificial nutrition and hydration under these circumstances";[27] and "[her] family is convinced that Nancy *would find* this state degrading."[28] But the nature of the counterfactual is never stated explicitly, and for good reason. To complete each of these sentences is to demonstrate the contradiction at the core of the opinion's rhetoric. Nancy "might choose to forego artificial nutrition" *if she were a person who could choose at all*—which, of course, she is not. She "would find this state degrading" *if she were a person capable of feeling, thinking, and wanting*—mental states that, tragically, she has lost the ability to experience.[29]

One might respond that even if the facts of this case make it a bad vehicle for announcing a "right to die," this defect in no way impeaches the validity of the right itself. But unfortunately, the problem runs deeper than this. The difficulty is not just that Ms. Cruzan herself was in no position to want, to feel, or to suffer. It

---

[27] Id at 2868 (emphasis added).

[28] Id at 2869 n 10 (emphasis added).

[29] Much of Justice Stevens's dissent is dominated by a similar contradiction. Justice Stevens asserted that "the Constitution requires the State to care for Nancy Cruzan's life in a way that gives appropriate respect to her own best interests." *Cruzan*, 110 S Ct at 2879 (Stevens dissenting). He concluded that there was overwhelming evidence supporting the view that her best interests would be served by the termination of life support treatment. Id. Yet on the same page on which this conclusion appears, he described Ms. Cruzan as "oblivious to her environment" and incapable of cognitive brain function beyond recognition of painful stimuli and apparent response to sound. Id. For the most part, his opinion leaves unexplained how a person in this state could have an interest in either life or death.

Occasionally, Justice Stevens suggested that Ms. Cruzan's state left her as a person without interests and, therefore, presumably, without rights. He suggested, for example, that Ms. Cruzan should not be thought of as "alive" in the usual sense, and that this is so because "[if] there is a shared thread among the various opinions on this subject, it may be that life is an activity which is at once the matrix for and an integration of a person's interests." Id at 2887. And he supported his argument with the assertion that "there is no reasonable ground for believing that Nancy Beth Cruzan has any *personal* interest in the perpetuation of what the State has decided is her life." Id at 2888. But this discourse is never reconciled with a competing discourse arguing that the state has violated Ms. Cruzan's rights by keeping her alive. The contradiction is encapsulated in a single sentence appearing toward the end of the opinion:

> If Nancy Cruzan's life were defined by reference to her own interests, so that her life expired when her biological existence ceased serving *any* of her own interests, then her constitutionally protected interest in freedom from unwanted treatment would not come into conflict with her constitutionally protected interest in life.

Id at 2889. The passage seems to suggest that Ms. Cruzan's life had expired because her existence was no longer serving any of her interests—leaving unexplained how a dead person could possibly be denied the right to die, or how a person no longer alive could have interests violated by the state's refusal to terminate treatment.

is that the very factor tending to support the removal of the feeding and hydration tubes in her case—her utter lack of consciousness—also renders incoherent the claim that she has a right to choose whether they should be withdrawn.[30]

Of course, whatever her status now, it cannot be doubted that Ms. Cruzan once had rights. It might be thought that this fact is sufficient to rescue Justice Brennan's dissent from incoherence. Much of that opinion is devoted to a discussion of Ms. Cruzan's past—of what she wanted, or what the dissent imagines she may have wanted, before her accident. Thus, the dissent argues that "[f]or many, the thought of an ignoble end, steeped in decay, is abhorrent,"[31] and that such a death is "for many, humiliating to contemplate, as is visiting a prolonged and anguished vigil on one's parents, spouse, and children."[32]

At first blush, these observations seem to suffer from the difficulty identified above. Surely the dissent is not asserting that Ms. Cruzan currently has thoughts of "an ignoble end" or that she is now feeling humiliated. Perhaps the claim is that Ms. Cruzan would have had these thoughts if, at some time in the past, she had known that the desire she then had to avoid an ignoble end would be frustrated. The dissent is on solid ground in believing that many people, whether rightly or wrongly, feel that they are somehow connected to the entity that they become when they lose consciousness. And there can be no doubt that many people, while conscious, care deeply about what will happen to their loved ones after they are no longer conscious and, indeed, after they are no longer alive.[33]

---

[30] There is, of course, more than a little controversy about the characteristics necessary for an entity to have rights. I make no assertion here about whether brain damaged individuals are, in general, appropriate rights bearers. Rather, my claim is only that there is a problem in asserting that people who are incapable of choice have a right to choose. For a similar argument, see Michael Tooley, *Abortion and Infanticide* at 121 (1983).

For a strikingly original argument that rights-bearing status is tied to our sense of human uniqueness and that the development of "artificial intelligence" will therefore lead to the abandonment of self-awareness as the touchstone for human life, see Steven Goldberg, *The Changing Face of Death: Computers, Consciousness, and Nancy Cruzan*, 43 Stan L Rev 659 (1991).

[31] *Cruzan*, 110 S Ct at 2868 (Brennan dissenting).

[32] Id at 2869 (Brennan dissenting).

[33] For an eloquent defense of family decision making premised on the assumption that most people share these emotions, see Nancy Rhoden, *Litigating Life and Death*, 102 Harv L Rev 375 (1988).

But these observations, while true enough, do not save the opinion. For it is obvious that no resolution of this case will affect what Ms. Cruzan thought, or might have thought, in the past. If she once feared a prolonged and undignified death, removing the feeding tubes now will not retroactively provide mental peace. Conversely, if she once experienced satisfaction because she believed that she would not burden her family in death, no prolongation of her parents' current agony can now deprive her of that past tranquility.

If there is a reason for respecting Ms. Cruzan's wishes, then, it is not that this respect will make things any different for her. It is, rather, that respecting them will make things different for other persons—persons who are now capable of feeling anxiety, fear, and impotence, and who might now experience these emotions if they think that, should they become incompetent, their wishes will be ignored.

This ancillary effect of disregarding Ms. Cruzan's putative former desires may or may not justify the dissent's position. But for present purposes, the crucial point is that this argument for ending life support has nothing to do with a claim that Ms. Cruzan has a "right to die." Indeed, the argument is inconsistent with the position that Ms. Cruzan is an appropriate rights bearer.

In order to see why this is so, it is necessary to examine more carefully what it means for an individual to have rights.

B

We might begin this examination by distinguishing between a public sphere, in which government decisions are determined by policy, and a private sphere in which they must be conditioned by the recognition of rights.[34] Most of constitutional law consists of an effort to delineate a boundary between these spheres, and much of the modern critique of constitutional law consists of an attack on the coherence of this boundary.

Despite this critique, I believe that the existence of such a boundary can be defended, at least if it is understood in a certain way.

---

[34] The argument summarized in the next several paragraphs is set out in much greater detail in Louis Michael Seidman, *Public Principle and Private Choice: The Uneasy Case for a Boundary Maintenance Theory of Constitutional Law*, 96 Yale L J 1006 (1987).

The defense begins with the insight that most people are caught between conflicting "public" and "private" sides of their own personalities. On some level, most of us believe that all individuals are entitled to equality of concern and respect. Yet most of us also believe that it is important for individuals to have special relationships of love and caring which are necessarily premised on inequality of concern and respect.

This contradiction can never be resolved, but it can be controlled by creating separate public and private spheres. In the public sphere, decisions should be premised on impersonal and equal beneficence. An ironic consequence of this equality is that when we are within this sphere, a welfare loss may be imposed on some individuals when this loss is necessary to achieve a greater welfare gain for other individuals. Indeed, the requirement of impersonal beneficence means that, at least in certain circumstances, some preferences held by the few *must* be frustrated so as to vindicate the preferences of the many.

In contrast, when decisions are located within a private sphere, they may be premised on special preferences for self, for family, for lovers, and for friends. It follows from this privileging that certain private sphere decisions must be immune from regulation even if they result in a net reduction in social welfare. People have a "right" to make such decisions because they should be allowed to treat themselves and those close to them not merely as means to the end of welfare maximization, but as ends in themselves.

I have argued elsewhere that much of constitutional law consists of an effort to delineate a contested and shifting boundary between these two spheres.[35] *Cruzan* presented the Court with just such a problem, and when Justice Brennan's dissent asserts that Nancy Cruzan had a "right to die," he is locating this decision squarely within the private sphere. He is claiming that her decision need not be justified by some overall utility calculus based upon an equal counting of everyone's welfare. Rather, she should be permitted to prefer her own welfare and that of her family—to decide for herself whether to die, without having to be accountable for the decision even if the decision can be shown to reduce overall social welfare.

---

[35] Id.

When one fully parses the logic of the dissent, however, the argument that ultimately emerges is not for this position at all, but rather for locating the decision in a public sphere. As I explained above, the dissent cannot be claiming that Ms. Cruzan *herself* would have her current desires frustrated by continued treatment. Patients in a persistent vegetative state have no current desires. The only sensible claim that can be made is that the failure to abide by Ms. Cruzan's previously experienced desires would reduce the sense of autonomy and well being experienced by other, conscious individuals who would now have good reason to fear that their current preferences will be disregarded in the future.

But it hardly follows from this that Ms. Cruzan has a "right" to die that *overrides* the public good. On the contrary, her treatment should be terminated because this course of conduct will *advance* the public good. Properly understood, Justice Brennan's claim is not that Ms. Cruzan is entitled to personal autonomy, but rather that the state is entitled to use Ms. Cruzan and her predicament as a means of advancing overall social welfare by alleviating the fear of others that they might someday lose their autonomy.

c

The following hypothetical—which disentangles Ms. Cruzan's autonomy claim from the effect on others of her continued treatment—tests this proposition. Suppose it could be shown empirically that disregarding Ms. Cruzan's previously expressed desires would not undermine the sense of autonomy experienced by currently conscious individuals. Those individuals might believe that their own situation was distinguishable from hers, for example. A defender of Ms. Cruzan's "rights" would nonetheless insist that the state was obligated to respect her previously expressed wishes. Conversely, a believer that patients in a persistent vegetative state have no rights would say that Ms. Cruzan's wishes could be overridden if the welfare of others (perhaps family members with a strong emotional and financial stake in the outcome) would thereby be maximized.

Reasonable people doubtless come down on both sides of this question. The public/private boundary is, after all, contested. But we have a fairly good idea where the Justices joining the Brennan dissent come down. They were the only Justices still sitting at the time of *Cruzan* who had also joined the majority opinion in *Roe v Wade*.[36] It is therefore important to understand that the problem posed in the previous paragraph *is* the abortion problem.

Fetuses can be aborted without interfering with their desires (since they have none) and, at least in our culture, without threatening the autonomy of most conscious people, who are quite confident that they will never again become fetuses. In contrast, disregarding the putative prior desires of brain damaged patients does threaten autonomy by raising doubts whether the desires of currently conscious people will be respected in the future.

Roe and the *Cruzan* dissent are therefore best reconciled on the assumption that neither fetuses nor permanently vegetative patients have rights. Indeed, the claim that brain damaged patients are rights bearers creates serious difficulties for adherents to *Roe*. That opinion treated fetuses as ranged along a continuum depending upon their state of development, with the state interest in preserving them from destruction growing more weighty as the fetus developed into an entity capable of independent thought and action.[37] On this logic the quintessential example of an individual asserting any right—including a "right to die"—would be a fully developed, fully competent, healthy adult who made a voluntary decision to commit suicide. Yet the *Cruzan* dissent carefully avoids any claim that state suicide statutes are unconstitutional—a reticence that Justice Scalia powerfully exploits in his concurring opinion. [38] Con-

---

[36] 410 US 113 (1973).

[37] The *Roe* Court held that the state's interest in the protection of the fetus "grows in substantiality as the woman approaches term" and reaches the "compelling" point at viability. 410 US at 162–63.

For an approach to abortion explicitly premised on the analogy between the beginning and end of life, see Gary B. Gertler, *Brain Birth: A Proposal for Defining When a Fetus Is Entitled to Human Life Status*, 59 S Cal L Rev 1061, 1071 (1986).

Of course, *Roe* is distinguishable from *Cruzan* because there is a fundamental individual liberty interest on the other side of the scale in the abortion context—viz., the interest of a woman in ridding herself of an unwanted pregnancy. The determination that previable fetuses are without rights—and that there is accordingly no need to balance their rights against those of the pregnant woman—was nonetheless crucial to the Court's holding. See *Roe*, 410 US at 156–57 ("If [the personhood of the fetus] is established, the appellant's case, of course, collapses, for the fetus' right to life would then be guaranteed specifically by the [Fourteenth] Amendment."). This is not to say that it plays a similarly crucial role in other defenses of the abortion right. See, for example, Judith Jarvis Thomson, *A Defense of Abortion*, 1 Phil & Pub Aff 47 (1971).

[38] See *Cruzan*, 110 S Ct at 2862 (Scalia concurring).

versely, the logic of *Roe* suggests that as sick patients at the end of their lives become more fetus-like—as they lose their capacity for independent thought, desire, and action—their rights should diminish as well. Yet it is precisely the fetus-like status of such patients that, in the dissent's view, gives them a right to die.

Thus, if brain damaged patients and fetuses are different, it is not because one but not the other has rights. Rather, it is because the putative desires of fetuses, unlike those of unconscious patients, can be disregarded without threatening the sense of autonomy enjoyed by others.

On this analysis the permissible status of abortion crucially rests on the empirical premise that insufficient numbers of people will perceive fetuses to be different from competent people, instead of treating the two as subgroups of some broader category. Irrespective of whether the distinction between fetuses and competent individuals is correct as a moral matter, it is a cultural fact that most people perceive them to be different. That, at least, is the implicit premise of this justification for abortion. If Missouri law provided that living wills written by redheads should be disregarded, many blonds and brunettes might feel that their autonomy interests were threatened. To most of us, there does not seem to be a relevant distinction between redheads and blonds. Because the distinction seems so arbitrary, action against one group will seem like the first step on a slippery slope that could well result in action against others. But the distinction between fetuses and competent persons is not perceived as being arbitrary in this way.

Thus, most advocates of abortion do not favor infanticide—even though competent adults can be assured that they will never again be infants—because in our culture, there is the perception of identity between infants and adults. It is hardly a coincidence that opponents of abortion effectively use slippery slope arguments—urging the arbitrariness of the distinction between fetus and infant and arguing that the practice of abortion ultimately threatens the lives of the old, the infirm, and the mentally impaired. These arguments are effective precisely because they challenge the categories that we use to organize our knowledge of the world. Threats directed against what was once perceived to be an alien "other" thereby become threats against ourselves.

It is possible to imagine a world where people thought of patients in a persistent vegetative state as sufficiently separated from themselves that their own autonomy would not be threatened by disregarding "living wills." If people perceived brain damaged individuals as different entities from the conscious people who once inhabited the same body, it would make no more sense to respect such a will than it would to enslave one individual to another.

But the very fact that people write such wills demonstrates that they do not see the world this way. So long as people perceive continuity between the conscious person they are and the unconscious entity they will someday become, Justice Brennan has a powerful argument for requiring deference to Nancy Cruzan's previous desires. But this is not an argument that incompetent and unconscious persons have a "right to die." It is an argument that such persons have no right to resist the use of their bodies in order to make the rest of us feel better about our own approaching impotence and death.

III

Justice Scalia's concurring opinion places decisions about life and death squarely within the public sphere. With characteristic verve and directness, he argues that the Constitution leaves the state free to make virtually any collective decision it chooses regarding the imposition of life supporting treatment on nonconsenting patients.[39] This broad power is conditioned only by the Equal Protection Clause, which "requires the democratic majority to accept for themselves and their loved ones what they impose on you and me."[40] Significantly, even this limitation constitutes a guarantee of the public quality of the decision. It amounts to an insistence that the decision be truly public in the sense that the government has neutrally and equally aggregated the preferences of all its constituents.

When one examines more closely the structure of Justice Scalia's argument, however, it becomes clear that he, like Justice Brennan, may have located his position on the wrong side of the public/private boundary. Properly understood, his reasoning lends little

---

[39] See id at 2859 (Scalia concurring) ("While I agree with the Court's analysis today, and therefore join in its opinion, I would have preferred that we announce, clearly and promptly, that the federal courts have no business in this field.").

[40] Id at 2863.

support to the claim that Ms. Cruzan lacks legal rights. The result below was correct not because she lacked a right to die, but rather because she had a right to live.

A

To see why this is so, I begin by asking: why does Justice Scalia think that the Constitution leaves the question of life and death in the public sphere? Parts of Justice Scalia's opinion suggest that the answer is in the text of the Constitution. Missouri is free to determine the issue collectively because "the Constitution says nothing about the matter."[41] But this view presupposes that the constitutional text carves out a domain of private rights against a background of pervasive public power: collective choice (at least by state governments) is the default position, assumed automatically when "the Constitution says nothing about the matter."

Justice Scalia advances no argument in defense of this position, however, and, on closer analysis of the opinion, it becomes apparent that it is not a view that he holds. He seems to believe that the presumption in favor of public power is not universally applicable and that textual silence is therefore not always determinative. His opinion acknowledges, albeit in backhanded fashion, that the Fourteenth Amendment's Due Process Clause protects a private sphere of rights that are not textually enumerated:

> The text of the Due Process Clause does not protect individuals against deprivations of liberty *simpliciter*. It protects them against deprivations of liberty "without due process of law." To determine that such a deprivation would not occur if Nancy Cruzan were forced to take nourishment against her will, it is unnecessary to reopen the historically recurrent debate over whether "due process" includes substantive restrictions. . . . *It is at least true that no "substantive due process" claim can be maintained unless the claimant demonstrates that the State has deprived him of a right historically and traditionally protected against state interference.*[42]

---

[41] Id at 2859 (Scalia concurring). See also id at 2863 (Scalia concurring):

What I have said above is not meant to suggest that I would think it desirable, if we were sure that Nancy Cruzan wanted to die, to keep her alive by the means at issue here. I assert only that the Constitution has nothing to say about the subject.

[42] Id at 2859–60 (Scalia concurring) (emphasis added).

The last sentence states the point negatively, but it is followed by a citation to Justice Scalia's own plurality opinion in *Michael H. v Gerald D.*,[43] and dicta in that opinion make the same point positively. Although the *Michael H.* plurality, like the *Cruzan* concurrence, ultimately rejected the due process claim advanced in the case, Justice Scalia's opinion in *Michael H.* nonetheless makes clear that he thinks such a claim would have been established if the claimant had succeeded in demonstrating that the right has historically been protected against state interference.[44]

B

It follows that, under his own approach, it is not sufficient for Justice Scalia to demonstrate that the constitutional text contains no explicit right to refuse lifesaving medical treatment. He must also show that this right has not been traditionally protected. His *Cruzan* concurrence accordingly launches into an extended historical analysis of laws prohibiting suicide and concludes that "there is no significant support for the claim that a right to suicide is so rooted in our tradition that it may be deemed 'fundamental' or 'implicit in the concept of ordered liberty.' "[45]

But the concession that tradition and not merely text determines the scope of constitutional rights goes further than Justice Scalia acknowledges to undermine his claim that the Constitution leaves Missouri free to determine the question in any way it chooses. This is true for a number of reasons.

First, the history that Justice Scalia cites arguably supports a stronger claim than he in fact makes. The nearly universal state intervention to prevent suicide suggests not just that there is no traditional right to commit suicide, but also that there is a traditional right to state protection against suicide. If there is such a

---

[43] 491 US 110 (1989).

[44] See *Michael H. v Gerald D.*, 491 US at 122–24 (citations omitted):

[T]he Due Process Clause affords only those protections "so rooted in the traditions and conscience of our people as to be ranked as fundamental." Our cases reflect "continual insistence upon respect for the teachings of history [and] solid recognition of the basic values that underlie our society. . . ." . . . .

Thus, the legal issue in the present case reduces to whether the relationship between persons in the situation of Michael and Victoria has been treated as a protected family unit under the historic practices of our society.

[45] See *Cruzan*, 110 S Ct at 2860. (Scalia concurring).

tradition, it follows from Justice Scalia's schema that Missouri is constitutionally obligated to protect Ms. Cruzan's life, even in the face of her considered decision that she would rather die.

Perhaps the recognition of such a tradition reads more into our history than is warranted. Certainly, it is possible, at least in principle, to distinguish between Justice Scalia's claim that there is no tradition permitting suicide and the further assertion that there is a tradition protecting against it. But a full defense of the view that the Constitution creates no rights pertaining to Ms. Cruzan's predicament would have to include a showing that state protection against suicide does not amount to traditional protection of a right to life, even in the face of one's own desire to die. Justice Scalia makes no such showing, and much of the evidence he cites, if not determinative, at least looks in the other direction.

Moreover, at this point, a second difficulty takes hold. Justice Scalia's argument from tradition is persuasive only if Ms. Cruzan's refusal of life supporting treatment is suicide. He must therefore meet petitioner's argument that this refusal is not suicide at all, but rather mere noninterference with the "natural" process of dying.

The Scalia concurrence responds to this argument by mounting a general attack on the action/inaction distinction.

> It would not make much sense to say that one may not kill oneself by walking into the sea, but may sit on the beach until submerged by the incoming tide; or that one may not intentionally lock oneself into a cold storage locker, but may refrain from coming indoors when the temperature drops below freezing. . . .
>
> It is not surprising, therefore, that the early cases considering the claimed right to refuse medical treatment dismissed as specious the nice distinction between "passively submitting to death and actively seeking it. The distinction may be merely verbal, as it would be if an adult sought death by starvation instead of a drug. If the State may interrupt one mode of self-destruction, it may with equal authority interfere with the other."[46]

This is a powerful critique. Indeed, it is more powerful than Justice Scalia imagines. For if the line between actively bringing

---

[46] Id at 2861 (Scalia concurring) (quoting from *John F. Kennedy Memorial Hosp. v Heston*, 58 NJ 576, 581–82, 279 A2d 670, 672–73 (1971).

about a death and passively allowing it to happen is as arbitrary as he asserts, it is hard to see how the state, any more than private individuals, can avoid responsibility for fatal nonfeasance. Just as there is no difference between an individual who kills herself and an individual who allows herself to die, so too, it would seem, there is no distinction between passive state acquiescence in the suicide of its citizens and active state assistance.

On the facts of *Cruzan*, this distinction seems especially arbitrary. Ms. Cruzan was in a state hospital and, by the time of the litigation, was already attached to feeding and hydration tubes. If Ms. Cruzan's parents had had their way, state doctors would have had to remove these tubes, thus taking "active" measures to bring about her death. Moreover, even if the resulting starvation was considered no more than the "passive" withholding of food, the distinction between a state hospital that kills its patients by passively starving them to death and a state hospital that kills them by actively poisoning them is every bit as arbitrary as the distinction between the individual who waits for the tide to come in and the individual who marches into the sea.

Once this distinction collapses, the claim that the Constitution does not speak to the *Cruzan* problem collapses as well. For whatever the status of a tradition favoring state protection against suicide, there is surely a strong tradition protecting sick, helpless, and innocent persons against state-sanctioned and assisted murder.

C

Justice Scalia's discussion of tradition creates still a third difficulty for him. He may be correct when he asserts that there is little support for the claim that a right to suicide is rooted in our traditions, but, as Justice Brennan forcefully argued, there is considerable support for a traditional right to avoid unwanted medical treatment.[47] Whether the Constitution speaks to Ms. Cruzan's predicament therefore depends upon which tradition one chooses to emphasize.

In a celebrated footnote in *Michael H. v Gerald D.*,[48] Justice Scalia squarely addressed the problem of choosing between conflicting

---

[47] See *Cruzan*, 110 S Ct at 2865 (Brennan dissenting).

[48] 491 US at 127 n 6 (plurality opinion by Scalia).

traditions for purposes of determining the scope of due process protection. Michael H., a natural father of a child born to a mother then married to another man, sought to rely on the traditional rights of natural fathers to support his constitutional claim to maintain a relationship with the child. Justice Scalia's plurality opinion rejected this claim because there was clearly no tradition granting such rights to *adulterous* natural fathers and, indeed, there was a tradition denying such rights. He suggested the following methodology for choosing between conflicting traditions:

> We refer to the most specific level at which a relevant tradition protecting, or denying protection to, the asserted right can be identified. If, for example, there were no societal tradition, either way, regarding the rights of the natural father of a child adulterously conceived, we would have to consult, and (if possible) reason from, the traditions regarding natural fathers in general. But there is such a more specific tradition, and it unqualifiedly denies protection to such a parent.[49]

Unfortunately, in *Cruzan*, it is far from clear which tradition is more specific and which more general. If one looks at the matter from a certain angle, one might say that Ms. Cruzan is not asserting a generalized right to end her life in all circumstances, but only a narrow, specific right to do so in circumstances where death results from abstinence from medical treatment. On this view, the right to refuse treatment is more specific and therefore should predominate. On the other hand, an opponent of such a right might plausibly respond that the narrow prohibition against suicide is more specific than a generalized right to determine medical treatment in all circumstances, including those not involving death. If this characterization is correct, then there is no right to refuse lifesaving treatment.

The analysis is further complicated by the fact that some traditions are permissive, while others are restrictive. Thus, there is a tradition permitting state regulation of suicide in tension with a tradition restricting state interference with private decisions to refuse treatment. Similarly, the tradition permitting the state to ignore the parental rights of adulterous fathers is in tension with the tradition restricting the state's right to interfere more broadly with family relationships.

---

[49] Id.

Some of Justice Scalia's writings suggest that permissive and restrictive traditions should not be given the same weight.[50] On this view, a restrictive tradition may or may not give rise to a constitutionally protected right, but it is at least true that there cannot be a constitutional right when the right would conflict with a permissive tradition.[51] It follows that when a permissive and restrictive tradition conflict, the permissive tradition should prevail, whether or not it is more specific. Thus, because the state has traditionally been permitted to regulate suicide, there cannot be a constitutional right to refuse lifesaving medical treatment even if the nonrecognition of this right would interfere with a restrictive tradition concerning state imposed medical treatment.

But this explanation for the *Cruzan* result only begs the central question. Justice Scalia never explains why permissive traditions are favored over restrictive traditions. This preference amounts to a privileging of the domain of collective public policy over the domain of private individual rights.[52] We are still left with the need to explain or justify the decision to place the decision in one sphere rather than the other. And once again, the reasons Justice Scalia offers simply do not support the conclusion he draws.

If one were a moral skeptic or agnostic on the subject of suicide, it might be sensible to adopt a preference for the public sphere. On this view, one might treat the Constitution as having "nothing to say" about the desirability of suicide because there simply is nothing to say about the subject. If choosing between life and death

---

[50] See *Burnham v Superior Court*, 110 S Ct 2105, 2115 (1990) (Scalia opinion for four Justices); *Rutan v Republican Party*, 110 S Ct 2729, 2748 (1990) (Scalia dissenting).

[51] See Justice Scalia's opinion in *Burnham v Superior Court*, 110 S Ct 2105, 2115 (1990) (quoting *Hurtado v California*, 110 US 516, 528 (1884)):

The distinction between what is needed to support novel procedures and what is needed to sustain traditional ones is fundamental, as we observed over a century ago:

"[A] process of law, which is not otherwise forbidden, must be taken to be due process of law, if it can show the sanction of settled usage both in England and in this country; but it by no means follows that nothing else can be due process of law."

Cf. Rutan v Republican Party, 110 S Ct 2729, 2748 (1990) (Scalia dissenting) ("[W]hen a practice not expressly prohibited by the text of the Bill of Rights bears the endorsement of a long tradition of open, wide-spread, and unchallenged use that dates back to the beginning of the Republic, we have no proper basis for striking it down.")

[52] See David A. Strauss, *Tradition, Precedent, and Justice Scalia*, 12 Cardozo L Rev 1699, 1708 (1991).

were like choosing between tuna salad and egg salad, one could defend collective decision making on the theory that democratic bodies are most likely to aggregate conflicting tastes in situations where everyone's desires cannot be satisfied.

But it is important to understand that Justice Scalia is not a moral skeptic on the subject of suicide. His opinion is bracketed by statements at the beginning and end making clear that he believes that there is a "right answer" to the suicide question.[53] His position stems not from the belief that there are no "right answers," but from the fear that courts are unlikely to discern the right answer:

> [T]he point at which life becomes "worthless," and the point at which the means necessary to preserve it become "extraordinary" or "inappropriate" are neither set forth in the Constitution nor known to the nine Justices of this Court any better than they are known to nine people picked at random from the Kansas City telephone directory; and hence . . . even when it *is* demonstrated by clear and convincing evidence that a patient no longer wishes certain measures to be taken to preserve her life, it is up to the citizens of Missouri to decide, through their elected representatives, whether that wish will be honored.[54]

This passage is puzzling in two, interlocking respects. First, it is hard to see why Justice Scalia thinks that the claim about "the Kansas City telephone directory" supports his position, rather than Justice Brennan's. Neither the Cruzan family nor Justice Brennan argued that it was the business of courts to determine when life was "worthless" or when medical treatment was "appropriate." On the contrary, they are the ones who wished to leave the matter to "people picked at random from the Kansas City telephone directory"—that is, to individuals making private choices about their own circumstances.

Second, it is hard to see why Justice Scalia thinks that the second clause in the passage follows from the first. There is simply no logical connection between the premise that Supreme Court Jus-

---

[53] Justice Scalia begins his opinion by observing that modern science is able to "keep the human body alive for longer than any reasonable person would want to inhabit it." *Cruzan*, 110 S Ct at 2859 (Scalia concurring). He ends by asserting that there are "obviously" "reasonable and humane limits that ought not to be exceeded in requiring an individual to preserve his own life." Id at 2863.

[54] Id at 2859 (Scalia concurring).

tices do not know the "right answer" to the suicide problem and the conclusion that the matter should be left to the collective judgment of the Missouri legislature, rather than to individuals, families, and doctors.

These non sequiturs are, in turn, symptomatic of a deeper confusion. They stem from the assumption that *Cruzan* is about the choice between judicial and legislative decision making. In fact the real issue posed by the case is the choice between the public and private sphere. To be sure, *if* the suicide question should be decided publicly, then perhaps there are strong reasons to give legislatures, rather than courts, the final word. But this observation offers no support for the conclusion *that* the matter should be publicly decided, rather than left in the private sphere. *If* this country were to have an established church, I suppose most people would agree that the religion to be established should be determined by the people's elected representatives. But it hardly follows *that* an established church is a good idea. Nor does judicial enforcement of the establishment prohibition (thereby leaving religion in the private sphere) mean that courts are assuming for themselves the power to choose an official religion.

So it turns out that the Scalia concurrence fails to provide a convincing argument for a public resolution of the *Cruzan* dilemma. On the contrary, the opinion inadvertently suggests a number of reasons why a private resolution might be preferable.

D

The irony is that Justice Scalia did not have to defend a public resolution in order to support his conclusion. The best argument for his position is not that the Constitution leaves the Missouri legislature with the power to resolve the *Cruzan* problem in any way that it chooses, but that the Constitution prohibits any governmental body from resolving it in a fashion that invades Ms. Cruzan's right to life.

It is not difficult to imagine the structure of such an argument. It rests on the core claim that individual, innocent human life should not be held hostage to the whims of legislative majorities. Even if it could be shown that overall social welfare would be maximized by killing a tiny and despised minority, thereby gratifying the sadistic desires of the majority, the Constitution surely would prohibit the slaughter. This is so because the Constitution does not permit the government to override the claim of each individual to a private sphere within which that person can act without regard to overall social welfare. And although the exact size and shape of this sphere is contested, it can hardly be doubted that it includes at least the right to life.

It may seem paradoxical to claim that the state is vindicating an individual's rights and protecting a private sphere when it prevents the individual from doing what she wishes. But there is no necessary identity between rights and desires, and no necessary contradiction in the claim that certain rights are inalienable. Even when the prohibition against suicide frustrates individual desires, it protects a "right" in this sense: it constitutes an insistence that the individual's life is not dependent on whether a governmental body decides that overall social welfare will be promoted by maintaining it. On this view, questions of life and death are simply outside the jurisdiction of public entities and can never be decided on the basis of welfare maximization.

Moreover, just as the right not to be enslaved entails a prohibition against a person selling herself into slavery, so too the right to life might be taken to mean that the state may not stand passively by while a person terminates her own life. There is a right to life because life is the necessary precondition for individual autonomy. The state's obligation to protect life is therefore not overridden merely because the individual decides to sacrifice her own autonomy.

It need hardly be added that these propositions are controversial. Not everyone would agree that this argument is the "right answer" to the suicide question. But the argument is at least consistent with the proposition that there *is* a right answer—something that cannot be said for the position actually advanced in the Scalia concurrence. One consequence of placing questions like suicide and abortion in the public sphere is that access to these procedures will be determined by the fortuities of time and geography. The rights of fetuses and incompetents—or, if you will, of pregnant women and the families of the terminally ill—will depend upon whether they happen to be in New York or New Jersey or on whether a procedure is to be performed before or after the effective date of a legislative change. Americans are sharply divided on the right answer to the abortion and termination of treatment issues, but they are largely united in the belief that these are questions of the utmost importance that turn on the resolution of central moral problems. Most people agree that, one way or the other, fundamental rights are at stake—rights which are wrongly trivialized by treating them as subject to legislative discretion.

Thus, if Justice Scalia had written in defense of a right to life, he might have defended the wrong "right" answer. But at least the opinion would have come to grips with what was really at stake in the case. By locating the *Cruzan* problem in the public sphere, he avoids a defense of the propositions that need to be defended and denigrates the powerful moral underpinnings of his own position.

IV

I have argued that the *Cruzan* debate was impoverished by a curious and reciprocal failure on the part of both sides to properly locate their position within the public or private sphere. In this final section, I want to offer a tentative explanation for this failure, as well as some ideas about its consequences for broader questions of constitutional law.

Since neither Justice Brennan nor Justice Scalia explicitly discusses his reasons for adopting his rhetorical strategies, any explanation for the structure of their opinions is necessarily speculative. I strongly suspect, however, that both opinions were substantially influenced by the obsessive and unfortunate preoccupation with judicial legitimacy that has dominated constitutional discourse since the New Deal. The unsatisfactory nature of both opinions, I believe, illustrates the price we have paid for this preoccupation.

For Justice Brennan, the problem stems from an assumption that if the treatment termination question were public—if there were no "right to die"—the question should necessarily be resolved by publicly responsive institutions. Failure to find a right to die thus leads ineluctably to the conclusion that the Court should uphold the Missouri statute—a result that he believed was wrong.

Oddly, Justice Scalia's difficulty stems from acceptance of precisely the same premise. He, like Justice Brennan, appears to think that the Court acts legitimately only when it protects a private sphere. Because Justice Scalia wished to uphold the statute, he felt it necessary to locate the problem within the public sphere, thereby undercutting the case for judicial intervention.

Both Justices are imprisoned by a box of their own making. There is no inherent reason why the Court should view its role as limited to protection of a private sphere. An important part of our constitutional tradition has involved judicial intervention designed to curb exercises of private power that threatened public values. Famous cases such as *Marsh v Alabama*,[55] stand for the proposition that the courts have an important role to play in keeping public institutions truly public and preventing them from ceding too much authority to private centers of power.

Nor need Justice Scalia fear that recognition of a private sphere necessarily requires judicial intervention. On the contrary, the Court might have upheld the Missouri statute precisely because it appropriately recognized the boundaries of a private sphere containing a right to life. Cases such as *Corporation of the Presiding Bishop of the Church of Jesus Christ of Latter-Day Saints v Amos*[56] fall squarely within this tradition.

To be sure, adopting this approach would have required Justices Brennan and Scalia to defend their positions on the merits. Justice Brennan would have had to justify the view that a truly "public" outcome would give primacy to the autonomy concerns of individuals fearing loss of control while in a persistent vegetative state rather than to the concerns of friends and relatives of the terminally ill, of other sick people competing for scarce medical resources, or, indeed, of bystanders who simply desire to live in a society where terminal illness is handled in a certain fashion. Justice Scalia, in turn, would have had to defend the view that even a voluntary and carefully considered suicide violates the rights of the person who chooses this course of conduct.

It is easy to see why both Justices would want to avoid coming to grips with these difficult and controversial substantive questions. But the ultimate lesson to be drawn from Justice Scalia's attack on the action/inaction distinction is that there is no way to avoid coming to grips with them. The Supreme Court, like a patient deciding whether to undergo treatment or a state hospital deciding whether to provide it, can find no shelter from the obligation of decision.

---

[55] 326 US 501 (1946) (First Amendment protects right of person distributing religious literature in privately owned town).

[56] 483 US 327 (1987) (upholding the constitutionality of the exemption for religious organizations from Title VII).

The Court must either invalidate the Missouri statute or leave it in place, and in either event, it has played a role in bringing about a state of affairs that must be defended on the merits.

The issues that divide Justices Brennan and Scalia are important and difficult. Perhaps it is demanding too much to expect the Justices to have comprehensive and persuasive theories that dictate resolution of these issues or to write opinions capable of persuading readers who begin with radically different premises. But it is not too much to expect that the opinions at least aid those starting with the same premises to see why a particular result will advance their position. It is time for the Justices to start talking coherently to those who share their values and to stop trying to change the subject.

ANGELA P. HARRIS

THE JURISPRUDENCE OF VICTIMHOOD

Q: Ms. Zvolanek, how has the murder of Nicholas's mother and sister affected him?

A: He cries for his mom. He doesn't seem to understand why she doesn't come home. And he cries for his sister Lacie. He comes to me many times during the week and asks me, Grandmama, do you miss my Lacie? And I tell him yes. He says, I'm worried about my Lacie.

Ms. GARDNER: Thank you. No further questions.[1]

I

At the end of its October 1990 Term, in *Payne v Tennessee*,[2] the Supreme Court held that the introduction of Mrs. Zvolanek's testimony at the penalty phase of a capital trial did not violate the Eighth Amendment. In doing so, the Court overruled its recent decisions in *Booth v Maryland*[3] and *South Carolina v Gathers*.[4] The Court concluded that evidence about the victim of a murder and the impact of the murder on the victim's family could legitimately be considered relevant to a jury's decision whether the death penalty should be imposed, and need not be treated differently from

Angela P. Harris is Acting Professor of Law, the University of California at Berkeley (Boalt Hall).

AUTHOR'S NOTE: I would like to thank John Dwyer and Catharine Wells for helpful conversations. All errors and implausibilities are mine.

[1] Joint Appendix, *Payne v Tennessee*, No 90-5721, at 3 (direct examination, sentencing phase).

[2] 111 S Ct 2597 (1991).

[3] 482 US 496 (1987).

[4] 490 US 805 (1989).

other relevant evidence.[5] *Payne* is not a surprising decision; it is consistent with the Court's policy this decade of "deregulating death."[6] More broadly, however, *Payne* promotes what might be called a jurisprudence of victimhood.

Other commentators have remarked on the Rehnquist Court's concern with the impact of affirmative action programs on innocent whites.[7] In the death penalty arena, the victims are easier to distinguish from the perpetrators. Yet even here the Court's perspective is troubling in its disregard for the ways in which crime and death are inseparable in this society from class and race. *Payne* portrays the capital sentencing trial as a contest between innocent victims and guilty defendants, in which the victims are often unfairly disadvantaged. In so doing, the Court reduces to a Manichaean struggle the ambiguous and complex politics of jury sympathy and perception. Even more seriously, the Court's jurisprudence of victimhood, in *Payne* as well as elsewhere, turns a blind eye to the larger social and historical context in which guilt and innocence are created and maintained. Like *McCleskey v Kemp*,[8] *Payne* submerges rather than acknowledges the equality issues embedded in decisions about death.

II

By 1990, the federal government and a majority of the states had passed some form of victims' rights legislation.[9] Included under

---

[5] *Payne v Tennessee*, 111 S Ct at 2609.

[6] Robert Weisberg, *Deregulating Death*, 1983 Supreme Court Review 305; see also William S. Geimer, *Death at Any Cost: A Critique of the Supreme Court's Recent Retreat from Its Death Penalty Standards*, 12 Fla St U L Rev 737 (1985).

[7] See, for example, Frances Lee Ansley, *Stirring the Ashes: Race, Class and the Future of Civil Rights Scholarship*, 74 Cornell L Rev 993, 1010–23 (1989), discussing the rhetoric of innocence in the Court's recent affirmative action cases.

[8] 401 US 279 (1987).

[9] The Victim and Witness Protection Act, 18 USC §§ 1512–15, 3579–80, was passed to serve as a model for legislation by state and local governments. See Note, *Victim Impact Statements and Restitution: Making the Punishment Fit the Victim*, 50 Brooklyn L Rev 301 (1984). The model has apparently been successful: in its amicus curiae brief in *Payne*, the State of California lists 47 states as having some form of "victim impact legislation." Brief of State of California, *Payne v Tennessee*, No 90-5721, at 3a; see generally National Organization for Victim Assistance, *Victim Rights and Services: A Legislative Directory* (1990). Other victims' rights projects have also begun at the federal level. For example, the Victims of Crime Act of 1984, 42 USC §§ 10601–04, established a fund making grants available to states for victim compensation, victim assistance programs, and child abuse prevention and treatment. In

the victims' rights rubric are statutes that amend substantive law in favor of crime victims; that authorize victim services such as restitution and counseling; and that allow for victim participation in various phases of the criminal justice process.[10] One of the most widespread innovations is the "victim impact statement," a written statement attached to the presentence report which describes the impact of the crime on the victim or the victim's family, or both.[11] The content of a victim impact statement varies, but most states require information on the seriousness of the victim's physical, emotional, and psychological injuries.[12] In addition, many states allow the report to include such matters as the victim's opinion of the offender, her fear of revictimization, her opinion on the recommended sentence, and even her own sentence recommendation.[13]

Booth considered the constitutionality of a state's use of a victim impact statement. The victims in that case were an elderly couple who were stabbed to death in their home during a robbery. The defendant and his partner were found guilty of first-degree murder,

---

1982, President Reagan's Task Force on Victims of Crime recommended that the Sixth Amendment be amended to guarantee victims "the right to be present and to be heard at all critical stages of [criminal] judicial proceedings." President's Task Force on Victims of Crime, *Final Report* (1982) at 114. For commentary on this proposal, see LeRoy L. Lamborn, *Victim Participation in the Criminal Justice Process: The Proposals for a Constitutional Amendment*, 34 Wayne L Rev 125 (1987). Several states have amended their constitutions to guarantee rights to crime victims. See David L. Roland, *Progress in the Victim Reform Movement: No Longer the "Forgotten Victim,"* 17 Pepperdine L Rev 35 (1989).

[10] For descriptions of the various forms of victims' rights legislation, see Edna Erez, *Victim Participation in Sentencing: Rhetoric and Reality*, 18 J Crim Just 19 (1990); Note, *Victim Impact Statements and Restitution: Making the Punishment Fit the Victim*, 50 Brooklyn L Rev 301 (1984); Lamborn, *Victim Participation in the Criminal Justice Process* (cited in note 9).

[11] The Victim and Witness Protection Act amended Rule 32 of the Federal Rules of Criminal Procedure to require a victim impact statement as part of the presentence report supplied to the sentencing judge. Dina R. Hellerstein, *The Victim Impact Statement: Reform or Reprisal?* 27 Am Crim L Rev 391, 394 (1989). Most states now either permit or require such a statement. One survey reports that as of summer 1987, "a victim role at sentencing had been authorized in over 96 percent of all states." Maureen McLeod, *An Examination of the Victim's Role at Sentencing: Results of a Survey of Probation Administrators*, 71 Judicature 162, 168 (1987). In some jurisdictions the victim also has the right to make an oral statement to the judge at the time of the sentencing. See Hellerstein, *The Victim Impact Statement: Reform or Reprisal?* 27 Am Crim L Rev at 399; Maureen McLeod, *Victim Participation at Sentencing*, 22 Crim L Bull 501 (1986).

[12] McLeod, *An Examination of the Victim's Role at Sentencing*, 71 Judicature at 166, table 1 (cited in note 11).

[13] For example, McLeod found that 26 percent of the probation administrators surveyed reported that the victim impact statement "must include" the victim's own sentence recommendation. Id.

and the prosecutor requested the death penalty, necessitating the preparation of a victim impact statement under Maryland law.[14] Instead of completing the form provided by the Department of Probation and Parole, the state probation officer submitted a 3½ page, single-spaced narrative based on interviews with the murder victims' son, daughter, son-in-law, and granddaughter. Some of the comments in the statement were directed toward describing the victims' personal qualities, such as the closeness of their relationship and their youthful spirit.[15] Other parts of the narrative described the anguished reactions of the victims' family to the death and their continuing grief.[16] Finally, the narrative described the family's feelings about the killers, including their inability to forgive them.[17] Agent Swann's narrative concludes:[18]

> As described by their family members, the Bronsteins were loving parents and grandparents whose family was most important to them. Their funeral was the largest in the history of the Levinson Funeral Home and the family received over one thousand sympathy cards, some from total strangers. They attempted to answer each card personally. The family states that Mr. and Mrs. Bronstein were extremely good people who wouldn't hurt a fly. Because of their loss, a terrible void has been put into their lives and every day is still a strain just to get through. It became increasingly apparent to the writer as she talked to the family members that the murder of Mr. and Mrs. Bronstein is still such a shocking, painful, and devastating memory to them that it permeates every aspect of their daily lives. It is doubtful that they will ever be able to fully recover from this tragedy and not be haunted by the memory of the brutal manner in which their loved ones were murdered and taken from them.

At the sentencing phase of the trial, over the objection of defense counsel, the statement was read to the jury in full. The jury recommended a death sentence.[19]

---

[14] Under Maryland law, a victim impact statement is required in any case in which the death penalty or life imprisonment without possibility of parole is requested. Md Ann Code Art 41, § 4-609(d) (1990).

[15] Victim Impact Statement, *Booth v Maryland*, 482 US at 510.

[16] Id at 511.

[17] Id at 512.

[18] Id at 514–15.

[19] See Joint Appendix, *Booth v Maryland*, No 86-5020, at 8–9.

In *Payne*, the murder victims were a young woman and one of her children, killed in an inexplicably brutal attack by a neighbor's boyfriend. The state of Tennessee had not explicitly provided for the introduction of victim impact statements in the sentencing phase of a capital trial, but the trial court permitted the mother and grandmother of the victims to testify movingly about the effect of the murder on the surviving child. The jury sentenced Payne to death.

III

Booth held that the admission of victim impact evidence in the sentencing phase of a capital murder trial created an impermissible risk of arbitrary decision making under the Eighth Amendment. Justice Powell, writing for the Court, began the opinion with the familiar principle that "a jury's discretion to impose the death sentence must be 'suitably directed and limited so as to minimize the risk of wholly arbitrary and capricious action.'"[20] The opinion then took a step further: "[W]hile this Court has never said that the defendant's record, characteristics, and the circumstances of the crime are the only permissible sentencing considerations, a state statute that requires consideration of other factors must be scrutinized to ensure that the evidence has some bearing on the defendant's 'personal responsibility and moral guilt.'"[21]

The Court then separated the victim impact statement at issue into two elements: information about the personal characteristics of the victims and the emotional impact of the crimes on the family, and information about the family members' opinions and characterizations of the crimes and the defendant.[22] The Court held that the first type of information was irrelevant to the death decision, because killers often do not know their victims, and "rarely select their victims based on whether the murder will have an effect on anyone other than the person murdered."[23] According to Justice Powell, "[a]llowing the jury to rely on a VIS therefore could result

---

[20] *Booth*, 482 US at 502, quoting *Gregg v Georgia*, 428 US 153, 189 (1976) (joint opinion of Stewart, Powell, and Stevens).

[21] *Booth*, 482 US at 502, quoting *Enmund v Florida*, 458 US 782, 801 (1982).

[22] *Booth*, 482 US at 502.

[23] Id at 504.

in imposing the death sentence because of factors about which the defendant was unaware, and that were irrelevant to the decision to kill. This evidence thus could divert the jury's attention away from the defendant's background and record, and the circumstances of the crime."[24] The Court conceded that in some cases the defendant will know something about the victim, and that "a defendant's degree of knowledge of the probable consequences of his actions may increase his moral culpability in a constitutionally significant manner."[25] However, this fact was outweighed by the "impermissible risk that the capital sentencing decision will be made in an arbitrary manner."[26]

In *South Carolina v Gathers*, the Court took the same approach, finding constitutionally impermissible the prosecutor's references to a pamphlet found on the victim's body called "The Game Guy's Prayer" because there was no evidence that the defendant knew anything about the content of the tract, let alone that it contributed to his decision to kill the victim.[27] The Court also rejected the argument that the contents of the pamphlet and the victim's other personal effects were relevant to the circumstances of the crime. In the Court's view, "the content of the various papers the victim happened to be carrying when he was attacked was purely fortuitous, and cannot provide any information relevant to the defendant's moral culpability."[28]

As Chief Justice Rehnquist, writing for the Court in *Payne*, later remarked, *Booth* and *Gathers* were based on two premises: "that evidence relating to a particular victim or to the harm that a capital defendant causes a victim's family do[es] not in general reflect on the defendant's 'blameworthiness,' and that only evidence relating to 'blameworthiness' is relevant to the capital sentencing decision."[29] Because neither of these premises is strongly founded in the Court's capital jurisprudence, the *Booth-Gathers* analysis is problematic.

---

[24] Id at 505.

[25] Id.

[26] Id.

[27] *South Carolina v Gathers*, 490 US 805, 811 (1989).

[28] Id at 812.

[29] *Payne*, 111 S Ct at 2605; see also *Booth*, 482 US at 516 (White dissenting).

A

The first premise of *Booth* and *Gathers* is that the harm caused by a murder to the victim and her family, beyond the fact of the killing itself, is not relevant to the issue of the defendant's blameworthiness. But in fact we do sometimes blame people for unforeseeable consequences of their actions, even while we simultaneously believe that to do so is inappropriate.

The harm a defendant actually does may well be different from the harm that she intends or consciously risks. The notion of blameworthiness in Anglo-American criminal law—sometimes described as *"mens rea* in its general sense"[30]—turns on the defendant's responsibility for her choices.[31] To base criminal punishment on the unforeseeable results of the defendant's conduct is therefore in tension with a fundamental principle of criminal liability.[32]

The criminal law does, however, often make culpability depend on the results of an action, even if the offender could not reasonably have foreseen them. The examples are familiar: the penalties for murder and attempted murder are different in most jurisdictions, even though the defendant's actions and intentions may have been the same; negligent conduct that might constitute a misdemeanor becomes involuntary manslaughter if the victim dies.[33] Despite the emphasis in the criminal law on notions of choice and intention, punishment often turns on events out of the defendant's control. Moreover, this is not simply a matter of wrongheaded doctrine but a problem deep within our notions of blame and responsibility. Philosophers use the term "moral luck" to describe a situation in which an actor is judged morally blameworthy even though the consequences of her actions are to a significant extent out of her control.[34] Buried in the tension between harm and culpability is the paradox of free will versus determinism, a paradox that "goes all

---

[30] See Sanford H. Kadish and Stephen J. Schulhofer, *Criminal Law and Its Processes: Cases and Materials* 217 (Little, Brown, 5th ed 1989).

[31] Id; see also H. L. A. Hart, *Punishment and Responsibility* at 28 (Oxford, 1968).

[32] See Stephen J. Schulhofer, *Harm and Punishment: A Critique of Emphasis on the Results of Conduct in the Criminal Law*, 122 U Pa L Rev 1497 (1974), pointing out the incompatibility of harm calculations with a *mens rea* theory of criminal responsibility.

[33] See id at 1498–99.

[34] Thomas Nagel, *Moral Luck* at 26, in *Mortal Questions* (Cambridge, 1979); see also Bernard Williams, *Moral Luck*, in *Moral Luck* (Cambridge, 1981).

the way down."[35] Despite the intuition that evidence of a particular victim's life or the unanticipated harm the defendant has caused should have no bearing on the defendant's responsibility, the existence of moral luck suggests that we do in fact blame· people for circumstances beyond their control.

Whether or not the problem of moral luck can be resolved as a matter of moral philosophy, its consequences are everywhere in the criminal law, and the Court has in other situations accepted them. For example, as Justice Scalia noted in his *Booth* dissent, if the harm a defendant causes is irrelevant to the death decision unless it reflects on her blameworthiness, then decisions like that in *Tison v Arizona*[36] are called into question.[37] *Tison* involved the capital murder convictions of two brothers who had helped their father escape from prison. In the course of the escape, the father and his cellmate kidnapped and murdered a married couple and two children.[38] The brothers and the cellmate were convicted of capital murder and sentenced to death on the basis of the Arizona felony murder doctrine, under which a killing occurring during the perpetration of robbery or kidnapping is capital murder, and the doctrine of accomplice liability, under which each participant in a crime is responsible for the acts of her accomplices. The Court held, 5–4, that the defendants' death sentences did not violate the Eighth Amendment proportionality principle, despite the fact that the defendants did not participate in the killing and testified that they were "surprised" by it.[39] As Justice Scalia later pointed out, the Tisons' death sentences were not based on their blameworthiness in the traditional sense, but rather on the degree of harm their actions ultimately caused.[40] If *Booth* and *Gathers* are correct and evidence related solely to the harm the murder has caused is irrelevant to the death decision, *Tison* is, to say the least, undermined.

Justice Souter gave different reasons for rejecting the premise that evidence of the harm a defendant causes does not reflect on the

---

[35] Nagel, *Moral Luck* at 37 (cited in note 34).

[36] 481 US 137 (1987).

[37] *Booth*, 482 US at 519 (Scalia dissenting); see also *Payne*, 111 S Ct at 2605; *Gathers*, 490 US at 818 (O'Connor dissenting); *Booth*, 482 US 517 (White dissenting).

[38] *Tison*, 481 US at 140–41.

[39] Id at 158.

[40] *Booth*, 1482 US at 520 (Scalia dissenting).

defendant's blameworthiness. In his concurrence in *Payne*, Justice Souter, joined by Justice Kennedy, argued that "evidence of the specific harm caused when a homicidal risk is realized is nothing more than evidence of the risk that the defendant originally chose to run despite the kinds of consequences that were obviously foreseeable."[41] It is a familiar maxim in criminal law that people intend the ordinary and natural (that is, foreseeable) consequences of their acts. But the maxim is not a substitute for the *mens rea* inquiry the death decision requires.[42] Moreover, this approach still leaves foreseeability to be determined. That a murder victim will leave behind a grieving family is foreseeable, but the specific form that grief will take is not. Justice Souter's approach would suggest that only the broad outlines of the family's loss could be used as evidence; but the power and poignancy of victim impact evidence is in its specificity and uniqueness.

B

The second premise of *Booth* and *Gathers*—that only evidence relating to the defendant's blameworthiness is relevant to the death decision—is similarly problematic. I have argued that because the borders of "blameworthiness" are so fuzzy, it does not follow from this premise that victim impact evidence should be inadmissible. In addition, the notion that individual blameworthiness is the touchstone of the death decision suggests a substantive theory of punishment based on some form of retribution. Although the Court has previously seemed to favor retribution as one of the most important justifications for the death penalty, if not the sole justification, the Court has been careful not to endorse a particular substantive theory of punishment.[43]

---

[41] *Payne*, 111 S Ct at 2616.

[42] See Wayne R. LaFave and Austin W. Scott, Jr., *Criminal Law* § 3.5 at 225 (West, 2d ed 1986), discussing the maxim as a permissive inference; Rollin M. Perkins and Ronald N. Boyce, *Criminal Law* at 812–13 (Foundation, 3d ed 1982) discussing it as a means of determining causation; and *Tison v Arizona*, 481 US at 150–51, distinguishing its use in the felony murder context from the intent inquiry as "generally understood in the common law."

[43] For example, the Court usually cites deterrence as an equally important goal of capital punishment. See *Spaziano v Florida*, 468 US 447, 462 (1984); *Enmund v Florida*, 458 US 782, 798 (1982); *Gregg v Georgia*, 428 US 153, 183 (1976) (joint opinion of Stewart, Powell, and Stevens). In *Jurek v Texas*, 428 US 262 (1976), the Court held that the likelihood that the

Finally, another case decided last Term suggests that an important source of support for the *Booth-Gathers* focus on personal blameworthiness has an uncertain future. The Court has held that punishment that is disproportionate to the crime is "cruel and unusual" within the meaning of the Eighth Amendment.[44] In evaluating the proportionality of the punishment, the Court has assessed the gravity of the individual defendant's offense, often explicitly in terms of retributivist principles.[45] The proportionality cases thus support the notion that individual blameworthiness must be at the center of the death decision.[46]

Last Term, in *Harmelin v Michigan*,[47] the Court upheld a statute that imposed a mandatory sentence of life in prison without the possibility of parole on a man who had been convicted of cocaine possession. Justice Scalia, who announced the judgment of the Court, and Chief Justice Rehnquist concluded after a long historical essay that the words "cruel and unusual" in the Eighth Amendment do not authorize any kind of proportionality analysis, but merely prohibit "barbaric" modes of punishment.[48] Although Justice Kennedy, joined by Justices O'Connor and Souter, would have adhered to precedent and retained a "narrow" proportionality principle, his opinion emphasized that the responsibility for determining and implementing the purposes of the penal system rests with legislatures, not the courts, and that "the Eighth Amendment does not mandate adoption of any one penological theory."[49] Five Justices, then, are willing either to abolish proportionality analysis altogether or to significantly reduce its scope in light of concerns about judicial competence. In light of these developments, the proposition that only evidence relating to blameworthiness is relevant to the death decision seems increasingly precarious.

---

defendant would commit additional crimes was a constitutionally acceptable reason for imposing the death penalty.

[44] See, for example, *Tison v Arizona*, 481 US 137 (1987); *Solem v Helm*, 463 US 277 (1983); *Coker v Georgia*, 433 US 584 (1977).

[45] See, for example, *Enmund*, 458 US at 798–800.

[46] Note, *The Significance of Victim Harm: Booth v Maryland and the Philosophy of Punishment in the Supreme Court*, 55 U Chi L Rev 1303, 1316 (1988).

[47] 111 S Ct 2680 (1991).

[48] *Harmelin*, 111 S Ct at 2695 (Scalia writing separately).

[49] Id at 2703–04 (Kennedy concurring in part).

IV

In *Payne*, the Court reviewed the widespread use of harm calculations in substantive criminal law and in sentencing practices and concluded that victim impact evidence is simply another form of bringing relevant information to the sentencer. Therefore, "[t]here is no reason to treat such evidence differently than other relevant evidence is treated."[50] Further, the introduction of victim impact evidence serves the purpose of humanizing the victim, just as the defendant is allowed a chance to be seen as a unique individual. The Court suggested that *Booth* had "unfairly weighted the scales in a capital trial" by eliminating such humanizing evidence on behalf of the victim, "while virtually no limits are placed on the relevant mitigating evidence a capital defendant may introduce concerning his own circumstances."[51]

Despite *Payne*'s acuity in pinpointing the flaws of *Booth* and *Gathers*, however, the opinion is ultimately unsatisfying. Like the cases it overrules, *Payne* shows little sensitivity to the problems of jury decision making in the context of the death decision. Even more troubling, *Payne* adopts reasoning and a rhetorical style that threatens to obscure the complex and serious issues involved in capital punishment with a jurisprudence of victimhood, which reduces the penalty trial to a contest between the innocent and the guilty.

A

A persistent problem in the Court's death penalty jurisprudence since *Furman v Georgia*[52] has been the fact that, as one commentator has written:[53]

> Capital punishment is at once the best and worst subject for legal rules. The state's decision to kill is so serious, and the cost of error so high, that we feel impelled to discipline the human power of the death sentence with rational legal rules. Yet a judge or jury's decision to kill is an intensely moral, subjective matter that seems to defy the designers of general formulas for legal decision.

---

[50] *Payne*, 111 S Ct at 2609.

[51] Id at 2607.

[52] 408 US 238 (1972).

[53] Robert Weisberg, *Deregulating Death*, 1983 Supreme Court Review 305, 308.

The open-textured, moral character of the death decision has daunted the Court's efforts to provide substantive guidelines for the jury in the penalty phase.[54] The demise of *Booth* and *Gathers* seems to indicate a similar withdrawal from procedural regulation of the penalty jury. But a close look at the work of the jury in the penalty phase of a capital trial reveals both the need for attention to the ways in which death decisions are made and some implications for the problem of victim impact evidence.

In the penalty phase of a capital trial, the defendant's guilt is no longer an issue. Instead, typically the jury considers both "aggravating" and "mitigating" factors in order to decide whether the defendant should receive the death penalty. In most jurisdictions, the aggravating circumstances the jury is asked to consider are enumerated by statute.[55] The Court, however, has held that in order to ensure that the defendant is treated as a "uniquely individual human being," no limit may be placed on the mitigating evidence that the jury can consider.[56] The jury's task is therefore to balance its list of aggravating circumstances (such as the defendant's record or the brutal nature of the crime) against an open-ended list of mitigating circumstances such as the defendant's childhood, present remorse, and degree of involvement in the killing.

It is difficult to fit this decision-making process into a formal, rule-governed model of decision making. There are no "rules" to apply to the facts; indeed, the Supreme Court has found mandatory death penalties unconstitutional.[57] It is not always clear whether a particular circumstance should be considered a mitigating or aggravating circumstance.[58] And empirical research indicates that juries in fact do not attempt to "weigh" or "balance" the statutory factors,

---

[54] See id at 395, arguing that "the Supreme Court seems to have decided that it no longer wants to use constitutional law to foster legal formulas for regulating moral choice at the penalty trial."

[55] In a few jurisdictions, the judge is the sentencing authority, or may override the recommendation of an advisory jury. See Stephen Gillers, *Deciding Who Dies*, 129 U Pa L Rev 1, 14 (1980); *Spaziano v Florida*, 468 US 447, 465 (1978).

[56] See *Payne*, 111 S Ct at 2609; *Penry v Lynaugh*, 492 US 302, 317 (1989).

[57] See, for example, *Sumner v Shuman*, 483 US 66, 85 (1987); *Roberts v Louisiana*, 431 US 633, 637 (1977); *Woodson v North Carolina*, 428 US 280, 305 (1976) (opinion of Stewart, Powell, and Stevens).

[58] See Note, *A Continuing Source of Aggravation: The Improper Consideration of Mitigating Factors in Death Penalty Sentencing*, 41 Hastings L J 409 (1990).

but rather base their decisions on factors which may or may not resemble the statutory list.[59]

The death decision is thus a form of "contextual" rather than "structured" decision making:[60] decision making that occurs at a lower level of abstraction than the legal ideal of applying a formal and universalized rule to a set of facts.[61] As Justice White emphasized in his dissent in *Booth*, " '[T]he decision that capital punishment may be the appropriate sanction in extreme cases is an expression of the community's belief that certain crimes are themselves so grievous an affront to humanity that the only adequate response may be the penalty of death.' "[62] In deciding whether the defendant should receive death, the penalty jury gathers a broad range of facts about the killing and ultimately makes a moral decision.[63]

In structured decision making, formal rules serve as a way of restraining the decision maker from making inappropriate decisions. In contextual decision making, where such formal rules are absent, the outcome depends more crucially on the character of

---

[59] See William S. Geimer and Jonathan Amsterdam, *Why Juries Vote Life or Death: Operative Factors in Ten Florida Death Penalty Cases*, 15 Am J Crim L 1 (1988).

[60] See Catharine Wells, *Situated Decisionmaking*, 63 S Cal L Rev 1727 (1990).

[61] Recently many legal scholars, drawing on various intellectual traditions, have begun to criticize the ideal of legal decision making as formalized, syllogistic, and rule-bound, and have substituted an ideal involving reliance on the particular rather than the abstract, recognition and acceptance of complexity, flexibility, and a concern for "context." Many of these writers draw on the Aristotelian concept of "practical reason." See, for example, William N. Eskridge, Jr. and Philip P. Frickey, *Statutory Interpretation as Practical Reasoning*, 42 Stan L Rev 321, 323, 371 (1990); Richard A. Posner, *The Jurisprudence of Skepticism*, 86 Mich L Rev 827, 838 (1988); Daniel A. Farber and Philip P. Frickey, *Practical Reason and the First Amendment*, 34 UCLA L Rev 1615, 1645–56 (1987); for a discussion of what Aristotle meant by practical reason, see Martha Nussbaum, *Non-Scientific Deliberation*, in *The Fragility of Goodness: Luck and Ethics in Greek Tragedy and Philosophy* at 290 (Cambridge, 1986). Other scholars draw on the feminist tradition. See, for example, Martha Minow and Elizabeth V. Spelman, *In Context*, 63 S Cal L Rev 1597 (1990); Margaret Jane Radin, *The Pragmatist and the Feminist*, 63 S Cal L Rev 1699 (1990). The call for context converges with the anti-foundationalist and pragmatist movements in philosophy. See, for example, Cornel West, *The Limits of Neopragmatism*, 63 S Cal L Rev 1747 (1990); Ruth Anna Putnam, *Justice in Context*, 63 S Cal L Rev 1797 (1990); Richard Rorty, *Consequences of Pragmatism* (Univ. of Minnesota, 1982).

[62] *Booth*, 482 US at 515 (White dissenting), quoting *Gregg v Georgia*, 428 US 153, 184 (opinion of Stewart, Powell, and Stevens).

[63] Of the current members of the Court, Justice O'Connor most consistently emphasizes the moral nature of the jury's death decision. See, for example, *Gathers*, 490 US at 814, 818, 819 (O'Connor dissenting); *California v Brown*, 479 US at 538, 545 (1987) (O'Connor concurring).

the decision maker.[64] Two matters of character seem especially important in the penalty phase of a capital trial: the jurors' ability to empathize and their ability individually and collectively to adopt a reflective and critical perspective toward their own intuitive judgments.[65] The procedural rules surrounding the trial can serve either to encourage or to retard the exercise of these capacities.

The Court has held that the Eighth Amendment requires an individualized assessment of the appropriateness of the death penalty.[66] In order to provide this assessment, the sentencing jury must be given access to any and all mitigating evidence.[67] According to the Court in *Woodson v North Carolina*,[68] this requirement reflects "the fundamental respect for humanity underlying the Eighth Amendment." The defendant, then, must be seen as a unique human being; and in light of the inherent difficulty of seeing a capital murderer this way,[69] the defense must be accorded a wide latitude in encouraging this process with the introduction of mitigating evidence.

But the killer's story is only part of the whole story of the murder; and in order to make a fully informed, sensitive moral decision, the jury should be able to see the victim as a human being as well. The purpose of victim impact evidence is not simply to provide the jury with information about the quantity and nature of the harm caused by the defendant, but to give the jury a sense of the unique humanity of the victim as well—thus *Payne*'s assertion that the rule in *Booth* and *Gathers* turned the victim of a murder into a " 'faceless stranger.' "[70] From the point of view of regulating the

---

[64] Aristotle took the view that the person of practical wisdom was a person of good character. See Martha Nussbaum, *The Fragility of Goodness* 306 (cited in note 61). See also Robin West, *Relativism, Objectivity, and Law*, 99 Yale L J 1473, 1501 (1990).

[65] See Wells, *Situated Decisionmaking*, 63 S Cal L Rev at 1734–35 (cited in note 60), describing the task of situated decision making as involving several steps, including "reconstructing the event from the perspectives of the various parties" and correcting intuitive responses through self-criticism.

[66] *Penry v Lynaugh*, 492 US 302, 317 (1989).

[67] See *Payne*, 111 S Ct at 2609; *Penry*, 492 US at 317, citing *Lockett v Ohio*, 438 US 586, 604 (1978) (plurality opinion).

[68] 428 US 280, 304 (1976) (plurality opinion).

[69] See Samuel H. Pillsbury, *Emotional Justice: Moralizing the Passions of Criminal Punishment*, 74 Cornell L Rev 655, 692 (1989), discussing the tendency to "demonize" the defendant who has committed a serious crime.

[70] *Payne*, 111 S Ct at 2608. Justice O'Connor also understands victim impact evidence to serve the function of "conveying to the jury a sense of the unique human being whose life

contextual decision-making process, the admission of victim impact evidence seems to aid the jury's task.

But the ability to reflect on one's intuitive and emotional reactions is as important a virtue in the penalty trial process as the ability to empathize. The process of applying external rules to a set of facts provides the structured decision maker with an opportunity for distance from her own judgments. The great danger of contextual decision making, in contrast, is the potential absence of any critical perspective.[71]

Here the admission of victim impact evidence seems threatening rather than helpful. First, self-criticism could be blocked by the overwhelming anger, revulsion, or other strong emotions that victim impact evidence may evoke in the individual juror. Second, and more subtly, self-criticism could be blocked by the reliance of victim impact evidence on social stereotypes that seem too "natural" to be subjected to critique. The Court has seen the first problem with respect to victim impact evidence, but not the second.

1. *Booth*'s analysis of the admissibility of family members' opinions and characterizations of the crimes, and recommendations as to the defendant's disposition, was succinct:[72]

> One can understand the grief and anger of the family caused by the brutal murders in this case, and there is no doubt that jurors generally are aware of these feelings. But the formal presentation of this information by the State can serve no other purpose than to inflame the jury and divert it from deciding the case on the relevant evidence concerning the crime and the defendant. As we have noted, any decision to impose the death sentence must "be, and appear to be, based on reason rather than caprice or emotion." The admission of these emotionally-charged opinions as to what conclusions the jury should draw from the evidence clearly is inconsistent with the reasoned decisionmaking we require in capital cases.

The nature of the Court's concern is clear: a jury that uncritically acts on the emotions evoked by a victim impact statement is too likely to send the defendant to death without reason or reflection, in violation of the Eighth Amendment principle prohibiting "arbi-

---

the defendant has taken," in order to assist the jury in its "profoundly moral" decision. *Gathers*, 490 US at 817 (O'Connor dissenting).

[71] See Wells, *Situated Decisionmaking*, 63 S Cal L Rev at 1735–36 (cited in note 60).

[72] *Booth*, 482 at 508–9 (citation omitted).

trary and capricious" decision making. The solution, however, is not simply to discredit "emotion" and exalt "reason."

To begin with, it is difficult to imagine any victim impact evidence that would not speak to the emotions. In addition, drawing a strict reason/emotion line would embroil the Court in choosing among possible justifications for the death penalty. The theory of retribution does not preclude and indeed may rely on the emotion of outrage.[73] Prohibiting the introduction of evidence that evokes outrage may therefore hinder the jury in the performance of its duty.

The problem is not the jurors' emotional reaction itself, but the likelihood that jurors will fail to reflect on and criticize their own judgments, including their emotional judgments. Emotions are not inimical to the reasoning process, particularly in a contextual decision-making situation. Rather, emotions, being partly cognitive, are partly intellectual and can serve as guides to reasoned decision making.[74]

The Court began to move closer to this idea—that reflective emotionality rather than nonemotionality is the goal—in *California v Brown*.[75] In that case, the sentencing jury in a capital murder trial heard mitigating evidence concerning both the defendant's capacity to commit the crime and his shame and remorse afterwards, including his own testimony asking for mercy.[76] The trial judge instructed the jury to weigh the aggravating and mitigating circumstances, but also warned that it "must not be swayed by mere sentiment, conjecture, sympathy, passion, prejudice, public opinion or public feeling."[77] Brown was sentenced to death. On appeal, the California Supreme Court reversed the death sentence on the ground that the Eighth Amendment requirement that the defen-

---

[73] See Samuel Pillsbury, *Emotional Justice: Moralizing the Passions of Criminal Punishment*, 74 Cornell L Rev 655 (1989).

[74] See, for discussion, Robert Solomon, *Emotions and Choice*, and Ronald De Sousa, *Self-Deceptive Emotions*, in Amelie Rorty, ed, *Explaining Emotions* (U Cal, 1980); Pillsbury (cited in note 73); Michael Moore, *The Moral Worth of Retribution*, in *Emotions, Character, and Responsibility* (Cambridge, 1982); Nussbaum, *The Fragility of Goodness* at 307–09 (cited in note 61).

[75] 479 US 538 (1987).

[76] *Brown*, 479 US at 539.

[77] Id at 542.

dant be entitled to present all mitigating circumstances precluded such an "anti-sympathy" instruction.

The United States Supreme Court, in a 5–4 decision, reversed. The Court, per Chief Justice Rehnquist in a somewhat strained opinion, held that, under the circumstances, a reasonable jury would not have understood the instruction to bar all sympathy for the defendant, but only "untethered" sympathy: that is, sympathy arising not from the evidence presented but from the juror's own pre-existing biases. The Court's conclusion—that there was no reasonable risk of jury misunderstanding—seems implausible. But the distinction between "tethered" and "untethered" sympathy holds promise as a more sophisticated approach to regulating the death decision than simply seeking to ban emotion.

Two issues remain, however. First, allowing the jury to hear families' opinions, characterizations, and recommendations might impermissibly encourage the jury to shirk its ultimate responsibility for the death decision and simply act as the agent of the grieving family. In *Caldwell v Mississippi*,[78] the Court ruled that the Eighth Amendment was violated by a prosecutor's suggestions that ultimate responsibility for a death sentence lay not with the jury but with the appellate court that would later review the case. Justice Marshall, writing for the Court, noted that its decisions have "taken as a given that capital sentencers would view their task as the serious one of determining whether a specific human being should die at the hands of the State."[79] In a situation where individual jurors are "placed in a very unfamiliar situation and called on to make a very difficult and uncomfortable choice,"[80] without much substantive guidance from the court, the temptation for jurors to minimize their own responsibility based on assurances from the prosecutor was too great. The *Caldwell* principle, logically extended, might well prohibit the admission of victim impact evidence that describes the recommendations of the victim's family, for reasons quite apart from the emotional impact of that evidence.

Second, some evidence may simply be so emotionally inflammatory that it creates a constitutionally unacceptable risk of arbitrary and capricious decision making. This problem, however, may be

---

[78] 472 US 320 (1985).

[79] Id at 329.

[80] Id at 333.

better handled by the trial court, with relief under the Due Process Clause available in egregious cases.[81]

2. A second source of problems raised by the admission of victim impact evidence is both more subtle and more troubling: jurors may fail to criticize their own judgments, not because of an inability to surmount strong emotional pulls, but because their judgments are invisible, perhaps preconscious.

In *Booth*, the Court noted that if victim impact evidence were admitted, death decisions might come to turn on "the perception that the victim was a sterling member of the community rather than someone of questionable character."[82] The Court added in a footnote: "We are troubled by the implication that defendants whose victims were assets to their community are more deserving of punishment than those whose victims are perceived to be less worthy. Of course, our system of justice does not tolerate such distinctions."[83]

Justice White in dissent responded that penal codes may constitutionally identify as particularly worthy of the death penalty the killing of certain high-status people such as government officials or law enforcement officers on active duty. His answer to the concern that the jury might be moved to rely on "impermissible factors such as the race of the victim" was that "there is no showing that the statements in this case encouraged this, nor should we lightly presume such misconduct on the jury's part."[84] Similarly, *Payne* rejected the concern that over the long run defendants whose victims were assets to the community would be punished more harshly than defendants whose victims were considered less worthy, noting that comparative judgments were not the aim of victim impact evidence.[85]

These responses, however, misconceive the nature of the problem. The danger is not that the jury's reasoning will be consciously skewed toward letting the killer of a vagrant, for example, go free; rather, the problem is that widely shared social constructions of

---

[81] See *Payne*, 111 S Ct at 2608.

[82] *Booth*, 482 US at 506.

[83] Id at n 8.

[84] Id at 2540.

[85] *Payne*, 111 S Ct at 2607.

what it means to be a victim enter into the decision-making process at the stage of forming an intuitive judgment, and may never reach the point of conscious scrutiny. At one level, contextual decision making generally and jury decision making in particular rely on the existence of these shared social constructs. At another level, these constructs can be problematic when they reflect shared values that are illegitimate.[86]

Trial attorneys persuade a jury by offering a narrative that makes sense of both the facts and what the jurors assume to be true about the world; and to the extent that a narrative is a familiar one, drawing upon widely shared stereotypes, it is all the more persuasive. In rejecting the concern that the killers of victims in good social standing would be punished more harshly than the killers of less productive members of society, the *Payne* Court relied on *Gathers*, asserting that the victim in that case was successfully portrayed as a unique and valuable individual.[87] But *Gathers* can also be used to illustrate the problem.

In *Gathers*, the victim was an unemployed, mentally handicapped man. During the penalty phase of the trial, the prosecutor read from a pamphlet found on the victim's body called "The Game Guy's Prayer." This pamphlet linked Christian living with the rules of being a "sport in this little game of life."[88] The prosecutor also commented on the fact that a voting registration card was found among the victim's personal effects. The prosecutor's closing statement ended, " 'And he believed that in Charleston County, in the United States of America, that in this country you could go to a public park and sit on a public bench and not be attacked by the likes of Demetrius Gathers.' "[89]

The success of this narrative does not so much rest on its ability to capture the victim as a unique human being, but rather on its ability to draw on shared social conceptions of goodness and innocence: Christianity, sports, citizenship, the essential value of the "little guy," and pride in being an American. The dark side of

---

[86] Compare Margaret Jane Radin, *The Pragmatist and the Feminist*, 63 S Cal L Rev 1699, 1710 (1990), describing as "bad coherence" the problem of widely shared, coherent beliefs that support practices of domination and oppression.

[87] *Payne*, 111 S Ct at 2607.

[88] *Gathers*, 490 US at 808.

[89] Id at 810.

contextual decision making in capital punishment cases, then, is that in the absence of precise rules to apply to certain facts, the jury is even less likely to see, let alone criticize, the spectacles through which it views the world.

3. Such narratives are probably inevitable, and in most cases unobjectionable. But victim impact evidence also provides an opportunity for the jury to use social constructs that are incompatible with ideals of equal justice. The most serious danger, given what we know about the history and administration of the death penalty, is that the introduction of victim impact evidence will allow prosecutors an opportunity to draw on social stereotypes of criminal victims and victimhood that are impermissibly intertwined with racism.

Although one could imagine a situation in which the jury's racism was explicitly appealed to, a different kind of scenario is more likely. For example, Stephen Carter has argued that the Bernhard Goetz case became so notorious because one narrative offered of the event—the story of a heroic individual defending himself against vicious, animal-like aggressors—successfully drew on a popular understanding of victimhood.[90] Carter argues that this understanding is based on "bilateral individualism"—the perception that victimization is "the result of concrete, individual acts by identifiable transgressors."[91]

Bilateral individualism is incompatible with a different understanding of victimization that is group-based, rather than individual-based, and that could be invoked to show that the aggressors are also victims. Failure to recognize this group-based concept of victimhood, in a world of systematic oppression of people on the basis of race, leads to a perspective in which black defendants are consistently thought of as predators, and the extent to which they may be victims is lost. This is not racism in the sense of conscious, intentional animus; rather, it is a seemingly neutral way of making sense of the world which nonetheless systematically disadvantages defendants who happen to be black.

A recent book by Patricia Williams also takes the Goetz case as paradigmatic. Williams notes "the degree to which Goetz's victims

---

[90] Stephen Carter, *When Victims Happen to Be Black*, 97 Yale L J 420 (1988).

[91] Id at 421.

were relentlessly bestialized by the public and by the media in New York: images of the urban jungle, with young black men filling the role of 'wild animals,' were favorite journalistic constructions; young white urban professionals were mythologized, usually wrapped in the linguistic apparel of lambs or sheep, as the tender, toothsome prey."[92] Williams points out that in such a rhetorical structure, "the meaning of any act by the sheep against the wolves can never be seen as violent in its own right, for it is inherently uncharacteristic, brave, irresistibly and triumphantly parabolic."[93] Victim impact evidence that draws on such a rhetorical structure may have an effect without deliberate, conscious appeals to racial hatred.

One response might be that any tendency of victim impact evidence to block jury self-criticism by invoking these stereotypical characterizations can be countered by the defense attorney in the course of the penalty trial. Part of a lawyer's job, after all, is to tell an effective story and to poke holes in the story of one's adversary. But this argument seems irresponsible in light of the documented problems of racism in capital punishment. The Baldus study considered by the Court in *McCleskey v Kemp*[94] suggested that killers of whites were 4.3 times more likely to be sentenced to death than killers of blacks,[95] and that blacks who killed whites were nearly three times more likely to be sentenced to death than killers of blacks.[96] Although *McCleskey* held that these statistics did not establish a constitutional violation, the Court accepted them as true.[97]

Part of the purpose of the criminal jury is to measure the defendant's conduct and character in light of shared community values. But when the decision at issue involves a capital crime, the jury's tendency to assess situations with reference to easily comprehended and widely shared stereotypes is in tension with the constitutional requirement that the defendant be seen as a " 'uniquely individual

---

[92] Patricia J. Williams, *The Alchemy of Race and Rights: Diary of a Law Professor* 74 (Harvard, 1991).

[93] Id at 75.

[94] 481 US 279 (1987).

[95] See *McCleskey*, 481 US at 355 (Blackmun dissenting).

[96] Id at 286. The studies indicated that blacks who killed whites were sentenced to death at nearly twenty-two times the rate of blacks who killed blacks and more than seven times the rate of whites who killed blacks. Id at 326 (Blackmun dissenting).

[97] Id at 291 n 7.

human being.' "[98] One result of *Payne* could be the intensification of the effects revealed by the Baldus study—effects that, whatever the doctrinal soundness of *McCleskey*, are in serious tension with the values underlying the Equal Protection Clause.[99]

In the end, perhaps the costs of retarding self-criticism by the admission of victim impact evidence in the penalty phase of a capital trial do not outweigh the benefits of encouraging empathy. What is most disappointing about *Payne*, however, is not the outcome it reaches but the Court's failure to acknowledge the difficulty and complexity of the issues. Rather than wrestle with the constitutional implications of admitting such evidence, the Court uses the case to further its jurisprudence of victimhood.

B

Justice Scalia, in his *Booth* dissent, remarked: "Recent years have seen an outpouring of popular concern for what has come to be known as 'victims' rights'—a phrase that describes what its proponents feel is the failure of courts of justice to take into account in their sentencing decisions not only the factors mitigating the defendant's moral guilt, but also the amount of harm he has caused to innocent members of society."[100] In the past two decades, the victims' rights movement has evolved into a powerful political force.[101] *Payne*, drawing on the rhetoric of victims' rights, effec-

---

[98] *Booth*, 482 US at 504, quoting *Woodson v North Carolina*, 428 US 280, 304 (1976).

[99] For a critique of the Court's equal protection analysis in *McCleskey*, see Randall Kennedy, *McCleskey v. Kemp: Race, Capital Punishment, and the Supreme Court*, 101 Harv L Rev 1388 (1988).

[100] *Booth*, 482 US at 520.

[101] See David L. Roland, *Progress in the Victim Reform Movement: No Longer the "Forgotten Victim,"* 17 Pepperdine L Rev 35 (1989); see also Brent L. Smith, John J. Sloan, and Richard M. Ward, *Public Support for the Victims' Rights Movement: Results of a Statewide Survey*, 36 Crime & Delinquency 488 (1990), finding broad support in Alabama for crime compensation, restitution, victim impact statements, victim notification and input at parole hearings, and the right of the victim to sit with the prosecutor throughout the defendant's trial.
The victims' rights movement draws strength from both liberals and conservatives. Some victims' rights advocates are feminists and traditional liberals seeking greater legal protection for rape victims and for battered women and children. See Josephine Gittler, *Expanding the Role of the Victim in a Criminal Action: An Overview of Issues and Problems*, 11 Pepperdine L Rev 117, 118 (1984). Concern for the victims of crime, however, is also attractive to conservatives with a get-tough, "crime control" agenda, and several writers have charged that conservative political forces have "co-opted" the victims' rights movement. See, for example, Lynne Henderson, *The Wrongs of Victims' Rights*, 37 Stan L Rev 937, 951 (1985); Emilio Viano, *Victim's Rights and the Constitution: Reflections on a Bicentennial*, 33 Crime & Delinquency 438, 444 (1987); Robert Elias, *The Symbolic Politics of Victim Compensation*, 8 Victimology 213 (1983).

tively creates a sentencing trial in which the adversaries are not the defendant and the state, but rather the defendant and the victim. The state's power is erased; the death penalty is privatized.

1. In *Booth*, the Court spent very little time describing the act that gave rise to the case.[102] In contrast, Chief Justice Rehnquist's opinion for the Court in *Payne* devotes six paragraphs to a vivid description of the killing. Creating an air of foreboding, the Court takes note of the fact that prior to the killing, the defendant had passed the morning and early afternoon injecting cocaine and drinking beer, then reading a pornographic magazine with a friend. The narrative then moves to the apartment complex where the victims (Charisse Christopher and her two-year-old daughter Lacie) and the defendant's girlfriend lived, and the defendant's sexual advances toward Charisse. Next, the opinion describes the "horribly loud," then "blood curdling" screaming from the victims' apartment, and the scene that the police reported finding, including descriptions of the defendant as "so covered with blood that he appeared to be 'sweating blood,' "[103] as having a " 'wild look about him,' "[104] and as "foaming at the mouth."[105] The opinion also describes in detail the victims' bloody and mutilated bodies, and the body of the surviving child, Nicholas, with a butcher knife "completely penetrated through his body from front to back."[106] The opinion even recounts the amount of blood required to transfuse Nicholas during surgery.[107]

The opinion in *Payne* is striking not simply for its descriptive detail, but also for the image of Payne as an animal—pupils contracting, foaming at the mouth, covered with blood, and barely able to speak. Unlike the murder in *Booth*, which is presented as

---

[102] *Booth*, 482 US at 497–98:

> In 1983, Irvin Bronstein, 78, and his wife Rose, 75, were robbed and murdered in their West Baltimore home. The murderers, John Booth and Willie Reid, entered the victims' home for the apparent purpose of stealing money to buy heroin. Booth, a neighbor of the Bronsteins, knew that the elderly couple could identify him. The victims were bound and gagged, and then stabbed repeatedly in the chest with a kitchen knife. The bodies were discovered two days later by the Bronsteins' son.

[103] *Payne*, 111 S Ct at 2601.

[104] Id at 2602.

[105] Id.

[106] Id.

[107] Id.

cold-blooded but rational, this murder is horrifying in its animal intensity and in its seeming arbitrariness. The opinion suggests that, primed as Payne was with pornography and cocaine, anyone could have been his victim.[108]

The difference in rhetoric between *Booth* and *Payne* is not limited to their characterizations of the crimes. In the *Booth* opinion, the victims' family, whose statements were at issue in the case, barely appeared except as tools of the prosecution. The dispute in the case is between the formal parties, the state and the defendant; the family's contributions are irruptions of emotion, understandable but finally irrelevant. In *Booth*, then, the crime victims and their family are treated rhetorically as they are often treated in the criminal justice system itself—as distractions from the real task at hand.

Justice Scalia's concurrence in *Payne* again makes reference to the victims' rights movement, stating that "*Booth*'s stunning *ipse dixit*, that a crime's unanticipated consequences must be deemed 'irrelevant to the sentence,' conflicts with a public sense of justice keen enough that it has found voice in a nationwide 'victims' rights' movement."[109] In *Payne*, the victims' family, barely visible in *Booth*, becomes visible to the point of eclipsing the state.

Thus, in *Payne* the Court states that the misreading of precedent in *Booth* so as to preclude evidence of the harm the defendant caused has "unfairly weighted the scales in a capital trial; while virtually no limits are placed on the relevant mitigating evidence a capital defendant may introduce concerning his own circumstances, the State is barred from either offering 'a glimpse of the life' which a defendant 'chose to extinguish,' or demonstrating the loss to the victim's family and to society which ha[s] resulted from the defendant's homicide."[110] The Court describes the character evidence introduced by the defendant at the sentencing phase, and contrasts it to the testimony of Nicholas's grandmother—"the only evidence of the impact of Payne's offenses during the sentencing

---

[108] Robin West argues that the Court's recent practice of beginning its death penalty cases with a narrative of the crime serves to "assign[] responsibility for the violent crime irrevocably and entirely to the individual defendant," in contrast to the dissenters' reliance on the abstract language of rights, which tends to make responsibility for the crime seem irrelevant. Robin West, *Narrative, Responsibility and Death: A Comment on the Death Penalty Cases from the 1989 Term*, 1 Md J Contemp Legal Issues 161, 168 (1990).

[109] 111 S Ct at 2613 (citation omitted).

[110] Id at 2607.

phase."[111] The Court goes on to quote the Tennessee Supreme Court's characterization of the *Booth* rule as "'an affront to the civilized members of the human race.'"[112]

This rhetoric, however, obscures the nature of the stakes in a death penalty proceeding. If the capital case is truly a contest between the innocent victims and the guilty killers, the evidentiary imbalance created by *Booth* seems grotesque. Indeed, the constitutional requirement that the defendant be permitted to present all relevant mitigating evidence makes no sense in this light, absent a requirement that the state be able to present all aggravating evidence as well.[113] But the contest is not simply between the victim and the perpetrator. A death penalty case is also a struggle between the killer as an individual citizen and the state; and in this light it is not only the victims who could be any of us, but the defendant as well.[114] But it is far easier to make the empathic link between ourselves and the victim than ourselves and the killer. As the *Booth* Court understood, the state is not in danger of becoming the underdog in a capital murder case. The difficulty is not in getting the jury to see the humanity in the innocent victims, but the humanity in the killer. The Court's rhetoric in *Payne* is ultimately at odds with the theory underlying the requirement that all mitigating evidence be presented—the notion that the jury should be allowed to see the sense in which the defendant's conduct was, if not wholly determined, also not wholly free.[115]

The Supreme Court's rhetoric, full of references to the defendant's "choice" to kill,[116] echoes with the conservative cry to hold the guilty responsible for their acts. Yet the instrument of that policy—the state—disappears in its rhetoric. The prosecutor in *Payne* urged the jury to make its decision "for Nicholas." The power of the state has been erased.

---

[111] Id at 2609. Of course, the jury had seen a color videotape of the crime scene which quite vividly and explicitly portrayed the bloody remains of the bodies.

[112] Id.

[113] Justice Scalia is prepared to abandon the constitutional requirement that the defendant be allowed to present all mitigating evidence, although he still stands alone on the Court on this issue. *Payne*, 111 S Ct at 2613 (Scalia concurring).

[114] Compare West, 1 Md J Contemp Legal Issues at 172–73 (cited in note 108); *Payne*, 111 S Ct at 2627 (Stevens dissenting).

[115] See, for example, *California v Brown*, 479 US at 545 (O'Connor concurring).

[116] See, for example, *Payne*, 111 S Ct at 2615, 2616 (Kennedy and Souter concurring).

V

In a sense, *Payne* represents not an authoritarian arrogation of power to restore moral order, but a deferral of power: the dismantling of the last regulations on death and the end of an era in which the Supreme Court had anything significant to say about the process. What is erased in the process is finally (as Justice Marshall says in his dissent) the Court's own sense of responsibility for the death penalty, for the sinister discourse of victimization, innocence, and race, and for the symbolic value of rights-talk. Both the language of rights and the language of responsibility have a place in the Court's death penalty jurisprudence.[117] Without a framework of principle, the death penalty process will dissolve into the pre-*Furman* world of arbitrary and capricious decisions (if, in fact, it ever escaped from that world). Without scrupulous self-criticism, the jury's death decision will ultimately be irresponsible; without scrupulous self-criticism, the Court's jurisprudence of death will be the same.

---

[117] See West, *Narrative, Responsibility, and Death*, 1 Md J Contemp Legal Issues at 168 (cited in note 108).

WELSH S. WHITE

REGULATING PRISON INFORMERS
UNDER THE DUE PROCESS CLAUSE

In October, 1988, Leslie Vernon White, a veteran jailhouse informer who had testified for the government in many highly publicized criminal cases, admitted that his testimony as to prisoners' incriminating statements was often completely fabricated.[1] In the wake of the White scandal, other prison informers also admitted giving false testimony.[2] Defense attorneys complained that such testimony has frequently resulted in miscarriages of justice.[3] While acknowledging that prison informers are often untrustworthy,[4] prosecutors assert that informers frequently are indispensable to solving crimes[5] and that precautionary measures, such as screening

Welsh S. White is Professor of Law, University of Pittsburgh.

AUTHOR'S NOTE: I would like to thank Albert Alschuler, Yale Kamisar, James Tomkovicz, and Rhonda Wasserman for their valuable comments on earlier drafts of this article and David Paul for his excellent research assistance.

[1] See Reinhold, *California Shaken Over an Informer*, New York Times, A1, Feb. 17, 1989.

[2] Los Angeles Times, A1, Mar. 4, 1990; Los Angeles Times, A1, April 16, 1989.

[3] Reinhold (cited in note 1). See also Curriden, *No Honor among Thieves*, ABA 52, 54, June, 1989 (Curriden I) (detailing the case of James Richardson, a Florida defendant who was convicted and given the death penalty on the basis of three prison informers' testimony and, after spending twenty-one years in prison, was released on the basis of one of the informer's recantations and another individual's confession that she committed the crime).

[4] Assistant District Attorney Curt Livesay of Los Angeles County characterized prison informers as "liars, cheaters, [who] will put their own mothers in prison in exchange for a deal." Los Angeles Times, A27, Dec. 11, 1989.

[5] New York Times, A14, Jan. 3, 1989. See also Curriden I at 55 (stating that Stephen Trott, a judge on the U.S. 9th Circuit Court of Appeals and former assistant attorney general for the criminal division, believes "the criminal-justice system would collapse without the use of informants" and that "[t]he system tolerates informants because they are necessary").

informers and carefully scrutinizing their testimony, can eliminate the worst abuses.[6] Since prosecutors continue to use the testimony of prison informers in a wide variety of contexts, determining the circumstances under which the informer's testimony will be admissible is an increasingly important issue in the administration of criminal justice. *Arizona v Fulminante*,[7] decided this past term, is the Court's most recent decision relating to this issue.

Significantly, the *Fulminante* decision does not address the special problems posed by prison informers. In the course of deciding three interrelated issues concerning the admissibility of a defendant's statement to a prison informer,[8] the Court pays almost no attention to the fact that the confession was given to a prison informer. Thus, *Fulminante* does not even attempt to come to grips with the problems presented when a prison informer testifies to incriminating statements by a fellow inmate. Instead, it utilizes an approach that was ineffective in regulating police interrogation of suspects at the stationhouse and is likely to be even less effective when applied to regulate the conduct of prison informers.

Fulminante's weaknesses may be attributed partly to the Court's lack of exposure to cases involving prison informers.[9] Although the Court has been involved in regulating the use of confessions obtained by government agents for more than half a century, most of its efforts have been directed to situations in which police officers (or other known government officials) interrogate criminal suspects. In the wake of the Wickersham Report, published in 1931,[10] the Court decided a series of cases,[11] culminating in *Miranda v Arizona*,[12] that were designed to curb coercive interrogation practices. Beginning with *Massiah v United States*[13] in 1964, the Court also

---

[6] Los Angeles Times, A1, Dec. 7, 1988.

[7] 111 S Ct 1246 (1991).

[8] See text at notes 72–75.

[9] Prior to *Fulminante*, the Court had decided only two cases that dealt with the admissibility of a prison informer's testimony: *Kuhlmann v Wilson*, 477 US 436 (1986); *United States v Henry*, 447 US 264 (1980).

[10] IV National Commission on Law Observance and Enforcement, Report on Lawlessness in Law Enforcement (1931) (Wickersham Report).

[11] See, for example, *Haynes v Washington*, 373 US 503 (1963); *Brown v Mississippi*, 297 US 278 (1936). See generally Kamisar, *Police Interrogation and Confessions: Essays in Law and Policy* 1 (1980) (Kamisar, *Essays*).

[12] 384 US 436 (1966).

[13] 377 US 201 (1964).

decided several cases in which government informers testified to incriminating statements by indicted defendants, including two in which the defendants were in prison at the time they made the incriminating statements to the informers.[14] In this situation, the Court has held that, because formal charges had been brought, the defendant's Sixth Amendment right to counsel barred the government from "deliberately eliciting" incriminating statements from the defendant.[15] Applying this test, the Court has admitted or excluded prison informers' testimony on the basis of an often problematic distinction—whether the informer actively induced the incriminating statements or was a passive listener who happened to overhear them.[16]

When a prison informer obtains incriminating statements that relate to a new offense rather than one with which the prisoner has already been charged, the Court has ruled that, because there is no formal adversary relationship between the government and the suspect, the government has greater freedom to use the informer's statement. *Illinois v Perkins*[17] held in 1990 that a government informer may directly question a prisoner in an effort to obtain incriminating statements relating to an uncharged offense. In *Arizona v Fulminante*,[18] however, the Court indicated that the Due Process Clause imposes some limits on the practices that government informers may use to obtain incriminating statements concerning uncharged offenses.

This article will focus primarily on situations in which a prison informer testifies to incriminating statements that do not relate to a crime for which the suspect has been formally charged. It will consider how the due process test was applied by the majority and dissent in *Fulminante*—and some other ways in which it might have been applied. The goal of the article is to assess the extent to which the Due Process Clause may be used to impose appropriate restraints on prison informers who seek to elicit incriminating state-

---

[14] See cases cited in note 9.

[15] See, for example, *Henry*, 447 US at 270; *Massiah v United States*, 377 US 201, 206 (1964).

[16] Compare *Kuhlmann*, 477 US 436 (agent who told defendant that his explanation of how the robbery occurred "didn't sound too good" held "passive" listener) with *Henry*, 447 US 264 (agent who engaged in conversations with defendant during the time the two were incarcerated together held to have "deliberately elicited" incriminating statements).

[17] 110 S Ct 2394 (1990).

[18] 111 S Ct 1246 (1991).

ments from suspects in prison. I conclude that neither the majority nor the dissent in *Fulminante* deals adequately with the problems presented in the prison context, and suggest a new approach, drawn from the Court's due process decisions in the area of identification procedures, that may better address the problem.

I. CONFESSION CASES PRIOR TO FULMINANTE

In the course of deciding approximately thirty state confession cases between 1936 and 1966,[19] the Court established the principle that the admission of an involuntary confession violates due process.[20] In applying this principle, the Court evaluated the "totality of circumstances."[21] It considered a variety of factors, including both the nature of the police practices and the individual characteristics of the defendant.[22]

Over the years, it became clear that the due process test applied by the Court was not an adequate means of regulating police interrogation practices. In 1963, Professor Yale Kamisar commented on the confusion produced by the due process cases. Kamisar observed that the Court's decisions—ostensibly focusing on such questions as whether the suspect's "will [was] overborne and his capacity for self-determination critically impaired"[23]—were unhelpful. They did little to explain the type of mental state a defendant would have to have to give a "voluntary" confession.[24] Further, the Court's formulations of the due process voluntariness test were misleading in that they failed to address the nature of the police practices used to induce the confession or the confession's reliability, two

---

[19] Kamisar, *Essays* 75 (cited in note 11).

[20] See, for example, *Culombe v Connecticut*, 367 US 568, 602 (1961); *Rogers v Richmond*, 365 US 534, 544 (1961). See generally Kamisar, *Essays* 1–25 (cited in note 11).

[21] See, for example, *Fikes v Alabama*, 352 US 191, 197 (1957).

[22] In *Spano v New York*, 360 US 315, 321–22 (1959), for example, the Court took into account the defendant's level of education and degree of experience with law enforcement, the defendant's mental state, the number of police present during questioning, the nature of the questioning (including the deceptive tactics employed), and the duration of the interrogation.

[23] Kamisar, *Essays* 14 (cited in note 11) (quoting *Culombe*, 367 US at 602, n 55).

[24] Kamisar, *Essays* 15 (cited in note 11). See also Benner, *Requiem for Miranda: The Rehnquist Court's Voluntariness Doctrine in Historical Perspective*, 67 Wash U L Q 59, 116 (1989). "[The Court's] Alice in Wonderland journey into the metaphysical realm of broken human 'wills' defied both scientific views of human behavior and common sense."

concerns that historically had been significant in shaping the voluntariness test.[25]

In addition to failing to provide clear guidelines for the police and lower courts, the due process test was ineffective because it did not take account of "monotonous swearing contests between police and defendant, and monotonous resolutions of those contests by state trial judges in favor of the police."[26] Even when the Court imposed a clear prohibition on police conduct—on using physical force to obtain a confession, for example[27]—this would not prevent the police from engaging in the prohibited conduct and then lying about it in court. Moreover, when this happened, it would often be difficult for even the most conscientious judge to resolve the credibility conflict in the defendant's favor. Since interrogation generally took place in secret, neither side would be likely to have any convincing corroborative evidence and the police were likely to appear more credible than the defendant. Thus, to the extent that the police were willing to lie, the protections afforded by the due process confession cases were nullified.[28]

Three years after Kamisar's article, *Miranda v Arizona*[29] seemed to eliminate the need for determining whether a confession was voluntary within the meaning of the Due Process Clause. *Miranda's* Fifth Amendment holding was premised on the view that police interrogation of suspects in the stationhouse is inherently coercive.[30] Accordingly, the Court imposed the rule that a suspect may not be subjected to "custodial interrogation" unless he is first given

---

[25] Kamisar, *Essays* at 15 (cited in note 11).

[26] Amsterdam, *The Supreme Court and the Rights of Suspects in Criminal Cases*, 45 NYU L Rev 785, 808 (1970).

[27] See, for example, *Watts v Indiana*, 338 US 49, 59–60 (1949) (dissenting opinion of Jackson, J.); *Brown*, 297 US at 286.

[28] The problems posed by the "swearing contest" will, of course, be likely to be present under any test where the fact-finder has to assess a government witness' credibility in order to determine the admissibility of a confession. See, for example, *Miranda*, 384 US 436 at 505 (dissent of Harlan, J.) (noting that the *Miranda* rule does not eliminate the problems posed by the swearing contest). The "swearing contest" problems are mitigated, however, when there is reliable evidence corroborating the government witness' testimony, see Kamisar, *Essays* at 129–37 (advocating that police interrogation of suspects be tape-recorded when feasible) or when safeguards are imposed to exclude a category of unreliable evidence without requiring a determination as to whether a particular witness' testimony is trustworthy.

[29] *Miranda*, 384 US 436.

[30] Id at 457–58.

some now familiar warnings[31] and makes a voluntary and intelligent
waiver of the rights described in those warnings.[32] Although the
Court did not say so, it undoubtedly believed that one of the advantages of *Miranda* was that it would displace the due process voluntariness test, thereby obviating the need to make both difficult
assessments of the circumstances of police interrogation and case-
by-case determinations of admissibility on the basis of vague and
confused legal standards.[33]

Miranda did not completely eliminate the need for determining
whether a confession is voluntary under the due process test, however. By its own terms, *Miranda* applies only when the suspect is
subjected to custodial interrogation.[34] Accordingly, if the suspect
is not in custody[35] or is not subjected to interrogation,[36] *Miranda*
does not apply. In these and other situations,[37] the due process
voluntariness test is likely to be the only governing constitutional
standard.[38]

Twelve years after *Miranda*, Kamisar argued that *Miranda* should
not apply when a prisoner confesses to a government informer.[39]

---

[31] Id at 478–79.

[32] Id at 475.

[33] Prior to *Miranda* at least one prominent commentator observed that the Court was
seeking "some automatic device by which the potential evils of incommunicado interrogation
[could] be controlled." Schaefer, *The Suspect and Society: Criminal Procedure and Converging
Constitutional Doctrine* 10 (1967).

[34] See 384 US at 478–79.

[35] The Court indicated in *Miranda* that custody occurred when the defendant was "deprived of his freedom of action in any significant way." 384 US at 444. In a later case,
however, the Court defined custody within the meaning of *Miranda* more strictly, focusing
on whether the defendant was subject to the functional equivalent of an arrest. See *Berkemer
v McCarty*, 468 US 420, 442 (1984).

[36] Interrogation within the meaning of *Miranda* was defined in *Rhode Island v Innis*, 446
US 291 (1980).

[37] The Court has also established certain exceptions to *Miranda*. In *New York v Quarles*,
467 US 649, 656 (1984), the Court held that *Miranda* does not apply when an officer's
question to a suspect is "prompted by a concern for the public safety." 467 US at 656.
Moreover, *Harris v New York*, 401 US 222 (1971) establishes that statements obtained in
violation of *Miranda* may be used for the purpose of impeaching a defendant's credibility if
he testifies in his own defense. For an ironic comment on these and other exceptions to
Miranda, see Alschuler, *Failed Pragmatism: Reflections on the Burger Court*, 100 Harv L Rev
1436, 1442–43 (1987).

[38] See generally Schulhofer, *Confessions and the Court*, 79 Mich L Rev 865, 877 (1981).

[39] See Kamisar, *Brewer v Williams, Massiah, and Miranda: What Is "Interrogation"? When
Does It Matter?*, 67 Georgetown L J 1 (1978) reprinted in Kamisar, *Essays* 200–01 (cited in
note 11).

Kamisar asserted that in this situation the interplay between police interrogation and police custody is not present, at least not "where it counts—in the suspect's mind."[40] Thus, he argued that the "inherently compelling" atmosphere that justified the *Miranda* warnings when known police officers interrogate a suspect at the stationhouse is not present when a "jail plant" in prison grey questions another inmate in a prison.[41]

Kamisar, however, addressed only the question whether "jail plant" questioning violates *Miranda*. He did not consider whether such questioning might independently violate the Due Process Clause. In an effort to fill this gap, I suggested at the time that the use of informers to obtain confessions from suspects in prison might be so unfair as to violate due process.[42] Drawing upon Supreme Court opinions that seemed to disapprove of certain forms of police trickery,[43] I emphasized not only the deceptive nature of the practice,[44] but also the coercive atmosphere of the prison environment[45] and the limited options available to the prisoner.[46] While not disagreeing with Kamisar's conclusion that *Miranda* is inapplicable to prison informer questioning, I argued that the government should be barred absolutely from using incriminating statements obtained by this tactic.[47] A decade later, in *Illinois v Perkins*,[48] the Court for the first time considered a case in which an undercover informer questioned a prison inmate about a crime for which he had not yet been charged. The case arose after a prison

---

[40] Kamisar, *Essays* 196 (cited in note 11).

[41] Id.

[42] See White, *Police Trickery in Inducing Confessions*, 127 U Pa L Rev 581, 604 (1979).

[43] See, for example, *Spano*, 360 US at 323 (evidencing distaste for the tactic of having defendant's childhood friend falsely tell the defendant that his job as a police officer would be in jeopardy if the defendant did not confess).

[44] White, 127 U Pa L Rev at 606 (cited in note 42).

[45] Id at 604.

[46] Id at 605: "Because the suspect's ability to select people with whom he can confide is completely within their control, the police have a unique opportunity to exploit the suspect's vulnerability. In short, the police can insure that if the pressures of confinement lead the suspect to confide in anyone, it will be a police agent." See also Dix, *Undercover Investigations and Police Rulemaking*, 53 Tex L Rev 203, 230 (1975) (making essentially the same point).

[47] White, 127 U Pa L Rev at 604 (cited in note 42). See also Dix, 53 Tex L Rev at 230 (cited in note 46) (reaching a similar conclusion on the basis of the Court's decision in *Massiah v United States*, 377 US 201 (1964)).

[48] 110 S Ct 2394 (1990).

inmate named Charlton reported to the police that Perkins, a fellow inmate, had told him in detail about a murder he had committed.[49] Some time after receiving this information, the police arranged for Charlton and a police officer named Parisi, both disguised as escapees from a work release program,[50] to be placed in the same cellblock with Perkins.[51]

While together, the three men discussed the possibility of escape. In the course of that discussion, Parisi asked Perkins whether he had ever killed anyone.[52] When Perkins replied affirmatively, Parisi asked several specific questions about the alleged murder.[53] Perkins's incriminating responses were admitted at his subsequent murder trial. The only issue before the Court was whether Perkins's incriminating statements were obtained in violation of *Miranda*.[54] In holding *Miranda* inapplicable, the Court accepted Kamisar's analysis. It emphasized that "when a suspect considers himself in the company of cellmates and not officers, the coercive atmosphere [described in *Miranda*] is lacking."[55] Justice Brennan, con-

---

[49] Id at 2396.

[50] Id. After Charlton gave the police information relating to Perkins, Perkins was released from prison and then rearrested and detained in the Montgomery County jail on a new charge.

[51] Id.

[52] Id.

[53] Id at 2401–02 (dissenting opinion of Marshall, J.).

[54] The lower court had excluded Perkins's confession on the basis that it was obtained in violation of *Miranda*. See *People v Perkins*, 531 NE2d 141, 145–46 (Ill 1988).

[55] 110 S Ct at 2397. *Perkins*'s conclusion that one prisoner's questioning of another is not inherently coercive within the meaning of *Miranda* is questionable. Kamisar's analysis, accepted by the Court, distinguished questioning by a prison informer from interrogation by a known police officer on the ground that "[t]here is nothing inherently compelling about talking with, or being talked to by, a prisoner in the same or an adjoining cell. For the suspect thinks he is dealing with an equal, not with his captors." Kamisar, *Essays* 196 (cited in note 11).

Kamisar seemed to assume that, in the absence of special circumstances, a talk with another inmate in prison is similar to a talk with an acquaintance outside of prison. Paul Keve's statement that "prison is a barely controlled jungle," Keve, *Prison Life and Human Worth* 54 (1974), calls that assumption into question. If the "jungle" atmosphere is pervasive, prisoners cannot be expected to enter into the casual relationships or friendships that might be found in normal society. The atmosphere of the prison, and the prisoner's place within the subculture that exists there, may dictate both the kinds of relationships that will be entered into and the nature of the interchanges prisoners will be likely to have. See Bowker, *Prison Victimization* 30–34; Keve 54–60.

Of course, it does not follow that an informer's questioning of an inmate will always be coercive. But, as the post-Warren Court has repeatedly recognized, see, for example, *Quarles*, 467 US at 654; *Michigan v Tucker*, 417 US 433, 443–45 (1974), police interrogation of a suspect at the stationhouse will not always be coercive either. *Miranda*'s safeguards were

curring in the result, observed that, on remand, the lower court would be free to determine whether the use of the undercover informer in the particular circumstances of the case violated due process.[56] The majority did not endorse this view, however. Justice Kennedy, writing for the Court, asserted that "[t]he statements at issue in this case were voluntary, and there is no federal obstacle to their admissibility at trial." [57] Thus, the Court went out of its way to suggest that use of a "jail plant" to induce a confession in prison does not in itself violate due process.

II. THE FULMINANTE DECISION

A. THE FACTS AND LOWER COURT DECISION

In 1983, Orestes Fulminante, convicted of possession of a firearm by a felon, was incarcerated in a Federal prison at Ray Brook, New York.[58] Anthony Sarivola, another convict, employed as a confidential informer by the FBI, was incarcerated in the same prison. The FBI was paying Sarivola for information "which they could corroborate and which they could prosecute or do something about." [59] In October 1983, Sarivola told FBI agent Ticano of rumors that Fulminante had killed Jeneane, his eleven-year-old stepdaughter, in Arizona.[60] In response, Ticano said to Sarivola, "[T]hat's just a rumor, you'll have to find out more about it." [61]

Sarivola and Fulminante subsequently met and had conversations in the prison. Sarivola claimed that in one of these conversations Fulminante admitted the killing of his stepdaughter; Fulminante denied that he ever made such an admission.[62] For purposes

---

adopted to reduce the possibility of coercive government questioning, to avoid the difficulties of determining on a case-by-case basis whether particular questioning was coercive, and to provide a bright line rule that could be easily followed by the police. See, for example, *Minnick v Mississippi*, 111 S Ct 486, 490 (1990); *Tucker*, 417 US at 443–45. Because these concerns are also present when a government informer questions a prison inmate, *Perkins*'s conclusion that a "jail plant's" questioning of a suspect should not be subject to a *Miranda*-type prohibition is questionable.

[56] *Perkins*, 110 S Ct at 2400–01 (concurring opinion of Brennan, J.).

[57] Id at 2399.

[58] *Arizona v Fulminante*, 111 S Ct 1246, 1250 (1991).

[59] Record, 12.

[60] Record, 10.

[61] Record, 10.

[62] Record, 38.

of the constitutional issue, however, the parties stipulated that Fulminante, who had earlier denied killing his stepdaughter, admitted
the killing to Sarivola after Sarivola had told him that "[Sarivola]
might be in a position to help protect [Fulminante] from physical
recriminations in prison, but that [Fulminante] must tell him the
truth."[63]

It was further stipulated that "[a]t no time did [Fulminante] indicate he was in fear of other inmates nor did he ever seek [Sarivola's]
'protection.'"[64] Nevertheless, the threat of "physical recriminations" from other inmates was apparently real. Child molesters are
typically despised by the prison population.[65] "[B]ecause [Fulmi-
nante] was an alleged child murderer, he was in danger of physical
harm at the hands of other inmates."[66] Moreover, Fulminante was
not physically well equipped to defend himself. He was forty-two
years old and "short in stature and slight in build."[67] In fact, Sarivola testified at trial that before he offered Fulminante protection,
Fulminante's situation in prison was such that "his time to keep
walking around was running short" and he was in danger of leaving
the prison "horizontally."[68]

Prior to trial, Fulminante moved to suppress his confession on
the grounds that it was obtained in violation of *Miranda* and was
involuntary. The trial judge denied both claims. At trial, Sarivola
testified to Fulminante's confession. Fulminante was convicted and
sentenced to death. On appeal, the Arizona Supreme Court held
that Fulminante's confession was involuntary.[69] Although it also
concluded that the admission of Fulminante's confession was harmless error because of the other evidence introduced at Fulminante's
trial,[70] the Arizona Supreme Court reversed Fulminante's conviction on the basis of a long line of Supreme Court precedent holding

---

[63] Record, 10.

[64] Record, 10.

[65] See generally Bowker at 27 (cited in note 55).

[66] *Fulminante*, 111 S Ct at 1252 (quoting *People v Fulminante*, 778 P2d 602, 608 (Ariz 1988)).

[67] *Fulminante*, 111 S Ct at 1252 n 2.

[68] Record, 28–29.

[69] *Fulminante*, 778 P2d 602.

[70] Id at 610–11. In reaching this conclusion, the Arizona Supreme Court particularly relied on the fact that Fulminante's later confession to Sarivola's wife was also introduced into evidence.

that the admission of a coerced confession can never constitute harmless error.[71]

B. THE COURT'S HOLDING

Three issues were potentially before the Court in Fulminante: first, whether admitting Fulminante's confession violated due process because the confession was coerced; second, whether the improper admission of a coerced confession can ever be harmless error; and, third, whether the introduction of Fulminante's confession was harmless error. Although the Court could have decided the case by deciding only two of the three issues,[72] it decided all three, each by a different five justice majority.

Justices White, Marshall, Blackmun, Stevens, and Scalia concluded that the confession had been coerced.[73] Justices Rehnquist, O'Connor, Kennedy, Scalia, and Souter held that a coerced confession can be harmless error.[74] Justices White, Marshall, Blackmun, Stevens, and Kennedy concluded that the admission of Fulminante's confession to Sarivola did not constitute harmless error.[75]

Commentators generally have viewed *Fulminante*'s ruling that the introduction of a coerced confession can be harmless error as the most significant aspect of the Court's decision.[76] In certain respects, this ruling is, indeed, important. The Court's eagerness to overrule a well established principle when it was not even necessary to reach the issue in order to decide the case[77] is suggestive both

---

[71] Id at 626. See *Mincey v Arizona*, 437 US 385, 398 (1978); *Chapman v California*, 386 US 18, 23 n 8 (1967); *Payne v Arkansas*, 356 US 560, 568 (1958).

[72] Since a majority of the Court held that the use of the coerced statements was not harmless, it was not essential in resolving the case before it to decide whether a coerced confession is susceptible to harmless error analysis. One commentator suggested that the Court's holding on the applicability of harmless error analysis to coerced confessions was "the sort of gratuitous advisory opinion that judicial conservatives have long condemned." See Greenhouse, *Conservatively Speaking, Its an Activist Supreme Court*, New York Times, May 26, 1991, Sec 4, p 1.

[73] *Fulminante*, 111 S Ct at 1252.

[74] Id at 1261.

[75] Id at 1260–61. On this issue, the vote was 5 to 3 because Justice Souter did not vote.

[76] Soon after the Court's decision, numerous editorials criticized this aspect of the decision; see, for example, Greenhouse (cited in note 72); Lewis, *Court in a Hurry*, New York Times, A29, April 26, 1991; Pillsbury, *Fifth Amendment Takes Another Blow*, Los Angeles Times, B7, March 29, 1991; Chicago Tribune, C22, March 28, 1991, without commenting on the other aspects of the Court's opinion.

[77] See note 72.

of the Court's overall direction and of its aggressiveness in approaching issues of criminal procedure. Despite its "conservative" tendencies, the Burger Court generally was reluctant to overrule the criminal procedure decisions of the Warren Court.[78] *Fulminante*'s harmless error ruling suggests that, in promoting its own criminal procedure agenda, the Rehnquist Court will go well beyond undoing the work of the Warren Court.[79]

Moreover, from a symbolic perspective, the connection between the public's outcry against the police officers who beat Rodney King and the Court's harmless error ruling in *Fulminante* is troubling.[80] As several commentators have noted,[81] *Fulminante* sends the "wrong" message to the police, for it suggests that for the police to coerce a confession from a suspect will, under certain circumstances, help obtain a conviction.[82]

Nevertheless, in terms of its actual impact on criminal trials, *Fulminante*'s harmless error ruling is likely to be of limited significance. Prior to *Fulminante*, reviewing courts apparently rarely concluded that coerced confessions had been improperly admitted into evidence,[83] instead affirming even questionable lower court determinations that confessions had not been coerced.[84] Thus, even after

---

[78] See Kamisar, *The Warren Court (Was It Really So Defense-Minded?), The Burger Court (Is It Really So Prosecution-Oriented?), and Police Investigatory Practices*, in V. Blasi, *The Burger Court: The Counter Revolution That Wasn't* 68 (1983).

[79] Justice Rehnquist's antipathy to the rule of automatic reversal in coerced confession cases apparently dates at least back to 1952 when he was a clerk for Justice Jackson. See New York Times, A18, May 1, 1991 (observing that, as a law clerk, Rehnquist wrote a memorandum urging that the Court abandon the automatic reversal rule in coerced confession cases).

[80] The court reversed its rule on the applicability of harmless error analysis to coerced confessions only a few weeks after the videotape of Los Angeles police officers beating Rodney King was shown on national television. For a comment on the disturbing implications of this proximity, see, for example, Chicago Tribune, C22, March 28, 1991.

[81] See, for example, Neisser, *Can Government Coercion Ever Be Harmless*, N.J.L.J. 13, April 25, 1991.

[82] It has been remarked that the *Fulminante* ruling on harmless error may also tempt prosecutors to "introduce questionable confessions in borderline cases in the hope that any resulting conviction will be upheld." Lacayo, *Confessions That Were Taboo Are Now Just a Technicality*, Time, 26, April 8, 1991.

[83] See, for example, White, *Defending Miranda: A Reply to Professor Caplan*, 39 Vand L Rev 1, 15 n 78 (1986) (White, *Miranda*) (observing that, over the six year period from June, 1960 to May, 1966, the Pennsylvania appellate courts did not hold a single confession to be involuntary).

[84] White, *Miranda* at 12 n 67 (identifying extreme examples in which appellate courts held confessions not coerced) (cited in note 83).

Fulminante, the question whether the admission of a coerced confession constitutes harmless error is likely to arise only infrequently. Moreover, on the rare occasion when that question does arise, *Fulminante* indicated that, in view of the powerful impact a confession is likely to have on the jury, a reviewing court should find the admission of a coerced confession harmless only in exceptional circumstances.[85]

C. THE COURT'S APPLICATION OF THE DUE PROCESS STANDARD

Although they adopted somewhat different perspectives on the due process issue, both the majority and the dissent in *Fulminante* employed approaches that already have proved inadequate in evaluating confessions obtained by the police. Given the nature of the interactions that take place in prison, there is little reason to believe that these approaches will be more effective in controlling the efforts of prison informers to elicit confessions than they were in regulating the police.

1. *The dissent's approach.* In view of the Court's long experience with the due process test, the dissent's approach seems especially misguided. Chief Justice Rehnquist sought to determine whether Fulminante's confession was actually coerced—that is, whether Fulminante had established by credible evidence that his "will was overborne" at the time he confessed to Sarivola.[86] Since Fulminante denied making a confession to Sarivola, he never testified "that he believed that his life was in danger or that he in fact confessed to Sarivola in order to obtain the proffered protection."[87] In Rehnquist's view, moreover, Sarivola's testimony did not establish that the confession was given in a coercive environment: the conversations with Fulminante were not lengthy; Fulminante was

---

[85] *Fulminante*, 111 S Ct at 1258.

[86] Id at 1261 (quoting *Culombe v Connecticut*, 367 US 568, 602 (1961)).

[87] *Fulminante*, 111 S Ct at 1262 (dissenting opinion of Rehnquist, J.). A defendant who claims that he didn't confess and, in the alternative, that his confession was coerced presents an interesting problem because, as Justice Rehnquist suggests, it is difficult to see how the defendant can establish his will was overborne when he claims that he did not in fact succumb to whatever pressure was exerted. In two earlier cases, however, the Court had held that "[t]he use in evidence of a defendant's coerced confession cannot be justified on the ground that the defendant . . . denied he ever gave the confession." *Ashcraft v Tennessee*, 322 US 143, 152 n 7 (1944). See also *White v Texas*, 310 US 530, 531–32 (1940). Accepting this principle, the *Fulminante* majority decided the confession issue before it on the assumption that Fulminante in fact made the confession.

free to leave Sarivola; Sarivola did not threaten Fulminante or demand that he confess; and Fulminante, "an experienced habitue of prisons," was "presumably able to fend for himself." [88] Thus, Fulminante failed to establish that his will [was] "overborne" at the time he confessed.

The fundamental difficulty with the dissent's approach is that, as an empirical matter, it is not meaningful to ask whether an individual's "will was overborne." As Kamisar has pointed out, every defendant who confesses in some sense makes a choice to confess; on the other hand, in litigated cases, few if any defendants have made spontaneous or unconstrained choices to admit their guilt.[89] Thus, the meaning of an "overborne will" depends on the normative question of how much mental freedom should be afforded the defendant who is confessing,[90] as well as an empirical assessment of how much freedom of choice he had at the time he made the incriminating statement. Unless a court first addresses the normative question, it cannot meaningfully determine whether the defendant's will was "overborne."

There is another difficulty with Rehnquist's due process inquiry. In applying the due process test, the Court traditionally has been concerned with regulating police practices as well as with protecting the mental freedom of individual suspects. Kamisar's analysis of the cases[91] demonstrates that, despite the Court's language about "voluntary" confessions and whether the defendant's "will was overborne," confessions are excluded because the particular police conduct either placed too much pressure on the suspect to confess[92] or offended some other norm of appropriate police conduct.[93] Rehnquist, however, apparently would not take into ac-

---

[88] *Fulminante*, 111 S Ct at 1263 (dissenting opinion of Rehnquist, J.).

[89] Kamisar, *Essays* 15 (cited in note 11).

[90] Grano, *Voluntariness, Free Will, and the Law of Confessions*, 65 Va L Rev 859, 885–86 (1979).

[91] See Kamisar, *Essays* 1–25 (cited in note 11).

[92] See, for example, *Culombe*, 367 US at 573–76. Determining whether the police placed too much pressure on the suspect to confess may seem similar to determining whether the defendant was coerced into confessing. The difference is that the focus is solely on the effect the police conduct might be expected to have on an ordinary person, not the effect it actually had on the defendant.

[93] See, for example, *Spano v New York*, 360 US 315, 320–21 (1959) ("the police must obey the law while enforcing the law"). Under this approach, a confession would be in violation of due process even though the police conduct was not coercive as long as it offended some

count the propriety of the informer's conduct unless it could be shown that such conduct played some part in rendering the confession a product of the defendant's overborne will.[94]

2. *The majority's approach.* Unlike the dissent, the majority did focus on the government conduct. Justice White concluded that the determination that Fulminante's confession was involuntary was justified by the state court's conclusion, "permissible on this record, that there was a credible threat of physical violence."[95] Essentially, the majority held that a government informer may not induce a confession by a promise to protect a prison inmate from physical violence if he confesses. This holding is analogous to early due process decisions holding that confessions are inadmissible when induced by threats of violence from either the police[96] or an angry mob.[97]

The *Fulminante* majority took pains to limit its holding, however. In ruling that Fulminante's confession was inadmissible, the Arizona Supreme Court cited and apparently relied on *Bram v United States*,[98] a 1897 decision holding that confessions must not be obtained by "any direct or implied promises, however slight, nor by the exertion of any improper influence[s]."[99] In his opinion for the

---

other societal norm. See Kamisar, *Essays* 15 (observing that a confession induced by an officer disguising himself as a priest so as to gain the suspect's confidence would violate due process) (cited in note 11).

[94] *Fulminante,* 111 S Ct at 1261 (dissenting opinion of Rehnquist, J.).

[95] Id at 1253.

[96] See *Beecher v Alabama,* 389 US 35 (1967).

[97] See *Payne v Arkansas,* 356 US 560, 564–65 (1958). *Fulminante* is arguably distinguishable from *Payne.* In *Payne,* the chief of police indicated to the defendant he would try to protect him from the angry mob only if the defendant made a confession. Because the chief clearly had a legal obligation to protect the defendant from the mob, he was implicitly threatening him with unlawful action if he didn't confess. In *Fulminante,* on the other hand, Sarivola had no legal obligation to protect Fulminante from the other prison inmates. Thus, Sarivola induced Fulminante's confession through an offer of help that he was not legally obligated to provide. From the defendant's point of view, however, the two situations are substantially similar. In both cases, the defendant is giving a confession in exchange for the promise of protection from physical harm. To the defendant, it makes no difference whether the government agent is legally obligated to provide such protection or not.

[98] *State v. Fulminante,* 778 P2d 602, 609 (Ariz 1988) (quoting *Bram v United States,* 168 US 532, 543 (1897) (prohibiting the introduction of confessions obtained by promises), and adding that "[t]hese standards also apply to the states through the fourteenth amendment").

[99] *Bram,* 168 US at 542–43. *Bram* was decided on the basis of the Fifth Amendment privilege against self-incrimination. Since *Bram* was a federal case, its holding was not even potentially applicable to state court confession cases until 1964 when *Malloy v Hogan,* 378 US 1 (1964) held that the Fifth Amendment privilege is applicable to the states.

majority, Justice White went out of his way to discredit *Bram*, stating that it "does not state the [current] standard for determining the voluntariness of a confession." [100]

Beyond the principle that the government may not induce a confession through a "credible threat of physical violence," however, the majority offered no standard of its own. It merely endorsed the "totality of circumstances" test as the proper means for determining whether a confession was obtained in violation of due process and characterized the issue in *Fulminante* as a "close" one. [101] Thus, although the majority did focus on government conduct in the prison context, it did not address the special problems posed in this setting or attempt to incorporate those problems into its analysis. Like the Court's early due process confession decisions, [102] *Fulminante* provides few guidelines for determining when government conduct violates due process.

III. OTHER POSSIBLE APPROACHES UNDER THE DUE PROCESS CLAUSE

The implication in *Perkins* to the contrary notwithstanding, [103] I continue to believe that the government's use of undercover agents to elicit incriminating statements from incarcerated suspects violates due process. Because the government can completely control the incarcerated "suspect's ability to select people with whom he can confide," it is "unfair to allow the government to exploit the suspect's vulnerability by trickery of this type." [104] *Perkins*, however, seems to have foreclosed such an approach. [105]

---

[100] *Fulminante*, 111 S Ct at 1251.

[101] Id at 1252.

[102] See generally Kamisar, *Essays*, 41–76 (cited in note 11); Stone, *The Miranda Doctrine in the Burger Court*, 1977 Supreme Court Review 99, 102–03.

[103] See text accompanying note 55.

[104] White, 127 U Pa L Rev at 605 (cited in note 42).

[105] A government informer's questioning of a criminal suspect also raises a Fourth Amendment issue because the government's use of an informer to obtain information arguably violates the "privacy upon which [the suspect] justifiably relied" and thus constitutes a search within the meaning of the Fourth Amendment. See *Katz v United States*, 389 US 347, 353 (1967). See generally Stone, *The Scope of the Fourth Amendment: Privacy and the Police Use of Spies, Secret Agents, and Informers*, 1976 Am Bar Found Res J 1193, 1220–29 (developing this argument). The Court has rejected this argument, however. See, for example, *United States v White*, 401 US 745 (1971); *Hoffa v United States*, 385 US 293 (1966).

Even if the government's use of prison informers is not a *per se* violation of due process, however, the Court's approach in *Fulminante* is flawed because it fails to consider the particular characteristics of the prison environment and the special problems posed by prison informers. In this part, I consider three approaches that take these factors into account. Although all three of these alternatives are preferable to the test applied in *Fulminante*, the third approach is, in my view, best calculated to deal with the most fundamental problem in prison informer cases.

A. ALTERNATIVE 1: THE STATE MAY NOT USE CONFESSIONS THAT
    ARE INDUCED BY A PRISON INFORMER'S PROMISES

Bram's prohibition of confessions induced by promises has deep historical roots. In 1783, an English court established the principle that "a confession forced from the mind by the flattery of hope . . . comes in so questionable a shape when it is considered as evidence of guilt, that no credit ought to be given to it; and therefore it is rejected." [106] During the nineteenth century, Anglo-American courts frequently held that "any threat or promise, any fear or hope, would exclude the confession irrespective of any attempt to measure its influence to cause a false confession," [107] a rule similar to the constitutional principle stated and applied by *Bram*. [108] Although the prohibition on confessions induced by promises was originally based on the rationale that such confessions are likely to be unreliable, [109] *Bram*'s analysis was premised on the view that even an implied promise of a benefit is likely to exert compulsion. As Professor Laurence Benner has said, *Bram* essentially held that "[if] an interrogation tactic, objectively viewed, was sufficient to engender hope or fear in the mind of the accused and thus exert

---

[106] *The King v Warickshall*, 1 Leach 263–64 (KB 1783).

[107] III Wigmore, Evidence § 861, 346 (Tillers rev 1983).

[108] In *Bram*, 168 US at 533, the defendant made an incriminating statement after the interrogating detective told him he was satisfied he had committed the offense and then said, "If you had an accomplice, you should say so, and not have the blame of this horrible crime on your own shoulders." The Court held that the detective's statement rendered Bram's statement involuntary because it "called upon the prisoner to disclose his accomplice, and might well have been understood as holding out an encouragement that by so doing he might at least obtain a mitigation of the punishment for the crime which otherwise would assuredly follow." Id at 565.

[109] See text accompanying note 114.

influence, however slight, upon his decision to speak, then it violated the fifth amendment prohibition against compelled self-incrimination." [110] In other words, when a defendant is interrogated by the police, the implied promise of a benefit is sufficient to engender hope and thereby constitute compulsion within the meaning of the Fifth Amendment privilege.

During the past half-century, the Court has reiterated *Bram*'s prohibition, [111] but has applied it sporadically, if at all. [112] Prior to *Malloy v Hogan*'s [113] holding that the Fourteenth Amendment Due Process Clause incorporates the Fifth Amendment privilege against compelled self-incrimination, [114] *Bram*'s Fifth Amendment holding was not applicable to the states. [115] Even before *Malloy*, however, the Court's due process confession cases indicated that a promise of leniency could be an important factor in the "totality of circumstances," [116] though rarely, if ever, sufficient in itself to render a confession involuntary. [117]

Malloy's ruling that the Fifth Amendment privilege applies to the

---

[110] Benner, 67 Wash U L Q at 109 (cited in note 24).

[111] See, for example, *Brady v United States*, 397 US 742, 754 (1970); *Malloy v Hogan*, 378 US 1, 7 (1964).

[112] See notes 113–28 and accompanying text.

[113] 378 US 1 (1964).

[114] Id at 6.

[115] Moreover, by the 1930s *Bram*'s prohibition on confessions induced by promises seems to have been largely disregarded even in federal cases. See, for example, *Shotwell Manufacturing Co. v United States*, 371 US 341 (1963) (holding *Bram* does not apply to a situation in which taxpayers made a disclosure of tax liability in response to the government's offer of immunity to any tax evader who made a voluntary disclosure of tax liability prior to an investigation); *United States v Lonardo*, 67 F2d 883 (2d Cir 1933) (refusing to apply *Bram* to a situation in which defendant confessed after a prosecutor told him he had been implicated by a co-defendant and that courts took into account the fact that a defendant plead guilty when imposing sentence). See generally Benner at 109–12 (cited in note 24).

[116] See, for example, *Lynumn v Illinois*, 372 US 528 (1963) (confession held involuntary under the "totality of circumstances" test where arresting officers told defendant she would lose her children and financial assistance if she did not confess and promised to recommend "leniency" if she cooperated); *Leyra v Denno*, 347 US 556 (1954) (police doctor's "promises of leniency" identified as a factor in determining confession was involuntary).

[117] Moreover, in *Stein v New York*, 346 US 156, 186 (1953), the Court seemed to indicate that the defendant's agreement to confess in exchange for the prosecutor's promise to alleviate his father's problems with parole authorities was a factor tending to show the defendant's confession was voluntary:

> [T]he spectacle of Cooper naming his own terms for confession, deciding for himself with whom he would negotiate, getting what he wanted as a consideration for telling what he knew, reduces to absurdity his present claim that he was coerced into confession.

states seemed to set the stage for applying *Bram*'s prohibition on confessions induced by promises to the states as well.[118] The post-Warren Court, however, has not accepted the principle that any interrogation that engenders hope or fear in the mind of the suspect constitutes compulsion within the meaning of the Fifth Amendment privilege.[119] Instead, the Court has conflated the concepts of compulsion and coercion, essentially holding that a confession is not obtained in violation of the Fifth Amendment privilege unless the defendant can establish that it was involuntary under the due process test.[120] Nevertheless, by paying at least lip service to *Bram*,[121] the post-Warren Court has indicated that in some situations a promise by an interrogating officer may have sufficient coercive effect to render a confession involuntary.

Justice White's dicta in *Brady v United States*[122] provides the most intriguing example. In *Brady*, the Court held that a guilty plea induced by the promise of a lesser sentence is not involuntary.[123] The Court concluded that *Bram*'s prohibition on confessions induced by promises was inapplicable because in *Bram*, unlike *Brady*, the defendant was alone and unrepresented by counsel.[124] Justice White explained *Bram*'s rationale:[125]

> In such circumstances, even a mild promise of leniency was deemed sufficient to bar the confession, not because the promise was an illegal act as such, but because defendants at such

---

[118] *Malloy*, 378 US at 7, indicated that *Bram*'s language excluding confessions "extracted by any sort of threats or violence . . . [or] obtained by any direct or implied promises, however slight," stated the applicable Fifth Amendment standard.

[119] See Benner, 67 Wash U L Q at 122–29 (cited in note 24).

[120] See, for example, *Oregon v Elstad*, 470 US 298, 306 (1985) ("The *Miranda* exclusionary rule . . . serves the Fifth Amendment and sweeps more broadly than the Fifth Amendment itself."); *New York v Quarles*, 467 US 649, 654 (1984) (making a similar point).

[121] See note 125.

[122] 397 US 742 (1970).

[123] In *Brady*, 397 US at 753, the defendant claimed that his guilty plea to kidnapping was involuntary because the federal kidnapping statute provided that the death penalty could be imposed only if the jury so recommended, thus insuring that a defendant who pled guilty would escape the death penalty. The Court rejected this argument, reasoning that, given the role of plea bargaining in our system of justice, "[a] contrary holding would require the States and Federal Government to forbid guilty pleas altogether." For an illuminating examination of the *Brady* case, see Alschuler, *The Supreme Court, the Defense Attorney, and the Guilty Plea*, 47 U Colo L Rev 1, 48–70 (1975).

[124] *Brady*, 397 US at 754 (noting that Brady had competent counsel).

[125] Id.

times are too sensitive to inducement and the possible impact
on them too great to ignore and too difficult to assess.

While this passage did not commit the Court to accepting *Bram*'s
prohibition in any circumstances, it did evidence a sensitivity to
the need to exclude confessions induced by promises in circumstances in which the promise is likely to exert significant pressure
on the suspect and its precise effect is difficult to gauge.

In light of the uniquely coercive atmosphere of prison, the Court
should apply *Bram*'s prohibition on confessions induced by promises in the prison context. As Paul Keve has observed, "Prison is
a barely controlled jungle where the aggressive and the strong will
exploit the weak, and the weak are dreadfully aware of it." [126] In
recent decades, various factors—including overcrowding[127] and the
higher proportion of violent offenders in most prisons[128]—have
made prison conditions even worse.

If Keve's description of the prison atmosphere is accurate, then
confessions induced by promises in prison should be highly suspect. When people live under conditions of extreme deprivation
and danger, gauging the probable coercive effect of a promised
benefit is virtually impossible. In this atmosphere, the smallest
material comfort may seem priceless and "protection" in any form
may appear indispensable. Although it may be possible in the conventional interrogation context to assess a promise's actual effect
on a suspect and to conclude it did not exert significant pressure,[129]
a prisoner's greater susceptibility to inducement renders this approach inappropriate. In the prison context, it may fairly be said
that the possible coercive impact of the promise of a benefit will
be "too great to ignore and too difficult to assess." [130]

One difficulty with this approach is that it would require the
Court to determine precisely what inducements constitute "promises of benefits" within the meaning of the prohibition. In my view,

---

[126] Keve at 54 (cited in note 55).

[127] See generally Bowker at 164–65 (cited in note 55).

[128] See, for example, Voorhees, *Double Trouble*, Manhattan Lawyer, May, 1991 (observing
that New York has "decided to reserve costly prison space for serious and violent offenders").

[129] Compare note 117.

[130] *Brady*, 397 US at 754. Compare Bowker at 79 (cited in note 55) (explaining how weaker
members of prison are induced to give up valuable goods in exchange for promises of
protection).

applying the rationale of *Bram*, as construed in *Brady*, to the prison context would require the prohibition of any offer of protection— even if the suspect is not in obvious danger—and any promise of material items—even those as seemingly insignificant as candy or cigarettes—for in the special circumstances of the prison environment the coercive impact of such promises is potentially great and difficult to assess.

There will be other circumstances, however, in which it is difficult to decide whether a particular inducement falls within the *Bram* prohibition. Suppose, for example, that a prison informer offers the suspect friendship in exchange for a statement about his crime? Arguably, this benefit is so elusive and intangible that the offer would not have a coercive effect. On the other hand, some prisoners may feel so isolated by the prison setting that the prospect of even a temporary ally would be an inducement that would be difficult to resist.[131]

Similarly, suppose a prison informer says, "I think you will feel better if you tell me what happened," or tells the suspect that if the suspect tells him his story, he will reciprocate and tell how he happened to be arrested and incarcerated. The inducements offered in these examples—subjective in the first situation, insubstantial in the second—seem too negligible to have any coercive effects. But even in these situations, a court would have to determine whether, viewed in context, the informer's statements promised a benefit that the informer could not legitimately offer to induce a confession. In the situation where the informer offers to exchange confidences, for example, it might be inferred that the informer was implicitly offering his friendship if, but only if, the latter told him about his crime. Depending on the circumstances, including the prisoners' respective positions in the prison hierarchy, the suspect might even perceive[132] the offer to share reciprocal confidences as an offer to enter into a relationship involving future obligations.

---

[131] Compare *Fulminante*, 111 S Ct at 1252 n 2 (noting that, during an earlier period of incarceration, Fulminante was placed in protective custody because he felt threatened by other inmates; while in protective custody, however, "he was unable to cope with the isolation and was admitted to a psychiatric hospital").

[132] The perception of the suspect or that of a reasonable person in the suspect's position would seem to be the appropriate standard. Compare *Berkemer v McCarty*, 468 US 420, 442 (1984) (in determining whether a defendant is in custody within the meaning of *Miranda* "the only relevant inquiry is how a reasonable man in the suspect's position would have understood his situation").

Such examples illustrate the difficulties the Court would face in applying a *Bram*-type prohibition to confessions induced by promises, even in the prison setting. Nevertheless, such a rule would provide more protection to prisoners than the due process test applied in *Fulminante* and would be consistent with the principle that the Constitution prohibits interrogation tactics that are likely to have an unduly coercive effect.[133]

B. ALTERNATIVE 2: THE STATE MAY NOT ENTER INTO CERTAIN
    ARRANGEMENTS WITH PRISON INFORMERS

Focusing on the fact that Sarivola was instructed to get information relating to a particular individual and was receiving "substantial financial and other incentives" to get incriminating statements from that individual,[134] Fulminante suggested in his brief to the Supreme Court that the lower court's judgment could be affirmed on the ground that Sarivola's superior, agent Ticano, engaged in "reprehensible conduct."[135] In deciding the case, however, the Court focused exclusively on the interaction between Sarivola and Fulminante, eschewing the invitation to consider Ticano's instructions to Sarivola or the nature of their relationship.

This was unfortunate, for rules regulating the interactions between government officials and informers will be more effective than rules regulating the interactions between informers and prisoners. There are two reasons for this: one concerning the relative capacities of government officials and informers to assimilate rules, the other concerning the effects that different types of rules are likely to have on informers' conduct.

---

[133] Compare *Miranda v Arizona*, 384 US 436, 449–58 (1966) (condemning tactics contained in manuals because they are likely to result in coercion). See generally White, 127 U Pa L Rev at 617–18 (cited in note 42).

[134] As Justice White said, "Sarivola received significant benefits from federal authorities, including payment for information, immunity from prosecution, and eventual placement in the federal Witness Protection Program." *Fulminante*, 111 S Ct at 1259. Although Sarivola was not offered a specific financial inducement to get information from Fulminante, he was being paid on the basis of the "quality of the information provided," and Ticano's instructions, see text accompanying note 61, indicated that Fulminante's "story" was important to the authorities. Moreover, Sarivola had important nonfinancial incentives to provide information relating to Fulminante. The FBI promised to inform other law enforcement agencies of his record of cooperation in the event that he was prosecuted for other offenses. Record, 112. In addition, at the time he gave the information relating to Fulminante, he was eager to obtain and had not yet obtained a place in the Federal Witness Protection Program. See *Fulminante*, 111 S Ct at 1259 n 9.

[135] Fulminante's Brief, p 20.

Even in the best of circumstances, Supreme Court decisions are likely to have only a limited effect on government interactions with criminal suspects.[136] The Court's decisions are more likely to affect police officers,[137] however, than prison informers, who are less likely to be familiar with the Court's decisions and have no institutional incentives to comply with them.[138] Moreover, rules restricting the types of arrangements officers may make with informers can effectively alter an informers' incentives to use impermissible means for obtaining information from prisoners and may more effectively control informers' behavior than rules that attempt more directly to restrict such behavior.

Fulminante provides an apt example. The FBI hired Sarivola on a contingent fee basis under which the amount of payment depended on the "quality of the information provided."[139] On October 23, 1983, after hearing some information relating to the murder of Fulminante's stepdaughter, agent Ticano gave Sarivola specific instructions: "I gotta know the whole story. Get me the whole story."[140] Given such powerful incentives to obtain incriminating statements, is it any wonder that, according to Ticano,[141] Sarivola had a real or fabricated incriminating statement from Fulminante within twenty-four hours?

Would Sarviola's conduct have been different if the Court had held that an informer is not allowed to induce a confession by a promise of "protection"? Or, if it had established additional restrictions on the means informers may use to induce confessions? Since Fulminante had shown he was reluctant to confess,[142] Sarivola may have believed that strong measures would be necessary to obtain

---

[136] See Amsterdam, 45 NYU L Rev at 786 (cited in note 25).

[137] See Kamisar, *Does (Did) (Should) the Exclusionary Rule Rest on a "Principled Basis" Rather Than an "Empirical Proposition"?*, 16 Creighton L Rev 565, 659–61 (1983); Orfield, *The Exclusionary Rule and Deterrence: An Empirical Study of Chicago Narcotics Officers*, 54 U Chi L Rev 1016, 1026–30 (1987).

[138] Compare Park, *The Entrapment Controversy*, 60 Minn L Rev 163, 229–31 (1976) (making a similar point with respect to rules relating to entrapment).

[139] Record, 79, 106.

[140] Record, 24.

[141] Record, 24, 144–48. Sarivola, however, testified that a few days elapsed between Ticano's instructions and Fulminante's incriminating statement. Record, 27–28.

[142] According to his testimony, Sarivola had talked to Fulminante about the Arizona murder on other occasions before he obtained the incriminating statement by offering Fulminante protection. On these occasions, Fulminante denied killing his stepdaughter. Record, 81–82.

one. In view of Sarivola's dubious character,[143] it seems unlikely that rules governing prison informers' conduct would have restrained him from doing whatever was necessary to obtain the substantial benefits that seemed likely to follow[144] if he obtained a confession from Fulminante.

Rules restricting the types of arrangements federal agents may enter into with informers might more effectively have restrained Sarivola's conduct. If Ticano had been prohibited from hiring informers on a contingent fee basis and/or from targeting particular prisoners for special efforts, Ticano would likely have complied with these strictures. In that case, Sarivola would have had less incentive to obtain particular incriminating statements and, therefore, would have been less likely to engage in improper conduct to obtain a statement or to lie about his interactions with Fulminante.

Under this approach, the Court would focus on the nature of the government-informer arrangement.[145] Targeting particular

---

[143] Justice White pointed out that "Sarivola's lack of moral integrity was demonstrated by his testimony that he had worked for organized crime during the time he was a uniformed police officer. His overzealous approach to gathering information for which he would be paid by authorities, . . . was revealed by his admission that he had fabricated a tape recording in connection with an earlier, unrelated FBI investigation." *Fulminante*, 111 S Ct at 1259 n 9. In addition, agent Ticano testified that Sarivola's participation in criminal activity prior to his entrance in the Witness Protection Program was "somewhat substantive." Record, 157. In particular, Sarivola was involved in extortion, and, according to Ticano, routinely used physical force or the threat of physical force in the collection of loan sharking debts. Record, 158.

[144] See note 134.

[145] Although it deals with a different constitutional issue, *United States v Henry*, 447 US 264, 270 (1980), has some bearing on the proposed approach. In holding that Henry's incriminating statements were introduced into evidence in violation of the Sixth Amendment, the Court focused more on the interaction between the government official and the informer Nichols than it did on the interchanges between Nichols and Henry. To support its conclusion that Nichols deliberately elicited incriminating statements from Henry, the Court emphasized that "Nichols and the agent [were] on a contingent fee basis," and that "the agent in his discussions with Nichols singled out Henry as the inmate in whom the agent had a special interest." Id at 271 n 8. Although its analysis was not entirely clear, the Court seemed to reason that these factors increased the likelihood that Henry's incriminating statements were made as a result of affirmative attempts to elicit information on the part of Nichols, and, therefore, the lower court's conclusion that deliberate elicitation occurred was permissible.

Henry does not, of course, suggest that the combination of a contingent fee arrangement and the targeting of a specific suspect is sufficient in itself to establish a Sixth Amendment violation. *Henry* determined that a Sixth Amendment violation because the government informer engaged in conduct that amounted to "indirect and surreptitious interrogatio[n]" of the defendant. Id at 273 (quoting from *Massiah v United States*, 377 US 201, 206 (1964)). The Court reserved decision on whether a Sixth Amendment violation would have occurred

prisoners and rewarding informers on a "contingent fee basis" are dangerous practices because they provide powerful incentives for informers to fabricate confessions or to induce them by improper practices. Indeed, the combination of a "contingent fee" arrangement and targeting particular suspects creates a potential for abuse even outside the prison context.[146] When these two practices are combined in the prison setting—where problems with the informer's reliability are exacerbated[147]—the potential for abuse is significant.

The Court has already recognized the dangers that "contingent fee" arrangements create in the system of criminal justice. *Tumey v Ohio*[148] held that the defendant's constitutional right to an unbiased judge is violated when the judge is paid only if the defendant is convicted.[149] In an opinion for a unanimous Court, Chief Justice Taft stated that such a practice deprives a criminal defendant "of due process of law," for it subjects "his liberty or property to the judgment of a court the judge of which has a direct, personal, substantial, pecuniary interest in reaching a conclusion against him in his case."[150]

Significantly, the danger that a financial incentive will induce improper conduct is even greater in the case of the informer. Given

---

if the government informer had been merely a passive listener to the defendant's incriminating statements. See *Henry*, 447 US at 271 n 9. Moreover, *Kuhlmann v Wilson*, 477 US 436, 459 (1986), held that, regardless of the government's arrangement with the informer, "the defendant must demonstrate that the police and their informant took some action, beyond merely listening, that was designed deliberately to elicit incriminating remarks." To that extent, *Henry* and its progeny rejects the proposed approach, establishing that the arrangement between the government and the informer will never be enough in itself to violate the Constitution.

[146] Compare *Williamson v United States*, 311 F2d 441, 444 (5th Cir 1962) (holding that "a contingent fee agreement to produce evidence against particular named defendants as to crimes not yet committed" invalidates resulting conviction because the arrangement creates the danger of a "frame-up" or entrapment).

[147] See text accompanying notes 162–78.

[148] 273 US 510 (1927).

[149] Id at 520. The relevant ordinance provided that the mayor sitting as judge "should receive or retain the amount of his costs in each case, in addition to his regular salary, as compensation for hearing such cases. But no fees or costs in such cases are paid him except by the defendant if convicted."

[150] Id at 523. *Tumey* was reaffirmed and expanded in *Ward v Village of Monroeville*, 409 US 57 (1972), in which the Court held that *Tumey* applies when the fines, forfeitures, costs, and fees imposed by the mayor sitting as judge in the mayor's court constitute a substantial portion of the municipality's funds.

their differing economic situations,[151] the informer generally will have more to gain by producing the evidence than the judge has by rendering a guilty verdict. In addition, the judge's conduct is more open to scrutiny—in that the evidence on which the judge acts is a matter of record, unlike the circumstances in which the informer obtains the evidence.[152] Thus, the rationale that underlies *Tumey* provides some basis for condemning the practice of rewarding informers on a contingent fee basis.

Moreover, the practice of targeting particular suspects exacerbates the problem because it narrows the informer's range of activity. While it is legitimate for law enforcement officers to target individuals for investigation,[153] targeting individuals for an informer who is paid on a "contingent fee" basis enhances the possibility of improper conduct. If, for example, an informer is told that he will be paid a specific sum to obtain information against a named individual,[154] the informer has a special incentive to produce evidence incriminating that individual because he knows evidence incriminating others will not be as lucrative.[155] Thus, the practice of targeting particular suspects for informers employed on a "contingent fee" raises such serious problems that there is a strong basis for condemning it as improper.

C. THE PROBLEM WITH ALTERNATIVES 1 AND 2: PRISON INFORMER
   UNRELIABILITY

Although both of these approaches are preferable to *Fulminante*'s due process approach, neither addresses a fundamental problem.

---

[151] Informers operating outside the prison sometimes become extremely wealthy because they are paid exorbitant fees for informing. See Curriden, *Making Crime Pay. What's the Cost of Using Paid Informers?*, 77 ABA J 43, 44, June, 1991 (Curriden II) (noting that many professional informers have six digit incomes). Nevertheless, the average informer (and certainly the average prison informer) has less financial assets to draw on than the average judge.

[152] The defense may, of course, cross-examine the informer for the purpose of exploring the circumstances under which the informer obtained the incriminating evidence. But because of the inadequacies of the litigation process, such circumstances are not likely to be fully revealed. See note 172 and accompanying text.

[153] See, for example, *United States v Allibhai*, 939 F2d 244 (5th Cir 1991) (law enforcement officers may target an individual for a "sting" operation even though they lack reasonable suspicion that he is engaged in any illegal activities).

[154] See *Williamson*, 311 F2d 441 (government promised informer $200 if he could catch one suspect and $100 if he could catch another one).

[155] Moreover, the informer may feel that he can fabricate evidence against the targeted individual with greater impunity because the government believes the individual is guilty and will be less likely to scrutinize the accuracy of evidence produced against him.

The difficulties associated with the litigation process—which thwarted the Court's efforts to administer the due process test in the pre-*Miranda* era[156]—are even more problematic in the prison context. As a result, even with the safeguards suggested above, prison informers' testimony may too often lead to miscarriages of justice.[157] The "swearing contest" between government agents and defendant, which made it difficult to determine the admissibility of confessions obtained by police interrogation, presents even greater problems when a prison informer testifies to a confession allegedly made by another prisoner. As in the stationhouse, the interaction between the informer and the prisoner usually takes place in secret. Indeed, in the typical case, where only one informer is involved, the defendant and the informer are usually the only witnesses to the relevant conversations. The absence of any corroborating evidence or witnesses[158] increases the likelihood that either the informer or the suspect will testify falsely.[159] Moreover, although the informer is a less trustworthy witness than a police officer, this does not make it easier for the judge to resolve the credibility dispute between the government witness and the defendant.[160] The defendant, after all, is an untrustworthy witness too. In addition, as in the stationhouse cases, political and other pressures[161] are

---

[156] See text at notes 26–28.

[157] See, for example, Curriden I at 52, 54 (recounting the case of James Richardson) and at 54–55 (noting other cases in which prison informers testimony probably led to the conviction of an innocent person) (cited in note 3).

[158] In the usual police interrogation case, numerous police officers may be available to corroborate part or all of each other's testimony.

[159] In police interrogation cases, the availability of several witnesses to the transaction— even if all but one is a police officer—is likely to provide some check against perjury. On the other hand, if an informer knows that he and the criminal defendant are the only witnesses to a conversation, no such check is present.

[160] The witnesses' dubious credibility is not the only problem. The participants in the critical conversations may find it difficult to recreate their interchanges accurately even if they are trying to be truthful. In the stationhouse context, the police can generally take notes or arrange to have the interrogation recorded. While it may still be impossible to capture the true atmosphere of the police interrogation, these aids will assist an honest officer in providing an accurate account of what happened. The prison informer, on the other hand, will find it difficult to utilize these devices because his enterprise (and possibly his life) depends upon deceiving the prisoner as to the true import of the conversations between them. Obviously, the prisoner is in an even worse position to recreate the critical conversations because he does not even know that the conversations he has with the informer will be relevant to subsequent litigation.

[161] See, for example, Schaefer, *Federalism and State Criminal Procedure*, 70 Harv L Rev 1, 5 (1956).

likely to increase the judge's natural tendency to resolve credibility conflicts in favor of the government.

There is, moreover, an added dimension to the "swearing contest." Although it is known that police sometimes commit perjury when testifying on a motion to suppress a confession,[162] empirical data indicate that officers are more likely to testify falsely with respect to the circumstances in which a confession was given than they are to fabricate the content of the confession or to lie about whether any confession was made.[163]

Prison informers, on the other hand, are unlikely to distinguish among these different types of false testimony. Their motive for presenting false testimony is simple: they hope to receive some benefit from the government.[164] In this respect, of course, prison informers are not distinguishable from other informers and witnesses, including expert witnesses, who expect to receive a benefit in exchange for presenting testimony favorable to the government. Nevertheless, the incentives offered a prison informer are of a different magnitude because of the informer's status as a prisoner. As a prominent defense attorney explained, "When you dangle extra rewards, furloughs, money, their own clothes, stereos, in front of people in overcrowded jails, then you have an unacceptable temptation to commit perjury."[165] Thus, unlike the officer, the informer is as likely to testify falsely about the content of the confession (or whether one was made) as he is about the circumstances in which it was given.

Empirical data suggest that this is a serious problem. After the Leslie White scandal,[166] a grand jury investigating the use of informers in Los Angeles County concluded that prison informers presented perjured testimony in an "extraordinary number of . . . instances."[167] One informer, an admitted perjurer, explained why, "Me and every other [informant] I've talked to have the same pol-

---

[162] See Orfield, 54 U Chi L Rev at 1051 (cited in note 137); Skolnick, *Justice Without Trial: Law Enforcement in Democratic Society* 214–15, 227–28 (1966).

[163] See Skolnick at 228 (cited in note 162).

[164] See text accompanying note 165.

[165] Reinhold (cited in note 1). As this comment suggests, even if the prison informer is offered a purely pecuniary incentive, the attractiveness of that incentive will be enhanced because of the informer's incarceration.

[166] See text accompanying note 1.

[167] Los Angeles Times, A1, July 10, 1990.

icy. The guy's guilty. Who gives a damn?"[168] Although more data would be helpful, the existing evidence supports the Los Angeles County District Attorney's judgment that prison informers' testimony is generally unreliable.[169]

Although the voluntariness test applied by the Court in confession cases may originally have been applied to exclude unreliable confessions,[170] that test, as it has evolved, is not well designed to deal with the problems of unreliability presented when an informer testifies to a prisoner's confession. In fact, when the claim is that the informer is testifying falsely to the content of the confession (as opposed to the circumstances under which it was made), the Court undoubtedly would hold that the credibility question is to be resolved by the jury deciding the case rather than by the judge applying the due process test to determine the admissibility of the confession.[171]

But in this context the notion that the jury can accurately determine an informer's credibility is an obvious fiction. When clever witnesses have powerful motives to lie and are able to testify so that their stories seem plausible,[172] some additional protection beyond those already provided by the normal operation of the adversary system is necessary to safeguard criminal defendants from miscarriages of justice.

The existing situation may be compared to the miscarriages of justice that occurred as a result of false testimony generated by the "reward" system in eighteenth-century England.[173] Under the "reward" system, Parliament offered rewards for apprehending and successfully prosecuting various criminals.[174] Tempted by these

---

[168] Los Angeles Times, A1, Mar. 4, 1990.

[169] See note 4.

[170] Kamisar, *Essays*, 11 (cited in note 11).

[171] See *Jackson v Denno*, 378 US 368, 386–87 n 13 (1964) (dicta). Compare *Colorado v Connelly*, 479 US 157, 167 (1986) (observing that a confession's reliability "is a matter to be governed by the evidentiary laws of the forum . . . and not by the Due Process Clause of the Fourteenth Amendment").

[172] In October, 1988, Leslie Vernon White demonstrated "that by using a jail telephone and pretending to be a bail bondsman, a prosecutor or police detective, he could gather enough information about a murder case to concoct for the authorities a confession by a defendant he had really never met." New York Times, A14, Jan. 3, 1989.

[173] Langbein, *Shaping the Eighteenth–Century Criminal Trial: A View from the Ryder Sources*, 50 U Chi L Rev 1, 105–12 (1983).

[174] Id at 106–07. See generally 2 L. Radzinowicz, *A History of English Criminal Law and Its Administration from 1750*, at 326–32, 337–39 (1948–68) (4 vols.).

financial inducements, individuals and gangs sometimes successfully framed innocent persons in order to gain the reward. The
MacDaniel scandal, which involved the apprehension and prosecution of a large gang that had benefited from the "reward" system by
presenting perjured testimony in a series of mid-eighteenth-century
cases,[175] awakened the public conscience as to the abuses generated
by the "reward" system and led eventually to reforms that precipitated that system's demise.[176]

Based on the Los Angeles County Grand Jury's report,[177] prison
informers as a group are at least as unreliable as the eighteenth-
century witnesses who presented testimony to obtain the pecuniary
benefit promised by the "reward" system. Moreover, at least in a
context where the prison informer obtains a statement admitting
an uncharged crime, the chances of a miscarriage of justice are
substantial because, aside from the informer's potentially unreliable
testimony, there may be no basis for prosecution.[178]

Because the approaches proposed above do not address the problem of the prison informer's lack of reliability,[179] they do not provide adequate safeguards against miscarriages of justices.

---

[175] Langbein at 110–14 (cited in note 173).

[176] Id at 114.

[177] See text accompanying note 167.

[178] This was the case in *Fulminante*. As Justice White said, in the absence of Fulminante's
confessions to Sarivola and later Sarivola's wife, "it is unlikely that Fulminante would have
been prosecuted at all, because the physical evidence from the scene and other circumstantial
evidence would have been insufficient to convict." *Fulminante*, 111 S Ct at 1258.

[179] Barring confessions induced by prison informers' promises does not address this problem at all. In view of the inadequacies of the litigation process, an informer's false testimony
that he did not induce the confession through a promise would be difficult to discredit.
Thus, this approach is not calculated to prevent convictions on the basis of false prisoner
informer testimony.

Regulating arrangements between the government and prison informers does have some
potential for preventing miscarriages of justice. Prohibiting arrangements under which informers are offered substantial incentives to produce evidence against suspects reduces the
possibility that informers will testify falsely against suspects in order to gain the incentive
offered by the government. Regulating arrangements between the government and informers
does not go far enough, however, because under our system of justice prison informers have
incentives to offer false testimony against prisoners even when they have not entered into
any specific arrangement with the government. Thus, in order to reduce the possibility of
convictions resulting from false testimony by prison informers, it is necessary either to
change the nature of our system of justice or to restrict the admissibility of unreliable
informer testimony.

D. ALTERNATIVE 3: STATE MAY NOT USE UNRELIABLE PRISON
   INFORMER TESTIMONY

The Court could safeguard against such miscarriages of justice
by restricting the admissibility of unreliable prison informer testimony. In so doing, the Court could draw on a due process principle
established to govern the admissibility of unreliable identification
evidence. In *Stovall v Denno*,[180] the Court held that the government's use of unreliable testimony induced by questionable investi-
gative procedures that create an unnecessary risk of erroneous fact-
finding violates due process. That principle should apply to the
present situation.

1. *The due process standard: Stovall and Brathwaite.* In a trilogy of
cases decided in 1967, the Court provided safeguards against the
use of identification evidence obtained as a result of suggestive
government procedures.[181] *United States v Wade*[182] held that an indicted defendant compelled by the government to participate in a
pretrial confrontation designed to elicit identification evidence has a
constitutional right to have counsel present at the confrontation.[183]
Wade's underlying concern was to reduce or eliminate miscarriages
of justice resulting from suggestive identification procedures.[184]
The right to counsel was designed to reduce unfairness at the pretrial confrontation and to allow a fuller exploration of the circumstances of the confrontation at trial.[185]

In *Stovall v Denno*,[186] the victim had been stabbed eleven times.
As a result, she was hospitalized for major surgery to save her life.
On the day after the victim's surgery, the police took the defendant
to the hospital and, while he was handcuffed to a police officer,

---

[180] 388 US 293 (1967).

[181] See *United States v Wade*, 388 US 218 (1967); *Stovall*, 388 US 293; *Gilbert v California*,
388 US 263 (1967).

[182] 388 US 218 (1967).

[183] Id at 228.

[184] The Court accepted a commentator's conclusion that "[t]he influence of improper suggestion upon identifying witnesses probably accounts for more miscarriages of justice than
any other single factor—perhaps it is responsible for more such errors than all other factors
combined." Id at 229, quoting Wall, *Eye-Witness Identification in Criminal Cases* 26.

[185] *Wade*, 388 US at 235.

[186] 388 US 293.

showed him to the victim who identified him as the perpetrator.[187] After concluding that the Sixth Amendment principle established in *Wade* was not applicable to the *Stovall* case,[188] the Court stated that testimony identifying a criminal defendant as the perpetrator of a crime is constitutionally inadmissible when the confrontation producing that testimony "was so unnecessarily suggestive and conducive to irreparable mistaken identification that [the defendant] was denied due process of law." [189] Applying this principle to the facts before it, the Court concluded that the confrontation in *Stovall* was not *unnecessarily* suggestive because, in view of the victim's precarious physical condition, "an immediate confrontation was imperative." [190]

In *Stovall*, as in *Wade*, the Court focused on the problem of providing safeguards against unduly suggestive identification procedures that might lead to misidentification. *Stovall* does not exist in isolation, however. Rather, it stands as the application of a broader principle of due process that extends to other situations as well. In *Wade*, the Court explained that it was necessary to establish safeguards relating to identification evidence because of the risk of miscarriages of justice.[191] In furtherance of this objective, *Stovall* articulated a standard for determining when identification evidence is so unreliable that it may not be admitted against a criminal defendant. *Stovall* suggested two key elements of the standard: first, unreliable evidence that the jury might view as reliable, and second, a government practice that unnecessarily contributed to the evidence's lack of reliability. These elements are, of course, vague. The Court did not explain in *Stovall* either the measure of unreliability[192] or the nature of the government's obligation to avoid practices that produce such unreliable evidence.[193] Moreover, the Court

---

[187] Id at 295.

[188] The Court concluded that *Wade* could not be retroactively applied to cases in which the pretrial confrontation took place prior to the date of the *Wade* decision. Id at 301.

[189] Id at 302.

[190] Id.

[191] *Wade*, 388 US at 228–29.

[192] Moreover, the Court does not explain what kind of empirical evidence must be adduced to establish either that the evidence is unreliable or that juries are likely to give it more credit than it deserves.

[193] In *Stovall*, the Court agreed that the procedure followed by the government—showing a single suspect to the witness for the purpose of identification—was likely to produce unreliable evidence. Nevertheless, the Court concluded that the procedure employed was

did not address the relationship between the two elements of its standard. In particular, it did not explain whether the government's obligation to avoid procedures that produce unreliable evidence is affected by either the degree of unreliability or the justifications for using the challenged procedure.

The Court modified *Stovall's* due process test in *Manson v Brathwaite*.[194] In *Brathwaite* the issue was whether the admission of a photo identification obtained as a result of an unnecessarily suggestive procedure violated due process.[195] Instead of holding that the unnecessarily suggestive procedure automatically rendered the identification inadmissible, the Court held that the identification's admissibility must be determined on the basis of its overall reliability. The Court explained that, in making this determination, a court must consider the corrupting effect of the suggestive identification procedure along with several other factors bearing on the identification's reliability[196] and exclude the identification evidence if it concludes that it is substantially likely to be unreliable.[197]

Brathwaite does not undermine the central principle of *Stovall*. When an unnecessarily suggestive government practice contributes to the production of unreliable evidence that the jury is likely to view as reliable, a due process issue arises. *Brathwaite* does modify *Stovall*, however, by holding that even if the requirements of *Stovall* are met, the admission of evidence will not violate due process in the absence of a particularized assessment that the evidence is substantially likely to be unreliable.

2. *Applying the due process test to prison informers' testimony.* Should the *Stovall* due process standard apply to prison informers' testi-

---

not "unnecessarily suggestive," because the government's need to obtain a prompt identification was "imperative." 388 US at 302. This analysis apparently indicates that the government will be allowed to employ procedures that are likely to obtain unreliable identification evidence when it is confronted with the choice between obtaining unreliable identification evidence or no evidence at all.

[194] 432 US 98 (1977).

[195] A police officer identified defendant as the person who sold him narcotics after the officer's superior showed him a single photograph of the defendant for purposes of making an identification. Id at 101. No explanation was given for the failure to utilize a photographic array or to conduct a line-up. Id at 102.

[196] The other factors to be considered were the witness' opportunity to view the criminal at the time of the crime, the witness' degree of attention, the accuracy of the witness' prior description of the criminal, the witness' level of certainty at the time of the confrontation, and the time between the crime and the confrontation. Id at 114.

[197] Id at 116.

mony as to prisoners' incriminating statements? In many such cases, the first element of *Stovall* is met. Although more empirical evidence relating to prisoner informer testimony needs to be collected, the Los Angeles grand jury's determination that prison informers presented perjured testimony in an "extraordinary number of . . . instances" [198] provides an adequate basis for concluding that in Los Angeles County at least prison informer testimony is highly unreliable. Since the existing empirical evidence suggests that the practices that produced unreliable prison informer testimony in Los Angeles also prevail in other jurisdictions, [199] it may be inferred that in many, if not most, jurisdictions such testimony is highly unreliable. [200]

Moreover, there is a grave danger that the jury will underestimate the unreliability of such testimony. Although cross-examination may be more effective in exposing false informer testimony than in exposing a mistaken identification because the mistaken identification witness often believes she is telling the truth, [201] the jury will also find it difficult to assess the credibility of a typical prison informer. That informer usually has had considerable experience in testifying, [202] has few scruples about perjuring himself, [203] and knows how to make his story appear convincing even if it is false. [204] In these circumstances, even cross-examination that effectively brings out the informer's incentives for obtaining the particular incriminating statements is unlikely to reveal to the jury the high probability that the informer's testimony is false.

Determining whether a government practice unnecessarily contributes to the prison informer testimony's unreliability is more problematic. If it is true that prison informers often testify falsely in order to gain rewards offered by the government, [205] then the

---

[198] See text accompanying note 167.

[199] See generally Curriden I at 56 (citing examples throughout the criminal justice system in which law enforcement officers " 'encourage[d]' criminals to snitch") (cited in note 3).

[200] See Reinhold (cited in note 1) (observing that "criminal lawyers have long suspected tainted testimony by informers in other states" besides California).

[201] See Williams & Hammelmann, *Identification Parades—I*, Crim L Rev 479, 479-80 (1962).

[202] See, for example, Los Angeles Times, A1, Mar. 4, 1990 (a "professional" prison informer, such as Leslie Vernon White, often testifies in numerous cases).

[203] See note 168.

[204] See note 172.

[205] See text at notes 164–69.

government practice of offering rewards for informers' testimony certainly contributes to the testimony's unreliability. It might be argued, however, that the practice of offering rewards for prison informer's testimony is not "unnecessary" because in the absence of such rewards virtually no informers would testify. This argument identifies a critical issue. What is the nature of the government's due process obligation to refrain from practices that contribute to the production of unreliable evidence? Does *Stovall* mean that the government must refrain from such practices only if it could employ another practice that would produce the same evidence in a more reliable form?[206] Or does *Stovall* mean that the government has some obligation to use procedures that minimize the use of unreliable evidence, even at the cost of losing some evidence that may be reliable?

Although *Stovall* itself does not speak to this issue, the rationale of the Court's identification cases suggests that the government does have at least some obligation to avoid practices that produce unreliable evidence even when the cost of avoiding such procedures is to lose some reliable evidence. *Stovall* and its progeny[207] established that the government may not employ suggestive identification procedures (i.e., "conducive to mistaken identifications") when nonsuggestive procedures could have been used instead. Obviously, nonsuggestive identification procedures are less likely than suggestive ones to result in an identification.[208] Moreover, some of the identifications resulting from suggestive procedures would in fact be reliable.

---

[206] When the government uses a suggestive identification procedure even though they would have had time to employ a nonsuggestive one, arguably the use of the suggestive procedure does not produce more evidence than the nonsuggestive procedure would. Utilizing the nonsuggestive procedure would still allow the witness an opportunity to identify the defendant and an identification given under these circumstances would be stronger evidence than one made pursuant to a suggestive procedure. Moreover, if the witness were unable to identify the defendant, this evidence also might be relevant to the issue of the defendant's guilt. From the government's point of view, however, substituting a nonsuggestive identification procedure for a suggestive one reduces the possibility of an identification and, over time, results in a net loss of admissible government evidence.

[207] See, for example, *Foster v California*, 394 US 440 (1969) (holding that a pretrial identification given after two line-ups and a one-on-one confrontation was so unnecessarily suggestive as to violate due process).

[208] By their nature, suggestive identification procedures increase the probability that the witness will identify the defendant. Moreover, as *Wade* pointed out, identifications made as a result of suggestive identification procedures will often constitute powerful evidence because the witness will be convinced as to the accuracy of her identification. *Wade*, 388 US at 229.

Thus, *Stovall* and its progeny imply that, in determining whether a government practice "unnecessarily" contributes to unreliable evidence, some kind of balancing must take place. The government cannot justify a practice that produces unreliable evidence on the ground that it also produces reliable evidence not otherwise obtainable if the dangers dwarf the benefits. Thus, *Stovall*'s due process principle should condemn government practices that produce unreliable evidence even when abandoning the practice involves some cost to the government. The crucial inquiry is whether the government practice strikes a reasonable accommodation between promoting the government's interest in obtaining evidence and avoiding a practice that produces evidence that is likely to skew accurate fact-finding.

The government practice of offering rewards to prison informers in exchange for their testimony precipitates unreliable prison informer testimony. When, as in *Fulminante*, the government employs an informer on a contingent fee, targets a particular suspect, and holds out the possibility of large rewards for incriminating testimony, the inducement to perjury is obvious.[209] Even if there is no contingent fee arrangement, if the government takes action—either through an explicit arrangement with the informer or by a pattern of rewarding other informers—that leads the informer to believe that he will receive an exorbitant reward for incriminating testimony, the inducement to commit perjury may be as great. Indeed, whenever the government provides rewards for prison informer testimony, there is a real inducement to perjury.

The government might reasonably claim that offering rewards for prison informer testimony is "necessary" because prison informer testimony is helpful to law enforcement and such testimony would dry up if prisoners had no incentive to inform. The government can also plausibly argue that the greater the reward, the more likely it is to produce testimony. In applying *Stovall*'s due process principle, however, the question is whether the offer of rewards for informer testimony creates such risks of unreliable testimony that the dangers dwarf the benefits.

---

[209] Compare *Hoffa v United States*, 385 US 293, 320 (dissenting opinion of Warren, C.J., arguing that in particular circumstances where the defendant was targeted and the informer was apparently offered inducements that included release from prison and the dismissal of very serious criminal charges, the government's use of the informer "evidence[s] a serious potential for undermining the integrity of the truth-finding process in the federal courts").

In my judgment, whenever the government offers exorbitant rewards for prison informer testimony, the risk of generating unreliable evidence far outweighs the benefits of the additional reliable testimony likely to be produced. In most circumstances, a nonexorbitant reward should be sufficient to induce prison informer testimony, and the temptation to perjury in order to obtain an exorbitant reward is too great to countenance.

The determination of whether a reward is "exorbitant" must be made from the perspective of the typical prisoner. In view of most prisoners' overwhelming desire to reduce their prison time, rewards that involve the dismissal of charges or the substantial reduction of prison time should generally be considered "exorbitant." Large sums of money or money that is paid on a contingent fee basis should also be viewed as "exorbitant" because such rewards are likely to constitute an extraordinary temptation to commit perjury.[210] On the other hand, employing a prisoner as a government informer with his salary to be the same whether or not he produces incriminating statements[211] or rewarding nongovernment informers with modest sums when they supply creditable incriminating testimony does not create the same incentive for perjury.[212]

---

[210] If the prisoner knows he will receive a large sum of money for any incriminating evidence, the temptation to commit perjury will occur because of the prisoner's knowledge that a large sum of money can be used to improve his conditions in prison. Even a smaller sum of money offered as a contingent fee for particular incriminating evidence would often constitute an exceptional temptation to commit perjury because the informer knows that producing incriminating information against that individual will maximize his chances of reward and minimize the risk that he will be accused of fabrication. See notes 154–55 and accompanying text.

[211] This approach will lead to other problems, however. If a salaried government informer really has no incentive to obtain incriminating evidence, there is a danger he will "rip the government off" by continuing to collect his salary without ever making the slightest effort to obtain incriminating evidence. This kind of cost is one that the government should be obligated to bear in order to reduce the risk of perjured prison informer testimony. On the other hand, an informer retained on a salary may believe that his continued employment is likely to depend on whether he regularly produces tangible results. If this is the case, this type of arrangement may still provide a considerable inducement to perjury.

[212] The empirical evidence may suggest that prison informers are highly likely to commit perjury when they know or expect that they will receive *any* reward in exchange for their testimony. If this is the case, then arguably the admission of informer testimony given with the expectation of obtaining a reward from the government violates the *Stovall* principle because opting for a practice that produces highly unreliable prisoner informer testimony rather than no such testimony at all does not strike a reasonable accommodation between promoting the government's interest in obtaining evidence and avoiding a practice that will skew accurate fact finding. The principle that protecting the innocent against wrongful conviction is a higher priority than convicting the guilty should lead to the conclusion that admitting no evidence is preferable to admitting highly unreliable evidence that may be misinterpreted by the jury.

Based on this analysis, *Stovall*'s due process principle would call into question any prison informer's testimony that was given in circumstances in which the informer knew or expected that he would obtain an exorbitant reward in exchange for the testimony. Under *Brathwaite*, a court in such circumstances must inquire into the overall reliability of the informer's testimony.[213] The court would have to determine whether there was a substantial likelihood that the testimony was unreliable.[214]

The effectiveness of this test would depend on the weight given to both the corrupting effect of the government practice and the other factors considered.[215] The existing empirical data indicate that prison informer testimony induced as a result of the government practice of offering exorbitant rewards for such testimony is highly unreliable.[216] Therefore, in such situations, testimony should be excluded unless the government presents affirmative evidence to establish that the informer's testimony is trustworthy.

Such evidence might take at least three forms: physical[217] or electronic evidence[218] corroborating the informer's account,[219] character evidence showing that the informer is especially credible,[220]

---

[213] Under this approach, judges might more readily determine particular rewards to be exorbitant because they would know that this determination would not necessarily lead to exclusion of the prison informer's testimony.

[214] See text at note 197.

[215] As applied in the lower courts, the *Brathwaite* test apparently seldom leads to the exclusion of identification evidence. See generally Sherwood, *The Erosion of Constitutional Safeguards in the Area of Eyewitness Identification*, 30 Howard L J 731, 749–52 (1987).

[216] See text accompanying notes 212–14.

[217] See, for example, *State v Arnold*, 657 P2d 1052, 1053 (Hawaii 1983) (defendant provided prison informer with map disclosing location of murder victim's body).

[218] There have been several cases in which electronic evidence corroborated an informer's account of his conversation with the defendant. See, for example, *Maine v Moulton*, 474 US 159 (1985); *Massiah v United States*, 377 US 201 (1964). Invariably, however, these cases have involved situations in which the informer was not in prison. Using electronic evidence when the informer is actually a prisoner would undoubtedly be more difficult but might be possible under some circumstances. In *Perkins*, for example, police apparently considered this possibility but rejected it as "impracticable and unsafe." *Illinois v Perkins*, 110 S Ct 2394, 2396 (1990).

[219] Following the scandal precipitated by Leslie Vernon White's revelations, see text accompanying note 1 and notes 182–85, the Los Angeles County district attorney's office issued new guidelines, apparently limiting situations in which prison informers will be permitted to testify for the government to cases in which this type of corroboration is available. See Los Angeles Times, November 18, 1988, B1.

[220] For example, evidence that a particular informer had an excellent track record in the sense that he had previously given information that was shown to be reliable could be considered in assessing his character.

or evidence that the reward offered by the government would not be as attractive to the prison informer involved as it would to others.[221] If the government introduces such evidence,[222] the court should then evaluate all the circumstances, including the nature of the reward offered to the informer,[223] in order to determine whether there is a substantial likelihood that the informer's testimony is unreliable.

IV. Conclusion

The need to regulate the use of prison informers' testimony is paramount, for empirical evidence indicates that such testimony is often false. *Fulminante* provided the Court with an opportunity to restrict the admissibility of prison informers' testimony in a context where the informer testifies to a statement from a prisoner relating to a crime with which the prisoner has not yet been charged. The Court wasted this opportunity, however, by essentially ignoring the fact that it was dealing with a case involving a prison informer. Instead, it decided the case by applying the due process voluntariness test, an approach that was ineffective in regulating the admissibility of statements obtained by police interrogation and is likely to be even less effective when applied to govern the admissibility of incriminating statements testified to by prison informers.

My primary goal has been to assess the extent to which the Due Process Clause imposes appropriate restraints on prison informers who seek incriminating statements from suspects in prison. Drawing upon the Court's decisions in *Stovall* and *Brathwaite*, I suggest

---

[221] A prison informer who had almost completed his sentence at the time he reported an incriminating conversation, for example, would arguably be less likely to be attracted by the prospect of a reward from the government because the reward could not be used to improve the informer's conditions of confinement. Evidence of this type could also be viewed as establishing that in the particular circumstances, the reward offered to the informer was not "exorbitant" and, therefore, the due process test should not be triggered.

[222] Evidence that the informer's account of the prisoner's confession corroborated details known to the police by other sources should not ordinarily be considered evidence of the informer's trustworthiness, however. Based on Leslie White's account of his experience as a prison informer, it is not difficult for a prisoner to obtain such details from the police. See note 172. Therefore, allowing the informer to establish his trustworthiness by providing such details would provide a significant opportunity for abuse.

[223] If the prisoner was targeted and the informer was offered a large reward, for example, these factors should weigh heavily against the government.

that the Due Process Clause imposes restrictions on the admissibility of evidence that is likely to skew accurate fact-finding when a government practice unnecessarily contributed to the evidence's lack of reliability. In this situation, the Due Process Clause at the very least requires a court to evaluate the reliability of testimony induced by the government practice and to exclude evidence that is substantially likely to be unreliable.

This test should govern the situation in which a prison informer testifies to a prisoner's incriminating statement. Since empirical evidence suggests that prison informer testimony induced by the government practice of offering exorbitant rewards for such testimony is highly unreliable, admitting such testimony violates due process unless special circumstances provide a basis for crediting the testimony. Moreover, the type of special circumstances to be considered should be limited to those that actually relate to the informer's trustworthiness or provide indisputable verification of his testimony. Such an approach would constitute at least a first step toward addressing the central problem posed by prison informers' testimony.

PAUL J. HEALD

THE VICES OF ORIGINALITY

Lately, the Constitution has become an unwelcome guest at the parties of those claiming rights lying on the periphery of intellectual property. Two terms ago, in *Bonito Boats, Inc. v Thunder Craft Boats Inc.*,[1] the Court held that federal patent law preempted a Florida statute forbidding the reproduction of boat hulls by use of any direct molding process. The Court's decision effectively provided a limited constitutional right to copy unpatented product shapes and designs.[2] Most recently, in *Feist Publications, Inc. v Rural Telephone Service, Inc.*[3] the Intellectual Property Clause[4] was held to create positive restraints on Congress's ability to provide copyright protection. In deciding that telephone directory white pages were uncopyrightable, the Court found that the Intellectual Property Clause imposed an originality requirement on authors seeking protection for their works. It held that Rural Telephone Service's white pages were not original enough to meet the new constitu-

---

Paul J. Heald is Assistant Professor of Law, University of Georgia.

AUTHOR'S NOTE: Thanks to Doug Baird, Richard Craswell, Craig Joyce, Ray Patterson, Jim Smith, and Michael Wells for insightful comments on earlier drafts. Any errors are undoubtedly theirs.

[1] 489 US 141 (1989).

[2] This right must be termed "limited" for two reasons. First, since the decision was based on the finding of a conflict between the state antimolding statute and the current federal patent statute, amendments to the federal statute might change its preemptive contours. Second, the copying privilege must be exercised with due regard for relevant prohibitions contained in federal trademark law. See Paul J. Heald, *Federal Intellectual Property Law and the Economics of Preemption*, 76 Iowa L Rev —— (1991).

[3] 111 S Ct 1282 (1991).

[4] US Const Art I, § 8, cl 8 (Congress shall have the power "to promote the Progress of Science and useful Arts, by securing for limited Times to Authors and Inventors the exclusive Right to their respective Writings and Discoveries.").

tional requirement. The Intellectual Property Clause, generally presumed to be nothing more than a grant of power to Congress,[5] suddenly grew some substantive claws.

The idea that only "original" works can be copyrighted is hardly novel. The 1976 Copyright Act[6] protects only "original works of authorship," as did its predecessor act as interpreted by courts and commentators.[7] Exactly what "original" meant in a work comprised of a compilation of facts was hotly debated. A unanimous Court in *Feist* dropped two bombshells in the middle of the debate. First, Justice O'Connor's opinion asserts, bludgeoning the point home in at least seven places, that originality exists as a constitutional requirement wholly apart from the Copyright Act.[8] Second, telephone white pages are not original enough to satisfy the new constitutional test. In other words, the familiar white pages are unprotected and Congress apparently can do nothing to render them protectable short of initiating a constitutional amendment.

The opinion is all the more interesting, because the Court bypassed at least four narrower grounds for reversing the Tenth Circuit's decision—the well-worn axiom militating against reaching constitutional questions except when necessary was nowhere to be seen. Doctrinally, these narrow grounds appear far more attractive than the rationale provided in Justice O'Connor's opinion. *Feist's* constitutionalization of the originality requirement is undesirable because it may frustrate the goals of the Intellectual Property Clause, as described by virtually all modern commentators and the Court itself. Although the likely contours of the post-*Feist* legal landscape are difficult to predict, Justice O'Connor's opinion in *Feist* has direct implications for the copyrightability of other types of statutory compilations, collections of facts found in noncompilations, and other works which evidence little originality such as maps and some computer programs. The opinion may also affect the copyrightability of broadcasts of sporting events and speeches, and raises the question of the legitimacy of a congressional attempt

[5] See Melville B. Nimmer & David Nimmer, 1 *Nimmer on Copyright* § 1.02 at 1-30 (1990) (hereinafter "Nimmer").

[6] 17 USC §§ 101 et seq (1976).

[7] See *Goldstein v California*, 412 US 546, 561 (1973); *Feist,* 111 S Ct at 1290, citing *Burrow-Giles v Sarony*, 111 US 53 (1884).

[8] See *Feist*, 111 S Ct at 1288, 1289, 1296, & 1297.

to circumvent the decision by enacting legislation under its power to regulate interstate commerce.

I. THE OPINION AND ALTERNATIVE HOLDINGS

The defendant in *Feist* produced a comprehensive white pages directory covering eleven different telephone service areas in northwest Kansas. It obtained permission from ten of eleven telephone companies to use their local listings to create an all-encompassing directory containing 47,000 alphabetically ordered listings. When Rural Telephone Service refused to grant permission to allow copying of any of its 7,700 listings, Feist used 1,309 of them anyway. Rural then brought suit in federal district court for copyright infringement, prevailing on a motion for summary judgment.[9] Later, the Tenth Circuit affirmed in a short unpublished per curiam opinion.[10] Both lower courts relied on consistent authority that white pages directories were copyrightable.[11] Since Feist readily admitted to copying some of Rural's listings, the lower courts had little problem finding Feist liable on the basis of precedent broadly protecting those who invest time and labor in the creation of factual compilations.

The Supreme Court, however, rejected this line of lower court cases by holding that telephone white pages are not "original," and therefore not copyrightable at all. The Court noted that cases finding white pages entitled to protection were based on the "sweat of the brow"/"industrious collection" theory[12] that rewards an author for her labor and not for her originality. After discussing the requirement of originality, the Court ruled that it was not met by showing that a great deal of labor and expense went into creating the work. Some degree of truly original expression must be present.

---

[9] 663 F Supp 214 (D Kan 1987).

[10] 916 F2d 718 (10th Cir 1990).

[11] See, for example, *Illinois Bell Tel. Co. v Haines & Co.*, 905 F2d 1081 (7th Cir 1990), vacated 111 S Ct 1408 (1991); *Hutchinson Tel. Co. v Fronteer Directory Co.*, 770 F2d 128 (8th Cir 1985); *Leon v Pacific Telephone & Telegraph Co.*, 91 F2d 484 (9th Cir 1937); *Southwestern Bell Tel. Co. v Nationwide Independent Directory Service, Inc.*, 371 F Supp 900 (WD Ark 1974).

[12] See *Jeweler's Circular Publishing Co. v Keystone Publishing Co.*, 281 F 83, 88 (2d Cir 1922) ("The right to copyright . . . does not depend upon . . . originality, either in thought or language, or anything more than industrious collection").

In the case of factual compilations, the Court stated that a modicum of originality as to selection, coordination, and arrangement would suffice to render most factual compilations copyrightable. However, the copyright so obtained would only extend to the selection, coordination, and arrangement—the facts themselves would fall in the public domain. Moreover, the Court found that alphabetized telephone white pages lacked the modicum of originality as to selection, coordination, and arrangement.

Most surprising was the Court's willingness to rely on constitutional rather than statutory grounds. Several nonconstitutional grounds are readily available. Obviously, the decision could have relied on the originality requirement found in the Copyright Act.[13] As several commentators and the Court have noted, the "sweat of the brow" theory is not easily teased out of the statutory language.[14] Without even mentioning the Constitution, the Court could have given as the sole basis for decision (it did only in passing) that the telephone white pages are not "original works of authorship"[15] in the language of the Act. Although the bottom line of such an opinion would have been the same as the one actually written— telephone white pages are wholly unprotected—Congress could have responded by amending the statute.

Alternatively, the Court could have held that the labor involved in collecting facts such as those found in telephone white pages did confer a sort of originality to the work. Such a finding of copyrightable through sweat, however, would not necessarily have resulted in a finding of copyright infringement on the facts of *Feist*. First, copyright law normally requires a finding of "substantial similarity" between the original and infringing works.[16] Given that Feist's unified directory of 47,000 names and addresses covering 11 telephone districts employed in scattered fashion only 1,309 of Rural's listings, the Court could have held that the activity engaged in by

---

[13] See 17 USC § 102(a).

[14] See William Patry, *Copyright in Compilations of Facts (or Why the "White Pages" are not Copyrightable)*, 12 Comm & L 37, 45–59 (1990); L. Ray Patterson & Craig Joyce, *Monopolizing the Law: The Scope of Copyright Protection for Law Reports and Statutory Compilations*, 36 UCLA L Rev 719, 757–77 (1989). Both articles were relied upon by the Court in *Feist*.

[15] 17 USC §§ 101 & 102.

[16] See Nimmer, 3 Nimmer § 13.03[A] at 13–23 (cited in note 5).

Feist was not actionable copying. The two works simply were not similar as a matter of law.

Third, the Court could have held that although Rural's white pages were copyrightable, Feist's independent checking of the information culled from Rural's work added enough of its own sweat to justify its "copying." Feist did not merely copy Rural's listings and print them as its own. Feist's investigators independently verified data culled from Rural's directory; as a result, Feist's listings often had the street addresses of Rural's subscribers while Rural's own listings did not. Feist worked hard and created a truly new and different work. Sanctioning its behavior by a finding of noninfringing use would arguably have advanced the statutory goal of encouraging new creations.

Finally, the Court could have resorted to the fair use doctrine.[17] The only material Feist took from Rural's white pages were raw facts which were themselves uncopyrightable.[18] Use of facts has traditionally been considered to be a fair use. Perhaps photocopying Rural's white pages and distributing them should be infringement (it is not under the Court's opinion as written), but merely using them as a reference work could easily suffice as fair use under section 107 of the Copyright Act.

However, rather than adopt any of these alternatives, the Court chose to rely on an interpretation of the originality requirement implicit in the Intellectual Property Clause of the Constitution. In holding that originality as a constitutional matter did not include a "sweat of the brow" component, the court harkened back over a hundred years to *Burrow-Giles Lithographic Co. v Sarony*[19] and the *Trade-Mark Cases*.[20] Neither decision compels (or forbids) the Court's approach in *Feist*. In considering the definition of "author" in the Intellectual Property Clause, the *Burrow-Giles* court found that copyright is meant to protect "original intellectual conceptions of the author."[21] It held that a carefully posed and artful studio

---

[17] See 17 USC § 107 ("the fair use of a copyrighted work . . . is not an infringement of copyright").

[18] See 17 USC § 102(b).

[19] 111 US 53 (1884).

[20] 100 US 82 (1879).

[21] 111 US at 58.

portrait of Oscar Wilde was original enough to be copyrighted.[22] However, after considering the copyrightability of mere "ordinary" pictures where the photographer's art was less apparent, the Court succinctly commented, "On the question as thus stated we decide nothing."[23] The decision therefore provided no minimum baseline for its requirement of "original intellectual conception" and clearly passed on the opportunity to declare purely mimetic works of image reproduction unoriginal and uncopyrightable.

In the *Trade-Mark Cases*, the Court struck down a nineteenth-century predecessor[24] to the Lanham Trademark Act[25] as unauthorized by either the Intellectual Property Clause or the Commerce Clause. In finding the Intellectual Property Clause an inappropriate source of congressional power, the Court held that trademarks are not works of authorship.[26] Trademarks were not found to be independent creations, "original . . . founded in the creative powers of the mind [or] . . . *the fruits of intellectual labor*."[27] This language is a bit more helpful. It at least tells us that trademarks are not original enough to merit protection under the Intellectual Property Clause.

A trademark, the Court explained, "is the adoption of something already in existence as the distinctive symbol of the party using it."[28] Trademarks embody the goodwill of a business or product:[29]

> The ordinary trade-mark has no necessary relation to investigation or discovery. The trade-mark recognized by the common

---

[22] The trial court had found as a matter of fact that the photo was a "useful, new, harmonious, characteristic, and graceful picture, and that plaintiff made the same . . . entirely from his own original mental conception, to which he gave visible form by posing the said Oscar Wilde in front of the camera, selecting and arranging the costume, draperies, and other various accessories in said photograph, arranging the subject so as to present graceful outlines, arranging and disposing the light and shade, suggesting and evoking the desired expression, and from such disposition, arrangement, or representation, made entirely by plaintiff, he produced the picture in suit." Id at 60.

[23] Id at 59.

[24] 19 Stat 141 (1876).

[25] 15 USC §§ 1051 et seq (providing for the registration of trademarks and remedies for their infringement).

[26] Remember the Intellectual Property Clause refers to advancing the useful arts by rewarding "authors."

[27] 100 US at 94.

[28] Id. The Court seemed to have only trade symbols in mind when it discussed the originality requirement, for example, the red triangle trademark of Bass Ale, reputedly the oldest registered trademark in England. See inscription on bottle of Bass Ale on file in author's refrigerator.

[29] Id.

> law is generally the growth of a considerable period of use, rather than a sudden invention . . . [a]t common law the exclusive right to it grows out of its *use*, and not its mere adoption.

Since the statute only authorized the registration of common law trademarks, what it sought to protect was something that attained its value through use, not through inspiration or laborious creation. A trademark becomes valuable when connected to a product in consumers' minds. The law aimed to protect the efforts of businessmen at promoting their goods—their efforts to develop good will, not their efforts to create interesting trademarks. The law was not proposed to stimulate the creation of interesting and original marks. The overtly commercial purposes of the Trade-Mark Act were ill-fitted to the creative goals of the Intellectual Property Clause.

Unfortunately, the Court's analysis in *Feist* does little to tell us why the telephone white pages resemble common-law trademarks. Applying copyright protection to some compilations might stimulate the "investigation or discovery" of works that may be valuable in and of themselves, unlike trademarks that have no value apart from products or businesses independently developed and promoted. The *Trade-Mark Cases* do tell us that the Constitution requires originality as a prerequisite to copyright protection; however, it does little to dispel the possibility that creations owing their existence to perspiration rather than inspiration might conceivably be defined as "original"[30] in order to advance the wealth-maximizing goals of the Intellectual Property Clause discussed below.

II. THE UNDESIRABILITY OF CONSTITUTIONALIZING THE ORIGINALITY REQUIREMENT

A. THE SPECIAL PROBLEM OF FACTUAL WORKS

Works consisting primarily of facts, such as the white pages directory at issue in *Feist*, have traditionally posed the thorniest copyright problems for the courts. Copyright law is supposed to stimulate creation, but facts are not "created." They already exist; therefore, one could conclude that primarily factual (low author-

---

[30] See *Jeweler's Circular Pub. Co. v Keystone Pub. Co.*, 281 F 83 (2d Cir 1922) (defining originality in terms of "industrious collection").

ship)[31] works should be utterly unprotected. However, what about facts that beg to be uncovered, collected, arranged, and made available to a needy public? Shouldn't the copyright system extend to provide proper incentives for their creation? The short answer is that it always has to varying degrees. The first copyright statute, enacted in 1790 by the first Congress, provided copyright protection for "any map, chart, book or books."[32] Maps are perhaps the quintessential factual work.[33] The closer a map depicts a precise physical reality, the better it is. Maps are protected under the current copyright statute, as are compilations of "preexisting materials."[34]

However, works of low authorship, including maps, have received inconsistent protection from copying. Some courts, sensitive to the danger of upholding claims that would take facts and ideas from the public domain, have allowed extensive copying. Other courts, sensitive to the need to protect expenditures of resources in developing valuable works of low authorship, have extended broad protection. The result has been chaotic. Courts have privileged some directories that appropriate large amounts of data from existing directories, while condemning others.[35] Some mapmakers have successfully based new maps directly from old ones, others have not.[36] Moviemakers are sometimes, but not always, privileged to borrow plots and storylines from books or plays.[37] Some sorts of information may be gleaned from published lists and tables,

---

[31] Professor Ginsburg has helpfully denominated primarily factual works (for example, factual compilations, maps, etc.) as those of "low authorship" and primarily fictive works (for example, novels, poetry, etc.) as those of "high authorship." I will use her terminology here. See Jane C. Ginsburg, *Creation and Commercial Value: Copyright Protection for Works of Information*, 90 Colum L Rev 1865, 1866 (1990).

[32] Act of May 31, 1790, ch 15, §I, I Stat 124.

[33] Robert A. Gorman, *Copyright Protection for the Collection and Representation of Facts*, 76 Harv L Rev 1569, 1571–76 (1962).

[34] 17 USC § 103.

[35] Compare *New York Times Co. v Roxbury Data Interface, Inc.*, 434 F Supp 217 (D NJ 1977), with *Illinois Bell Tel. Co. v Haines & Co.*, 905 F2d 1081 (7th Cir 1990) (vacated in light of *Feist*, see 111 S Ct 1408 (1991)), and *Leon v Pacific Tel. & Tel. Co.*, 91 F2d 484 (9th Cir 1937).

[36] Compare *Amsterdam v Triangle Publications, Inc.*, 189 F2d 104 (3d Cir 1951), with *Rockford Map Publishers Inc. v Directory Serv. Co.*, 768 F2d 145 (7th Cir 1985), and *United States v Hamilton*, 583 F2d 448 (9th Cir 1978).

[37] Compare *Miller v Universal City Studios, Inc.*, 650 F2d 1365 (5th Cir 1981), with *Sheldon v Metro-Goldwyn Pictures Corp.*, 81 F2d 49 (2d Cir 1936) (aff'd 309 US 390 (1940)), and *Nichols v Universal Pictures Corp.*, 45 F2d 119 (2d Cir 1930).

while virtually indistinguishable information is privileged.[38] Prints[39] and biographies[40] have suffered similar seemingly random fates.

In a recent article, Professor John Wiley proposes an imaginative explanation to illustrate this confused state of copyright jurisprudence as related to the protection of facts, ideas, and expressions. He blames the opaque state of the law on Duncan Kennedy traveling backward in time to plant the seeds of a subversive plant of copyright indeterminacy which would grow to be "discovered" by his CLS followers decades later.[41] Indeed, the body of law concerning the scope of copyright protection afforded works of "low authorship" at issue in *Feist* is a morass of elusive and manipulable doctrine and counterdoctrine.

Several indeterminate yet widely accepted doctrines govern disputes involving the copyrightability of materials containing primarily facts. The idea/expression and fact/expression dichotomies teach that the particular expression of ideas and facts, but not the ideas and facts themselves, are copyrightable.[42] The merger doctrine tells us that when ideas or facts must inevitably be expressed in a particular manner, content and form are said to "merge" rendering the expression itself unprotected.[43] As noted above, the originality requirement requires that a copyrighted work be, well, original.[44] Further explanation of these governing "principles" need not be discussed in detail because they are essentially indeterminate and contentless.[45] They can be defined and discussed in the ab-

---

[38] Compare *Financial Information Inc. v Moody's Investors Serv.*, 808 F2d 204 (2d Cir 1986), with *Eckes v Card Prices Update*, 736 F2d 859 (2d Cir 1984), and *National Business Lists Inc. v Dun & Bradstreet, Inc.*, 552 F Supp 89 (ND Ill 1982).

[39] Compare *Gracen v Bradford Exchange*, 698 F2d 300 (7th Cir 1983), with *Alfred Bell & Co., Ltd. v Catalda Fine Arts, Inc.*, 191 F2d 99 (2d Cir 1951).

[40] Compare *Toksvig v Bruce Publishing Co.*, 181 F2d 664 (7th Cir 1950), with *Rosemont Enterprises v Random House, Inc.*, 366 F2d 303 (2d Cir 1966).

[41] John S. Wiley Jr., *Copyright at the School of Patent*, 58 U Chi L Rev 119, 126 (1991).

[42] See *Feist*, 111 S Ct at 1290; *United Video v FCC*, 890 F2d 1173, 1191 (DC 1989).

[43] See *Shaw v Lindheim*, 919 F2d 1353, 1360 (9th Cir 1990).

[44] See *Feist*, 111 S Ct at 1294 (a work must "display some minimal level of creativity").

[45] For a sample of the voluminous criticism of these doctrines see Wiley, 58 U Chi L Rev at 120–27 (cited in note 41); Ginsburg, 90 Colum L Rev at 1913–16, 1927 (cited in note 31); Jessica Litman, *The Public Domain*, 39 Emory L J 965, 968, 1012 (1990); Gorman, 76 Harv L Rev at 1570 & 1572 (cited in note 33); Robert C. Denicola, *Copyright in Collections of Facts: A Theory for the Protection of Nonfiction Literary Works*, 81 Colum L Rev 516 (1981); *Nichols v Universal Pictures Studio Corp*, 45 F2d 119 (2d Cir 1930) (Hand, J.).

stract, but they fail to generate consistent results in like cases.[46] Saying that only original expressions, but never facts or ideas, are copyrightable proves to be far easier than applying the notion consistently and coherently. Although commentators and the courts generally agree that the purpose of copyright law as a whole is to establish incentives for the creation of works which because of their public goods aspects might otherwise go uncreated,[47] the rules supposedly advancing that uncontroversial goal are incoherent. Interestingly, the cases themselves demonstrate a keen awareness of the haphazard nature of the results, "Obviously, no principle can be stated as to when an imitator has gone beyond copying the 'idea,' and has borrowed its 'expression.' Decisions must therefore inevitably be *ad hoc*."[48]

The cases undeniably fail to articulate a rationale that helps resolve the tension inherent in the controversies. The tension arises due to the dual needs to maintain public access to important facts and to stimulate the discovery and publication of those facts through the grant of exclusive rights. A broad doctrine such as the idea/expression dichotomy recognizes the tension, but provides no clue as to how the balance should tip in a particular case.

B. RECONSTRUCTING COPYRIGHT LAW

The problems inherent in evaluating the copyrightability of low authorship works has stimulated several interesting proposed solutions worthy of very brief summary to illustrate the unsatisfactory nature of the Court's approach in *Feist*. Professor Wiley has suggested that copyright law has much to learn from patent law. He argues for a functional approach to defining the originality of and therefore the protectability of works of low authorship: "Copyright courts, then, should define as original any work whose creation requires enough effort to deter the creative act absent the copyright's exclusive promise."[49] If this results in the protection of

---

[46] See notes 35–40.

[47] See generally William M. Landes & Richard A. Posner, *An Economic Analysis of Copyright Law*, 18 J L Stud 325 (1989); Wiley (cited in note 41); Litman (cited in note 45); Ginsburg (cited in note 31); Denicola (cited in note 45); Gorman (cited in note 33). See also *Mazer v Stein*, 347 US 201, 219 (1954); *Sony Corp. v Universal Studios, Inc.*, 464 US 417, 429 (1984).

[48] *Peter Pan Fabrics, Inc. v Martin Weiner Corp.*, 274 F2d 487, 489 (2d Cir 1960) (Hand, J.).

[49] Wiley, 58 U Chi L Rev at 148 (cited in note 41).

works more the result of their authors' labor and research than their personalities, so be it—as long as the public receives in return a creation it otherwise would not have.

Professor Ginsburg offers the "high authorship"/"low authorship"[50] distinction and argues that two different sets of rules should govern her categories. She contends that protecting low authorship works from any substantial borrowing would diminish the net information available to society, while the absence of protection for low authorship works would not provide adequate incentives for their creation. She concludes that a compulsory licensing scheme for low authorship works would create the most efficient set of incentives. Professors Patterson and Joyce disagree, believing that works of low authorship are probably overprotected. In an influential article[51] criticizing the important *West Publishing*[52] case, they assert that any protection afforded the pagination of West's National Reporter System volumes "turns copyright law upside down: it inhibits the promotion of learning by taking public domain materials which have no author and subjecting them to the monopoly of copyright."[53]

Professor Litman is also concerned with nurturing the public domain. Like Wiley, she views the originality requirement as "an apparition [that] cannot provide a basis for deciding copyright cases."[54] She argues forcefully that most works are unoriginal in any real sense. Even works of so-called "high authorship" are full of stock characters, scenes, themes, and motifs that have long been part of our rich public domain. She redefines the notion of originality to better "reserv[e] the raw material of authorship to the commons."[55] On the other hand, Professors Denicola[56] and Gorman[57] are less concerned about the public domain and more concerned with rewarding the industrious efforts of authors who create pri-

---

[50] See note 31.

[51] See Patterson & Joyce, 36 UCLA L Rev 719 (cited in note 14). The Court's opinion in *Feist* cites the article on five occasions.

[52] *West Publishing Co. v Mead Data Central Inc.*, 799 F2d 1219 (8th Cir 1986).

[53] Patterson & Joyce, 36 UCLA L Rev at 810 (cited in note 14).

[54] Litman, 39 Emory L J at 1023 (cited in note 45).

[55] Id.

[56] See Denicola, 81 Colum L Rev 516 (cited in note 45).

[57] See Gorman, 76 Harv L Rev 1569 (cited in note 33).

marily factual works: histories, biographies, and news of the day, as well as maps, directories, and forms. They fear the misapplication of copyright doctrine would result in seriously diminished incentives for creation.

On the other extreme is former professor, now First Circuit Judge, Stephen Breyer.[58] He is skeptical about the notion of copyright in general. He would agree with Professor Wiley that protection should be provided when it results in the creation of a work that otherwise would go uncreated. However, he is not convinced as an empirical matter that many such potential works need the prodding of the copyright monopoly.[59] He occupies the far fringe of the antiprotectionist position.

Although commentators disagree on precisely how to reform copyright law, they all agree that copyright law is a complex system of incentives designed to advance knowledge and therefore the public welfare. Contrary to frequent assertions by the publishing industry, copyright is not a natural law right of the author[60]—it exists as positive law "to promote the Progress of Science and useful Arts."[61] And it does so by establishing a balance between the monopoly costs of the copyright grant and the benefits of creations stimulated thereby.[62] They all tend to see the balance as out of whack due the incoherence of the originality requirement and the idea/expression dichotomy. They disagree on whether the current confusion results in too little or too much protection for works of low authorship; however, the goal of reform seems to be the same: maximize public welfare through a coherent system of incentives.

This is, of course, more easily said than done. As Breyer pointed out twenty years ago, the question of the proper scope of copyright protection is primarily empirical and difficult to quantify.[63] In the absence of convincing studies, it is unclear whether the courts

---

[58] Stephen Breyer, *The Uneasy Case for Copyright: A Study of Copyright in Books, Photocopies, and Computer Programs*, 84 Harv L Rev 281 (1970).

[59] Id at 351.

[60] At least one recent commentator makes rights-based arguments, however. See Alfred C. Yen, *Restoring the Natural Law: Copyright as Labor and Possession*, 51 Ohio St L J 517 (1990).

[61] US Const, Art I, § 8, cl 8.

[62] The most formal presentation of the theory is found in Landes & Posner, 18 J Legal Stud at 333–44 (cited in note 47).

[63] Breyer, 84 Harv L Rev at 351 (cited in note 58).

should be left to continue to forge a common law of copyright within the wide interstices of the Copyright Act or whether Congress should step in and try to legislate the efficient answer. The fact situation in *Feist* provides a good hypothetical: To what extent should telephone white pages be protected from copying? Most commentators agree that the correct answer would be: "To the extent necessary to maximize public welfare." The discussion would then center around what that answer necessitates: no protection; protection only from competing uses; protection only from substantially similar uses; protection from all uses. Of course, the lack of empirical evidence would allow for a wide diversity of opinion. Focusing on public welfare hardly guarantees correct answers in the absence of convincing empirical evidence. But it is at least the proper focus.

C. THE STRANGE ROAD TAKEN

On the surface, *Feist* recognizes the welfare goals of the Intellectual Property Clause. As she did in *Bonito Boats, Inc. v Thunder Craft Boats Inc.*,[64] Justice O'Connor asserts the primacy of the public interest as the basis for creating rights to intellectual property. She reaffirms the notion expressed in *Wheaton v Peters*[65] that copyright is a statutory grant of limited power, not a recognition of the natural law right of the author. This acknowledgment is crucial to any reform. In *Feist* and *Bonito Boats*, Justice O'Connor may have the Court pointed in the right direction—the public will almost certainly benefit from the copying blessed by the two cases. In fact, we may be seeing the dawning of a new era of "user's rights." However, the *Feist* decision prevents Congress from focusing directly on the public welfare question when it considers copyrights for works of low authorship formerly protected under the "sweat of the brow"/"industrious collection" doctrine.

In handcuffing Congress with a version of the originality requirement that absolutely forbids protection based on the value of an author's research or labor, the Court clearly rejected the "sweat of the brow"/"industrious collection" rationale for protection:[66]

---

[64] 489 US 141 (1989).

[65] 8 Peters 591 (1834).

[66] *Feist*, 111 S Ct at 1291–92.

> The "sweat of the brow" doctrine had numerous flaws, the most glaring being that it extended copyright protection in a compilation beyond selection and arrangement—the compiler's original contribution—to the facts themselves . . . "[s]weat of the brow" courts thereby eschewed the most fundamental axiom of copyright law—that no one may copyright facts or ideas . . . [w]ithout a doubt, the "sweat of the brow" doctrine flouted basic copyright principles.

As stated earlier, a strong argument can be made that under the current copyright statute, the Court is correct. Section 103 states that factual compilations are copyrightable, but "factual compilation" is defined as a work "selected, coordinated, or arranged in such a way that the resulting work as a whole constitutes an original work of authorship."[67] The statute can plausibly be read to exclude completely protection of any factual information contained in a work. Whether the Constitution mandates such a result, however, is less clear.

The constitutional question can be posed by a brief examination of two appellate cases, the first of which, *Miller v Universal City Studios*,[68] the Court relied on in *Feist*. In *Miller*, the plaintiff coauthored a book with the victim of a bizarre Georgia kidnapping. After Universal, drawing heavily on the book as a reference, made a television motion picture about the crime, Miller sued for copyright infringement alleging that Universal had appropriated many of the details uncovered in his research. The Fifth Circuit reversed a jury verdict for Miller, holding that the trial court erred in instructing the jury that the Copyright Act protected Miller's research as opposed to merely its literal expression. The Fifth Circuit rejected the sweat of the brow rationale, reasoning that no amount of labor in and of itself was sufficient to confer copyright protection.

Does the Constitution mandate the same result? The Intellectual Property Clause suggests that the inquiry should center on whether providing copyright protection would advance the public welfare. In other words, would Miller have created the work in the absence of protection against the sort of behavior engaged in by Universal?

---

[67] 17 USC § 101.

[68] 650 F2d 1365 (5th Cir 1981), discussed in *Feist*, 111 S Ct at 1288–89, 1291, 1295.

Let's assume the answer is yes.[69] After all, Miller's research consisted primarily in interviewing his coauthor about her experiences—not an overly burdensome or expensive task. In addition, Universal's film did not directly compete with Miller's book. Book sales were probably not adversely affected.[70] Although it has been argued that an author's right to produce derivative works provides a marginal creative stimulus,[71] it would seem unlikely that Miller's book would have gone unwritten due to the fear that an unauthorized film will appear.

One can imagine, however, a case where a disincentive to borrow factual information might be necessary to stimulate creative activity. In *Toksvig v Bruce Publishing Co.*,[72] the plaintiff traveled to Europe to collect and translate original sources relevant to her biography of the life of Hans Christian Andersen. Much of the information presented in the biography was a direct result the plaintiff's time, labor, expense, and fluency in Danish.[73] After the plaintiff's biography was published, defendant published a biography of Andersen which drew broadly from plaintiff's work. The Seventh Circuit held that the subsequent biographer had infringed plaintiff's copyright. The facts of *Toksvig* provide a better ground upon which to argue that protection was necessary to stimulate creation.

---

[69] And let's also assume, as the framers of the Constitution apparently did, that encouraging authors to create artistic works tends to advance the public welfare. In other words, we assume that Miller would not have discovered a cure for cancer had he not been writing his book. Technically, the public welfare should be measured by taking the *difference* between the social utility of the authored work and the social utility of the other opportunities of the author. In other words, a work should be copyrightable only if necessary to encourage the work *and* the work is more socially useful than whatever else the writer would choose to do, for example, child rearing or brickmasonry. Unfortunately, the ramifications of this insight into the marginal utility of creativity in the copyright context have never been fully explored and will not be so here. Cf. Richard A. Posner, *Economic Analysis of Law* 37 (3d ed 1986) (noting in the patent context that "[t]he costs of the patent system include . . . inducing potentially excessive investment in inventing"); Janusz A. Ordover, *Economic Foundations and Considerations in Protecting Industrial and Intellectual Property*, 53 Antitrust L J 503, 507 (1984) (patent law "may lead to excessive investment in the creation of intellectual and industrial property").

[70] The movie even may have stimulated sales to those wanting to learn more about the crime. Of course, others, having seen the movie, may not have wanted to buy the book.

[71] See Landes & Posner, 18 J Legal Stud 353–57 (cited in note 47).

[72] 181 F2d 664 (7th Cir 1950).

[73] As any person fluent in a foreign language can attest, language acquisition represents a substantial investment in resources. Of course, writing the biography was not the plaintiff's sole motivation for learning Danish.

The plaintiff may very well have eschewed the travel, time, expense, and labor involved in researching the book in the absence of the certain ability to reap the full profit of her labor. Affording protection to the sort of research engaged in by Toksvig may very well increase public welfare.

The *Toksvig* argument, however, is difficult to make on the facts of *Feist*. A Kansas statute mandated that Rural publish its directory. In addition, it distributed its directory for free. The argument that Rural needed a copyright monopoly to stimulate the creation of its directory is almost impossible to make.

Note we have discussed whether *Miller*, *Toksvig*, and *Feist* are consistent with the constitutional mandate "to promote the Progress of Science and useful Arts" without mentioning the originality requirement or the idea/expression dichotomy. They seem irrelevant when conducting a direct inquiry into whether protecting a particular type of work from a particular type of borrowing is necessary to promote the public welfare. Unfortunately, *Feist* frustrates Congress from conducting this direct inquiry regarding "unoriginal works."

Under the Intellectual Property Clause, Congress is charged to increase public welfare by providing incentives for creation. Congress might do this in several ways respecting low authorship works. It might find that: (1) low authorship works in general require strong incentives for creation and provide broad protection to labor and research; (2) only certain types of very labor-intensive and expensive-to-produce works of low authorship require the incentive of copyright protection; (3) virtually no protection should be afforded to labor and research because the cost of such protection is simply too high; or (4) general guidelines suffice and the courts should be left to establish the proper balance of incentives on a case by case basis. According to the *Feist*, the current copyright statute should most closely embody option 3.

As long as Congress is seeking to realize the constitutional mandate to promote public welfare, then the choice of any of these four options should be constitutional. The Constitution gives Congress the job of initially performing the cost-benefit analysis inherent in copyright law. Traditionally, congressional fact-finding is accorded great weight. Congress may or may not succeed in providing an efficient set of incentives, but in the absence of strong empirical data to the contrary, who can say it will not? Tinkering with copyright law seems properly left to Congress (who under option 4 might punt to the courts).

The primary vice of *Feist* is that it locks Congress into option 3. The Court could not have made it clearer that the Constitution forbids protection of labor, research, or industrious collection: in simple terms, "sweat." Even if Congress identifies works which would not be created but for the grant of copyright protection, Congress may not protect them. If Congress determines option 1, 2, or 4 above would maximize the public welfare, Congress may not act. Rather than permitting Congress to scrutinize the market and establish protection for works that merit stimulation, the Court cordoned off a forbidden zone. Looking at the facts of *Feist* illustrates the point. Although probably unlikely, assume that after the *Feist* decision some telephone companies stopped producing white pages directories, and other parties did not fill the void by producing their own white pages and selling them because such works were utterly unprotected. Consistent with its constitutional mandate, Congress might decide to amend the copyright statute to stimulate the creation of what is clearly a valuable resource. The Court's finding of a constitutional prohibition in *Feist*, as opposed to a statutory prohibition, would prevent Congress from doing precisely that.

One can find some solace in the fact that many white pages directories are required by state statute to be produced and distributed, but many other sorts of valuable low authorship works may require the carrot of the copyright monopoly. Protecting labor and sweat requires the protection of facts and information to a certain degree. The best way to protect the research and labor of Ms. Toksvig may be to protect some biographic material that is entirely factual. Sometimes the only way to stimulate investments in labor and research may be to provide limited protection to the facts and information thereby produced. The fair use doctrine traditionally has provided appropriate limitations to avoid the impoverishment of the public domain.

Would providing protection to the primarily factual fruits of industrious labor generate wealth or impoverish the public domain? Who knows? The salient point is that the debate ended prematurely. Congress is stymied and may not provide any such protection even if it has irrefutable evidence that "the Sciences and useful Arts" would be promoted. In addition, the courts are saddled with a definition of originality that seems only negative in conception. All we know is that sweat and labor do not confer it.

III. The Post-Feist Terrain

Not all low authorship works are endangered by *Feist*. Although facts themselves are never protected, an original selection, coordination, and arrangement of facts can still be copyrighted. Presumably, the decision in a case like *Adventures in Good Eating v Best Places to Eat*[74] is still good law. In *Good Eating*, the plaintiff had prepared a list of restaurants from around the country. He selected a discrete group out of the hundreds of thousands available and provided information on location, menu items, and prices. Such a work easily demonstrates the modicum of originality as to selection, coordination, and arrangement demanded by *Feist*. Other more formulaic works, however, may be in trouble. In the first appellate decision published after *Feist*, the Second Circuit held that a newsletter organizing facts from horse racing results relevant to the selection of winning numbers in illegal lottery operations was not entitled to copyright protection. It noted that all other publishers of such charts used the same format, describing them as "purely functional grids that offer no opportunity for variation."[75] Although the plaintiff "engaged in a certain degree of labor to compile his charts, his labor [was] irrelevant to the central question of whether his work displayed some modicum of originality entitling it to copyright protection."[76] Obviously, *Feist* will have an impact on other works of low authorship as well.

A. LAW REPORTS

The Eight Circuit's decision in *West Publishing Co. v Mead Data Central, Inc.*[77] is almost certainly a casualty of *Feist*. In *West*, the court held that Mead Data's Lexis computerized legal research service could not reference page numbers contained in volumes of West reporters, other than the first page of a case.[78] In other words,

---

[74] 131 F2d 809 (7th Cir 1942).

[75] *Victor Lalli Enter., Inc. v Big Red Apple, Inc.*, 936 F2d 671, 673 (2d Cir 1991).

[76] Id at 674.

[77] 799 F2d 1219 (8th Cir 1986).

[78] West did not seek to protect the numbers of the initial page of cases it publishes.

Lexis could not provide "pinpoint" or "jump-cites" to cases published by West without its permission. Although the cases themselves are not copyrightable,[79] the Eight Circuit enjoined Mead Data's jump-cite service on the basis that it infringed West's copyright in the arrangement of its cases.[80] The case was vigorously attacked in an article[81] which apparently impressed the *Feist* Court.

Is there anything original about labeling consecutively the pages of the *Feist* opinion in volume 111 of the Supreme Court Reporter from 1282 through 1297? Certainly no more than choosing to follow "Anne Zwerling" by "Mark Zwolak" in my local telephone white pages.[82] Perhaps West's arrangement of cases in F2d is copyrightable, but that should only prevent Mead Data from putting out competing reporter volumes with the same arrangement.[83] Its mere lifting of the fact that a particular set of words rests on a particular page of a West reporter clearly would seem to be privileged by *Feist*. Mead borrowed numbers that are ordered in West's volumes from smallest to largest. Given the Court's finding that alphabetical arrangement is unprotected, it is hard to see how the Eighth Circuit's protection of numeric arrangement can survive *Feist*.

B. THE YELLOW PAGES

Telephone directory yellow pages present a slightly different problem than the white pages. They are not merely alphabetized listings of all the businesses in a particular area. The yellow pages typically contain advertisements, artwork of various sorts, and other material arranged alphabetically along with phone numbers and addresses within particular subject headings. Obviously, a greater opportunity for original selection, arrangement, and coordination exists. Most yellow pages would seem to be copyrightable.

---

[79] See *Wheaton v Peters*, 8 Peters 591 (1834).

[80] 799 F2d at 1224. Mead has since agreed to pay West tens of millions of dollars to obtain a license. See Patterson & Joyce, 36 UCLA L Rev at 722 n 6 and accompanying text (cited in note 14).

[81] See Patterson & Joyce, 36 UCLA L Rev 719 (cited in note 14).

[82] Athens, Georgia, Phone Directory at 156 (BellSouth 1990).

[83] Federal Reporter (Second) volumes are arranged in roughly chronological order. But see *Boeving v United States*, 650 F2d 493 (8th Cir June 17, 1981), which is in between *NLRB v Kiawah Island Co., Ltd*, 650 F2d 485 (4th Cir May 27, 1981), and *Federal Leasing, Inc. v Underwriters at Lloyd's*, 650 F2d 495 (4th Cir June 2, 1981).

However, under *Feist*, copyrightability does not mean full protection under all circumstances. The Court made it clear that only selection, arrangement, and coordination are protectable. For example, although BellSouth's Athens, Georgia, yellow pages are copyrightable, the facts contained therein can be used for any purpose. Since "[t]he originality requirement 'rule[s] out protecting . . . names, addresses, and telephone numbers,'" only a reproduction of original elements of yellow pages formatting is prohibited.[84]

Several courts have held that a directory publisher may not use the listings contained in an existing yellow pages to produce a competing product.[85] This conclusion now seems highly questionable. Under *Feist*, names and addresses are not copyrightable, so any competitor can feel free to use an existing yellow pages to compile a list of potential advertisers in its own yellow pages. A slightly more difficult question involves whether the competing yellow pages can utilize the same subject headings as the existing directory. Through the work of the National Yellow Pages Service Organization, virtually all yellow pages in the United States adhere to a standardized format. Therefore, the standard format is unprotectable as a practice "firmly rooted in tradition and so commonplace that it has come to be expected as a matter of course."[86] A final sticking point may arise when a business wishes to use the same advertisement in both yellow pages. Must the producer of the competing yellow pages demand that its customers invent new advertisements for its directory? The answer is probably "no," given that the copyright to the advertisement belongs to the business and not the producer of the first yellow pages.[87] Contrary to prior lower court precedent, *Feist* clearly sanctions the production of competing yellow pages as long as the second-comer's product does not substantially reproduce the individual page-by-page arrangements of materials found in the first (something only likely to result from photocopying).

---

[84] See *Feist*, 111 S Ct at 1296, citing Patterson & Joyce, 36 UCLA L Rev at 776 (cited in note 14).

[85] See *BellSouth Advertising & Pub. Corp. v Donnelly Information Pub., Inc.*, 933 F2d 952 (11th Cir 1991).

[86] *Feist*, 111 S Ct at 1297.

[87] See 17 USC § 201(b).

C. MAPS

The most troubling victim of the *Feist* opinion may be the map-making industry. Cartographers typically expend painstaking time, energy, and expense in making accurate representations of parcels of terrain. When their surveys are finished, their ability to recoup their investment is enhanced by the power to exclude unauthorized copying. However, this merely suggests that we might increase public welfare by affording copyright protection to maps; it does not tell us that a map is original under *Feist*.

Unfortunately for modern-day Amerigo Vespuccis, the map is one of the least original works protected by pre-*Feist* copyright law. Although a great deal of expense, labor, and sweat go into creating a map, a good map is usually not original. Its subject matter is certainly not a creation of its author, and its formatting is usually dictated by standard mapmaking conventions. One can imagine maps that might be original; for example, the famous humorous rendition of the map of the world as seen by New Yorkers, consisting 90 percent of oversized images of New York City with tiny figures labeled "Texas" and "Pacific Ocean" in the far background. Or perhaps a map that listed streets as "Puddings" and schools as "Grapefruit" might be original. Maybe the choice to include certain street names or use a particular scale or typeface might consist of a sort of originality as to selection. But once selection is made, arrangement and coordination are completely dictated by physical reality.

The most endangered map is probably the most useful: the technical survey plat. These maps are carefully produced in a standardized manner sometimes dictated by law.[88] Before *Feist*, the Seventh Circuit recently confirmed the copyrightability of plat maps.[89] That decision may also be on our endangered list, although it hardly seems conceivable that the Court would completely deny protection to a type of work mentioned specifically by Congress in 1790 as being one of the three objects of the first copyright act. In fact, given the presence of some of the framers of the Constitution in that first Congress, the conclusions reached in *Feist* regarding the availability of sweat-based copyright protection seem even more suspect.

---

[88] See, for example, OCGA § 15-6-67 (1990).

[89] See *Rockford Map Publishers Inc. v Directory Serv. Co.*, 768 F2d 145 (7th Cir 1985).

D. NEW USES FOR EXISTING DATA

Given that *Feist* protects only the selection, arrangement, and coordination of low authorship works, it seems generally to authorize the incorporation of existing data in dissimilar works. For example, in *National Business Lists, Inc. v Dun & Bradstreet, Inc.*[90] ("NBL") the court enjoined a creator of business mailing lists from using information copied from Dun & Bradstreet credit reports. The information taken from Dun & Bradstreet was entirely factual. The mailing list compiler did not produce competing business credit reports—it created a different product with a different purpose. When factual information is used to create a work that lacks substantial similarity to a prior work, then the selection, arrangement, and coordination have not been copied. In a case like *NBL*, *Feist* would seem to permit the copying because "[t]he originality requirement 'rule[s] out protecting . . . names, addresses, and telephone numbers of which the plaintiff by no stretch of the imagination could be called the author.' "[91]

E. LIVE BROADCASTS

One of the most surprising casualties of *Feist* may by the copyright currently afforded certain live television and radio broadcasts. Under sections 101 and 102 of the Copyright Act, broadcasters of live events on television and radio receive a copyright on the broadcast that permits them to prevent unauthorized taping, simultaneous broadcasting, or taped rebroadcasting of the event. For example, the Seventh Circuit has held that Major League Baseball owns the copyright to broadcasts of professional baseball games.[92] This is somewhat curious given that the games themselves (as opposed to the broadcasts) are clearly not copyrightable, not because they are not original, but because they are not authored.[93] A contrast with ballet is instructive on this point. A ballet is scripted before it is performed—the movements of the dancers are planned in

---

[90] 552 F Supp 89 (ND Ill 1982).

[91] *Feist*, 111 S Ct at 1296, quoting Patterson & Joyce, 36 UCLA L Rev at 776 (cited in note 14).

[92] *Baltimore Orioles, Inc. v Major League Baseball Players Assoc.*, 805 F2d 663 (7th Cir 1986).

[93] See 1 Nimmer §§ 108[c][2] at 1-49 to 1-54 & 209[f] at 2-138 to 2-138.6 (cited in note 5).

advance[94] and painstakingly rehearsed. A choreographer may therefore obtain a copyright in an original work of dance.[95] It is truly a work of authorship as demanded by the Intellectual Property Clause.

Consider, however, a typical baseball game. No one knows what will happen next. No single author or group of authors is orchestrating, planning, or scripting the game. It may be original, but it is not authored. Something different happens every game. Will the pitcher strike out the lead-off hitter or will the batter hit a home run? How many pitches will he foul off? If he gets a base hit, will he steal a base? Given the proper conditions, a baseball game is not unlike a thunderstorm: it just happens. Therefore, both events are uncopyrightable. Under the current statute, however, the electronic broadcasts of both a baseball game and a thunderstorm are copyrightable merely by the fact of their transmission over the airwaves. The legislative history indicates that Congress thought that some broadcasting was original enough to confer copyright protection even when the underlying work was uncopyrightable due to lack of authorship:[96]

> When a football game is being covered by four television cameras, with a director guiding the activities of the four cameramen and choosing which of their electronic images are sent to the public and in which order, there is no doubt that what the cameramen and the director are doing constitutes authorship.

This rationale seems to comport with *Feist*'s emphasis on originality in selection, arrangement, and coordination when the underlying materials are uncopyrightable works. Although the underlying game is uncopyrightable (as are facts in compilations), some elements of the broadcast may be sufficiently original to merit a copyright.

This rationale explains why the broadcasting of an entire game may well pass constitutional muster, but at the same time it casts doubt on whether bits and pieces of games, like individual facts in a compilation, are protected. The originality requirement of *Feist* may well provide for more leeway in the borrowing of unoriginal

---

[94] I suppose with the exception of some totally freeform modern dancing.

[95] See *Horgan v Macmillan, Inc.* 621 F Supp 1169 (SDNY 1985) (George Balanchine production of "The Nutcracker" copyrightable).

[96] HR Rep No 94-781 at 52, 98th Cong, 2d Sess (1981).

individual clips of athletic performance without the broadcaster's permission—for example, a clip of Nolan Ryan striking out his 4,000 batter taken entirely from the standard behind-the-plate camera location. Much more seriously endangered are cases affording broad protection to television news broadcasts.[97]

Take, for example, typical nightly newsfare: a live speech by a candidate for political office. Normally there will be no coordination of cameras, no real choices as to where to point the camera, no arrangement of images to consider. The task of the cameraman is to stand in the back of the room and transmit images. The event is purely factual; therefore, under *Feist*, only originality as to selection, coordination, and arrangement of the broadcast speech is entitled to protection. Many televised speeches and interviews presumably lack the requisite originality. Unlike broadcasts of some athletic events, the goal of a televised speech or interview is not originality, but mere transmission of facts. This is not to say that television stations should not be rewarded for the enormous effort and expense entailed in broadcasting the news. This section simply notes that *Feist* makes it clear that originality and not effort is the constitutional prerequisite for protection.

In rejecting the sweat of the brow doctrine, the Court noted its historical refusal to allow the news of the day to be copyrighted.[98] This suggests a hostility to the notion that standard and pedestrian broadcasting of a speech or interview should be protected absent the sort of originality as to selection, arrangement, and coordination described above in reference to the filming of some sporting events. Originality must be the public's reward when protection renders news of the day less available. Surely, some live news broadcasting meets the low threshold established by the Court. Equally surely much does not. The sort of protection afforded any broadcast of television news interviews and speeches by the Eleventh Circuit in *Pacific and Southern Co. v Duncan*[99] certainly is overbroad.

---

[97] See *Pacific and Southern Co., Inc. v Duncan*, 792 F2d 1013 (11th Cir 1986) (affirming permanent injunction against the taping of WXIA newscasts).

[98] 111 S Ct at 1292, citing *International News Serv. v Associated Press*, 248 US 215, 234 (1918). Ironically, the Court in *INS* did provide limited protection to news of the day by finding a proprietary interest worthy of short-term protection under pre-*Erie* federal law of unfair competition.

[99] 792 F2d 1013 (11th Cir 1986).

In *Pacific and Southern*, the court affirmed an injunction against a service that copied news broadcasts and sold tapes to the subjects of the broadcasts. It held, "Television interviews with or speeches by public officials, for example, seem to us . . . likely to qualify as the work of WXIA staff—who make audio, filming and editing choices in the presentation of this material."[100] Although the court's focus on "choices" seems well placed, it granted complete protection to all past and future news broadcasts without regard to the "choices" it thought the station would make (analyzing past broadcasts would have been impossible because the plaintiff television station routinely destroyed all its tapes within seven days after they were made). The court's permanent injunction as to future copying can only be read to establish a per se copyright to WXIA's broadcasts without proof of originality.

F. COMPUTER PROGRAMS

Feist's implications for the computer industry are largely beyond the scope of this article. However, the decision does add some ammunition to those who attack the copyrightability of screen displays that are dictated primarily by function.[101] The alphabetical listing of the telephone white pages in *Feist* was unoriginal in large part because it was "practically inevitable."[102] This same argument against the protection of computer screen displays has arisen in cases such as *Lotus Development Corp. v Paperback Software Intern.*[103] The content of many screen displays is dictated by function rather than the imagination of the programmer. *Feist* suggests that whenever the choices made by a programmer are "inevitable," the constitutionally required modicum of originality may very well be absent.

Although the impact of *Feist* is difficult to predict, case law protecting law report pagination, telephone yellow pages, and existing data from new uses appears to be jeopardized. Broadcasters and computer programmers may also find that standard, routine, or

---

[100] Id at 1014 n. 1.

[101] Comment, *Lotus Development Corp. v Paperback Software International: Broad Copyright Protection for User Interfaces Ignores the Software Industry's Trend toward Standardization*, 52 U Pitt L Rev 689 (1991).

[102] 111 S Ct at 1297.

[103] 740 F Supp 37 (D Mass 1990).

inevitable aspects of their works have entered the public domain. In theory, the most endangered class of creations should be maps; however, it would be surprising to find courts stripping protection away from one of the recipients of the original 1790 copyright grant. Finally, even when works of low authorship are entitled to a copyright, the protection extends only to selection, arrangement, and coordination. This narrow scope of protection may often prevent little more than photocopying or verbatim transcription.

IV. ALTERNATIVES OPEN TO CONGRESS

Although *Feist* constitutionalizes the originality requirement, Congress may have several options if it finds *Feist*'s regime overly restrictive.

A. COMMERCE CLAUSE

The opinion in *Feist* makes it clear that the Intellectual Property Clause does not authorize Congress to protect works of low authorship under a sweat of the brow rationale. Whether the opinion prevents Congress from providing protection under its general power to regulate interstate commerce[104] is a difficult question. Representatives of the publishing industry have urged Congress to overrule *Feist* before its own ink dried. If Congress chooses to respond, it could attempt to negate *Feist* on its facts by passing a law forbidding the copying of telephone white pages, or it could enact a broader unfair competition statute prohibiting the copying of any "industrious collection."

No cases have expressly held that Congress can resort to the Commerce Clause to evade limitations present in the Intellectual Property Clause.[105] Such a question would have presented itself in another context, if, for example, Congress had ever attempted to use the Commerce Clause to justify the grant of an eternal patent. The Intellectual Property Clause authorizes Congress to promote science by granting monopoly rights to inventors "for limited times." A law granting an eternal patent would clearly contravene

---

[104] US Const Art I, § 8, cl 3.

[105] See 1 Nimmer § 1.09 at 1-60 (cited in note 5) ("no judicial or legislative authority exists for this proposition").

the express language of the clause. According to *Feist*, a law protecting the white pages or any other "unoriginal" writings would directly contravene the implicit language of the clause.

This interpretation suggests that section 8 of Article I does more than grant Congress a laundry list of powers—it also places substantive limitations on Congress. This interpretation is plausible on the face of section 8, which contains several other express limitations on the federal legislative power. For example, the first clause of section 8 grants Congress the power to levy taxes, but requires that "all Duties, Imposts and Excises shall be uniform throughout the United States." Clause 4 establishes congressional power to enact bankruptcy laws, provided they are "uniform." Clause 12 authorizes Congress to raise armies, but provides that "no appropriation of Money to that Use shall be for a longer Term than two years." Similarly, clause 17 provides for the creation of the District of Columbia in a size "not exceeding ten Miles square." Such limitations on Article I power recently were illustrated—at least nominally—by the Court's decision in *Railway Executors Ass'n v Gibbons*,[106] holding that the substantive limitation against nonuniform bankruptcy laws could not be overridden under the general commerce power.

We should recognize, however, that the limitations in clauses 1, 12, and 17 seem further removed from the Commerce Clause than the Intellectual Property or Bankruptcy Clauses. Although we might imagine Congress enacting legislation providing for nonuniform duties and taxes in order to regulate interstate commerce in some way (thereby conflicting with clause 1) or annexing an extra square mile of Maryland in order to build a new headquarters for the ICC (thereby conflicting with clause 17), an attempt to protect the telephone white pages is arguably closer to the core of the commerce power. Congress' bankruptcy power contained in clause 4 similarly seems to overlap its power to regulate commerce. Not surprisingly, then, the interrelation of the Bankruptcy and Commerce Clauses canvassed by the Court in *Gibbons* provides clear guidance in evaluating the Intellectual Property Clause/Commerce Clause conflict that would arise from the enactment of a statute purporting to override *Feist*. The Intellectual Property/Commerce

---

[106] 455 US 457 (1982).

Clause problem, however, was partially addressed by the Court in the Trade-Mark Cases,[107] where we should first turn.

In 1870, Congress passed the first law providing for the federal registration of trademarks. Although the law purported to find its basis in the Intellectual Property Clause,[108] the Court held that the clause did not authorize the statute. In response to the argument that the Commerce Clause could serve as an alternative basis for the legislation, the Court found fault with the wording of the statute which was interpreted to provide for registration of trademarks whose use was wholly intrastate. However, the Court strongly suggested that the Commerce Clause could properly authorize the registration of marks used in interstate commerce.[109] Because of this suggestion, the case arguably stands for the broad proposition that Congress may do under the Commerce Clause what it may not do under the Intellectual Property Clause.

Because such a reading of the case would nullify the substantive limitations contained in the Intellectual Property Clause, closer reading of the decision is warranted. Of particular importance is why a statute providing for the federal registration of trademarks failed as a matter of Congress' power to grant copyrights. As discussed earlier,[110] the Court in the *Trade-Mark Cases* adhered to traditional notions of what constitutes a trademark. Under the traditional view, a trademark does nothing more than embody the good will of a business: "Good will and its symbol, a trademark, are inseparable. A trademark has no independent significance apart from the good will it symbolizes. If there is no business and no good will, a trademark symbolizes nothing."[111] This understanding

---

[107] 100 US 82 (1879).

[108] Id at 92. See 16 Stat 198 (1870) ("An act to revise, consolidate, and amend the statutes relating to patents and copyrights.").

[109] Id at 95–99. Of course, the Lanham Act, 15 USC §§ 1051 et seq., which currently provides for the federal registration, is based on the Commerce Clause. See, for example, J. Thomas McCarthy, 2 *Trademarks and Unfair Competition* § 25:15 at 270 (1984); *Purolator, Inc. v Efra Dist.*, 687 F2d 554 (1st Cir 1982). The Court has never directly confronted the constitutionality of the Lanham Act, but it has presumed it in a number of recent cases. See *San Francisco Arts & Athletics Inc. v United States Olympic Committee*, 483 US 522 (1987); *Park 'N Fly, Inc. v Dollar Park & Fly, Inc.*, 469 US 189 (1985). It cannot be seriously doubted that the commerce power extends to the protection of trademarks.

[110] See text accompanying notes 24–29 above.

[111] McCarthy, 1 *Trademarks* § 2.8 at 76 (cited in note 109). See also Comment, *Money Damages and Corrective Advertising: An Economic Analysis*, 55 U Chi L Rev 629, 642–58 (1988) (discussing the economic value of good will and function of trademarks); *Trade-Mark Cases*,

of the function of trademark law explains the Court's holding that
a trademark cannot be "original." In layman's terms, a trademark
often is original. Many trademarks are new and different—the result of hours of creative labor. However, according to the Court,
the value of a trademark is a result of its use and not its design.
Even if a trademark is attractive and artistic, its merit cannot be
separated from consumer perceptions of the business or product it
serves to identify. The purpose of trademark law is to protect the
integrity of that perception by preventing confusing uses of similar
trademarks.

Imagine "Mona Lisa" beer, the product of a micro-brewery that
utilizes a picture of the Mona Lisa as its trademark. Under the
Trade-Mark Cases, Congress may find in the Intellectual Property
Clause the power to grant Da Vinci (if he were still alive) a copyright for his painting. Congress clearly advances the arts by providing such protection. However, if Congress provides protection for
the use of the Mona Lisa as a trademark on a bottle of beer, it is
advancing a different interest. Federal registration of the Mona
Lisa beer trademark will help protect the trademark owner and
consumers from competitors wishing to capitalize on the Mona Lisa
Company's good will by selling an inferior product under the Mona
Lisa label. Trademark law protects the ability of a consumer to
identify products and also provides incentives for the creation of
higher quality products.[112] Although trademark law, like copyright
and patent, is concerned with economic efficiency and the creation
of wealth, it does not accomplish its goals by advancing "Science
and Useful Arts." Therefore, the Intellectual Property Clause does
not authorize the protection of a trademark no matter how new,
different, elaborate, or artistic it may be. When the Court said a
trademark is not "original," therefore, it meant that the values protected by trademark law are not *"the fruits of intellectual labor. . .
depend[ing] upon novelty, invention, discovery, or any work of
the brain."*[113] Trademark law does not protect creativity per se, but

---

100 US at 93–94. For the minority contrary position, see Frank Schecter, *The Rational Basis
for Trademark Protection* (1927) (some trademarks may be so distinctive that they are valuable
even before they are used and good will can attach). Cf *Mishawaka Rubber & Woolen Mfg.
Co. v S. S. Kresge Co.*, 316 US 203 (1942) (discussing the psychological attraction of some
distinctive marks).

[112] Why incur the increased cost of creating a high quality product if the competition can
produce an inferior version and attract consumers by using the same trademark?

[113] 100 US at 94.

rather consumer perceptions and quality incentives. Since creativity is at the heart of copyright protection, trademark protection rightfully falls outside its ambit.

The crucial question, however, is whether the Intellectual Property Clause contains an express limitation on the protection of trademarks that should prevent their protection under the Commerce Clause. Such a limitation is difficult to find. As noted above, the Intellectual Property Clause authorizes Congress to "promote the Progress of Science and useful Arts" by granting limited and exclusive rights to creators. Given the Court's understanding of trademark law, the limitations inherent in that authorization seem inapposite. Trademark law does not hinder the progress of the Arts and Sciences, nor does it grant rights to authors. It merely protects convenient source identification devices, as evidenced by the fact that nonconfusing uses of another's trademark are not actionable under federal law. Use of the Commerce Clause to authorize the protection of trademarks would not seem to conflict with the language, goals, or purpose of the Intellectual Property Clause.[114]

Legislation protecting telephone white pages or other works of low authorship under the Commerce Clause poses more serious difficulties because the Court made it clear in *Feist* that such protection would directly conflict with the purpose of the Intellectual Property Clause. According to the Court, the clause not only tells us what may be protected, but what must remain in the public domain. The progress of the arts and sciences would be impeded if a healthy public domain were not maintained. The primary inhabitants of that domain are facts and ideas that may be copied at will. This result is neither unfair nor unfortunate—it is the means by which copyright advances the progress of science and art.[115] To that end, the Court labels as a "constitutional requirement" that "much of the fruit of the compiler's labor may be used by others without compensation."[116] The Court sees, although perhaps incorrectly, that the protection of works such as the white pages would

---

[114] This formulation sounds a bit like preemption analysis. In a sense, the Constitution limits (preempts) congressional action in the same way that congressional action can preempt state action. There is a presumption against both sorts of limitations, and the key is finding a frustration of purpose or a direct conflict in goals.

[115] 111 S Ct at 1289–90.

[116] Id.

frustrate the goals of the Intellectual Property Clause by diminishing the raw materials available for others' creations.

Given the Court's recognition of the danger of protection, it seems unlikely it would permit its perception of the framer's vision of the public domain to be circumvented. Unlike trademark law, a statute providing protection for industrious collections that flunk *Feist*'s originality test would seem to run directly counter to the goals of the Intellectual Property Clause as defined by the Court.

Some support for this proposition may be gleaned from a surprising source, the Bankruptcy Clause. In 1980, Congress attempted to protect the employees of the bankrupt Rock Island railroad by authorizing payments to them out of the railroad's estate in bankruptcy. Since the law applied only to the Rock Island estate, and not to other railroad bankruptcies, it was not "uniform" as mandated by the Bankruptcy Clause. In *Railway Labor Executors Assn v Gibbons*,[117] the Court considered whether Congress could enact this nonuniform bankruptcy legislation under the Commerce Clause. A unanimous Court answered negatively: "if we were to hold that Congress had the power to enact non-uniform bankruptcy laws pursuant to the Commerce Clause, we would eradicate from the Constitution a limitation on the power of Congress to enact bankruptcy laws."[118]

In *Feist* the Court similarly held that the originality requirement was a limitation on Congress' power to enact copyright legislation. *Gibbons* provides strong support for the proposition that Congress may not circumvent that limitation through the Commerce Clause despite the implications of the *Trade-Mark Cases* discussed above. The same rationale that prevents Congress from enacting nonuniform bankruptcy laws should prevent it from enacting laws protecting unoriginal creations.

The history of the Intellectual Property Clause sheds additional light on the propriety of the Court's insistence that it functions as not only a grant of power but a strong substantive limitation. The language of the clause is almost certainly borrowed from the Statute of Anne,[119] which was enacted in response to problems which

---

[117] 455 US 457 (1982). See Douglas G. Baird, *Bankruptcy Procedure and State-Created Rights: The Lessons of* Gibbons *and* Marathon, 1982 Supreme Court Review 25.

[118] *Gibbons*, 455 US at 468–69.

[119] 8 Anne ch 21 (1710). See generally L. Ray Patterson, *The Statute of Anne: Copyright Misconstrued*, 3 Harv J Leg 223 (1966).

arose during the pendency of the copyright monopoly enjoyed by the London Stationer's Company. The Stationer's copyright "was used as an instrument of both monopoly and press control until the last of the English censorship acts."[120] The Statute of Anne "was designed to ensure that the statutory copyright would be used for neither purpose."[121] The Statute of Anne led to the end of the Stationer's monopoly, helped increase the public domain, and enhanced the free flow of information.

This lesson was not lost on the framers of the Constitution. They worded the Intellectual Property Clause to prevent abuses like those perpetrated when the Stationer's Company exercised complete control over publishing in England. According to the clause, only authors may be granted a copyright, only for a limited time, and only for original works. Most importantly, the copyright law should promote the progress of science, which in the eighteenth century sense meant "knowledge."[122] This progress is meant to benefit the public as a whole, and the Court has often spoken in economic terms to describe the benefit: "The economic philosophy behind the clause empowering Congress to grant patents and copyrights is the conviction that encouragement of individual effort by personal gain is the best way to advance public welfare."[123] The rationale for copyright protection fails without "public access to the products of [authors'] genius."[124] Public access "is the means by which copyright advances the progress of science and art."[125]

Therefore, the clause can properly be seen to tie Congress' hands to a certain extent. The systematic grant of monopoly rights should be designed to ensure the public welfare, not profit the few at the expense of the many. History indicates that any use of the Commerce Clause to subvert that end should be rebuffed. This is not to say that the Court is correct in its assertion that the sweat of the brow rationale inevitably diminishes public wealth. Strong arguments can be made that the Court has made a grave mistake in holding the rationale unconstitutional. However, once the Court

---

[120] Patterson & Joyce, 36 UCLA L Rev at 785 (cited in note 14).

[121] Id.

[122] See Ginsburg, 90 Colum L Rev at 1876 (cited in note 31).

[123] *Mazer v Stein*, 347 US 201, 219 (1954).

[124] *Sony Corp. v Universal Studios, Inc.*, 464 US 417, 429 (1984).

[125] *Feist*, 111 S Ct at 1290.

finds that the Intellectual Property Clause forbids the protection of works under a sweat of the brow rationale, Congress cannot avoid the holding by resorting to the Commerce Clause. History demonstrates that Congress does not have carte blanche—in order to promote the public welfare, the Intellectual Property Clause tells Congress what it may not do.

B. DIRECT SUBSIDIES

In *New Energy Co. of Indiana v Limbach*,[126] the Court considered an incentive taxation scheme enacted by Indiana to encourage its budding ethanol industry, and struck down the Indiana law as discriminating against interstate commerce in violation of the Commerce Clause. However, Justice Scalia, writing for the majority, noted that direct subsidies of the state's ethanol producers would not be unconstitutional. Although *Limbach* deals with the question of what states may do under the Constitution, its reasoning may be applicable to how Congress can respond to *Feist*. Rather than enacting a potentially unconstitutional statute granting monopoly rights to producers of telephone white pages, Congress might choose to subsidize their production if it determined such a subsidy would be necessary to ensure their continued existence. Given that many telephone companies are required by state law to compile and publish alphabetical lists of their subscribers, such a subsidy program would not seem necessary in the case of telephone white pages. However, it might be necessary to ensure the production of other valuable works of low authorship.

The suggestion—that subsidizing works ineligible for copyright protection would be constitutional—may seem somewhat paradoxical. However, the Court has never taken an active role in policing congressional action taken under the spending clause. Congress subsidizes numerous sorts of production through its power of the purse. The Intellectual Property Clause should only be implicated when Congress acts through the grant of monopoly power.

C. CIRCUMVENTION OF FEIST BY THE STATES

Although Congress is powerless to protect "unoriginal" works, the possibility of a response to *Feist* by the states remains. Since

---

[126] 486 US 269 (1988).

the limitations present in the Intellectual Property Clause are found in the enumeration of powers of the federal Congress in Article I, the states could plausibly argue that they are free to provide a different scope of protection for "unoriginal" works. This issue, however, is unlikely ever to arise. Since the Copyright Act itself contains an originality requirement, under *Bonito Boats, Inc. v Thunder Craft Boats, Inc.*[127] any state law protecting unoriginal creations would be preempted as conflicting with the goals and purposes of the Act's originality requirement. In *Bonito Boats*, the Court struck down a Florida statute prohibiting the duplication of boat hulls by any direct molding process. The Florida statute frustrated the purpose of federal patent law because it provided protection without requiring satisfaction of any of the qualitative criteria (novelty, nonobviousness, or usefulness) present in the patent law. Similarly, a state law protecting unoriginal creations would run afoul of the originality criteria contained in the Copyright Act.

This analysis, however, does not apply to all types of creations, only those categorized in sections 102 and 103 of the Act.[128] In *Goldstein v California*,[129] which was cited with approval in *Bonito Boats*, the Court held that states may protect categories of works (in that case sound recordings before they were protected under the Act) left unregulated by Congress. For example, although a state may not protect an unoriginal literary work, piece of music, or compilation, it may protect something like a right of publicity which Congress has not yet made a category of work eligible for protection. So, an unoriginal work of a type not yet categorized in sections 102 and 103 of the Copyright Act might be amenable to protection by the states. Given the difficulty of imagining such a work, it seems safe to say generally that state attempts to circumvent *Feist* will be futile.

V. Conclusion

Before *Feist* was decided, a sophisticated scholarly debate raged about the need to protect low authorship works. Although

---

[127] 489 US 141 (1989). See generally John S. Wiley Jr., *Bonito Boats: Uninformed But Mandatory Innovation Policy*, 1989 Supreme Court Review 283.

[128] Listing literary works, musical works, dramatic works, pantomimes, choreographic works, motion pictures, sound recordings, compilations, and pictorial, graphic, and sculptural works.

[129] 412 US 546 (1973).

no agreement was reached on the contours of the necessary protection, a general consensus found that valuable works of low authorship should be protected if they would otherwise go uncreated. The debate focused on the proper balance of incentives necessary to increase public wealth. Originality was recognized to be a term of art: works worth protecting were original; those not needing protection were not. As the opinion recognizes, telephone directory white pages are almost certainly not worth protecting from the sort of activity engaged in by Feist. However, other works that are the product of perspiration rather than inspiration might be. The primary vice of *Feist* is its broad language forbidding Congress from protecting any sweat of the brow works or industrious collections in the future. This flaw is especially glaring given that copyright law as currently enacted clearly does not provide for such protection, and therefore the decision could have rested on purely statutory grounds.

The potential effect of *Feist* may well be far-reaching. Its particular definition of originality casts doubt on the copyrightability of maps, systems, lists, tables, historical works and research, and pagination of law reports. Perhaps the most interesting question left after *Feist* is not what works will be cast to the public domain, but whether Congress can constitutionally overrule the decision.

LARRY KRAMER

VESTIGES OF BEALE: EXTRATERRITORIAL APPLICATION OF AMERICAN LAW

Appellate courts are supposed to keep the law consistent and coherent, which can be difficult because decentralized, adversarial adjudication tends to stretch statutes and precedents in different directions. The same principle will often be applied in different contexts and may develop along different lines. The differences, unfortunately, are not always a product of careful deliberation or self-conscious choice. So periodically the highest court of a jurisdiction is called upon to revisit an issue and sort through the disparate strands to restore order. In this way, the law evolves and improves; but not always.

Consider, for example, the problem of extraterritorial application of American law. In 1909, Justice Holmes wrote for the Supreme Court in *American Banana Co. v United Fruit Co.* that "in case of doubt . . . any statute [should be interpreted] to be confined in its operation and effect to the territorial limits over which the lawmaker has general and legitimate power."[1] This principle was then followed in a number of cases for three more decades.[2]

Larry Kramer is Professor of Law, University of Michigan Law School.

Author's Note: I am grateful to Alex Aleinikoff, Lee Bollinger, Lea Brilmayer, Anne-Marie Burley, Heidi Feldman, Don Herzog, John Jackson, Harold Maier, Richard Posner, Eric Stein, Joseph Weiler, and Louise Weinberg for comments on an earlier draft.

[1] 213 US 347, 357 (1909).

[2] See, for example, *New York Central R.R. v Chisolm*, 268 US 29 (1925) (FELA); *Blackmer v United States*, 284 US 421 (1932) (allowing extraterritorial service of a subpoena where expressly provided by statute); *Foley Bros. v Filardo*, 336 US 281 (1949) (maximum hours law).

Inconsistencies began to appear in the mid-1940s. While faithfully applying Holmes's principle in antitrust cases, the Court had rephrased it in terms of power to control combinations that "affect" United States commerce.[3] Although probably not meant to change the doctrine, these statements provided authority for Learned Hand's notorious *Alcoa* opinion,[4] which applied the Sherman Act to conduct abroad that is intended to and does affect United States commerce—the very interpretation rejected by Holmes.

The approach developed in the antitrust area was subsequently extended to cases involving the antifraud provisions of the Securities Exchange Act.[5] At the same time, courts continued to apply the presumption against extraterritoriality in other areas, including labor relations, civil rights, and environmental law.[6] In still other areas, the presumption was replaced by a more flexible analysis of state interests.[7] Hence, different approaches to extraterritoriality evolved in different substantive contexts with significantly different consequences for legislative policy.

Last Term, the Supreme Court rendered a decision apparently intended to resolve these inconsistencies. But rather than articulate a new approach to problems of extraterritoriality, the Court opted to restore the original presumption to full vigor. In *EEOC v Arabian American Oil Co. (Aramco),*[8] an American citizen employed in Saudi Arabia brought suit under Title VII alleging that he was fired because of his race and religion. Although the defendant was also American, the Court affirmed the dismissal of plaintiff's claim on the ground that the alleged discrimination occurred in Saudi Ara-

---

[3] *Thomsen v Cayser,* 243 US 66, 88 (1917); *United States v Sisal Sales Corp.,* 274 US 268, 275–76 (1927).

[4] See *United States v Aluminum Co. of America,* 148 F2d 416, 444 (2d Cir 1945).

[5] *Schoenbaum v Firstbrook,* 405 F2d 200, rev'd on other grounds, 405 F2d 215 (2d Cir 1968); *Bersch v Drexel Firestone, Inc.,* 519 F2d 974 (2d Cir 1975).

[6] See, for example, *Benz v Compania Naveria Hidalgo,* 353 US 138 (1957) (LMRA); *McCulloch v Sociodad Nacional,* 372 US 10 (1963) (NLRA); *Boureslan v Aramco,* 857 F2d 1014, aff'd en banc, 892 F2d 1271 (5th Cir 1990), aff'd, 111 S Ct 1227 (1991) (Title VII); *Cleary v United States Lines, Inc.,* 555 F Supp 1251 (DNJ 1983), aff'd, 728 F2d 607 (3d Cir 1984) (ADEA); *Natural Resources Defense Council, Inc. v Nuclear Regulatory Comm'n,* 647 F2d 1345 (DC Cir 1981) (NEPA). These cases are discussed in Jonathon Turley, *"When in Rome": Multinational Misconduct and the Presumption against Extraterritoriality,* 84 Nw U L Rev 598, 608–34 (1990).

[7] *Lauritzen v Larsen,* 345 US 571 (1953) (Jones Act); *Romero v International Terminal Operating Co.,* 358 US 354 (1959) (same).

[8] 111 S Ct 1227 (1991).

bia. The Court based its decision entirely on the presumption against extraterritoriality.

Before proceeding further, we need to clarify the meaning of "presumption against extraterritoriality." One could say that a nation has "territorial" authority over anything connected to its territory. This might include the fact that one of the parties resides in or is a citizen of the nation, that some of the acts complained of occurred there, or that the effect of those acts is felt within the nation or by its citizens. As traditionally used by judges and commentators, however, "territoriality" referred to acts occurring within the nation and was meant to exclude assertions of authority based on nationality or effects. On this view, which appears to be that of the Court in *Aramco*, there are multinational cases that do not involve an "extraterritorial" assertion of power, as when a nation regulates the conduct of foreign nationals within its borders. Conversely, regulating action abroad is "extraterritorial" even if all the parties involved or affected are citizens of the regulating state. The presumption against extraterritoriality, in other words, refers to a presumption that laws regulate only acts occurring within the United States.[9]

Aramco is especially noteworthy for the weight the Court was willing to give this presumption. Thus, the plaintiff argued that Congress expressed its intent to protect United States citizens abroad by extending coverage to commerce "between a State and any place outside thereof" and by expressly exempting employers from liability only "with respect to the employment of aliens outside any State."[10] Plaintiff also cited EEOC guidelines supporting his interpretation of Title VII, arguing that these are entitled to judicial deference. All this, the Court replied, "is insufficiently weighty to overcome the presumption against extraterritorial application" and "falls short of demonstrating the affirmative congres-

---

[9] The meaning of "territorial" and hence "extraterritorial" is purely conventional, and these words have therefore been used in different ways at different times and in different contexts. For example, some courts justified effects-based assertions of power as an application of the territorial principle. See Restatement (Third) of the Law of the Foreign Relations of the United States § 402, comment d (1986). Similarly, international law recognizes differences between prescriptive, adjudicatory, and enforcement jurisdiction, and uses slightly different definitions of "extraterritorial" in all these contexts. See id §§ 401–33. For purposes of this paper, however, the definition in text will suffice.

[10] Id at 1231, 1233 (citing 42 USC §§ 2000e(g), 2000e-1).

sional intent required to extend the protections of Title VII beyond our territorial borders."[11]

The Court did not explicitly say it was reestablishing the presumption against extraterritoriality across the board. Nonetheless, the opinion's broad, uncompromising language makes this the likely effect.[12] And while Congress acted quickly to overturn the particular result in *Aramco*,[13] adjusting the scope of Title VII still leaves the general presumption in place. *Aramco* thus has important implications for American policy. Cases with foreign elements may once have been marginal, but events since World War II have deeply entangled the United States in the world's political and market economies. The most obvious example is antitrust, where extraterritorial enforcement has become a central tenet of American policy. But multinational cases affect American interests in a growing number of other areas as well, including environmental law, labor law, corporate governance, and securities regulation.

It does not follow, of course, that because multinational cases are important so, too, is a presumption against extraterritoriality. The Court did not hold, after all, that Congress cannot extend American law to cases with foreign elements—only that if this is what Congress wants to do, it must say so clearly. As the Court observed in justifying another clear statement rule, "Whatever we say regarding . . . a particular statute can of course be changed by Congress. What is of paramount importance is that Congress be able to legislate against a background of clear interpretive rules, so that it may know the effect of the language it adopts."[14] *Aramco* is thus of a piece with much of the Court's recent jurisprudence on statutory interpretation, which seeks to limit judicial discretion

[11] Id at 1231, 1235.

[12] Some lower courts have already read *Aramco* as establishing a broad, general presumption against extraterritoriality. See, for example, *Cruz v Chesapeake Shipping, Inc.*, 932 F2d 218 (3d Cir 1991).

[13] See Civil Rights Act of 1991, § 109, Pub L 102–66, 105 stat 1071, 1076, codified at 42 USC §§ 2000e(f), 2000e-1.

[14] *Finley v United States*, 109 S Ct 2005, 2010 (1989) (Congress must clearly indicate its desire to confer pendent or ancillary jurisdiction). Congress overruled *Finley* by providing that statutes granting jurisdiction should be interpreted to confer supplemental jurisdiction to the full extent permitted by Article III unless Congress provides otherwise. See 28 USC § 1367.

and in this way to shift responsibility for articulating details to Congress.[15]

Reality, unfortunately, is more complicated than the Court seems willing to acknowledge. Legislation is not enacted in a Coasean universe of no transaction costs. Congress conducts an enormous amount of business under complex political pressures. Much of this work, including virtually all of the drafting, is handled by an extensive bureaucracy whose membership changes constantly. Legislation originates in a myriad of committees and subcommittees, and there is little centralized control over the drafting process—particularly when it comes to technical questions (like extraterritorial scope) that are relevant to a variety of legislation. Mistakes and oversight are common and to be expected, and legislative inertia inevitably impedes the process of ongoing supervision.[16]

For these reasons, the content of a presumption matters—more so as the presumption is made stronger. And *Aramco* makes the presumption against extraterritoriality very strong indeed. If experience is any guide, this means that general language will be interpreted narrowly and that Congress must get very specific about exactly when it wants United States law to apply.[17] But Congress will often find it difficult to specify extraterritorial scope in detail. More important, the need for international application may not be apparent at the time of enactment and, as just noted, will often be overlooked anyway. As a practical matter, then, the presumption against extraterritoriality is bound to restrict the enforcement of American law in many areas.

This, of course, is the whole purpose of a presumption: to identify a generally desirable outcome and force the legislature to go out of its way to do something different. To be sure, some pre-

---

[15] See Nicholas S. Zeppos, *Justice Scalia's Textualism: The "New" Legal Process*, 12 Cardozo L Rev 1597, 1614–20 (1991).

[16] See Report of the Federal Courts Study Committee 91 (April 2, 1990); Larry Kramer, *"The One-Eyed Are Kings": Improving Congress's Ability to Regulate the Use of Judicial Resources*, 54 L & Contemp Probs 73, 78-80 (1991). There are support agencies within Congress responsible for drafting and law revision, but these have neither the authority nor the status to exercise control and simply take orders from the decentralized committees and subcommittees of Congress.

[17] See, for example, cases deciding whether Congress has abrogated the states' sovereign immunity from suit in federal court. *Dellmuth v Muth*, 109 S Ct 2397 (1989); *Welch v State Dept. of Highways & Pub. Transp.*, 107 S Ct 2941 (1987). See also *Kent v Dulles*, 357 US 116 (1958) (narrowly interpreting the power of the Secretary of State to deny passports).

sumptions are said merely to provide a means of ascertaining "unexpressed congressional intent."[18] But this is just a coy way of soft-pedaling the conclusion that judges have found a particular policy normatively superior: having decided which course of action is generally preferable, courts assume that this is what "reasonable" lawmakers would want. The only real difference between strong clear statement principles and weaker presumptions of legislative intent is the amount of evidence required for the court to accept a contrary legislative decision—a measure of the strength of the judicial preference. And, as noted above, *Aramco* establishes a strong preference that can be overcome only by unequivocal language.

The Court's decision thus reflects a normative judgment that it is preferable to restrict American law. Given the importance of multinational cases, the wisdom of this judgment must be evaluated. In my view, the *Aramco* Court made a bad choice. Instead of learning from the diversity of views that emerged from Justice Holmes's germinal opinion, the Court thoughtlessly attempted to revive the original principle. As the discussion below explains, however, the world in which a presumption against extraterritoriality made sense is gone—and for good reasons. The Court's decision is an anachronism.

I

A

The presumption against extraterritoriality made its first formal appearance in somewhat remarkable circumstances. An American businessman named McConnell bought a banana plantation in Panama, then still part of Colombia. He was quickly contacted by the United Fruit Company, a New Jersey corporation aggressively seeking to monopolize the Central American banana trade. United Fruit told McConnell that he could either deal with it or go out of business. Instead, McConnell began constructing a railway to carry his bananas for export. In June, 1904, McConnell sold the plantation to the American Banana Company, a newly established Alabama concern organized to harvest and sell Central American bananas.

---

[18] *Aramco*, 111 S Ct at 1237 (Marshall, dissenting) (quoting *Foley Bros.*, 336 US at 285). See also Cass Sunstein, *After the Rights Revolution: Reconceiving the Regulatory State* 153–54 (Harvard, 1990).

In July, Costa Rica invaded Panama (by then an independent state), allegedly at the behest of United Fruit. Costa Rican soldiers seized American Banana's plantation and conveyed it to one Astua, who promptly sold it to United Fruit. Costa Rican forces remained on the plantation to ensure that these transfers were carried out.

Having lost that battle, American Banana shifted theatres and brought an antitrust action against United Fruit in New York. In addition to alleging defendant's use of the government of Costa Rica, which seemed at the time to present difficulties under the act of state doctrine, American Banana charged United Fruit with more conventional anticompetitive acts: conspiring with other banana producers, interfering with American Banana's contracts, below-cost bidding, and the like. The complaint was dismissed by the trial judge, and the case made its way by writ of error to the Supreme Court.

Writing for the Court, Justice Holmes observed: "It is obvious that, however stated, the plaintiff's case depends on several rather startling propositions. In the first place, the acts causing the damage were done, so far as appears, outside the jurisdiction of the United States and within that of other states. It is surprising to hear it argued that they were governed by the act of Congress."[19] The surprise, Holmes continued, comes from the fact that[20]

> the general and almost universal rule is that the character of an act as lawful or unlawful must be determined wholly by the law of the country where the act is done. *Slater v. Mexican National R.R. Co.*, 194 U.S. 120, 126. This principle was carried to an extreme in *Milliken v. Pratt*, 125 Massachusetts, 374. For another jurisdiction, if it should happen to lay hold of the actor, to treat him according to its own notions rather than those of the place where he did the acts, not only would be unjust, but would be an interference with the authority of another sovereign, contrary to the comity of nations, which the other states concerned justly might resent. *Phillips v. Eyre*, L.R. 4 Q.B. 225, 239; L.R. 6 Q.B. 1, 28; Dicey, Conflict of Laws (2d ed.), 647.

These considerations, Holmes concluded, "would lead in case of doubt to a construction of any statute as intended to be confined

---

[19] 312 US at 355.

[20] Id at 356.

in its operation and effect to the territorial limits over which the lawmaker has general and legitimate power."[21] Hence, when Congress uses language like "every contract" or "every person who shall monopolize," courts should presume that what Congress means is every contract or person in the United States.[22]

Holmes's analysis of this case is pure conflict of laws. The prevailing theory of the time—today associated primarily with Joseph Beale—was built on the territorial principle: in Justice Story's words, that "every nation possesses an exclusive sovereignty and jurisdiction within its own territory" and that "it would be wholly incompatible with the equality and exclusiveness of the sovereignty of all nations, that any one nation should be at liberty to regulate either persons or things not within its own territory."[23] In the area of torts, this meant that "[t]he existence and nature of a cause of action . . . is governed by the law of the place [of the] wrongful act or omission."[24] Therefore, "[i]f by the law of the place where the defendant caused an event to happen this event created no right of action in tort, no action can be brought on account of the event in another state although it would create a cause of action by the law of that other state."[25] This last proposition was picked up by Holmes in *American Banana:* "For again, not only were the acts of the defendant in Panama or Costa Rica not within the Sherman Act, but they were not torts by the law of the place and therefore were not torts at all, . . ."[26]

Any doubt about the fact that Holmes saw *American Banana* as a conventional conflict of laws problem is removed by the authorities he cites. Holmes supports the opinion's central proposition— that enforceable rights are ordinarily determined by the law of the place where an act occurs—with his own decision in *Slater v Mexican National R.R.*, "[t]he classic judicial formulation" of traditional conflicts theory.[27] Holmes then illustrates the governing principle with *Milliken v Pratt*—an essential chestnut in any choice of law

---

[21] Id at 357.

[22] Id.

[23] Joseph Story, *Commentaries on the Conflict of Laws* 19, 21 (Hilliard, Gray & Co., 1834).

[24] 2 Joseph Beale, *Treatise on the Conflict of Laws* 1289 (Baker, Voohris & Co., 1935).

[25] Id at 1290–91.

[26] 213 US at 357.

[27] Eugene Scoles & Peter Hay, *Conflict of Laws* 14 n 2 (West, 1982).

course. Finally, he adds citations to a leading English conflicts case and the leading conflict of laws treatise of the day, that of his friend A. V. Dicey.

B

To understand the decision in *American Banana*, it is important also to understand the legal environment in which Holmes was writing. Territoriality was the cornerstone of a framework developed to regulate sovereign relations in a number of areas, of which choice of law was merely one. Thus, Justice Story borrowed the territorial principle from Ulrich Huber's seventeenth-century tract "De Conflictu Legum Diversarum in Diversis Imperiis" (On the Conflict of Different Laws in Different States), which was a single chapter in a larger work on the functioning of nation-states defined by territorial boundaries.[28] Read in this light, Huber's territorial maxim becomes a sweeping proposition with broad political significance. And, indeed, territoriality became the central concept in political and legal thinking about public international law generally. In the United States, this principle received authoritative endorsement from Chief Justice Marshall in *The Schooner Exchange v M'Faddon:* "The jurisdiction of the nation within its own territory is necessarily exclusive and absolute. It is susceptible of no limitation not imposed by itself."[29]

Nor did the importance of the territorial principle end with foreign affairs. Anyone who has taken first-year civil procedure, for example, is familiar with *Pennoyer v Neff*, which limited adjudicatory jurisdiction to persons or property in a state in accord with the "universal" principle that "[t]he authority of every tribunal is necessarily restricted by the territorial limits of the State in which it is established. Any attempt to exercise authority beyond those limits would be deemed in every other forum, as has been said by this court, an illegitimate assumption of power, and be resisted as mere abuse."[30]

---

[28] The chapter on conflicts was published in Volume II, Book 1, title iii of Huber's *Praelectiones Juris Romani et Hodierni* (1689). See generally Hessel Yntema, *The Historic Bases of Private International Law*, 2 Am J Comp L 297 (1953); D. J. Llewelyn Davies, *The Influence of Huber's "De Conflictu Legum" on English Private International Law* 18 Brit YB Int'l L 49, 65 (1937).

[29] 7 Cranch 116, 136 (1812).

[30] 5 Otto 714, 720 (1877).

I offer these quotations both to suggest the relationship between public international law, adjudicatory jurisdiction, and conflict of laws, and to underscore the centrality of the territorial premise in nineteenth-century thinking about them. Many commentators have seen connections between these fields,[31] but the literature has for the most part been concerned more with differences than similarities. These are, in fact, all variations on a single theme—that of accommodating conflicting policies of independent sovereigns.

The point is straightforward: Laws are means to an end. Lawmakers prescribe legal rules to achieve some objective, choosing an enforcement scheme to implement that objective effectively (which does not necessarily mean to the fullest extent possible). A "public" enforcement scheme utilizes the government's own bureaucracy; a "private" scheme leaves affected individuals to fend for themselves by suing in courts. Conflicts arise because one government or its citizens may have dealings with another government or its citizens, and the two nations may have inconsistent policies. But whether a conflict arises between two governments (usually a matter of public international law), between a government and a foreign national (also typically a matter of public international law), between citizens of two nations (a question of conflict of laws), or between citizens of the same nation acting in a foreign nation (also conflict of laws), the problem is the same: to find a way to accommodate the conflicting policies by deciding whose should prevail or arranging some other acceptable compromise.

This is true, moreover, whether the conflict concerns prescriptive or adjudicatory jurisdiction. If one nation's law is applied, the other nation's law is not; if one nation's courts decide the dispute, the other nation's courts do not. If both nations want their law

---

[31] See, for example, Lea Brilmayer, *Extraterritorial Application of American Law*, 50 L & Contemp Probs 11 (1987); Andreas Lowenfeld, *Public Law in the International Arena: Conflict of Laws, International Law, and Some Suggestions for Their Interaction*, 163 Recueil Des Cours 311 (1979-II); Harold Maier, *Extraterritorial Jurisdiction at a Crossroads: An Intersection between Public and Private International Law*, 76 Am J Comp L 280 (1982); Daniel Chow, *Rethinking the Act of State Doctrine: An Analysis in Terms of Jurisdiction to Prescribe*, 62 Wash L Rev 397 (1987); Harold Maier & Thomas McCoy, *A Unifying Theory for Judicial Jurisdiction and Choice of Law*, 39 Am J Comp L 249 (1991). Other commentators deny that these problems are related. See, for example, Karl Meessen, *International Law Limitations on State Jurisdiction*, in Cecil J. Olmstead, ed., *Extra-territorial Application of Laws and Responses Thereto* 38-44 (Int'l Law Ass'n, 1984); Friedrich Juenger, *Constitutional Control of Extraterritoriality?: A Comment on Professor Brilmayer's Appraisal*, 50 L & Contemp Probs 39, 41–42 (1987).

applied or their courts to decide, we have a conflict and must find some way to resolve it.[32]

The territorial principle was supposed to solve all these problems. By establishing a priori that only the nation where an event occurs has power, it limited states' lawmaking competence so that conflict was practically impossible. Only one state could regulate events, either directly or by creating rights for private parties to enforce in a legal action. Similarly, only the state where a party (or that party's property) was located could exercise jurisdiction to adjudicate a dispute. The rationale was simple: because sovereignty is defined by territorial control, any other principle would be a source of friction and discord "inconvenient to the commerce and general intercourse of nations."[33] Given such a worldview, Justice Holmes's reliance on territoriality to delimit the scope of American law in multinational cases hardly comes as a surprise.[34]

c

Implementing the territorial principle was not so simple in practice, and the complications eventually led courts to abandon the idea of territoriality as the sole justification for exercising state power. To begin with, despite the unqualified language used by Story and others, the territorial principle was never followed universally. Even during its heyday there were exceptions. Nations sometimes asserted prescriptive jurisdiction based on nationality, for example, and the applicable law in many contexts turned on a

[32] It is possible for courts in more than one nation to adjudicate the same dispute, and it is not uncommon for courts to decline to enforce a foreign judgment. But this itself raises the stakes in a controversy and becomes a source of conflict. The objective in international (as in interstate) litigation is thus to find a single forum whose adjudication is acceptable to both nations.

[33] Ulrich Huber, *De Conflictu Legum*, reprinted in translation in Davies, 18 Brit YB Int'l L at 66 (cited in note 28). See also *American Banana*, 213 US at 356; Joseph Story, *Commentaries on the Conflict of Laws*, at 5 (cited in note 23). There is a tension implicit in the territorial principle: to say that a forum court must apply the law of another nation where events occurred seems inconsistent with the exclusive sovereignty of the forum nation. Story and Huber explained this limitation as a matter of comity, a choice made by the forum in the interests of international order. Dissatisfied with the amount of discretion this left, later commentators such as Beale and Dicey substituted the notion of vested rights.

[34] What is surprising is to see this formalistic reasoning invoked by the author of *The Common Law* and *The Path of the Law*. Commentators have long puzzled over the inconsistency between Holmes's general jurisprudence and his analysis in choice of law cases. See, for example, G. Kenneth Reiblich, *The Conflict of Laws Philosophy of Mr. Justice Holmes*, 28 Geo L J 1 (1939).

party's domicile rather than on where the party acted. Beale and Holmes both recognized that legislatures did sometimes assert extraterritorial jurisdiction, which is why they offered their rules as interpretive guides that could be overcome by a sufficiently clear legislative statement.[35]

More important, the commitment to territoriality never actually succeeded in eliminating conflicts. For example, while the territorial principle worked fine in cases like *American Banana*, where all the relevant acts occurred in another state, it worked less well where these acts occurred in more than one jurisdiction. In such cases, the principle could logically be understood to permit either both states or neither to regulate.

Traditional conflicts theory avoided this conundrum and preserved the myth of no conflicts by declaring (rather arbitrarily) that a tort occurred at the place of the last event necessary to make an actor liable.[36] When this problem arose in a subsequent antitrust case, however, the Supreme Court ignored the established choice of law convention and instead adopted a principle allowing both nations' laws to apply. *United States v Pacific & Arctic Ry.*[37] involved an alleged conspiracy by Canadian carriers to monopolize transport on certain routes between the United States and Canada. Citing *American Banana*, the defendants argued that the Sherman Act did not apply to acts by foreign corporations outside the United States.[38] The Court agreed that "laws have no extra-territorial operation," but rejected the defendants' argument on the ground that "it would put the transportation route . . . out of the control of either Canada or the United States."[39] Focusing instead on the fact that the conspiracy included the carriage of goods in the United States, the Court held: "If we may not control foreign citizens or

---

[35] See Restatement of the Law of Conflict of Laws § 5, comments a–d (1934); *American Banana*, 213 US at 356–57.

[36] Restatement of Law of Conflict of Laws § 377. The last event test is arbitrary because there is no claim unless all the elements are established. A tort may be *consummated* where the last act occurs, but it is *being committed* from the first to the last act and thus "occurs" at all these places. See Comment, *Jurisdiction over Interstate Felony-Murder*, 50 U Chi L Rev 1431, 1442–43 (1983).

[37] 228 US 87 (1913).

[38] Id at 100.

[39] Id at 106.

corporations operating in foreign territory, we certainly may control such citizens or corporations operating in our territory, . . ."[40]

The same problem arose four years later in *Thomsen v Cayser*.[41] Once again, the defendants were charged with conspiring to monopolize the carriage of goods, this time between the United States and South Africa. Once again, the defendants argued that their actions were outside the scope of the Sherman Act because the combination was formed abroad, and once again the Supreme Court rejected the claim, now citing *Pacific & Arctic Ry*. This time, however, the Court put the principle somewhat differently. Defendant's actions were subject to liability under American antitrust laws, the Court said, because "the combination affected the foreign commerce of this country and was put into operation here."[42] The Court stated the point in essentially the same way a few years later in *United States v Sisal Sales Corp.*, holding that defendants' acts here and abroad created liability because they "brought about forbidden results within the United States."[43]

This seemingly inadvertent reformulation in terms of effects was picked up by Learned Hand in the notorious *Alcoa* case.[44] A group of foreign corporations formed a cartel to regulate competition in the aluminum industry. No acts in furtherance of this combination occurred in the United States, though American companies bought and sold aluminum from cartel members. The court held that United States law applied—citing *American Banana* for the proposition that limitations on extraterritorial application "generally correspond to those fixed by the 'Conflict of Laws,'" and citing *Pacific & Arctic Ry.*, *Thomsen v Cayser*, and *Sisal Sales Corp.* for the proposition that the Sherman Act reaches agreements intended to affect and affecting United States commerce.[45] "[A]ny state," Judge Hand wrote, "may impose liabilities, even upon persons not within its allegiance, for conduct outside its borders that has consequences within its borders that the state reprehends. . . ."[46]

---

[40] Id.
[41] 243 US 66 (1917).
[42] Id at 88.
[43] 274 US 268, 276 (1927).
[44] *United States v Aluminum Co. of America*, 148 F2d 416 (2d Cir 1945).
[45] Id at 443–44.
[46] Id at 443.

At first sight, this conclusion looks rather disingenuous. The American Banana Company had made the same argument, only to have it rejected by Justice Holmes on the ground that what matters is where an act occurs, not where its effects are felt. None of the subsequent cases cited in *Alcoa* questioned this principle. They simply recognized that territoriality was broad enough to permit a state to regulate when only part of the conduct in question occurred within its borders. Judge Hand takes these statements out of context and uses them to establish a new ground for exercising prescriptive jurisdiction.

On the other hand, Hand's reasoning probably seemed quite natural in context. It was 1945, and territoriality was already giving way in other contexts. Traditional choice of law theory had been thoroughly dismantled by a realist critique demonstrating (among other things) that the territorial principle reflected neither what states do nor what they should necessarily want in multistate situations.[47] Learned Hand had made significant contributions to this debate.[48] It took a few more years before state courts accepted the critique,[49] but the Supreme Court had already done so in decisions recognizing that the Constitution permits a state to apply its law on grounds other than territoriality so long as the state has a legitimate "interest."[50] Similarly, the territorial limitation in customary international law had already been expanded to include effects in the landmark case of the *S.S. Lotus*.[51] And, of course, 1945 was the year of *International Shoe*,[52] in which the Supreme Court abandoned the strict territoriality of *Pennoyer* for a flexible approach to adjudi-

---

[47] See, for example, Walter Wheeler Cook, *Logical and Legal Bases for the Conflict of Laws* (Harvard, 1942); Ernest G. Lorenzen, *Selected Essays on the Conflict of Laws* (Yale, 1947); David F. Cavers, *A Critique of the Choice of Law Process*, 47 Harv L Rev 173 (1933). Many of the particular arguments made against the territorial principle are discussed in Part IIIB.

[48] See, for example, *Guinness v Miller*, 291 Fed 769 (SDNY 1923); *Scheer v Rockne Motors Corp.*, 68 F2d 942 (2d Cir 1934); and *Siegmann v Meyer*, 100 F2d 367 (2d Cir 1938). David Cavers thoughtfully analyzes Judge Hand's opinions in *The Two "Local Law" Theories*, 63 Harv L Rev 822 (1950).

[49] Rejection of the traditional approach to choice of law in the state courts is generally dated from the decision of the New York Court of Appeals in *Babcock v Jackson*, 12 NY2d 473, 240 NYS2d 743, 191 NE2d 279 (1963).

[50] *Pacific Employers Ins. Co. v Industrial Acc. Comm'n*, 306 US 493 (1939); *Alaska Packers Ass'n v Industrial Acc. Comm'n*, 294 US 532 (1935). See Paul Freund, *Chief Justice Stone and the Conflict of Laws*, 59 Harv L Rev 1210 (1946).

[51] PCIJ Ser A, No 10 (Judgment of September 7, 1927).

[52] *International Shoe Co. v Washington*, 326 US 310 (1945).

catory jurisdiction. Thus, in reinterpreting cases like *Thomsen v Cayser* and *Sisal Sales Corp.*, Learned Hand was simply doing what great judges have always done: reshaping the law to preserve its sense and rationality in light of evolving understandings.

The problem was that *Alcoa* went too far. Foreign acts deliberately affecting United States commerce are often intended also to affect foreign commerce—sometimes with the approval or even the encouragement of foreign governments. *Alcoa* thus did precisely what the territorial principle was designed to prevent: create conflicts with foreign nations that caused tension in international relations. To avoid these problems, courts in subsequent cases moderated the *Alcoa* doctrine by recognizing that deference to foreign law is sometimes appropriate despite effects in the United States.[53] Self-consciously maintaining the link to conflicts, these courts adopted a balancing approach similar to that in section 6 of the Restatement (Second) of Conflict of Laws.[54] This approach, or one substantially equivalent to it, was subsequently extended to the extraterritorial regulation of securities under the Securities Exchange Act.[55]

Note that these developments were confined to the lower courts. That is, while *Alcoa* has acquired a sort of quasi–Supreme Court status,[56] the Supreme Court has never actually endorsed either Hand's interpretation of the Sherman Act or its extension to the Securities Exchange Act.[57] The Supreme Court has, however, applied *Alcoa*'s reasoning to the Lanham Act. In *Steele v Bulova Watch Co.*,[58] Bulova alleged that Steele was making and selling watches

[53] Timberlane Lumber Co. v Bank of America, 549 F2d 597, 608–15 (9th Cir 1976); Mannington Mills, Inc. v Congoleum Corp., 595 F2d 1287, 1297–98 (3d Cir 1979).

[54] See *Timberlane Lumber Co.*, 549 F2d at 613–15 ("We believe that the field of conflict of laws presents the proper approach . . .").

[55] See Turley, 84 Nw U L Rev at 613–17 (cited in note 6).

[56] This is due not only to the fact that *Alcoa* is the seminal American case establishing effects-based jurisdiction, but also because the case was referred to the Second Circuit by the Supreme Court for lack of a quorum. See *Alcoa*, 149 F2d at 421.

[57] The Court has reaffirmed the holdings of *Pacific & Arctic Ry.*, *Thomsen v Cayser*, and *Sisal Sales Corp.* that a conspiracy to monopolize trade "is not outside the reach of the Sherman Act just because part of the conduct complained of occurs in foreign countries." See *Continental Ore Co. v Union Carbide & Carbon Corp.*, 370 US 690, 704 (1962) (citing *Alcoa*); *Pfizer, Inc. v India*, 434 US 308 (1978).

[58] 344 US 280 (1952).

stamped with its name. Steele defended on the ground that he produced the watches in Mexico. The Court held that Bulova could state a claim because Steele's acts had effects in the United States.[59]

More interesting was the Court's dismissal of Steele's invocation of the standard justification for the presumption against extraterritoriality: that United States law should be interpreted narrowly to avoid conflicts with Mexico. Noting that Steele's mark had already been nullified in Mexican proceedings, the Court explained that "there is thus no conflict which might afford petitioner a pretext that such relief would impugn foreign law."[60] This response, familiar in choice of law as "false conflict" analysis, suggests that deference to foreign law can be limited to cases where foreign law actually applies.

A number of the Court's other cases in this period similarly show the influence of the new thinking in jurisdiction and choice of law. *Vermilya-Brown Co. v Connell*[61] involved the applicability of the Fair Labor Standards Act on an American army base located on land leased from England. The Act regulates commerce among the states, defined to include "any Territory or possession of the United States."[62] The question was whether the leased base was a "possession"—a question made difficult, the Court observed, by the fact that possession is "not a word of art, descriptive of a recognized geographical or governmental entity."[63]

Of course, this would not have made the case difficult twenty or thirty years earlier: to the extent the statute was ambiguous, the Court would have interpreted it narrowly based on the presumption against extraterritoriality. Now, however, the Court ignored the presumption and—again speaking a familiar choice of law language—explained:[64]

> [O]ur duty as a Court is to construe the word "possession" as our judgment instructs us the lawmakers, within constitutional limits, would have done had they acted at the time of the legislation with the present situation in mind.

---

[59] Id at 286–88 (citing *Alcoa* and distinguishing *American Banana*).

[60] Id at 289.

[61] 335 US 377 (1948).

[62] 29 USC § 203(c).

[63] 335 US at 386.

[64] Id at 387–88, 390.

. . . .

[] It depends on the purpose of the statute. Where as here the purpose is to regulate labor relations in an area vital to our national life, it seems reasonable to interpret its provisions to have force where the nation has sole power, rather than to limit the coverage to sovereignty.

Most striking of all are the Court's decisions in *Lauritzen v Larsen*[65] and *Romero v International Terminal Operating Co.*,[66] both involving the extraterritorial scope of the Jones Act. These cases should have been easy. The Jones Act merely extends the Federal Employer's Liability Act (FELA) to seamen, and the Court had already ruled in *New York Central R.R. v Chisolm*[67] based on the presumption against extraterritoriality that the FELA applies only to injuries in the United States. In *Lauritzen* and *Romero*, the Court acknowledged *Chisolm*, and then ignored it—plainly influenced by developments in other areas to adopt a different approach.

In *Lauritzen*, a Danish seaman was injured on a Danish ship while in port in Cuba. He sued for compensation, basing his claim on the fact that he joined the crew in New York. Justice Jackson begins by observing that reading the unqualified language of the Jones Act literally will produce needless conflicts with other nations. The question is, what limits should the Court read into the law? Justice Jackson's answer has nothing to do with presumptions against extraterritoriality. Rather, in a scholarly opinion that canvasses many of the leading authorities on developments in jurisdiction and choice of law, he explains:[68]

> Maritime law, like our municipal law, has attempted to avoid or resolve conflicts between competing laws by ascertaining and valuing points of contact between the transaction and the states or governments whose competing laws are involved. The criteria, in general, appear to be arrived at from weighing of the significance of one or more connecting factors between the shipping transaction regulated and the national interest served by the assertion of authority.

After careful consideration of the relevant contacts, Justice Jackson found "an overwhelming preponderance" in favor of Danish law.[69]

---

[65] 345 US 571 (1953).

[66] 358 US 354 (1959).

[67] 268 US 29 (1925).

[68] 345 US at 582.

[69] Id at 592–93.

In *Romero*, the Court applied the "broad principles of choice of law . . . set forth in *Lauritzen*" to deny a similar claim where the injury occurred in United States waters.[70] Rather than a presumption against extraterritoriality, the Court held that "in the absence of a contrary congressional direction, we must apply those principles of choice of law that are consonant with the needs of a general federal maritime law and with due recognition of our self-regarding respect for the relevant interests of foreign nations in the regulation of maritime commerce as part of the legitimate concern of the international community."[71] Such concerns, Justice Frankfurter explained, are distorted by "mechanical" doctrines like *lex loci delicti*, and require a more discriminating investigation into the interests of the concerned nations.[72] On the particular facts in *Romero*, which involved a Spanish seaman injured on a Spanish ship docked in Hoboken, New Jersey, the Court found the shared nationality of the parties controlling: "The amount and type of recovery which a foreign seaman may receive from his foreign employer while sailing on a foreign ship should not depend on the wholly fortuitous circumstance of the place of injury."[73]

Brainerd Currie described *Lauritzen* and *Romero* as textbook illustrations of how properly to analyze a choice of law problem after discarding the traditional theory.[74] That claim may be debated, but clearly the Court in these decisions has abandoned the presumption against extraterritoriality. To be sure, neither case applies United States law (as *Romero* should have done if the Court were following the presumption). Nor does either case expressly repudiate *American Banana* or any of the cases following it. Nevertheless, the Court's analysis fundamentally rejects both the presumption against extraterritoriality and its premises.

While the evolution of the law respecting extraterritorial regulation in these cases tracks developments in jurisdiction and choice of law generally, in some areas of substantive law this process of updating failed to occur. The question of extraterritorial labor regulation, for example, was first raised in 1918, in *Sandberg v*

---

[70] 358 US at 382–84.

[71] Id at 382–83.

[72] Id at 383–84.

[73] Id at 384.

[74] Brainerd Currie, *Selected Essays on the Conflict of Laws* 361–75 (Duke, 1963).

McDonald.[75] British sailors sued their British vessel while in an American port, seeking to have wage advances declared unlawful under the Seaman's Act of 1915. The Court easily disposed of their claim, citing *American Banana* for the proposition that, absent clear language to the contrary, the Act is presumed to cover only contracts made in the United States.[76]

Sandberg was the first in a line of cases construing federal labor laws narrowly in accordance with the traditional rule of territoriality. *Jackson v S.S. "Archimedes"*[77] relied on *Sandberg* and *American Banana* to hold the Merchant Marine Act of 1920 inapplicable to contracts made outside the United States. *Benz v Compania Naveriera Hidalgo, S.A.*[78] relied on *Sandberg* and *Jackson* to withhold the protection of the Labor Management Relations Act from foreign seamen having a contract dispute with their foreign vessel. *McCulloch v Sociedad Nacional*[79] relied on Benz in giving the same interpretation to the National Labor Relations Act. Finally, *Windward Shipping Ltd. v American Radio Ass'n*[80] relied on *Benz* and *McCulloch* in holding that the Labor Management Relations Act does not reach contract disputes between foreign seamen and foreign employers even when American unions participate in order to protect American jobs and wages.

Other labor cases followed suit. *Foley Bros. v Filardo,*[81] for example, relied on the presumption against extraterritoriality to deny a claim under the Eight Hour Law by American citizens working in Iraq and Iran. Justice Reed did not cite any of the cases discussed above, instead finding the presumption against extraterritoriality in *Blackmer v United States*, a rare case in which the presumption was deemed adequately rebutted.[82]

The Court's treatment of the presumption against extraterritoriality in these labor cases is perfunctory. There is no rethinking

---

[75] 248 US 185 (1918).

[76] Id at 195–96.

[77] 275 US 463, 466–68 (1928).

[78] 353 US 138, 144–47 (1957).

[79] 372 US 10, 18–22 (1963).

[80] 415 US 104, 109–15 (1974).

[81] 336 US 281, 285–86 (1949).

[82] 284 US 421 (1932). *Blackmer* upheld service of a subpoena on an American citizen living abroad under a statute expressly providing for such service.

going on here, no process of reevaluating the justification for the presumption in light of subsequent developments. Most of the opinions are short and merely restate and apply the *American Banana* rule (though citation to *American Banana* itself is soon replaced by citations to later cases applying it). The few opinions that bother to explain why a presumption against extraterritoriality makes sense merely repeat Justice Holmes's claim that the presumption is needed to avoid conflict and discord in the "delicate field of international relations."[83]

II

This, then, was the somewhat confused state of the law when the Court granted certiorari in *Aramco*. The facts of the case are straightforward: Ali Boureslan, a naturalized United States citizen born in Lebanon, was hired in Texas by a subsidiary of Aramco, the Aramco Service Company (ASC); both ASC and Aramco are Delaware corporations. After working for ASC for approximately a year, Boureslan requested a transfer to Aramco's office in Saudi Arabia, where he worked until he was discharged in 1984. Boureslan sued Aramco and ASC, alleging that he was fired because of his race, religion, and national origin. The district court dismissed on the ground that Title VII does not protect citizens employed abroad. The court of appeals affirmed en banc.

The Supreme Court also affirmed, resting its decision on the "longstanding principle of American law 'that legislation of Congress, unless a contrary intent appears, is meant to apply only within the territorial jurisdiction of the United States.'"[84] This

---

[83] *Benz v Compania Naviero Hidalgo*, 353 US at 146–47. See also *McCulloch v Sociedad Nacional*, 372 US at 21–22 (quoting *Benz*); *Windward Shipping Co.*, 415 US at 110–11 (same). It is tempting to explain the Court's adherence to the presumption against extraterritoriality in the labor context as motivated by concern for the ability of American employers to compete abroad. I find this "realist" explanation rather unrealistic, however. If that were the Court's motivation, one would have expected it to say so at some point. None of the opinions makes such an argument, and it seems unlikely that so many judges were moved silently by this consideration for 40 or 50 years. As a general matter, I find invisible-hand explanations dubious and unpersuasive—particularly in a post-realist world where it is proper and acceptable to make policy arguments openly. Note also that, as a normative matter, it is difficult to justify giving more protection to American companies operating abroad than to those operating within the United States but facing foreign competition. On balance, the more "realistic" explanation is that the labor cases are a product of unreflective judging. Cf. Turley, 84 Nw U L Rev at 638–55 (cited in note 6).

[84] 111 S Ct at 1230 (quoting *Foley Bros.*, 336 US at 285).

presumption, the Court explained, "serves to protect against unintended clashes between our laws and those of other nations which could result in international discord."[85] For authority, Chief Justice Rehnquist selected *Foley Bros.*, *Benz*, and *McCulloch*.

The Court had little trouble distinguishing the various cases rejecting the presumption against extraterritoriality because, with one exception, it simply ignored them. The parties and *amici* had cited these decisions, so it is not as if the Court was not aware of the inconsistencies. The choice not to mention the antitrust cases is perhaps forgivable because, as noted above, these are lower court decisions that have not been expressly endorsed by the Supreme Court itself.[86] The decision similarly to ignore *Vermilya-Brown*, *Lauritzen*, and *Romero* is harder to explain.

The Court did address the impact of *Steele v Bulova Watch Co.*, explaining that because the Lanham Act expressly reaches "all commerce" that Congress may lawfully regulate, "the Court in *Steele* concluded that Congress intended that the statute apply abroad."[87] Chief Justice Rehnquist does not support this reading of *Steele* with a citation to the case—perhaps because *Steele* did not make much of this fact. Rather, as noted above, the Court in *Steele* based its decision on the reasoning of the antitrust cases, holding that "[u]nlawful effects in this country . . . are often decisive" and that American law may therefore be applied if the particular facts reveal no conflict with foreign law.[88]

In any event, establishing a presumption against extraterritorial applications did not fully dispose of Boureslan's claim, for he and the EEOC made a strong argument that the presumption was rebutted in Title VII. Plaintiffs noted first that Title VII prohibits discriminatory acts by employers engaged in "commerce," defined to include activity "between a State and any place outside thereof." Because the definition of state already includes territories and the District of Columbia, they argued, "any place outside thereof" must refer to foreign commerce. Aramco responded that this simply establishes a jurisdictional nexus under the commerce clause

[85] Id.

[86] See supra notes 56–57 and accompanying text.

[87] 111 S Ct at 1232–33.

[88] 344 US at 288–89; see supra notes 58–60.

and has nothing to do with the scope of liability. The Court found it unnecessary to choose between these interpretations:[89]

> Each is plausible, but no more persuasive than that. The language relied upon by petitioners—and it is they who must make the affirmative showing—is ambiguous, and does not speak directly to the question presented here. The intent of Congress as to the extraterritorial application of this statute must be deduced by inference from boilerplate language which can be found in any number of congressional acts, none of which have ever been held to apply overseas.

Plaintiffs' best argument was based on Title VII's so-called alien exemption, which provides that the statute "shall not apply to an employer with respect to the employment of aliens outside any State."[90] Reasoning that there would have been no need to exempt aliens abroad unless the statute had extraterritorial applications, plaintiffs argued that the logical inference is that Title VII protects Americans employed "outside any State."

The Court disagreed, explaining that if Title VII extends to employers overseas "we see no way of distinguishing in its application between United States employers and foreign employers. Thus, a French employer of a United States citizen in France would be subject to Title VII—a result at which even [plaintiffs] balk."[91] If Congress had contemplated extraterritorial applications, Chief Justice Rehnquist continued, it would have included provisions for handling conflicts with foreign laws and procedures: "Without clearer evidence of congressional intent, we are unwilling to ascribe to that body a policy which would raise difficult issues of international law by imposing this country's employment-discrimination regime upon foreign corporations operating in foreign commerce."[92]

Finally, plaintiffs argued that the Court should defer to EEOC guidelines interpreting Title VII to protect Americans employed abroad. The Court responded that these guidelines have little authority because the EEOC has no formal rulemaking power and because the agency's early interpretations did not refer to extrater-

---

[89] 111 S Ct at 1231–32.

[90] 42 USC § 2000e-1.

[91] Id at 1234.

[92] Id.

ritorial applications. Having thus diminished the importance of the guidelines, the Court concluded that "even when considered in combination with [plaintiffs'] other arguments, the EEOC's interpretation is insufficiently weighty to overcome the presumption against extraterritorial application."[93]

Justice Scalia concurred separately in order to make clear his view that the EEOC is entitled to as much deference as any other agency. But, he concluded, given the requirement that extraterritorial applications be clearly expressed, "it is in my view not reasonable to give effect to mere implications from the statutory language as the EEOC has done."[94]

Justice Marshall dissented, joined by Justices Blackmun and Stevens. Rather than challenge the presumption against extraterritoriality, Justice Marshall argued that the Court's decisions actually establish two distinct doctrines. Cases like *Foley Bros.* establish a gap-filling presumption to be used if congressional intent remains unclear after traditional methods of interpretation are exhausted.[95] Cases like *McCulloch* and *Benz*, in contrast, recognize a strong clear statement principle to be used where extraterritorial applications threaten executive control over foreign affairs.[96] Because "[n]othing nearly so dramatic is at stake when Congress merely seeks to regulate the conduct of United States nationals abroad,"[97] only the weaker presumption of *Foley Bros.* applies. But that principle never comes into play with Title VII, because the provisions cited by plaintiff clearly indicate that Congress intended to protect Americans employed abroad.[98]

III

Aramco is a disappointing and unsatisfactory decision. The problem is not just that the Court ignored inconsistencies in existing case law and failed to justify (or even to explain) such a strong presumption. It is more that the entire history and development of

---

[93] Id at 1235.
[94] Id at 1237.
[95] Id.
[96] Id at 1239.
[97] Id.
[98] Id at 1240–46.

the doctrine suggested analyzing the case differently. As we have seen, the strict territorial definition of jurisdiction was part of a nineteenth-century system for regulating intersovereign relations that has been abandoned in every area in which it was employed. The process began in conflict of laws, with a vigorous realist critique that was picked up first by the Supreme Court, in cases interpreting the full faith and credit clause, and later by the states.[99] Territoriality was then abandoned in adjudicatory jurisdiction beginning with *International Shoe*, and in American foreign relations law beginning with *Alcoa*. The Court's more recent cases on the extraterritorial application of federal statutes begin to reflect these developments, but none of them contains the sort of unequivocal declaration needed to lay the presumption against extraterritoriality to rest. *Aramco* thus presented the Court with a perfect opportunity to complete the process of modernization begun in *Vermilya-Brown*, *Steele*, *Lauritzen*, and *Romero*. Instead, the Court slipped back to the nineteenth century, seemingly unaware that it was doing so.

It is possible, of course, that the decision in *Aramco* simply reflects the current Supreme Court's hostility to civil rights generally and employment discrimination claims in particular. On this view, the Court's easy acceptance of the presumption against extraterritoriality expresses nothing more than indifference to the doctrinal question in the face of political distractions. But while such a reading is plausible (certainly the Court's distaste for antidiscrimination law seems palpable enough), it does not mean that we can ignore the opinion. Even a Court determined to reach the result in *Aramco* could have shown a better grasp of developments in this area, suggesting that the Court really does not understand the issues. Moreover, the broad and unequivocal language of the *Aramco* opinion will make it difficult to ignore in subsequent cases that do not involve civil rights. So whatever the Court's underlying objectives or motivations, its handling of the problem of extraterritoriality remains problematic.

At the same time, the suggestion that the Court should have used *Aramco* to repudiate the presumption against extraterritoriality

---

[99] The traditional approach to choice of law has not been abandoned in all of the states but is still followed in a (steadily shrinking) number of them. See Herma Hill Kay, *Theory into Practice: Choice of Law in the Courts*, 34 Mercer L Rev 521, 582–84 (1983); P. John Kozyris & Symeon C. Symeonides, *Choice of Law in the American Courts in 1989: An Overview*, 38 Am J Comp L 601, 602–04 (1990).

remains incomplete for at least two reasons. First, more needs to be said about why territoriality is so bad. Yes, the fact that territoriality has been abandoned in so many areas suggests that it must have real disadvantages. But legal evolution is not always progressive. Perhaps territoriality still provides the best definition of legislative jurisdiction, and the Supreme Court has the right idea in pushing its restoration.

Second, the desirability of abandoning the presumption against extraterritoriality depends on what is to replace it. But what will that be? The cases rejecting the presumption discussed in Part I employ several methods. Nor is there a clearer consensus in other areas. Rather, traditional choice of law rules have been replaced by at least six alternatives;[100] *Pennoyer* has been displaced by an uncertain minimum contacts approach;[101] and international law remains in flux, though the trend appears to favor some form of balancing.[102] Before abandoning the presumption against extraterritoriality, then, we need to think about how multinational cases should be handled.

A

The first step in addressing these concerns is to make sure we understand the problem. Everyone agrees that extraterritorial scope is a question of congressional intent.[103] But what kind of question? Justice Holmes treated it as a straightforward choice of law question, as did Learned Hand and Justices Jackson and Frankfurter. Yet this connection seems somehow to have gotten lost by the time of *Aramco*. As we shall see below, not only was Holmes correct, but understanding why he was correct helps to frame the issue properly and points the way toward a more satisfying resolution.

---

[100] See Herma Hill Kay, 34 Mercer L Rev 521 (cited in note 99).

[101] See, for example, *Asahi Metal Indus. Co. v Superior Court*, 480 US 102 (1987).

[102] See Ian Brownlie, *Principles of Public International Law* 309–11 (Clarendon, 4th ed, 1990); Restatement (Third) of the Foreign Relations Law of the United States §§ 401–423 (1986); Gary Born & David Westin, *International Civil Litigation in United States Courts* 432–88 (Deventer, 1989).

[103] A statement to this effect introduces the Supreme Court's analysis in all the cases discussed in Part I. See, for example, *Aramco*, 111 S Ct at 1230; *Benz*, 353 US at 142; *Steele*, 344 US at 282–83; *Blackmer*, 284 US at 437. See also Brilmayer, 50 L & Contemp Probs at 14 (cited in note 31).

Consider a simple choice of law problem involving two states within the United States. Suppose, for instance, that Boureslan was fired by ASC while still working in Texas and that he brought a wrongful discharge claim under Delaware law. The question would be whether Delaware gives Boureslan a cause of action in this situation.

Answering this question would be easy if Delaware law expressly stated its scope in multistate cases—for example, by listing the contact or contacts with Delaware necessary to state a claim. We can probably assume, however, that the statute is silent in this regard; most laws are silent when it comes to multistate cases, because lawmakers typically work with wholly domestic situations in mind. The court must therefore define the law's multistate reach through interpretation. The interpretive problem has two levels. First, there is the question of what the Constitution permits the Delaware legislature to do. Second, within the range of constitutional possibilities, there is the question of what the legislature has done—or, since legislators may not have thought about the problem, what a court should do.

Interpreting the statute may still be easy if the constitutional constraints on legislative action are sufficiently restrictive. Under traditional territorial theory, for example, a state can apply its law only if the wrongful act occurs within its borders. Consequently, if territoriality is the constitutional rule, statutory silence will not matter much because the potential scope of state laws will necessarily be confined to narrowly defined situations.

As noted above, however, the Court long ago repudiated this view and allowed states considerably greater leeway in legislating.[104] Basically, a state can exercise prescriptive jurisdiction whenever it has a contact that might implicate a material domestic policy. Thus, a state can apply its law not only if acts occur within the state, but also if the effects of those acts are felt there, if the party to be burdened is from the state, or if the party to be benefited is from the state and the burdened party has minimal contacts with it.[105]

---

[104] See supra note 50 and accompanying text. The reasons for abandoning territoriality and expanding the scope of adjudicatory and prescriptive jurisdiction are discussed infra notes 111–23 and accompanying text. For now, the important point to see is how relaxing these constraints shapes the interpretive problem before the court.

[105] See, for example, *Allstate Ins. Co. v Hague*, 449 US 302 (1981); *Clay v Sun Ins. Office*,

It makes sense to assume that lawmakers do not intend to violate the Constitution, at least not unless the language of a statute makes this conclusion unavoidable. Accordingly, we can presume that a law applies only when the state has constitutionally sufficient contacts. Does it follow that the law applies whenever the state has such contacts? Such an interpretation is consistent with a plain meaning approach to statutory construction, something the present Supreme Court seems generally to favor.[106] The legislature used unqualified language. And while it may be permissible to read in limitations required by fundamental law, if there are to be further qualifications on matters within legislative discretion, the legislature must say so in the statute's text.

The problem with plain meaning in this context is that it maximizes conflicts with other states—which is why only one court has ever taken this position.[107] Instead, judges generally assume that they can and should establish further limitations on the scope of state laws in multistate cases. These may then be overturned by the legislature if lawmakers conclude that the court made a mistake.

This process of specifying limitations is merely the familiar one of defining the elements of a claim. Laws are targeted at particular problems. My hypothetical wrongful discharge statute, for example, targets a particular employment practice and gives victims an opportunity to obtain relief. To recover, the claimant must demonstrate that his or her situation is one of those targeted by the legislation: Was the plaintiff an employee of the defendant? Was she or he discharged? Was the discharge unjustified? Plaintiff can recover under the law only by alleging facts sufficient to satisfy these requirements, whatever they may be.

Ltd., 377 US 179 (1964); *Watson v Employers Liab. Assur. Corp.*, 348 US 66 (1954). See generally Lea Brilmayer et al., *An Introduction to Jurisdiction in the American Federal System* 267–73 (Michie, 1986). The question whether a state may apply its law solely because the party invoking that law is a resident is unsettled. Compare *John Hancock Mutual Life Ins. Co. v Yates*, 299 US 178 (1936) (postoccurence change of residence alone is insufficient to justify applying forum law), with *Phillips Petroleum Co. v Shutts*, 472 US 797 (1985) (Kansas can apply its law to leases made in Kansas or to leases made by Kansas residents).

[106] See Frederick Schauer, *Statutory Construction and the Coordinating Function of Plain Meaning*, 1990 Supreme Court Review 231.

[107] See *Arnett v Thompson*, 433 SW2d 109, 113 (Ky 1968); Robert Sedler, *Judicial Method Is "Alive and Well": The Kentucky Approach to Choice of Law in Interstate Automobile Accidents*, 61 Ky L J 378 (1973). When it comes to adjudicatory jurisdiction, in contrast, many states interpret long-arm statutes to permit service to the extent permitted by the Due Process Clause. See John Cound, Jack Friedenthal, Arthur Miller & John Sexton, *Civil Procedure: Cases and Materials* 101 (West, 5th ed 1989).

Territorial scope is an aspect of this inquiry, one element of the claim. If laws are to be interpreted not to reach as far as the Constitution permits, we must define the more limited class of persons or conduct covered: Does the law protect only persons employed by Delaware companies? Does it protect anyone employed or fired in Delaware? Does it protect Delaware citizens regardless of where they are employed or fired? What, in other words, are the defining spatial characteristics or other contacts with the state required to establish a claim under this statute?

We will return to this question in a moment. For now, the important point to see is that the nature and structure of the problem does not change if we move from an interstate to an international situation. The particular policies involved may be different, and the process of defining limits is undoubtedly more complex because of questions of national pride, differences in language and culture, and the absence of formal enforcement mechanisms. But the basic question is the same: Congress has enacted a statute without specifying its reach in multinational situations. To interpret such unqualified language literally would make the statute universally applicable, violating international law and possibly also due process constraints on federal lawmaking.[108] Even with these limits, the statute is potentially applicable in an enormous number of cases, for international constraints on jurisdiction to prescribe are at least as permissive as those found in domestic law.[109] As in the domestic context, then, interpreting American law to reach as far as the Constitution or international law permits will generate a great many conflicts with other nations, and it makes sense to read some further limitation into the statute.

Put another way, federal courts in international cases face a task similar to that faced by state courts in interstate cases. Defining the scope of American law in cases with multinational contacts is, as Justice Holmes recognized, a choice of law problem. The federal

---

[108] See Lea Brilmayer & Charles Norchi, *Federal Extraterritoriality and Fifth Amendment Due Process*, 105 Harv L Rev 1217 (1992).

[109] See Restatement (Third) of the Foreign Relations Law of the United States §§ 401–402. On their face, the limits imposed by foreign relations law appear identical to those found in domestic law, except that a nation can clearly apply its law solely because the victim is one of its citizens in limited circumstances. Compare note 105 supra. But these are formal limitations; foreign relations law is considerably more flexible in practice and in this sense may actually be broader than domestic law. See Matthias Herdegan, *Book Review*, 39 Am J Comp L 206, 209–10 (1991).

courts must therefore address problems that have long troubled
their state counterparts and attempt to fashion a workable choice
of law system.[110]

B

Now consider the question deferred above: how should courts
define the limits of American law in multinational cases? This
brings us back to territoriality, which is, after all, one possible
approach to the problem. The Court in *Aramco* held that federal
statutes should be interpreted to apply only when the conduct
being regulated occurs in the United States. This simultaneously
defines the scope of American law and provides a rule to resolve
conflicts with foreign law: if the conduct at issue occurred abroad,
American law does not apply; if it occurred in the United States,
American law applies notwithstanding another nation's inconsistent law. The question is whether this is a sensible choice of law
regime.

Understanding the problem as one of choice of law makes this
question seem very surprising indeed: its first important choice of
law case in more than 30 years (since *Romero*), and the United States
Supreme Court actually reverted to Joseph Beale's First Restatement! For most scholars in the field, even those unhappy with
the modern alternatives, this is as "startling" a proposition as its
opposite (that this approach should not be used) was to Justice
Holmes in 1904.[111] Nonetheless, the decision in *Aramco* makes it
necessary briefly to recount the reasons Beale's approach was abandoned.

The first point to understand is that territoriality did not origi-
nate in choice of law as a reflective policy choice among plausible
alternatives. The territorial principle emerged in the sixteenth
century as the defining characteristic of sovereignty. It served an
important political need at the time, justifying local control as the

---

[110] My earlier observation about how choice of law, adjudicatory jurisdiction, and public
international law are similar remains true. See supra Part IB. Thus, while *Aramco* involves
private law enforcement, the analysis would be the same if the question was the authority
of public agencies to act or of courts to adjudicate. These are all activities defined by law.
Insofar as the question is whether an actor has rights or can act in cases with international
contacts, it is first and foremost a question of interpreting the law on which they rely. This,
in turn, requires defining the scope of these laws to determine when there is a conflict, and
developing principles of accommodation to resolve whatever conflicts arise.

[111] See *American Banana*, 213 US at 355 (quoted supra note 19).

hold of the Papacy and the Holy Roman Empire weakened in medieval Europe. Driven by this need, and accompanying the rise of the nation-state, the stature of territoriality grew until it became the exclusive justification for any exercise of state power—the argument being that since only the sovereign can control what happens in its territory, no other state can have any legitimate interest or concern in such matters.[112] One sees this idea clearly expressed, for example, in the excerpts quoted above from Story's *Commentaries* and Marshall's opinion in *The Schooner Exchange*.[113]

By the early twentieth century, the notion of territorial exclusivity had come to seem increasingly implausible. As noted above, there always were exceptions to the territorial principle: situations in which states regulated acts occurring elsewhere or persons or property outside the state.[114] For a long time, these exceptions were treated as nothing more than that, and no one asked whether their existence challenged the validity of territoriality. The same was true of various "escape devices" (like public policy and renvoi) that were frequently used to avoid the territorial principle. This all changed with the emergence of legal realism, however, as commentators finally examined the exceptions and began to question whether they really were exceptions or whether they indicated the need for an altogether different understanding of sovereignty.[115]

The realists drew attention to another, more profound failing of the territorial principle. Suppose Pat lives in the United States and owns Whiteacre in Canada. Disposition of Pat's rights in that property by either nation will necessarily intrude on the supposedly exclusive sovereignty of the other. If a Canadian court awards Whiteacre to Terry, Pat's rights are affected even though Pat is in the United States; if an American court makes this award, Canada's control over land situated within its borders is diminished. This is

---

[112] See Yntema, 2 Am J Comp L at 305–08 (cited in note 28) (discussing influence of Bodin, Grotius, Huber, and Story); Lorenzen, *Selected Essays* at 138–39 (cited in note 47); Joel Paul, *Comity in International Law*, 32 Harv Int'l L J 1, 14–17 (1991).

[113] See supra notes 23, 29 and accompanying text.

[114] See supra note 35 and accompanying text.

[115] See, for example, Lorenzen, *Territoriality, Public Policy and the Conflict of Laws*, 33 Yale L J 736 (1924), reprinted in Lorenzen, *Selected Essays* at 1–18 (cited in note 47). This reexamination of territoriality was not a purely intellectual development, but had a material basis as well. In particular, the development of an increasingly integrated international market system and the growth of multinational firms helped focus intellectual energy on problems with the formal territorial system.

unavoidable—a necessary consequence of the fact that disposing
of property affects persons who have rights to that property and
vice versa.[116] For a long time, courts and commentators denied that
there was any inconsistency between the principle of territoriality
and the fact of extraterritorial effects—usually by *ipse dixit*.[117] Eventually, however, this view yielded to reality and the conclusion
that limitations on state power "are not based upon, nor are they
derivable from, any uniform theory of territoriality."[118]

This investigation of the territorial principle—itself merely a
facet of the larger realist critique—changed the way we think about
state power in a number of ways, two of which are relevant for
present purposes. First, the necessitarianism of nineteenth-century
thinking was abandoned. Courts and commentators no longer
talked as if the power to regulate follows naturally and inevitably
from some self-evident theory. Ernest Lorenzen expressed the new
understanding:[119]

> Nothing can be gained by hiding the truth and making it appear
> that certain rules govern in the nature of things . . . . The
> common law has not hidden in its bosom a logical set of rules
> which can be derived from its notion of territoriality. Sound
> progress in this field of law, as in all other departments of
> knowledge, can be made only if the actual facts be faced, which
> show that the adoption of the one rule or the other depends
> entirely upon considerations of policy which each sovereign
> state must determine for itself.

Second, as Lorenzen suggests, the understanding of when a state
could properly assert jurisdiction was revised to conform to practice and reexplained in this light. Territoriality was abandoned and
the theory of "interests" emerged—not Brainerd Currie's governmental interest analysis, which came later and built on these earlier
developments, but the idea that a state may exercise authority over
persons or acts that impinge on its sphere of legitimate concern.
This includes territoriality, since a state is legitimately concerned

---

[116] See Walter Wheeler Cook, *Logical and Legal Bases* at 48–70 (cited in note 47).

[117] See, for example, *Pennoyer v Neff*, 5 Otto 714, 723 (1877) ("To any influence exerted
in this way . . . no objection can be justly taken" because "the exercise of this jurisdiction
in no manner interferes with the supreme control [of] the state within which [the persons
or property are] situated.").

[118] Lorenzen, *Selected Essays* at 9 (cited in note 47).

[119] Id at 11.

with what happens in its territory. But it also includes such matters as the regulation or protection of nationals and the prevention or encouragement of consequences within the state.

Defining jurisdiction this way may seem tautological, and it is—but only from the perspective of one looking for an a priori theory to explain state power. The post-realist understanding of prescriptive and adjudicatory jurisdiction is based instead on recognition that limits on state power vis-à-vis other states are a function of practice and convention. The legitimate grounds for exercising power, in other words, are those that states recognize as legitimate, and this includes grounds other than controlling acts within one's borders.

These were the arguments that led to the relaxation of constitutional and international limitations on extraterritoriality discussed above.[120] It seems unlikely that the Supreme Court in *Aramco* meant either to question these developments or to suggest that territoriality defines the complete scope of national power. Rather, the Court apparently favors territoriality on the policy level, as a matter of expediency. Expanding the grounds for asserting jurisdiction increases the number of situations in which conflicts may potentially arise, making it necessary to construct some system to identify and resolve them. This being so, one might still defend territoriality's presumptively favored status on the ground that it remains useful to reduce and resolve the conflicts that will otherwise ensue. This, in fact, appears to be the position of the Court in *Aramco*. The justices recognize Congress's broad power to legislate extraterritorially, but say that (absent clear language to the contrary) we should assume that federal laws apply only within the territorial jurisdiction of the United States "to protect against unintended clashes between our laws and those of other nations which could result in international discord."[121]

Defending territoriality on this ground, however, is scarcely more persuasive than defending it on the ground that sovereignty is limited as a matter of definition to control over acts within one's borders. Indeed, while much of modern conflicts theory remains unsettled, if anything is established, it is that across-the-board ter-

---

[120] See supra notes 47–52, 99 and accompanying text.

[121] 111 S Ct at 1230.

ritoriality is a poor system for resolving conflicts.[122] The argument is simple: because laws are enacted for reasons, they should be interpreted in light of their objectives. It follows that extraterritorial application may make sense whenever the aim of a law is to prevent or encourage consequences that may be caused by acts outside the state, or to protect a class of persons who may need protection for or from things that happen outside the state. Put another way, it may make sense to apply a law to acts outside the state whenever the fact that these acts occurred outside the state is irrelevant to achieving the law's domestic objective.[123]

This understanding suggests a number of flaws in the *Aramco* Court's rationale for favoring territoriality, First, territoriality does not avoid all conflicts. A conflict exists whenever the facts in a particular case affect the policies of more than one nation, and these policies are inconsistent. There are cases in which the United States has an interest in applying its laws to acts abroad and cases in which foreign nations have an interest in applying their laws to acts that occur here. A territorial approach does not avoid such conflicts. It simply resolves them a particular way: by preferring the law of the place where the acts occurred. But this assumes that territorial interests always take precedence—an assumption that has yet to be explained and that certainly is not obvious.

Second, at least some of these cases will present what Brainerd Currie called "false conflicts"[124]—that is, cases where the fact that conduct occurred in the United States creates no interest in applying American law, or the fact that conduct occurred abroad creates no interest in applying foreign law. Applying the law of the place where conduct occurred in such cases needlessly subordinates the law and policy of the other nation. To illustrate, suppose that two corporations take action in the United States that will give

---

[122] A string cite here could go on for pages. The classic treatment of the point is Brainerd Currie's, see *Selected Essays* at 77–187 (cited in note 74). Even commentators unpersuaded to adopt Currie's alternative approach generally concede the effectiveness of his critique of territoriality.

[123] The point is not that it makes sense for a nation to apply its law in *all* such cases. As discussed below, the fact that there is a conflict with international law or with the domestic law of another nation, or the desire to advance certain multinational policies, may lead the court not to apply forum law. See Part IIIC infra. The point here is simply that a blanket assumption that a law should not apply whenever the acts in dispute occurred abroad does *not* make sense.

[124] Currie, *Selected Essays* at 81–121 (cited in note 74).

them a monopoly in some foreign market but have no effect on the American market. The mere fact that they acted here need not trigger antitrust liability, for as Learned Hand recognized in *Alcoa*, the object of the Sherman Act is to protect competition in American markets. Thus, while the Sherman Act might come into play if United States trade was restrained, there is no reason to apply American law in the absence of such an effect. On the contrary, if the nation whose market is affected would permit the monopoly, applying American law constitutes needless interference.[125]

There are also false conflicts involving acts abroad that only the United States is interested in regulating. *Steele v Bulova Watch Co.* was such a case, since (according to its own courts) Mexico had no interest in protecting Steele's use of Bulova's name even though he was manufacturing watches in Mexico.[126] Moreover, since foreign law is as diverse in its purposes as American law, there should be many instances in which the fact that action was taken in a foreign nation gives that nation no interest in regulating the action or in preventing the United State from doing so.

Third, while restricting American law to conduct in the United States does avoid some conflicts, it does so in a manner that is often arbitrary. Once again, this is true for any law whose purpose focuses on consequences or on protecting a class of individuals. To restrict such laws to acts committed within the territorial limits of the United States may avoid some conflicts, but in a senseless fashion: lopping off a portion of the cases in which the law sensibly applies for reasons having nothing to do with attaining its objectives. The Court might just as well say that to avoid conflicts American law shall not apply whenever the events that give rise to a claim occur on Monday, Tuesday, or Wednesday.

---

[125] As several colleagues have observed, nations sometimes assert sovereignty without regard for any material policy concerns—taking offense at another nation's effort to enforce legal regulation simply because it relates to acts in its territory. In this sense, I am told, interstate and international cases may differ

As a descriptive matter, this is undoubtedly correct. There was a time, however, when states too took offense at another state's imposition of legal consequences for acts within their borders. If that attitude has faded, it is partly because territoriality has been abandoned as the exclusive basis for exercising sovereignty. This difference between international and interstate cases is thus itself a vestige of the territorial system in the international context. But the hold of territoriality has weakened considerably over the last fifty years, and I see no reason to doubt the continuation of that trend. My argument includes a normative dimension in that I am suggesting that courts give no weight to such non-policy based assertions of prescriptive jurisdiction.

[126] See supra notes 58–60 and accompanying text.

The point, more generally, is that using the territorial principle to define the limits of all American laws is like trying to fit pegs of many different shapes into the same square hole. For some laws, territorial limits make sense. The United States is obviously interested in regulating activity in the United States, and the applicability of many laws should be triggered and limited by whether conduct occurred here. But not all laws, and not all the time.

C

1. This brings us to the question of alternatives. Grant that territoriality has these disadvantages, how should courts define the limits of American law in multinational cases? A complete answer to this question is, unfortunately, beyond the scope of this article, but I do want to suggest a way to think about it. The basic premise, implied already in the analysis above, is that the court should determine what policy a law was enacted to achieve in wholly domestic cases and ask whether there are connections between the case and the nation implicating that policy. If the purpose of the Sherman Act is to preserve a competitive market, the critical contact in triggering antitrust liability is not where the acts in question occur, but whether these acts affect American markets. If Congress adopted worker's compensation in the FELA and Jones Act to protect injured railroad and maritime workers, what matters is not where a claimant was injured, but whether he or she is within the class of workers Congress sought to protect, presumably United States residents (including resident aliens[127]) and employees of American companies. The alternative to territoriality, in other words, is to make the applicability of American law turn on whether the contacts with the United States—be they the residence or nationality of the parties, the place where the conduct occurred, or the place where its effects were felt—are relevant in terms of the domestic policy underlying the law in question.

The limiting principle implicit in this approach is that American law should apply only when this advances the policies that led Congress to pass a statute for wholly domestic cases. Its justification is straightforward. On the one hand, the positive law of a

---

[127] For an argument in favor of extending the protections of United States law to resident aliens, see Alex Aleinikoff, *Citizens, Aliens, Membership and the Constitution*, 7 Const Comm 9 (1990).

nation reflects the judgment of that nation's lawmakers about the best way to organize society. On the other hand, these lawmakers presumably recognize that lawmakers in other nations may have different views about what is best. The presumption that American law may apply whenever its underlying domestic policy is affected reflects the former principle.[128] The presumption that it does not apply when domestic policy is not affected reflects the latter. Presuming that a nation's law reaches only cases affecting domestic policy thus avoids conflicts while faciliting each nation's ability to achieve its domestic objectives.

This justification shares with territoriality the assumption that United States law should be confined to situations in which the United States has a genuine stake. The difference is that, whereas territoriality assumes that lawmakers are always most concerned with regulating conduct within the nation's borders, the principle of interpretation discussed above looks to the actual policies underlying particular laws. Since some laws have objectives that are not territorially based, there is no reason to interpret them with a territorial rule.

Note that in determining what contacts make a particular law applicable, the court is not limited to identifying a single purpose. Many laws have several objectives, in which case a number of contacts with the United States may make them applicable. Title VII, for example, both protects specified classes of individuals and deters conduct deemed wrongful and undesirable. Consequently, under the approach described above, Title VII would apply either when a United States resident is a victim of impermissible discrimination or when the discriminatory conduct occurs within the United States.

Note also that this approach does not entail forgoing clear rules for some hopelessly confusing, ad-hoc alternative. Rather, the choice is between an approach that interprets every statute according to a territorial rule, and an approach in which different statutes are interpreted according to different rules, depending on their purpose. Both approaches read an implied term into laws that are silent with respect to extraterritorial scope. Applying a

---

[128] This formulation is qualified by "may" because, as discussed below, the fact that another nation's law also applies should sometimes lead the courts to apply foreign law. See infra Part IIIC(3).

territorial rule to the Sherman Act is like reading it to proscribe "every contract in restraint of trade that is made in this country." My point is simply that for many laws, a different implied limitation makes more sense. It makes more sense, for example, to read the Sherman Act to prohibit "every contract that restrains trade in the United States." And instead of implying that workers must be injured in the United States to recover under the FELA or Jones Act, it makes more sense to require the claimant either to reside in the United States or to work for a United States employer. For any particular law, in other words, this approach provides a solution as clear and as easy to follow as the territorial approach. That being so, I see no reason to think that all laws must receive the same (territorial) interpretation.

2. Interpreting laws in the manner described above will resolve many cases, for factual contacts will often be distributed in such a way that only American law or only foreign law applies, and the court should rule accordingly.[129] *Aramco* is such a case.[130] To begin with, the applicability of American law seems clear, for Title VII appears to be one of the relatively rare statutes (outside the trade

---

[129] There is some confusion about what this ruling should be. Many cases, including *Aramco*, treat the applicability of American law as a question of subject matter jurisdiction. See, for example, *Boureslan v Aramco*, 653 F Supp 629 (SD Tex 1987), aff'd en banc, 892 F2d 1271 (5th Cir 1990); *Steele v Bulova Watch Co.*, 344 US 280, 282 (1952); Born & Westin, *International Civil Litigation in United States Courts*, at 444 (cited in note 102); Note, *Extraterritorial Application of United States Laws: A Conflict of Laws Approach*, 28 Stan L Rev 1005 (1978). As the analysis above makes clear, this is simply incorrect: the question of extraterritorial application goes to whether the plaintiff has pleaded a proper cause of action. Holding that American law does not apply because, for example, the conduct at issue occurred abroad means that the plaintiff cannot establish an essential element of the claim. The complaint should therefore be dismissed under FRCP 12(b)(6) for failure to state a claim upon which relief can be granted—unless, of course, the plaintiff can establish a claim under foreign law. See *Romero*, 358 US at 359 ("the question whether jurisdiction exists has been confused with the question whether the complaint states a cause of action"); *Lauritzen*, 345 US at 575 ("A cause of action under our law was asserted here, and the court had power to determine whether it was or was not well founded in law and in fact"); *American Banana*, 213 US at 353.

At the same time, finding American law inapplicable will often lead to dismissal for lack of subject matter jurisdiction. First, such a holding may eliminate the only federal question from the case, requiring dismissal unless there is diversity; in *Aramco*, for example, dismissal was proper because Boureslan and ASC were both "citizens" of Texas. Second, many multinational cases involve penal, tax, or regulatory laws, and it is well established that courts will not take jurisdiction to enforce these types of foreign laws. See Brilmayer, 50 L & Contemp Probs at 13 (cited in note 31). The question whether American law applies is not itself a question of subject matter jurisdiction, however, and in many cases the court should retain jurisdiction to resolve the dispute under foreign law.

[130] See Louise Weinberg, *Against Comity*, 80 Geo L J 53, 73–74 (1991).

context) in which Congress actually addressed the question of extraterritorial application. As plaintiff pointed out, after defining "State" to include territories and the District of Columbia, Congress exempted employers "with respect to the employment of aliens outside any State."[131] Viewing this language without the distorting lens of a strong judicial presumption, its obvious implication is that Title VII applies abroad but only protects American citizens. The legislative history supports this interpretation. In the only discussion of the provision, the House Committee on Education and Labor explained that "The intent of the . . . exemption is to remove conflicts of law which might otherwise exist between the United States and a foreign nation in the employment of aliens outside the United States by an American enterprise."[132]

The Court points out that the alien exemption leaves many questions unanswered.[133] The criticism is a fair one: Congress did not, for example, indicate what courts should do in cases involving foreign employers who discriminate against aliens in the United States or against United States citizens abroad. But while the exemption may be a poor or incomplete conflicts provision, leaving courts some difficult issues to resolve, it does plainly suggest that Title VII protects American employees (like Boureslan) from discrimination by their Americans employers (like Aramco) even in foreign lands.

The Supreme Court reached a different conclusion. Relying on the presumption against extraterritoriality, the Court construed the incompleteness of the alien exemption to indicate that Congress did not think about extraterritorial applications (though what the Court thinks Congress did have in mind when it added this provision remains unclear). But even if Congress overlooked the question, it would still make sense to apply Title VII in a case like *Aramco*. As noted above, one of Title VII's purposes is to protect specified classes of individuals from conduct deemed wrongful and undesirable. This policy is implicated whenever a United States resident is a victim of discrimination, regardless of where the act occurs.

---

[131] 42 USC §§ 2000e(i), 2000e-1.

[132] Equal Employment Opportunity Act of 1963, HR Rep No 88-570, 88th Cong, 1st Sess 4 (1963).

[133] 111 S Ct at 1234.

The Court worried that such an interpretation might lead to conflicts with foreign law. It might, and we may need to interpret the statute differently when it does.[134] But before restricting American law to avoid conflicts with foreign law, we should make sure that there is a conflict. In fact, nothing in the record gives even the slightest hint that applying Title VII in *Aramco* would have conflicted with the law of Saudi Arabia.[135] As noted above, the mere fact that conduct occurs in a foreign nation need not give that nation an interest in regulating the conduct or in preventing the United States from doing so. Saudi Arabia may not prohibit the same discriminatory conduct as the United States, but as far as one can tell neither does it encourage or desire such conduct. Consequently, applying Title VII to prevent an American employer from discriminating against an American employee is not inconsistent with Saudi law, and the plaintiff should have been permitted to seek relief.[136]

3. While many cases may be resolved in this fashion, there will inevitably be cases in which the facts are distributed so that both American and foreign law apply, what Brainerd Currie called "true conflicts."[137] These will not be the same cases as under a territorial approach, because different contacts will trigger the applicability of many American laws. But altering the method of defining when American law might apply cannot avoid all conflicts; nothing can. Conflicts are inherent in a world in which there are multinational

---

[134] This problem is considered infra notes 137–54 and accompanying text.

[135] In interstate cases, the defendant must argue that the plaintiff's claim fails because foreign law applies. In international cases with potential foreign policy implications, however, or where the question of whose law applies is seriously in doubt, the court may want to act on its own initiative, including to invite representatives of the involved nations to offer their views.

[136] The fact that there is no law either allowing or prohibiting certain activity does not necessarily mean that a nation is indifferent to that activity. It may not always be necessary to promulgate a specific positive enactment to permit activity a nation finds desirable. On the other hand, not everything that is permitted is actually desired in this sense, and a nation may in fact be indifferent to some activity. Determining whether this is so is itself part of the interpretive process of deciding whether there is a conflict. The question, of course, is not whether one can imagine a policy that will generate a conflict (clever lawyers can always do that), but whether such a policy makes sense given the nation's laws and background social practices. In *Aramco*, for example, Boureslan alleged that he was a victim of discrimination based on his religion (Moslem) and his nationality (Arab). Saudi Arabia has no law expressly prohibiting such discrimination. Nonetheless, applying American law on these facts should have been unproblematic.

[137] Currie, *Selected Essays* at 119 (cited in note 74).

transactions and different nations have different laws and different policies. A mature choice of law system thus requires a second step to choose a law when more than one applies.

The best way to resolve such problems would be through bilateral or multilateral negotiations with other nations.[138] Negotiated agreements could set forth clear ground rules and provide solutions that avoid potential controversy precisely because they are established by mutual consent. The European Community has a number of such agreements, and these have generally succeeded in solving choice of law problems.[139] The United States, in contrast, has seldom followed this practice, instead leaving courts to resolve multinational cases as a matter of federal common law.[140] Unfortunately, as the discussion in Part I demonstrates, the courts have not done a very good job of organizing or systematizing practice in this area.

Be that as it may, until Congress or the Executive acts, courts have no choice but to do the best they can. Cases will continue to arise and must be resolved somehow. We must therefore try to identify the best solution, trusting to the fact that if the courts make a mistake, the political branches can correct them.

Several alternatives are available in lieu of formally negotiated treaties. The easiest solution is simply to decline to choose among conflicting laws and apply American law. This can be justified on the ground that courts lack competence to measure the relative importance of American and foreign interests. Applying American law in a true conflict will (by definition) advance that law's underlying domestic policy. That being so, one may argue, any decision to qualify this policy in deference to foreign interests should be made by legislative or executive officials.[141] Such an approach has

---

[138] See Paul, 32 Harv J Int'l L at 76 (cited in note 112); Harold Maier, *Interest Balancing and Extraterritorial Jurisdiction*, 31 Am J Comp L 579 (1983); see also Larry Kramer, *On the Need for a Uniform Choice of Law Code*, 89 Mich L Rev 2134 (1991).

[139] See, for example, EEC Convention on the Law Applicable to Contractual Obligations (1980). The Uniform Commercial Code serves a similar function among the states of the United States.

[140] The United States recently took a step in the right direction, negotiating an agreement with the European Community on antitrust enforcement. See US/EC Agreement on Antitrust Cooperation and Coordination, 61 BNA Antitrust & Trade Reg Rep 382 (Sept 26, 1991).

[141] See Harold Maier, *Resolving Extraterritorial Conflicts, or "There and Back Again,"* 25 Va J Int'l L 7, 23–24, 29–30 (1984).

the additional advantage of being simple to administer, since it limits the court's task to ascertaining whether the United States has an interest.

A solution based on preferring forum law in true conflicts is usually associated with Brainerd Currie, who recommended this approach in the interstate context.[142] But state courts overwhelmingly rejected his suggestion,[143] and Currie himself subsequently conceded that courts could and sometimes should defer to foreign law.[144] Surprisingly, choosing forum law appears to be the solution favored by the Supreme Court in *Aramco*. That is, having defined the prima facie scope of American law in territorial terms, the Court would apply that law whenever the conduct at issue occurred in this country, notwithstanding inconsistent foreign law. We do not know this for sure, of course, since *Aramco* did not present the problem, but this is how the territorial principle traditionally operated. Moreover, Chief Justice Rehnquist's analysis of Boureslan's argument suggests that it would be improper to vary the applicability of American law on the ground that foreign law also applies. Thus, the Court says it is reluctant to apply Title VII to employers overseas because then even "a French employer of a United States citizen in France would be subject to Title VII."[145] But France may have an interest in such a case that it lacks in cases involving only parties from the United States, and one can argue that this interest justifies treating the cases differently.

The Court's failure to see the possibility of treating true and false conflicts differently is puzzling. The Court recognizes that when a statute is silent with respect to extraterritorial scope, judges can and should infer reasonable limitations. Hence, the Court does not hesitate to impute territorial limits (and for the same reason should not hesitate to impute limits based on residence, nationality, or effects as well). The fact that another nation's law applies is simply one more relevant consideration: applying American law to further American interests is more problematic when foreign law applies than when it does not. So if the Court can read in terms

---

[142] See Currie, *Selected Essays* at 117–21, 169, 184 (cited in note 74).

[143] See John Hart Ely, *Choice of Law and the State's Interest in Protecting Its Own*, 23 Wm & Mary L Rev 173, 175 (1981); Kay, 34 Mercer L Rev at 538–52 (cited in note 99).

[144] Brainerd Currie, *The Distinterested Third State*, 28 L & Contemp Probs 754, 757 (1963).

[145] 111 S Ct at 1234.

like "when the conduct occurs in the United States" or "when the parties are from the United States," it can also read in a further limitation along the lines of "unless another nation's law applies, in which case . . . ."

Moreover, inferring some such limitation makes considerable sense. Ignoring foreign law whenever the United States has an interest will cause precisely the sort of "clashes" and "international discord" the Court rightly wants to avoid.[146] This may be less true in a purely territorial regime, since the long tradition of favoring this interest helps legitimate subordinating foreign law. But even here there may be controversy if acts in one nation create a strong regulatory interest in another, as when foreign companies manipulate American markets through their activities abroad or vice versa. And once we shift to a system that is not strictly territorial, controversial exercises of jurisdiction may become more frequent. Furthermore, always applying American law may ultimately undermine American interests. If other nations follow the same practice, American law will be applied only in true conflicts litigated in American courts. Yet these may not be the majority of cases or the most important ones. It may therefore be in the United States' own interest to defer to foreign law in some cases to encourage other nations to do the same.

The chief alternative to always applying forum law is to balance the interests involved in the particular case and defer to foreign law where foreign interests are paramount. This is the practice followed by courts in the antitrust context, where it has been endorsed by the Justice Department.[147] Indeed, the Supreme Court itself adopted a balancing approach for questions of extraterritorial discovery (yet another departure from the presumption against extraterritoriality that *Aramco* ignores).[148] Balancing is, moreover, favored by prominent commentators and endorsed by the American

---

[146] See 111 S Ct at 1230. It is not clear just how serious this concern really is. Writing about the potentially more controversial act-of-state doctrine, a number of commentators have observed that adjudication has not embarrassed American foreign policy and argued that courts can remain sensitive to this consideration without sacrificing their independence. See, for example, Monroe Leigh & Michael D. Sandler, *Dunhill: Toward a Reconsideration of Sabbatino*, 16 Va J Int'l L 685 (1976).

[147] See supra notes 53–54 and accompanying text; US Dept of Justice, Antitrust Enforcement Guidelines for International Operations (1988).

[148] *See Societe Nacionale Industrielle Aerospatiale v United States District Court*, 482 US 522 (1987).

Law Institute in its influential Restatement (Third) of the Foreign Relations Law of the United States.[149]

As a conceptual matter, interest balancing seems attractive. What could be better, after all, than an approach that enables the judge to take all relevant considerations into account and tailor them to the particular case? But balancing tends not to work so well in practice.[150] The considerations being weighed are usually imprecise enough to permit several answers, and to dictate none. As a result, there is no greater certainty about the correctness of particular outcomes—only more uncertainty about what these outcomes are likely to be. In choice of law, the problems are exacerbated by the often imponderable nature of the interests being weighed, by the fact that the stakes frequently depend on outcomes in many cases rather than on the disposition of any particular case, and by the difficulty courts face in ascertaining and evaluating the interests of foreign nations. For these reasons, interest balancing and other forms of case-specific analysis have consistently disappointed in choice of law.

A third alternative can be constructed on the basis of a few straightforward observations.[151] First, it is impossible for every nation fully to achieve the objectives of its laws in multinational true conflicts: by definition, both nations have an interest in applying their law, these laws are inconsistent, and applying one nation's law means not applying the other's. It does not follow, however, that choice of law is a zero-sum game. Each nation presumably cares more about some true conflicts than others, because some true conflicts affect more important purposes of the nation's laws or affect these purposes in more important ways. The best way to resolve true conflicts is thus to determine which cases nations care about most, and arrange trade-offs that secure the application of each nation's law in as many of these as possible. In this way, we can maximize the extent to which each nation achieves its objectives.

---

[149] See Restatement (Third) Foreign Relations Law of the United States § 403 (1987); Lowenfeld, 163 Recueil de Cours at 330–44 (cited in note 31). Cf. Maier, 25 Va L Rev at 40–41 (cited in note 141).

[150] See *Laker Airways Ltd. v Sabena, Belgian World Airlines*, 731 F2d 909 (DC Cir 1984); Born & Westin *International Civil Litigation in United States Courts*, at 461–65 (cited in note 102); Maier, 31 Am J Comp L at 591–95 (cited in note 138).

[151] See Larry Kramer, *Rethinking Choice of Law*, 90 Colum L Rev 277 (1990); Larry Kramer, *Return of the Renvoi*, 66 NYU L Rev 979 (1991).

As with balancing, the considerations involved in determining which nation has the stronger policy commitment are too complex for courts to calculate on a case-by-case basis. Rather, maximizing the interests of different nations can be done better on a wholesale basis: by identifying generally shared policies or policy preferences and constructing rules that systematically advance these. Suppose, for example, that two nations generally favor a particular policy; each recognizes different exceptions to this policy, some deliberately created, others a product of judicial or legislative inertia. A rule calling for courts in both nations to apply the law reflecting the generally preferred policy—regardless of whose law it is in any particular case—should benefit both nations over time: each nation forgoes the opportunity to enforce its exceptions in some multinational true conflicts but gains by the other nation's reciprocal forbearance. Over the course of many cases, such a rule will maximize the extent to which both nations achieve their preferred objectives in multinational situations, thus minimizing friction without sacrificing any nation's domestic policies more than is necessary.

Developing rules that satisfy this criterion will not be easy. The task is difficult enough even among the states of the United States, where cultural differences are few and there are many shared policy commitments. In the international context, the problems are considerably more complicated. In addition to the sheer complexity of identifying mutually advantageous policy tradeoffs, the rules require reciprocity to work, and this is difficult to obtain among nations. Nonetheless, as the existence of customary international law and other forms of non-negotiated reciprocity illustrate, it can be done. Making the effort to develop appropriate rules thus seems better than either a uniform preference for forum law or the open-ended balancing of the Third Restatement.

Unfortunately, a complete discussion of how courts can articulate workable rules and why other nations may be expected to reciprocate is beyond the scope of this article.[152] At this point,

---

[152] I have developed the general theoretical framework elsewhere. See authorities cited supra note 151. Although these articles concern interstate problems, much of the theory is drawn from the international law literature, and the theory should work just as well in that context. The basic premise is that choice of law presents a problem akin to an iterated prisoner's dilemma, in which the indefinite repetition of cases creates the condition for developing cooperation even without formal negotiations. The stability of this cooperation is further strengthened by certain unique characteristics of the judicial process, such as written opinions and appellate review.

morcover, I am not entirely sure what these rules would or should look like in the international context. If the territorial principle is as entrenched as some commentators believe, we may end up with rules that favor territorial contacts in true conflicts.[153] Alternatively, Anne-Marie Burley suggests distinguishing between the treatment of liberal and non-liberal nations.[154] According to Burley, courts can make relatively nuanced trade-offs with other liberal nations (since shared interests and approaches are widespread), but something cruder may be necessary when it comes to non-liberal nations. The proposal is an interesting one, and deserves further investigation.

For present purposes, it is enough to recognize that courts have many resources to draw upon. Practices and conventions already followed in foreign nations provide a valuable source of information, as do existing treaties and agreements made by this and other countries. International law can be consulted for solutions to some problems, and while multinational cases raise unique issues, practice among the states may also be relevant. Even academics have a role to play: offering their expertise in particular areas to provide courts with the information and analysis needed to establish sensible international choice of law rules. With these sources, courts should be able to establish a system of rules through conventional common law adjudication—the same way they have developed substantive principles of customary international law, and the same way courts in the states and in other nations have developed choice of law rules. The federal courts may be late in entering the field, but better late than never.

IV

The argument made here is simply this: we need a federal choice of law system for multinational cases, but not the nineteenth-century system adopted by the Supreme Court in *Aramco*. That system proved inadequate long ago, and for this reason has been abandoned everywhere else. The federal courts should develop something more functional, something more attuned to

---

[153] This would still be an improvement over the present system in all those cases that, like *Aramco*, present false conflicts.

[154] Anne-Marie Burley, *Liberal Internationalism and the Act of State Doctrine* (forthcoming).

contemporary understandings of legislative jurisdiction and statutory interpretation.

This still leaves the problem of *Aramco*. Congress has amended Title VII,[155] but this is not enough, for there is still the matter of the general presumption against extraterritoriality with its broader implications for American legislative policy. We could just leave the presumption in place and ask Congress to be more careful in passing laws. Or, we could wait for Congress to enact a federal choice of law code or for the Executive to negotiate agreements with other nations. But none of these solutions seems likely to materialize in the foreseeable future, leaving a practical problem in the meantime.

In my view, *Aramco* should either be overruled or confined to its facts. The Court made a mistake—one it is in the best position to correct. This is not like a judicial misinterpretation of a particular statute, where the usual rule is to wait for Congress to make the needed correction. The Court in *Aramco* formulated a general rule of federal common law, applicable in a wide range of contexts. But it is a bad rule, and it would be irresponsible to dismiss the problem with the excuse that Congress can always fix things. Judges are supposed to administer the law sensibly, and a presumption against extraterritoriality simply is not sensible.

---

[155] See supra note 13.

THOMAS W. MERRILL

THE CONSTITUTIONAL PRINCIPLE

OF SEPARATION OF POWERS

I. Introduction

The Supreme Court has had many occasions in recent years to consider what it calls "the constitutional principle of separation of powers."[1] The principle in question has been effusively praised[2] and on occasion vigorously enforced.[3] But just what is it? The Court clearly believes that the Constitution contains an organizing principle that is more than the sum of the specific clauses that govern relations among the branches. Yet notwithstanding the many testimonials to the importance of the principle, its content remains remarkably elusive.

The central problem, as many have observed,[4] is that the Court

---

Thomas W. Merrill is Professor of Law, Northwestern University School of Law.

AUTHOR's NOTE: This paper has benefited from comments on a previous draft by Gary Lawson and participants in a Northwestern constitutional theory workshop.

[1] The phrase appears in the Court's statement of the question presented in *Metropolitan Washington Airports Auth. v Citizens for Abatement of Aircraft Noise, Inc.*, 111 S Ct 2298, 2301 (1991).

[2] See, e.g., *Freytag v Commissioner of Internal Revenue*, 111 S Ct 2631, 2634 (1991) ("the central guarantee of a just government"); *Mistretta v United States*, 488 US 361, 380 (1989) ("essential to the preservation of liberty").

[3] On five occasions in recent years, the Court has invalidated federal legislation on separation-of-powers grounds: *Metropolitan Washington Airports Auth. v Citizens for Abatement of of Aircraft Noise, Inc.*, 111 S Ct 2298 (1991); *Bowsher v Synar*, 478 US 714 (1986); *INS v Chadha*, 462 US 919 (1983); *Northern Pipeline Construction Co. v Marathon Pipe Line Co.*, 458 US 50 (1982); and *Buckley v Valeo*, 424 US 1 (1976).

[4] See, e.g., Martin H. Redish and Elizabeth Cisar, *"If Angels Were to Govern": The Need for Pragmatic Formalism in Separation of Powers Theory*, 41 Duke L J 449 (1991); Rebecca L. Brown, *Separated Powers and Ordered Liberty*, 139 U Pa L Rev 1513, 1522–31 (1991); Harold J. Krent, *Separating the Strands in Separation of Powers Controversies*, 74 Vir L Rev 1253 (1988);

has employed two very different conceptions of separation of powers in recent years. On the one hand, there is the "formal" understanding, emphasizing that "[t]he Constitution sought to divide the delegated powers of the new Federal government into three defined categories, Legislative, Executive, and Judicial, to assure, as nearly as possible, that each branch of government would confine itself to its assigned responsibility."[5] On the other hand, there is the "functional" understanding, stressing that the three branches do not "operate with absolute independence," and that the Constitution requires only that "the proper balance between the coordinate branches" be maintained.[6] The Court has alternated between the formal and the functional constructions, with a swing group of Justices evidently happy to embrace one or the other as suits the needs of the moment.[7]

When we step back from the doctrinal inconstancy and examine the outcomes of the Court's recent separation-of-powers decisions, however, a readily discernible pattern emerges. The formal theory is regularly used in evaluating (and invalidating) attempts by Congress to exercise governmental power by means other than the enactment of legislation;[8] the more elastic functional approach is favored in reviewing (and approving) duly-enacted legislation that regulates or reallocates the functions performed by the other two branches.[9] Unfortunately, this pattern does not follow from the

---

Cass R. Sunstein, *Constitutionalism after the New Deal*, 101 Harv L Rev 421, 493–96 (1987); Peter L. Strauss, *Formal and Functional Approaches to Separation-of-Powers Questions—a Foolish Inconsistency?* 72 Cornell L Rev 488 (1987); Thomas O. Sargentich, *The Contemporary Debate about Legislative-Executive Separation of Powers*, 72 Cornell L Rev 430, 433 (1987).

[5] *INS v Chadha*, 462 US 919, 951 (1983).

[6] *Morrison v Olson*, 487 US 654, 694, 695 (1988), quoting *United States v Nixon*, 418 US 683, 707 (1974) and *Nixon v Administrator of General Services*, 433 US 425, 443 (1977).

[7] On the last day of the 1985 Term, the Court handed down two separation-of-powers decisions. One, *Bowsher v Synar*, 478 US 714 (1986), applied a highly formal analysis to invalidate part of the Gramm-Rudman-Hollings Act; the other, *Commodity Futures Trading Comm'n v Schor*, 478 US 833 (1986), adopted a functional understanding to uphold the jurisdiction of an administrative agency over common-law counterclaims. Chief Justice Burger, Justice Powell, Justice Rehnquist, and Justice O'Connor joined both majority opinions.

[8] *Bowsher v Synar*, 478 US 714 (1986) (congressional agent cannot control execution of the laws); *INS v Chadha*, 462 US 919 (1983) (one-House legislative veto unconstitutional); *Buckley v Valeo*, 424 US 1 (1976) (members of Congress cannot exercise appointments power over nonlegislative officers).

[9] *Mistretta v United States*, 488 US 361 (1989) (Sentencing Commission with rulemaking powers permissible as part of judicial branch); *Morrison v Olson*, 487 US 654 (1988) (federal court may appoint independent counsel to investigate and prosecute crimes by high execu-

tenets of either formalism or functionalism. Applied consistently, formalism would impose strict limitations on efforts to scramble executive and judicial functions,[10] and functionalism would probably lead the Court to uphold at least some of the extra-legislative congressional controls that have been disapproved.[11] All of which suggests that neither formalism nor functionalism provides a satisfactory account of the constitutional principle of separation of powers—at least as it operates in practice.

In the 1990 Term the Court decided two cases that required it to revisit the constitutional principle of separation of powers— *Metropolitan Washington Airports Authority v Citizens for the Abatement of Aircraft Noise, Inc.*[12] and *Freytag v Commissioner of Internal Revenue.*[13] In terms of doctrinal development, neither decision does much to clear up the "incoherent muddle"[14] of recent years. But in terms of outcomes, we see the same pattern repeated once again. In *Washington Airports*, the Court reviewed another attempt at extra-legislative Congressional control: legislation that would allow members of Congress, serving as a state "Board of Review," to veto decisions of a regional airports authority. True to pattern, the Court invoked the constitutional principle of separation of powers and struck it down. By contrast, *Freytag* involved a challenge to the allocation of functions between the executive and judicial branches: whether the Chief Judge of the Tax Court (a non–Article III tribunal) was either a "Head of Department" or "Court of Law" for

---

tive officials); *Commodity Futures Trading Commission v Schor*, 478 US 833 (1986) (administrative agency may adjudicate common-law couterclaim); *Nixon v Administrator of General Services*, 433 US 425, 443 (1977) (controls on disposition of Presidential papers permissible). The principal exception is *Northern Pipeline Construction Co. v Marathon Pipe Line Co.*, 458 US 50 (1982), where Justice Brennan's plurality opinion used a formal analysis to invalidate portions of the jurisdiction of the bankrupcty courts as being inconsistent with the judicial function of Article III courts. This aspect of *Northern Pipeline*, however, does not appear to have survived subsequent decisions. See note 91.

[10] This is the view of Justice Scalia, the Court's most consistent champion of formalism. See *Morrison*, 487 US at 703–15 (Scalia dissenting); *Mistretta*, 488 US at 413–27 (Scalia dissenting). See also Gary Lawson, *Territorial Governments and the Limits of Formalism*, 78 Cal L Rev 853 (1990) (detailing the impact that a rigorous formalism would have on territorial courts).

[11] This is the position of Justice White, the one Justice who has steadfastly endorsed a functional approach. See *Washington Airports*, 111 S Ct at 2317–21 (White dissenting); *Bowsher*, 478 US at 776 (White dissenting); *Chadha*, 462 US at 998–1002 (White dissenting).

[12] 111 S Ct 2298 (1991).

[13] 111 S Ct 2631 (1991).

[14] Brown, 139 U Pa L Rev at 1517 (cited in note 4).

Appointments Clause purposes.[15] Although the Court split 5–4 over the answer to this question, not a single vote could be mustered to endorse the formalist answer urged by the petitioners: that the Chief Judge was neither, and hence that the appointment authority was unconstitutional. Last Term's cases thus deepen the paradox of the Court applying a "notorious inconsistency of method"[16] to generate quite consistent outcomes.

In this article, I will argue for a new understanding the constitutional principle of separation of powers, what I will call the "minimal" conception. I developed this alternative inductively, by reflecting on what theory, if applied consistently, might generate a pattern of results similar to the one reached by the Court. I do not, however, suggest that the minimal conception supplies a positive explanation for the Court's decisions; there may be a variety of reasons that account for the Court's performance.[17] Instead, I offer it as a possible understanding of what the constitutional principle of separation of powers should mean, and will argue that, if adopted as a normative standard for decision-making, it would outperform formalism and functionalism on a number of fronts, including but not limited to its capacity to generate outcomes congruent with those of the past.

The foundation of the minimal conception is a simple rule: there are only three branches of government, and every federal office must be accountable to one of these branches. Thus, an attempt by Congress to create a "Fourth Branch" of the federal government would be unconstitutional. Moreover, because every federal office must be located "in" one of the three branches, each office is subject to whatever specific constitutional limitations apply to action by its branch. For example, a federal office that is an agent of Congress (like the Board of Review in *Washington Airports*) would be subject to the same Bicameral and Presentment requirements that apply to Congress itself. Because such an agent could not comply with these requirements, it would be unconstitutional.

---

[15] The Appointments Clause permits Congress to vest the appointment of "inferior officers" (such as the Special Trial Judge at issue in *Freytag*) "in the President alone, in the Courts of Law, or in the Heads of Departments." US Const Art II, § 2, cl 2.

[16] Geoffrey P. Miller, *Rights and Structure in Constitutional Theory*, 8 Social Philos & Policy 196, 201 (1991).

[17] See text at note 105.

Like formalism, the minimal conception rests on a rule-like understanding of the constitutional principle of separation of powers. But unlike both formalism and functionalism, the minimal conception would reject the idea that separation of powers is concerned with achieving a particular allocation of "legislative," "judicial," and "executive" functions among the three branches. Instead, it would treat questions about the correct definition of the governmental powers mentioned in the Vesting Clauses of Articles I, II, and III, and their assignment to different branches, to be nonjusticiable political questions consigned to the discretion of Congress. Thus, under the minimal understanding Congress would be free to delegate "functions" any way it wants, but would be strictly limited in its options as to who could receive the deletation: only the three constitutional branches and their agents.

I will argue that the minimal conception would avoid the more glaring problems associated with formalism and functionalism, and would have several other attractive features as well. Because it would produce results consistent with the outcomes of virtually all the Supreme Court's major separation of powers decisions, it would provide a substantial measure of continuity with established understandings about the structure of government. Moreover, because it would prevent evasion of specific clauses of the Constitution that limit the power of the branches, and would promote a diffusion of power among the branches, it would achieve important purposes traditionally associated with the doctrine of separation of powers. Finally, it would be broadly consistent with both the text of the Constitution and with James Madison's explanation of how the structural features of that document would work to preserve liberty.

II. Unpacking Formalism and Functionalism

Part of the problem in trying to make sense of the Court's recent separation-of-powers jurisprudence is that the two doctrines deployed by the Court and commentators—formalism and functionalism—are complex rather than simple ideas.[18] Although

---

[18] For a compendium of the literature on formalism versus functionalism, see Brown, 139 U Pa L Rev at 1522–31 (cited in note 4). The tenets of formalism are spelled out more fully in Lee S. Liberman, *Morrison v Olson: A Formalistic Perspective on Why the Court Was Wrong,*

nearly always treated as alternatives along a single dimension,[19] the formal/functional dichotomy in fact operates at two different levels. At one level, it refers to different methods of justification employed by the Court, and mirrors the more general distinction in law between formal and functional styles of legal reasoning.[20] At another level, however, the dichotomy refers to different substantive interpretations of the Constitution. Although the two levels of the formal/functional distinction are closely linked in the cases and commentary, it is useful to unpack them, if only because doing so reveals the possibility of adopting a substantive interpretation of the constitutional structure different from those embedded in the current understandings of formalism and functionalism.

At the methodological level, the formal/functional dichotomy parallels the familiar division in law between rules and standards. Here, the formalist insists that the structural provisions of the Constitution establish a set of rules—an "instruction manual"[21]—that must be followed whatever the consequences. The formalist thus adopts what amounts to a deontological theory of justification: separation of powers is a rule that must be followed because it is laid down in the Constitution and the Constitution is supreme law.[22] The rule may have a higher-order justification—such as diffusing power the better to protect liberty. But, for the formalist, realization of such an end is seen as depending in good part on preserving the rule-like quality of the inquiry.[23] As the Court stated in *Chadha*, "the fact that a given law or procedure is efficient, convenient, and useful in facilitating functions of government, standing alone, will not save it if it is contrary to the Constitution."[24]

---

38 Am U L Rev 313 (1989); Gary Lawson, 78 Cal L Rev 853 (cited in note 10); David P. Currie, *The Distribution of Powers after Bowsher*, 1986 Supreme Court Review 19. For a thoughtful defense of functionalism, see Peter Strauss, *The Place of Agencies in Government: Separation of Powers and the Fourth Branch*, 84 Colum L Rev 573 (1984).

[19] See, e.g., Strauss, 72 Cornell L Rev at 488 (cited in note 4).

[20] See generally, Frederick Schauer, *Formalism*, 97 Yale L J 509 (1988).

[21] Gary Lawson, *In Praise of Woodenness*, 11 Geo Mason L Rev 21, 22 (1988). See also Sargentich, 72 Cornell L Rev at 458 n 31 (cited in note 4).

[22] Sunstein, *Constitutionalism after the New Deal*, 101 Harv L Rev at 493; see also Stephen Carter, *From Sick Chicken to Synar: The Evolution and Subsequent De-Evolution of the Separation of Powers*, 1987 BYU L Rev 719, 735–43 (describing "de-evolutionary" tradition); Geoffrey P. Miller, *Independent Agencies*, 1986 Supreme Court Review 41, 53–58 (describing "neoclassical" approach).

[23] Redish & Cisar, 41 Duke L J at 127–28 (cited in note 4).

[24] *Chadha*, 462 US at 944.

The functionalist, in contrast, argues that structural disputes should be resolved not in terms of fixed rules but rather in light of an evolving standard designed to advance the ultimate purposes of a system of separation of powers.[25] Accordingly, the functional approach adopts a consequentialist theory of justification: the task of the court is to judge institutional arrangements in terms of their contribution toward attaining certain ends. The Court's functionalist opinions have consistently described the underlying purpose of a system of separation of powers in terms of preserving individual liberty;[26] functionally oriented commentators have proposed variations on this theme.[27] But all functionalists agree that legislation should be invalidated only when it disserves these ultimate ends.

At the second level, the formal/functional distinction reflects different substantive interpretations of the Constitution. At this level, interestingly, formalists and functionalists start with the same premise: that the constitutional principle of separation of powers is concerned with the allocation of governmental functions among the different branches of government. Indeed, both groups generally agree with the traditional understanding that governmental activities can be classified under three functional headings — legislative, executive, or judicial—with each function associated with one of the three branches of government.[28] Where they disagree is over what sorts of deviations are permitted from the one function–one branch equation.

A pure formalist embraces what I will call an "exclusive functions" interpretation of the relationship between functions and branches. On this view, each of the three branches has exclusive

---

[25] Sunstein, 101 Harv L Rev at 495 (cited in note 22); see also Carter, 1987 BYU L Rev at 722–35 (describing "evolutionary" tradition) (cited in note 22); Miller, 1986 Supreme Court Review at 41 (cited in note 22) (describing "pragmatic" approach).

[26] *Freytag*, 111 S Ct at 2634; *Mistetta*, 488 US at 380; *Youngstown Sheet & Tube Co. v Sawyer*, 343 US 579, 635 (1952) (Jackson concurring); *Myers v United States*, 272 US 52, 294–95 (1926) (Brandeis dissenting).

[27] See Brown, 139 U Pa L Rev at 1516 (cited in note 4) (ultimate question is "the potential effect of the arrangement on individual due-process interests"); Paul Verkuil, *Separation of Powers, the Rule of Law, and the Idea of Independence*, 30 Wm & Mary L Rev 301 (1989) (basic purpose is to avoid conflicts of interest). Some commentators have also posited that a central purpose of separation of powers is to control rent-seeking factions. See Miller, 8 Social Philos & Policy 196 (cited in note 16).

[28] See, e.g., *Humphrey's Executor v United States*, 295 US 602, 630–32 (1935); *Myers v United States*, 272 US 52, 161 (1926); *Massachusetts v Mellon*, 262 US 447, 488 (1923); *Wayman v Southard*, 10 Wheat 1, 46 (1825).

authority to perform its assigned function, unless the Constitution itself permits an exception.[29] In effect, the Vesting Clauses of Articles I, II, and III are construed as establishing a prima facie allocation of a single function to each of the branches of government. This allocation may be ignored only if a specific clause of the Constitution authorizes a deviation. For example, the Vesting Clause of Article I establishes a prima facie allocation of "all legislative power" to the Congress. Under the Presentment Clause,[30] however, the President is expressly permitted to participate in the legislative power by exercising the veto. Absent some such exception grounded in constitutional text, however, the proper classification of any governmental activity according to its function establishes which branch may exclusively perform it.

The substantive constitutional theory of the functionalists is harder to pin down. All functionalists reject the exclusive functions idea, and believe that many governmental activities can be categorized as falling within more than one function; they would have courts defer to the allocation established by Congress in these doubtful cases.[31] And all functionalists believe that the primary objective of judicial review in separation of powers cases is to insure that each branch retains "enough" governmental power to permit it to operate as an effective check on the other branches of government.[32] In the most extreme version of functionalism, the idea of a specified allocation of functions would disappear altogether, leaving only the notion of a general diffusion or balancing of power among the branches. Separation of powers would on this view become indistinguishable from a free-floating checks and balances.[33] Most functionalists would not go that far, but would instead embrace a "core functions" theory.[34] This posits the existence of a nucleus of

---

[29] *Mistretta*, 488 US at 426 (Scalia dissenting); Redish & Cisar, 41 Duke L J 449 (cited in note 4); Lawson, 78 Cal L Rev at 857–58 (cited in note 10). The formal theory is equivalent to what M. J. C. Vile calls the "pure doctrine" of separation of powers, with the addition of the qualification that text-based exceptions are permissible. See M. J. C. Vile, *Constitutionalism and the Separation of Powers* 13 (1967).

[30] Art I, § 7, cl 2.

[31] See Brown, 139 U Pa L Rev at 1527–29 (cited in note 4).

[32] Id at 1527.

[33] Sargentich, 72 Cornell L Rev at 433 (cited in note 4).

[34] See *Bowsher*, 478 US at 776 (White dissenting); *Chadha*, 462 US at 1000 (White dissenting); *Nixon v Administrator of General Services*, 433 US 425, 443 (1977).

activities that uniquely belongs to each of the three branches, and that cannot be reassigned by Congress. Although courts would defer to Congress outside these areas, they would step in to prevent any tampering with the core.[35] The reason for preserving such a core, however, is again to insure that a balance or equilibrium of power is maintained among the branches.

Two important insights emerge from breaking formalism and functionalism down into their composite elements in this fashion. First, we can see that the criticisms most commonly leveled against formalism and functionalism are attributable more to their substantive theories than their methodological commitments. Formalism is often attacked on the ground that the definitions of the legislative, executive, and judicial powers are elusive and lead to a question-begging analysis.[36] The elusiveness of the functional categories poses special difficulties for formalism, however, only because of the assumption of its substantive theory that each function is uniquely assigned to one branch. For example, in *INS v Chadha*,[37] the same activity—determining whether deportation of an alien should be suspended—was described by Chief Justice Burger as "legislative" when performed by one House of Congress, and as "executive" when performed by the Attorney General.[38] For good measure, Justice Powell in his concurring opinion described it as "adjudicatory."[39] Since the classification of House's decision as a "legislative act" was critical to the outcome under the formal theory, commentators had a field day lampooning the Court's reasoning.[40]

---

[35] Moreover, most functionalists probably believe it is permissible for Congress to assign certain activities to entities that operate outside the chain of command of the three constitutional branches, as long as the core functions of the constitutional branches are not violated. Indeed, the creation of a Fourth Branch of government (or a Fifth or Sixth Branch) may be viewed as salutary, insofar as it creates yet another power center that can check and balance concentrated power.

[36] As Justice Stevens has wryly noted, "a particular function, like a chameleon, will often take on the aspect of the office to which it is assigned." *Bowsher*, 478 US at 749 (Stevens concurring).

[37] 462 US 919 (1983).

[38] Id at 952, 953 n 16.

[39] Id at 964.

[40] See Laurence H. Tribe, *The Legislative Veto Decision: A Law by Any Other Name?* 21 Harv J Legis 1 (1984); E. Donald Elliott, *INS v Chadha: The Administrative Constitution, the Constitution, and the Legislative Veto*, 1983 Supreme Court Review 125; Girardeau A. Spann, *Deconstructing the Legislative Veto*, 68 Minn L Rev 473 (1984).

Formalism is also attacked on the ground that it tends "to strait-jacket the government's ability to respond to new needs in creative ways, even if those ways pose no threat to whatever might be posited as the basic purposes of the constitutional structure."[41] Again, the exclusivity postulate of formalism's substantive theory is the root of the problem. If each branch has only one function (absent a constitutional exception), then multifunctional enti-ties—for example, administrative agencies that perform all three functions—would be unconstitutional.[42] To avoid this extreme conclusion, formalists are forced to adopt a grandfather strategy, preserving past deviations from formalist purity (like administrative agencies) based on stare decisis or a principle of historical settle-ment, while subjecting new innovations to scrutiny under a rigor-ous exclusive functions canon.[43] This solution, however, leads di-rectly to the "straitjacket" that the functionalists complain about. As Justice White has asked, if in the past the Court has sanctioned deviations from constitutional purity, and those deviations are grandfathered, how do we know the proper response to new devia-tions should be automatic disapproval—especially if a plausible case can be made that the new deviation is designed to correct an imbalance caused by the old one?[44]

The principal criticism leveled against functionalism is not that it is too rigid but that it is not rigid enough.[45] The problem, again, derives largely from the substantive theory, and in particular from the nebulousness of the concepts of "diffusion of power" and "core functions." Because these concepts are so indeterminant, the judi-cial reaction will almost always be to defer to the judgments of

---

[41] Brown, 139 U Pa L Rev at 1526 (cited in note 4).

[42] Id at 1524; Harold Bruff, *Presidential Power and Administrative Rulemaking*, 88 Yale L J 451, 498–99 (1979); Strauss, 84 Colum L Rev at 596 (cited in note 18).

[43] This is the strategy pursued by Justice Brennan's plurality opinion in *Northern Pipeline Co. v Marathon Pipe Line Co.*, 458 US 50 (1982). There, Justice Brennan asserted that the adjudicatory function belongs exclusively to Article III courts, subject to three exceptions designed to cover preexisting deviations: territorial courts, military courts, and tribunals considering questions involving "public rights." Id at 63–70. Because the adjudication of common law claims did not fall within any of the three exceptions, the *Northern Pipeline* plurality reasoned that the power to hear such claims could not be given to the Bankruptcy Court, a non–Article III tribunal.

[44] See *Chadha*, 462 US at 1002–03 (1983) (dissent).

[45] Redish & Cisar, 41 Duke L J 449 (cited in note 4); Stephen Carter, *Constitutional Improprieties: Reflections on Mistretta, Morrison, and Administrative Government*, 57 U Chi L Rev 357, 375–76 (1990).

other branches when separation of powers controversies arise. The arguments in support of innovation will be concrete and immediate, while the case for preserving "diffusion" or the "core" will seem abstract and remote.[46] Thus, the "core" functions notice is unlikely to achieve its stated aim: the preservation of a system of separated and balanced powers as a guarantee of liberty.[47]

Unpacking the strands of formalism and functionalism also allows us to see that although there is a natural affinity between the methodological and substantive sides of each understanding, the linkage is contingent rather than logically compelled. For the formalist, the exclusive functions construction posits that the constitutional structure incorporates a complex rule subject to many text-based exceptions. This rule-like understanding is obviously congenial to a deontological method of justification. On the functional side, the substantive theory eschews bright line rules in favor of more judgmental concepts like diffusion of power and core functions. These concepts invite a consequentialist methodology that examines every challenged institution or practice in terms of its impact on the overall purpose of a system of separation of powers. But notwithstanding these natural affinities between legal method and substantive theory, there is no reason in principle why some other substantive theory of the constitutional principle of separation of powers could not be adopted. Such a theory might avoid the more glaring problems generated by the substantive theories associated with formalism and functionalism. And it could be implemented with either a formal or a functional method of justification, or perhaps some combination of both.

III. The Minimal Conception of Separation of Powers

One pathway to a new substantive theory of separation of powers would be to break away from the shared preoccupation with the functional classification of government activities, and focus instead on the three branches of government as distinct organizations subject to specific constitutional limitations on how they

---

[46] See *United States v Nixon*, 418 US 683, 712–13 (1974) (President's interest in confidential communications is "general in nature" as opposed to the need for relevant evidence which is "specific and central to the fair adjudication of a particular criminal case").

[47] Redish & Cisar, cited in note 4.

exercise governmental authority.[48] Specifically, if we start with the substantive theory of the formalists, and drop the concern with the division of functions, what we would be left with is a "minimal conception" of separation of powers that would insist that there are only three branches of government, and that every federal office must be located in one of the three branches. The substantive interpretation of the constitutional principle of separation of powers would reduce to a single, simple rule: Congress may not create a Fourth Branch of the federal government.

In effect, under the minimal conception, all questions about the correct definition of the "legislative," "executive," and "judicial" powers, and about how those powers should be allocated among the branches, would become nonjusticiable political questions confined to the discretion of Congress.[49] Thus, Congress would be free to assign any function to any of the three branches of government. What Congress could not do would be to assign functions to an entity that is not accountable to one of the three constitutional branches, and hence not subject to the specific constitutional limitations that apply to each branch.[50]

In terms of legal methodology, the central proposition of the minimal conception would operate in a highly formalistic fashion. The idea that there are only three branches of government, and that every federal office must be accountable to one branch, would be regarded as a fixed rule derived from the text and structure of

---

[48] For another attempt along these lines, which has helped clarify my own thinking, see Krent, 74 Vir L Rev 1253 (cited in note 4).

[49] Alternatively, one could posit that questions about the definition and allocation of functions should be answered by the "core functions" theory of formalism, which would almost always result in their being upheld. See text at note 46. In fact, if I were tasked with implementing the minimal understanding, I would not say that the definitional and allocational questions are nonjusticiable, but would follow the functionalists and say that courts should intervene to decide these questions when core functions are threatened. Keeping the core functions idea around would provide some rhetorical continuity with the past, and would offer a "failsafe" should Congress in the future ever attempt severely to cripple the ability of either the executive or judicial branch to function. See note 115. For heuristic reasons, however, I will confine myself here to developing the case for a pure minimal approach, which would treat these questions as nonjusticiable.

[50] Because it would require strict judicial enforcement of the three-branches rule, the minimal approach would be quite different from those theories that would treat all questions about the horizontal division of powers as nonjusticiable. See Jesse H. Choper, *Judicial Review and the National Political Process* 260–379 (1980). Cf. Michael J. Perry, *The Constitution, the Courts, and Human Rights* 49–60 (1982) (arguing that separation-of-powers disputes should not be justiciable if the political branches agree about the proper resolution).

the Constitution and not subject to judicial waiver. The further steps in the inquiry, such as attributing federal offices to particular branches, and determining whether branch-specific constitutional limitations have been violated, could be decided either formalistically or under a more flexible, functional inquiry.

In practice, the minimal conception would require courts to make three determinations in any separation-of-powers case. First, the court would have to assign the office whose action is being challenged to one of the three constitutional branches (or determine that it constitutes an unconstitutional attempt to create a Fourth Branch). Second, it would have to determine if the action violates any specific constitutional limitations that apply to its assigned branch. Third, if the action transgresses any branch-specific limitation, the court would have to consider whether there is any basis for concluding that the action should be exempt from these limitations. A brief elaboration of each step is appropriate at this point; I will then offer some illustrations of how the approach would be employed in resolving recent separation-of-powers controversies.

A. ATTRIBUTION RULES

The first and in many respects key step under the minimal conception would require the Court to develop rules for assigning federal offices[51] to the three constitutional branches of government. The rules for identifying the components of the constitutional branches themselves—members of Congress, the President, and federal judges—are set forth with some particularity in the Constitution itself, and generally should not be problematic.[52] The rules for identifying federal offices that are agents of one of the branches are less self-evident. The Court's decision in *Bowsher v Synar*[53] sug-

---

[51] By "federal offices" I mean both principal and inferior offices. I will not here discuss the important question of how one distinguishes persons holding federal offices from other persons performing functions under federal law, such as state officers carrying out federal statutory directives or private citizens suing to enforce federal rights. See generally Harold J. Krent, *Fragmenting the Unitary Executive: Congressional Delegations of Administrative Authority Outside the Federal Government*, 85 Nw U L Rev 62 (1990). Obviously, my thesis presupposes that this can be done, otherwise the constitutional principle of separation of powers could be circumvented simply by allocating federal functions to private corporations or state entities.

[52] US Const, Art I, § 2, cl 5; Amend XVII; Art II, § 2, cl 2; Art II, § 3; Art III, § 1.

[53] 478 US 714 (1986).

gests that this inquiry could also be governed by a formal rule: an office is an agent of a branch if the members of the branch have the power to remove the incumbent officer.[54] *Washington Airports*, in contrast, suggests more of an all-things-considered standard for resolving this question. Justice Stevens noted that the Board of Review at issue in that case was "an entity created at the initiative of Congress, the powers of which Congress has delineated, the purpose of which is to protect an acknowledged federal interest, and membership in which is restricted to congressional officials."[55] He also noted that Congress as a whole could effectively remove a member of the Board.[56] Without suggesting that any one of these factors was determinative, he concluded that the Board should be regarded as exercising federal power as an agent of Congress. My own inclination would be to adopt a formal test for attributing offices to particular branches, and to make the power to remove the exclusive criterion. A simple removal test not only has the advantage of reducing uncertainty and litigation costs, it also reflects institutional reality. As the Court noted in *Bowsher*, once an officer is appointed, "it is only the authority that can remove him, and not the authority that appointed him, that he must fear and, in the performance of his functions, obey."[57]

For present purposes, however, it is not necessary to choose between formal and functional methodological approaches to this question. I would only note that to the extent the power to remove is a relevant factor—as it surely is under either approach—it would not necessarily mean the power to remove at will. *Bowsher* held that the Comptroller General is an agent of Congress, even though he is removable by Congress only for cause. And *Morrison v Olson*[58] expressly disapproved statements in *Myers v United States*[59] to the

---

[54] The Comptroller General (whose powers were at issue in *Bowsher*), like all other "civil officers," was removable by impeachment. US Const Art II, § 4. But the Court quite rightly did not suggest that this made him an agent of Congress. Because impeachments are so rare, this power does not act as a realistic day-to-day restraint on the behavior of federal officers.

[55] *Washington Airports* at 2308.

[56] Id ("Control over committee assignments also gives Congress effective removal power over Board members because depriving a Board member of membership in the relevant committees deprives the member of authority to sit on the Board.").

[57] *Bowsher*, 478 US at 726, quoting *Synar v United States*, 626 F Supp 1374, 1401 (D DC 1986); cf. *Mistretta*, 488 US at 423 (Scalia dissenting) ("It would seem logical to decide the question of which Branch an agency belongs to on the basis of who controls its actions.").

[58] 487 US 654 (1988).

[59] 272 US 52 (1926).

effect that all executive officers must be removable at will by the President. In effect, *Morrison* placed the independent counsel whose office was at issue in that case in the executive branch even though the Attorney General could remove her only for "good cause."

The effect of the attribution exercise would be to place most federal governmental entities in the executive branch. The congressional staff and a few offices like the General Accounting Office and the Congressional Budget Office would be deemed agents of Congress. The Administrative Office of the United States Courts, law clerks, and clerks of court would be agents of the federal courts. But most of the entities whose parentage has been a matter of controversy in the past—including the independent regulatory agencies like the FCC and SEC and Article I courts like the Tax Court—would become part of the executive branch. Ironically, the event that makes this allocation of offices even thinkable is the decision in *Morrison*—thought by most formalists to be a defeat for executive power. Before *Morrison*, it was assumed that all executive officers had to be removable at will by the President, a rule incompatible with the tenure rights enjoyed by the commissioners of independent agencies and judges of Article I courts.[60] But now that *Morrison* has established that some executive officers can be protected by a good cause removal requirement, reconceiving the independent agencies and Article I courts as part of the executive branch would not be that disruptive to settled institutional arrangements.

B. BRANCH-SPECIFIC LIMITATIONS

Next, having placed the office in one of the three branches, the Court would have to determine whether the actions required of that office transgress any constitutional limitations specific to the branch to which the office is assigned. As Harold Krent has observed, each branch of government is subject to certain "procedural" limitations reflected in the text of the Constitution.[61] Congress may generally act only in conformance with the Bicameral

---

[60] Hence in *Humphrey's Executor v United States*, 295 US 602 (1935) and *Wiener v United States*, 357 US 349 (1958), the Court upheld restrictions on the President's removal power only after finding that the offices involved were engaged in "quasi-legislative" or "quasi-judicial" rather than "executive" functions.

[61] See Krent, 74 Vir L Rev 1253 (cited in note 4).

and Presentment Clauses.[62] The executive branch, consistent with the Take Care Clause, may act only pursuant to authority given by legislation or an enumerated constitutional power.[63] And the federal courts may act only through the adjudication of "cases" and "controversies."[64] Thus, the process of placing an office in a particular branch will generally result in imposing at least one set of constitutional limitations on actions taken by that office.

The procedural limitations identified by Krent do not necessarily exhaust the constitutional constraints on action taken by any particular branch. Other clauses, like the Appointments Clause, the Incompatibility Clause, and the Speech or Debate Clause, also impose constraints on action by one branch affecting one or more of the others. In addition, the Court could conceivably recognize implied branch-specific limitations. For example, one could read the *Myers* case, even after the qualifications of *Morrison*, as establishing that all principal officers of the executive branch (as opposed to inferior officers like the independent counsel in *Morrison*) must be removable at will by the President. Alternatively (or in addition), one could reason from the Constitution's creation of a unitary executive that the President must be able to issue orders to any subordinate officer in the executive branch, and deem the failure to obey such an order "good cause" for removal.[65] It could also be that the judicial branch, like the executive, has no inherent power to create rules of decision, but must derive its authority to act from some source in enacted law, such as the Constitution or a federal statute.[66]

For present purposes, the point is not to develop a complete catalogue of all limitations specific to the actions of each branch. It is sufficient to note that there is at least one recognized limitation

---

[62] *Chadha*, 462 US 919 (1983).

[63] This is the lesson generally drawn from the *Steel Seizure* case, *Youngstown Sheet & Tube Co. v Sawyer*, 343 US 579 (1952). See, e.g., Currie, 1986 Supreme Court Review (cited in note 18).

[64] *Mistretta*, 488 US at 385, 389; *Morrison*, 487 US at 677; *Allen v Wright*, 468 US 737, 750 (1984).

[65] See Steven Calabresi and Kevin Rhodes, *The Structural Constitution: Unitary Executive, Plural Judiciary*, 105 Harv L Rev (forthcoming 1992); Liberman, 38 Am U L Rev at 316–17 (cited in note 18); Miller, *Independent Agencies*, 1986 Supreme Court Review at 86–87 (cited in note 22).

[66] As I argue in Thomas W. Merrill, *The Judicial Prerogative*, 12 Pace L Rev (forthcoming 1992); see also Currie, 1986 Supreme Court Review at 25 (cited in note 18).

applicable to each branch, and that the task of the Court under the minimal conception, once it attributes the actions of an office to a particular branch, is to determine whether any applicable limitations have been transgressed.

C. EXCEPTIONS

Finally, the Court would have to consider in some cases whether an exception from the usual limitations on branch action may be applicable. The primary constraints—the Bicameral and Presentment Clauses, the Take Care Clause, and the Cases or Controversies limitation—should be construed as applying only to exercises of governmental authority by each branch. As the Court said in *Chadha*, the Bicameral and Presentment rules apply when a component of Congress takes action that has "the purpose and effect of altering the legal rights, duties and relations of persons . . . outside the Legislative Branch."[67] By negative implication, actions that do not affect the "rights, duties and relations of persons" outside the legislative branch would be exempt from these constitutional procedures. Thus, rules relating to parliamentary procedures, congressional staff, and use of congressional facilities presumably could be adopted by Congress or a designated component of Congress without complying with the Bicameral and Presentment Clauses. Similarly, internal operating rules having no impact on the public can be adopted by the other branches without complying with specific constitutional constraints.[68] In addition, specific Clauses of the Constitution may create other exceptions. For example, there are several express exceptions to the Bicameral and Presentment requirements.[69] Again, the point is not to offer an exhaustive list of exceptions, but merely to note their role in a fully formed federal offices conception of separation of powers.

---

[67] 462 US at 952.

[68] Thus, for example, the courts can be empowered to adopt rules of procedure through a rulemaking process, as authorized by the Rules Enabling Act, 28 USC § 2072 (1988), without offending the Cases or Controversies limitation. The key question would be whether such rules are "governmental" or "nongovernmental," that is, whether they are designed to control primary (prelitigational) behavior or to control the behavior of attorneys and other persons engaged in litigation. Cf. *Hanna v Plumer*, 380 US 460 (1965). Fairly clearly, such an exception would have to be developed in a methodologically functional rather than a formal fashion, that is, it would have to be developed in light of the purpose of the exception (to limit the Cases or Controversies limitation to exercises of governmental authority).

[69] See *Chadha*, 462 US at 955 (listing exceptions).

D. ILLUSTRATIONS

In order to clarify the way in which the minimal conception would operate, it may be useful to indicate how that approach would resolve some recent separation-of-powers controversies.

Last Term, *Washington Airports* involved the question whether Congress can use its power over the disposition of federal property to induce a state to create an institution exercising what is in effect a Congressional veto. Assuming that the financial inducement was sufficient to establish that the Board was a federal agency,[70] then the key question under the minimal conception would be attribution. Since Congress as a whole could remove members of the Board by taking them off the relevant Congressional committees, under the formal criterion the Board would be regarded as an agent of Congress. As we have seen, Justice Stevens engaged in an all-things-considered inquiry, and reached the same conclusion.

Once the attribution question is resolved, then the case becomes easy. As an agent of Congress, the Board was subject to the same constitutional limitations that apply to Congress. Since a decision by Congress disapproving action by a regional airports authority would have to be approved by both Houses and presented to the President for his signature or veto, decisions of the Board must also comply with these requirements. Given that the Board could not possibly comply with these limitations, the legislation creating it should be deemed unconstitutional.

Mistretta v United States[71] concerned the constitutionality of the United States Sentencing Commission, an entity composed in part of sitting federal judges and given broad powers to prescribe binding federal sentencing guidelines. Under the minimal conception, the initial task would be to determine where the Commission fits in the tripartite constitutional structure. Although described by the

---

[70] Given that the federal legislation took the form of a conditional grant of federal property (a long-term lease of National and Dulles Airports), the Court could easily have required more evidence of federal "coercion" of Virginia before attributing the actions of the state-created Board to Congress itself. Although the issue is beyond the scope of this paper, the implicit conception of "coercion" in *Washington Airports* seems to be closer to the notion of irresistible financial inducement invoked in *United States v Butler*, 297 US 1 (1936), than to the stricter notion of coercion employed in *South Dakota v Dole*, 483 US 203 (1987) and *Steward Machine Co. v Davis*, 301 US 548 (1937). Whether this portends a permanent shift in the Court's atttitude toward conditional grants of money and property remains to be seen.

[71] 488 US 361 (1989).

legislation establishing it "as an independent commission in the judicial branch of the United States,"[72] under the minimal conception the Commission should be regarded as part of the executive branch. All members of the Commission are subject to removal by the President "for neglect of duty or malfeasance in office or for other good cause shown."[73] Under the formal approach to attribution, this would settle the matter. The fact that the statute required that three members of the Commission be active federal judges— although perhaps raising a question under the Appointments Clause[74]—would not change this result. The relevant question is whether the office is accountable to the President, not whether the President has the power to remove the incumbent officer from all forms of government service. The President clearly has the power to remove the Article III judges acting in their capacity as Sentencing Commissioners, and so they should be regarded as part of the executive branch.

Under a more contextual analysis, the same conclusion should be reached. All Commission members, including the three sitting federal judges, are appointed by the President. And it is clear that the Commission operates independent of direction from the Chief Justice, the Judicial Conference, or any other judicial body. Thus, the Commission is quite unlike other entities, such as the Administrative Office of the United States Courts or the Federal Judicial Center, that are generally regarded as being part of the judicial branch.[75]

Once is it clear that, for separation-of-powers purposes, the Sentencing Commission is an agent of the executive branch, then the other issues in the case are straightforward. The various challenges to the Commission based on the anomaly of rulemaking by an entity in the judicial branch would be serious only if the Commission were in fact located in the judicial branch.[76] The nondelegation

---

[72] 28 USC § 991(a) (1988).

[73] Id.

[74] See *Public Citizen v United States*, 491 US 440, 488–89 (1989) (Kennedy concurring) (arguing that the textual commitment of the appointments power to the President prohibits any legislative interference with the President's discretion in selecting nominees).

[75] See Brief for the United States, at 39–40, *Mistretta v United States*.

[76] Congress' designation of the Commission as an independent commission in the judicial branch, 28 USC § 991(a), might still be important for statutory purposes, such as determining whether the Commission is subject to the Freedom of Information Act. See 5 USC 552(f) (1988).

doctrine challenge necessarily fails because it rests on the notions about the proper allocation of the "legislative function" rather than some specific constitutional limitation. And the fact that Article III judges were included on the Commission is of no significance, since the Incompatibility Clause applies only to Members of Congress, and does not prohibit Article III judges from simultaneously serving in the executive branch.[77] The minimal conception thus confirms that the Court was correct in upholding the constitutionality of the Sentencing Commission.

Morrison v Olson,[78] which considered the constitutionality of the independent counsel provisions of the Ethics in Government Act, is somewhat more difficult. The attribution question may hinge on whether one adopts a formal criterion, or a contextual approach. The independent counsel is removable by the Attorney General for "good cause," thus satisfying the formal criterion for placement in the executive branch. But in other respects, the counsel's allegiance is divided between the executive and the judicial branches. The counsel must abide by the policies of the Justice Department where possible.[79] But an Article III court—the Special Division of the D.C. Circuit—confirms the counsel's jurisdiction and has the power to terminate an investigation.[80] If one concludes that, on balance, the counsel is an agent of the judicial branch, then the statute would be unconstitutional under the minimal approach, because the counsel is not confined to the adjudication of cases and controversies or permissible internal functions of the judicial branch.

On the other hand, if one finds that the independent counsel is an agent of the executive branch—as the formal criterion suggests—then most of the provisions of the Act should survive a challenge based on the principle of separation of powers. The good cause limitation on the power to remove the independent counsel is acceptable, as long as the President is afforded other means of assuring ultimate control over executive branch officers. And the claim that the Act as a whole unduly interferes with "executive" functions necessarily fails, because questions about where Congress

---

[77] See *Mistretta*, 488 US at 398.

[78] 487 US 654 (1988).

[79] 28 USC § 594(f) (1988).

[80] 28 USC § 596(b)(2) (1988).

places executive powers are nonjusticiable. The provision giving the Special Division the power to terminate the office of the independent counsel, however, would appear to be unconstitutional because it transgresses the cases and controversies limitation on the judicial power.[81] To this limited extent, then, the federal officers approach would indicate a result contrary to that reached by the Court.[82]

IV. THE ADVANTAGES OF THE MINIMAL CONCEPTION

Even if it is possible to state a third conception of the constitutional principle of separation of powers, and to show that it could be implemented as a legal doctrine, the question remains: what claim would it have to our allegiance? Fairly clearly, the minimal conception would eliminate the most glaring problems associated with formalism and functionalism. Because it would consider questions about the proper definition and allocation of "legislative," "executive," and "judicial" power to be nonjusticiable, it would avoid the source of the question-begging analysis that plagues formalism. Also, by eschewing any review of the questions about the distribution of functions, it would permit considerable experimentation with new forms of multifunctional entities, at least those located in the executive branch. Thus, it would eliminate the main cause of the "straightjacket" on governmental innovation associated with formalism. On the other hand, the three-branches rule at the core of the minimal understanding would provide clear signals to the judiciary and other actors in government about the outer limits of structural experimentation, and thus would avoid the vacuity associated with functionalism.

In addition, there are three positive reasons why the minimal conception presents an attractive alternative to formalism and functionalism. First, the minimal conception, unlike both formal-

---

[81] See Krent, 74 Vir L Rev at 1319–21 (cited in note 4).

[82] The consitutionality of the Act was also challenged under the Appointments Clause on the grounds that the Special Counsel is a principal officer requiring presidential appointment, and that the Appointments Clause does not permit "cross branch" appointments of inferior officers. On both scores, I find the reasoning of Justice Scalia's dissent and the D.C. Circuit more persuasive than the majority's opinion. See *Morrison*, 487 US at 715–23 (Scalia dissenting); *In re Sealed Case*, 838 F2d 476 (D C Cir 1988). But since these issues are extraneous to the question of the meaning of the constitutional principle of separation of powers, I will not elaborate on them here.

ism or functionalism, is consistent with the outcomes (but not the reasoning) of virtually all the Supreme Court's major decisions on separation of powers. Second, the minimal conception would further two general purposes of a doctrine of separation of powers: preventing evasions of specific clauses limiting the powers of the branches, and encouraging a diffusion of power. Third, the minimal conception is consistent with the text of the Constitution, and is in some respects more faithful to the original understanding than are its principal rivals.

A. CONGRUENCE WITH SUPREME COURT OUTCOMES

While the Court has struggled with the yin and yang of formalism and functionalism, the outcomes it has reached have been intriguingly consistent. The Court has nearly always rejected claims based on the improper assignment of executive and judicial functions,[83] but has regularly sustained claims based on Congressional attempts to exercise governmental power in violation of the requirements for enacting valid legislation.[84] The same pattern of results would be reached under the minimal conception. The minimal conception would treat questions about proper allocation of functions as nonjusticiable; thus, like the Court, it would not overturn legislation on the ground that it improperly assigns the executive or judicial functions. On the other hand, the minimal conception would strictly enforce the requirements of the Bicameral and Presentments Clauses, and thus like the Court would invalidate attempts by Congress to assert extra-legislative governmental power. I would go further, however, and argue that the minimal conception would produce outcomes that are congruent with virtually all of the judgments rendered by the Supreme Court in its leading separation-of-powers decisions.

1. *Nondelegation doctrine.* The Supreme Court has steadfastly maintained that only Congress can exercise the legislative power.[85] Nevertheless, under the rubric of the nondelegation doctrine, the Court has also said that Congress may confer significant discretion

---

[83] See *Freytag* and cases cited in note 8.

[84] *Washington Airports* and cases cited in note 7.

[85] *Touby v United States*, 111 S Ct 1752, 1755 (1991); *Mistretta*, 488 US 371–72; *Field v Clark*, 143 US 649, 692 (1892).

on the other branches, so long as it "lay[s] down by legislative act an intelligible principle to which the person or body authorized to [act] is directed to conform."[86] Application of this "intelligible principle" doctrine, in turn, has resulted in widespread transfers of power to administrative agencies to promulgate "legislative rules"[87] functionally indistinguishable from statutes. In the last fifty years, the Court has consistently declined to interfere with such transfers,[88] to the point where, realistically speaking, there is no meaningful judicial limitation on Congressional decisions to delegate legislative power to other branches. The minimal conception would of course reach the same result by declaring the issue nonjusticiable.

2. *Non–Article III courts.* In no area of constitutional law is there a greater or more persistent deviation from formal or functional theories than that involving the assignment of the judicial function. The Supreme Court has permitted controversies between adverse parties under federal law to be decided by territorial courts, military courts, District of Columbia courts, various "legislative" courts like the Tax Court, and administrative agencies.[89] The one exception here is *Northern Pipeline,*[90] where the Court invalidated a portion of the jurisdiction of the bankruptcy courts as being inconsistent with the vesting of judicial power in Article III courts. But recent decisions make clear that the analysis employed by the plurality in *Northern Pipeline* has been confined to its facts.[91] Taken together, the decisions approving a wide variety of non–Article III courts overwhelmingly suggest that there is no judicially enforced limitation on assignment of the "judicial" function. The minimal conception would reach this same conclusion by declaring such questions nonjusticiable.

---

[86] *J.W. Hampton, Jr. & Co. v United States,* 276 US 394, 409 (1928).

[87] See *Batterton v Francis,* 432 US 416, 425 n 9 (1977).

[88] For the most recent decisions that reach this conclusion, see *Touby v United States,* 111 S Ct 1752 (1991) (upholding delegation of power to criminalize possession of drugs); *Skinner v Mid-America Pipeline Co.,* 490 US 212 (1989) (upholding delegation of power to set rates of taxation); *Mistretta* (upholding delegation of power to set criminal sentencing guidelines).

[89] See generally Lawson, 78 Cal L Rev 853 (cited in note 10); Richard H. Fallon, Jr., *Of Legislative Courts, Administrative Agencies, and Article III,* 101 Harv L Rev 916 (1988).

[90] 458 US 50 (1982).

[91] See *Freytag,* 111 S Ct at 2644 ("judicial power" may be given to non–Article III court); *Commodity Futures Trading Comm'n v Schor,* 478 US 833 (1986) (administrative agency may adjudicate common-law claim); *Thomas v Union Carbide Agricultural Products Co.,* 473 US 568 (1985) (value of trade secrets may be fixed by non–Article III forum).

3. *Removal cases.* The Court has decided four major cases that consider whether a congressional restriction on the President's power to remove subordinate officers interferes with the "executive power" given to the President by Article II. In one—*Myers v United States*[92]—the Court held that the restriction was unconstitutional. In the remaining three cases[93] the restriction was upheld. Although the reasoning of these four decisions is impossible to reconcile, the outcomes all comport with those that would be reached under the minimal conception. In *Myers*, the restriction took the form of a requirement that any removal of a postmaster first class be confirmed by the Senate.[94] This was a legislative veto, unconstitutional under the Bicameral and Presentment Clauses. In the other three cases, the restriction took the form of limiting the President's power of removal to a finding of good cause, and in each case the restriction was upheld. Thus, when the sole foundation for the claim is interference with the assignment of the executive function to the President, the claim has been rejected, consistent with the minimal conception.

4. *Legislative attempts to execute the laws.* On several other occasions, the Court has invalidated legislation said to permit the legislature to perform executive functions.[95] But the holdings of each of these cases can be explained on the basis of specific constitutional limitations: in each case Congress either transgressed the Bicameral and Presentment Clauses,[96] or violated an expressly enumerated Presidential power, such as the Appointments Clause or the Pardon Power.[97] Thus, the results in these cases would not be disturbed under the minimal conception, which would not permit Congress to transgress express constitutional limitations on its power.

5. *Executive privilege cases.* In three cases involving former President Nixon, the Court has recognized an "executive privilege"

---

[92] 272 US 52 (1926).

[93] *Morrison v Olson*, 487 US 654 (1988); *Wiener v United States*, 357 US 349 (1958); *Humphrey's Executor v United States*, 295 US 602 (1935).

[94] See 272 US at 107.

[95] *Washington Airports*, 111 S Ct at 2312; *Bowsher*, 478 US at 726; *Buckley v Valeo*, 424 US 1, 140 (1976); *Springer v Philippine Islands*, 277 US 189, 205–06 (1928); *United States v Klein*, 80 US 128, 148 (1872).

[96] *Washington Airports*, 111 S Ct at 2312; *Bowsher*, 478 US at 754–56 (Stevens concurring); *Springer*, 277 US at 203.

[97] *Buckley*, 424 US at 143; *Klein*, 80 US at 147–48.

based on general considerations of separation of powers.[98] Such a privilege has no express textual foundation, and would have to be grounded in an understanding of the President's assigned responsibility to perform "executive" functions. Recognition of such a privilege runs counter to the minimal conception, but the ultimate holding of two of these cases was to deny the Presidential claim.[99] Although the claim was sustained in the third, the Court reserved the question whether Congress could override the privilege, suggesting that the holding was not constitutionally compelled.[100] Thus, the actual outcome reached in these cases does not necessarily conflict with the minimal conception.

6. *Foreign affairs cases.* Finally, in the foreign affairs and national defense context, there are statements suggesting that the President may act in exigent circumstances without specific legal authorization, contrary to the implication that the minimal conception would draw from the Take Care Clause.[101] However, most of the decisions in this area can be explained on alternative grounds—either the President's action could be sustained under a specific clause of the Constitution, such as the Commander-in-Chief or Receiving Ambassadors provisions,[102] or under existing statutory authority, broadly construed.[103] Thus, the actual holdings of the cases are not necessarily inconsistent with an understanding that the Take Care Clause imposes a general limitation on executive action.

* * *

We can thus see that the Supreme Court's leading separation of powers decisions trace a generally consistent pattern overall. Claims grounded solely on an assertion about the correct allocation of functions among branches almost invariably fail; claims based

---

[98] *Nixon v Fitzgerald*, 457 US 731 (1982); *Nixon v Administrator of General Services*, 433 US 425, 446–55 (1977); *United States v Nixon*, 418 US 683 (1974).

[99] *Nixon v Administrator*, 433 US at 455; *United States v Nixon*, 418 US at 713.

[100] *Nixon v Fitzgerald*, 457 US at 748 n 27.

[101] *United States v Curtiss-Wright Corp.*, 299 US 304, 319–20 (1936); *The Prize Cases*, 2 Black 635, 668 (1863).

[102] For example, *United States v Belmont*, 301 US 324, 330 (1937) (power to enter into executive agreements derived from Receiving Ambassadors Clause); *The Prize Cases*, 2 Black at 668 (power to act in military emergency supported by President's power as Commander-in-Chief).

[103] E.g., *Dames & Moore v Regan*, 453 US 654 (1981).

on the violation of a specific textual limitation on action by a branch
will succeed if the Court concludes that the limitation has in fact
been transgressed.[104] There may be a variety of explanations for
this phenomenon. It could be, for example, that the presence of a
specific clause like the Presentment Clause or the Appointments
Clause increases the Court's confidence about interposing its judgment against that of the political branches. Or it could be that
the pattern reflects a bias in favor of the executive branch.[105] The
important point, for present purposes, is that the pattern is fully
consistent with the results that would be reached under the minimal conception, which would make questions about the definition
and allocation of functions nonjusticiable, but would strictly enforce specific limitations on the branches.

At a theoretical level, how much significance one attributes to
this congruence depends on how one conceives of the role of the
Supreme Court in interpreting the Constitution, and one's theory
of precedent. If one regards the Supreme Court's decisions as authoritative, and adopts a theory of precedent that stresses the judgments reached in light of the material facts,[106] then the evidence
of consistency would be very powerful support for the minimal
conception. But if one does not regard Supreme Court decisions
as authoritative (as opposed to, say, the original intentions of the
Framers), or if one adopts a theory of precedent that stresses the

---

[104] Individual Justices have also perceived this pattern. See *Chadha*, 462 US at 999 (White
dissenting) ("The separation-of-powers doctrine has heretofore led to the invalidation of
Government action only when the challenged action violated some express provision in the
Constitution."); *Public Citizen v United States*, 491 US 440, 484–85 (1989) (Kennedy concurring) (noting that the Court employs a "balancing test" where the power at issue is "thought
to be encompassed within the general grant to the president of the 'executive Power,' " but
that "where the Constitution by explicit text commits the power at issue to the exclusive
control of the President, we have refused to tolerate *any* intrusion by the Legislative
Branch").

[105] See Erwin Chemerinsky, *A Paradox Without a Principle: A Comment on the Burger Court's
Jurisprudence in Separation of Powers Cases*, 60 S Cal L Rev 1083 (1987). The pro-executive
bias explanation was dealt a severe setback by *Morrison*, where the Court, over the vigorous
objections of the Solicitor General, curtailed the scope of the President's removal power
recognized in *Myers*. The Court also rejected the position of the Solicitor General in *Mistretta*, *Freytag*, and *Washington Airports*, although in the last case the effect of the Court's
decision was to give the executive more protection against Congressional aggrandizement
than it sought.

[106] See Arthur L. Goodhart, *Determining the Ratio Decidendi of a Case*, 40 Yale L J 161
(1930). For a recent discussion, see Charles W. Collier, *Precedent and Legal Authority: A
Critical History*, 1988 Wis L Rev 771.

reasons given by the Court rather than the judgments rendered on material facts, then the evidence would be less than compelling.

On a more practical level, however, the congruence must be regarded significant, if only as a measure of continuity with our institutional past. As Justice Frankfurter once observed in this context, "[d]eeply embedded traditional ways of conducting government" represent "the gloss which life has written" on the words of the Constitution.[107] The outcomes the Court has reached in resolving major separation-of-powers controversies reflect that gloss and in turn shape it. Ordinarily, of course, the articulated understanding of the Supreme Court is also an important ingredient in comprehending the past and providing guidance for the future. But where the Court has developed two rivalrous understandings of the constitutional principle of separation of powers, neither of which can account for the full range of its judgments, the Court's reasons naturally play a less significant role. Because the minimal understanding would reach essentially the same outcomes the Court has arrived at (by whatever means), it would largely preserve the settled pattern of institutional arrangements under our Constitution.

B. PROMOTING THE PURPOSES OF SEPARATION OF POWERS

The minimal construction would also advance two important purposes associated with a doctrine of separation of powers: it would prohibit evasion of the specific clauses of the Constitution that limit the governing authority of the branches, and it would promote a diffusion of power among the branches. If Congress were free to create a Fourth Branch of government, that is, an entity not accountable or subject to the limitations that apply to the three constitutional branches, then it would be easy to circumvent these provisions altogether. For example, Congress could bypass the Cases or Controversies limitation of Article III by enacting a statute making the Justices of the Supreme Court an independent agency with power to render advice to the President. Alternatively, Congress could evade the Presentment Clause by constituting both Houses of Congress an independent agency and delegating to that agency the power to promulgate legislative rules.

---

[107] *Youngstown Sheet & Tube Co. v Sawyer*, 343 US 579, 610 (1952) (concurring opinion).

The decisions in *Chadha*, *Bowsher*, and *Washington Airports* suggest that the Court is sensitive to the problem of evasion. When Congress adopts legislation delegating governing authority to a sub-unit of Congress or a Congressional agent, such legislation does not literally violate the Bicameral and Presentments Clauses. The statutes incorporating the delegations (which are the statutes held unconstitutional) technically comply with the Clauses—they have been passed by both Houses and signed by the President.[108] The problem is that these statutes set up institutional mechanisms that would permit wholesale evasion of these Clauses in the future. Thus, the Court has invalidated statutes that permit Congress to assert extra-legislative governmental authority because "[a]ny other conclusion would permit Congress to evade the 'carefully crafted' constraints of the Constitution."[109]

The minimal conception of separation of powers, by forcing all federal offices into one of three constitutional branches, would function more generally to prevent evasion of the specific clauses of the Constitution. Because every federal office would be located in one of the branches, every office would be subject to one set of constitutional limitations—those that apply to the branch to which it belongs. To be sure, by transferring functions back and forth among the branches, Congress would have the power to shift from one set of limitations to another. But it could never circumvent the constitutional limitations altogether, and assuming that it was forced to give some functions to each branch (as I shall argue momentarily it would be), each limitation would be given effect.

The minimal conception would also create a dynamic tension between Congress and the other branches of government that would serve the central end of a system of separation of powers—the diffusion of power to "protect the liberty and security of the governed."[110] Perhaps the easiest way of seeing this is to consider

---

[108] See *Chadha*, 462 US at 980 (White dissenting).

[109] *Washington Airports*, 111 S Ct at 2308. Admittedly, the Court has been less vigilant about the possibility of evasion with respect to the Cases or Controversies limitation on the judicial branch. The decision in *Mistretta*, for example, seems to suggest that Article III judges may in special circumstances participate in legislative rulemaking. But at least at the rhetorical level, the Court has continued to insist that Article III courts are constitutionally restricted to deciding cases and controversies, see *Morrison* 487 US at 677, suggesting that at some point it would invalidate attempts to bypass this limitation too.

[110] *Washington Airports*, 111 S Ct at 2310. See also cases cited in note 26 .

the structure of options that the minimal understanding would present to Congress. This approach would give Congress unreviewable discretion to delegate functions, but would impose strict limits on who may receive the delegation. Congress (*a*) could not delegate governing authority to a subunit of itself or to a Congressional agent, (*b*) could delegate to the federal courts only on the understanding that they would be limited to deciding cases and controversies, but (*c*) could make virtually unlimited delegations to the executive branch. How would Congress respond to this menu of options?

Consider, first, the possibility that Congress might decide to assign all functions to itself. Because there would be no judicially enforced limits on the allocation of functions, it would be free to do this. But any governmental action by Congress (or an agent of Congress) must comply with the Bicameral and Presentment Clauses, and Congress is severely limited in the number of times it can surmount these cumbersome barriers in any legislative session. Because the legislative agenda is a scarce resource, one would predict that Congress, if it wanted to maximize its own influence within the tripartite system, would typically use the legislative process to promulgate general rules for the governance of society, and would resist requests to engage in the more routine and high-volume activities traditionally associated with the executive and judicial functions. The great reluctance of Congress to conduct impeachment proceedings,[111] and the self-imposed limitations it has adopted on the use of private bills,[112] tend to confirm these observations.

Once Congress decides to delegate most routine functions outside the legislative branch, its only options would be the judicial branch and the executive branch. Because courts cannot act expeditiously or on their own initiative, and could make law only through the development of federal common law, the best choice for most purposes would be the executive branch. But the President is historically the principal constitutional rival of the Congress, and so Congress would be reluctant to give unconstrained discretion to the executive. Thus, the minimal understanding would provide an

---

[111] Mitch McConnell, *Reflections on the Senate's Role in the Judicial Impeachment Process and Proposals for Change*, 76 Ky L J 739 (1987–88).

[112] Note, *Private Bills in Congress*, 79 Harv L Rev 1684, 1688–93 (1966).

THE SUPREME COURT REVIEW

incentive for Congress to make key policy decisions itself through legislation—probably far more of an incentive than the toothless nondelegation doctrine provides. In addition, Congress would want some assurance that those executive entities that receive delegated power respect its intentions as set forth in general law.[113] Given that Congress is severely limited in its ability to enact remedial legislation correcting executive interpretations, the only effective monitoring device would be to provide for judicial review by Article III courts.[114] Thus, Congress would almost surely want to give the independent judiciary significant power to review executive action.

In short, given the three branches rule and the procedural limitations that attach to each branch, the most logical choices for Congress in disbursing functions would be to keep large elements of the lawmaking function for itself, give important elements of the case deciding function to the Article III courts, and transfer what is left over to the executive. The resulting allocation of powers would look very much like those that the formal and functional theories would have the judiciary impose directly through enforcement of some constitutionally compelled allocation of functions.

For the same reasons that Congress would want to call upon the aid of each of the other two branches, it is not plausible that Congress would want seriously to "encroach" on their capacity to function effectively. Thus, although it is possible to hypothesize various horribles—Congress demanding that C-Span be allowed to broadcast from the Oval Office, or from the Conference Room of the Supreme Court—it is highly unlikely that any of these horribles would ever materialize. Because Congress would want each of the other branches to perform efficiently in order to realize its own objectives, it could not afford to adopt measures that would cripple the ability of the executive or the courts to function.[115]

---

[113] William Landes and Richard Posner, *The Independent Judiciary in an Interest Group Perspective*, 18 J Law & Econ 875 (1975).

[114] See Thomas W. Merrill, *Judicial Deference to Executive Precedent*, 101 Yale L J 969, 993–98 (1992); Cynthia R. Farina, *Statutory Interpretation and the Balance of Power in the Administrative State*, 89 Colum L Rev 452 (1989).

[115] If one thinks that the dynamic incentives created by the minimal construction are not enough to insure against congressional mischief, there is no reason why it could not be "backstopped" by some version of the core functions understanding. See note 49. Under such a dual theory, most of the work of preserving equilibrium among the branches would

In sum, the incentive structure created by the minimal understanding would establish a dynamic tension that should lead Congress to allocate significant powers to all three constitutional
branches. Because it would not trust the executive and judiciary
with all functions of government, Congress would want to retain
significant powers for itself. Yet because of the Bicameral and Presentment Clauses, it would have to give significant powers away.
Given its rivalry with the President, it would want to provide for
a substantial measure of judicial review of executive action. And
because of the disability of courts to govern other than through the
cases or controversies, it could not dispense with the executive for
most of what we regard as executive functions. Thus, the minimal
understanding should lead to a dispersion of power among the
branches—not because of direct judicial enforcement of an allocation of governmental functions, but because of the incentive structure presented to Congress. This dispersion, in turn, would provide the foundation for the checking and balancing of governmental
power that both the formalists and the functionalists seek as means
of protecting liberty.

C. TEXT AND ORIGINAL UNDERSTANDING

What about the ultimate touchstone of constitutional law: the
text and original understanding of the Framers? The minimal conception of separation of powers would seem to be consistent with,
but admittedly not compelled by, the text of the Constitution. To
be sure, the opening clauses of Articles I, II, and III each speak in
terms of the vesting certain "powers" in each of the three departments of government: "All legislative Powers herein granted" are
vested in the Congress;[116] "The executive Power" is vested in the
President;[117] and "The judicial Power" is vested in the Supreme
Court and "in such inferior Courts as the Congress may from time
to time ordain and establish."[118] These clauses provide some sup-

---

be performed by the minimal understanding. But the core functions idea would be kept
around, like an old gun in the closet, just in case this prediction proved wrong and Congress
in a fit of pique tried to cripple one of the other branches. If this happened, the Court could
declare an invasion of a "core" function not supported by adequate justification, and strike
the encroachment down.

[116] US Const Art I, § 1.

[117] Art II, § 1.

[118] Art III, § 1.

port for the shared assumption of the formalists and the functionalists that the constitutional principle of separation of powers is concerned with the division of powers or functions among the branches
of government, not just the assignment of federal offices to
branches.

But the text provides very little support for the further proposition that the Constitution adopts a fixed definition or allocation of
the three powers, certainly not to the degree necessary to support
judicial enforcement comfortably. The Constitution makes no effort to define the "legislative," "executive," and "judicial" powers.
Instead, it specifically confers power on Congress "[t]o make all
laws which shall be necessary and proper for carrying into Execution the foregoing [legislative] powers, and *all other powers*
vested by this Constitution in the Government of the United
States. . . ."[119] Thus, the text plausibly can be read as committing
questions about the definition and allocation of the three great powers to Congress, not the courts.

Nor does the federal Constitution, like some of the state constitutions of the period, contain a clause requiring that the functions or
powers given to the different branches remain separate.[120] Indeed,
an amendment that would have committed the national government to something like the exclusive functions construction[121] was
proposed as part of the package of provisions that became the bill
of rights, but was rejected by the Senate.[122] The failure of such an
amendment is notoriously ambiguous: it could either mean that the
Senate thought the principle of strict functional division ought not
to be in the Constitution, or that it thought it was already reflected

---

[119] Art I, § 8, cl 18 (emphasis added).

[120] For example, the Virginia Constitution of 1776 provided: "The legislative, executive,
and judiciary department, shall be separate and distinct, so that neither exercise the powers
properly belonging to the other: nor shall any person exercise the powers of more than one
of them, at the same time. . . ." 7 Francis N. Thorpe, *The Federal and State Constitutions,
Colonial Charters, and Other Organic Laws of the States* 3815 (1909).

[121] The Sixteenth Article of Amendments approved by the House on August 24, 1789,
provided:

The powers delegated by the Constitution to the government of the United States,
shall be exercised as therein appropriated, so that the Legislative shall never exercise the powers vested in the Executive or Judicial; nor the Executive the powers
vested in the Legislative or Judicial; nor the Judicial the powers vested in the
Legislative or Executive.

Daniel A. Farber & Suzanna Sherry, *A History of the American Constitution* 436 (1990).

[122] Edward Dumbauld, *The Bill of Rights and What It Means Today* 46–47 (1957).

in the Constitution, making the amendment unnecessary. But given that the first Congress did not shy away from adopting two other "truistic" or "redundant" amendments—the Ninth and the Tenth[123]—it is plausible to think that some persons may have regarded the proposed separation-of-powers amendment not just as clarifying what was already implicit in the document but rather as imposing an unwanted restriction on congressional discretion to organize the new government.

On the other hand, the text of the constitution is surely consistent with the proposition that there are only three branches of government. The first three articles of the Constitution are not just about "powers," they are about institutions. At the highest level there are only three institutions: "a Congress of the United States,"[124] "a President of the United States of America,"[125] and "one supreme Court."[126] A number of other institutions are also mentioned: "Departments," "the Army," "the Navy," and "inferior Courts." But it is clear from context that, three of these subordinate institutions—"Departments," "the Army," and "the Navy"—are accountable to the President. The Departments are at one point referred to as *executive* Departments," where it is further specified that the President may require the opinion in writing of the principal officer of each on any subject relating to the duties of his office.[127] And the President is expressly made the commander-in-chief of the Army and Navy.[128] The other named institution—the inferior courts—is expressly placed in the judicial branch. Thus, it is entirely natural to construe the Constitution as creating a government with three and only three branches of government.

What we know of the drafting history sheds virtually no light on whether the Framers would have preferred a functions-oriented

---

[123] See *United States v Darby*, 312 US 100, 124 (1941) ("The [Tenth] Amendment states but a truism that all is retained which has not been surrendered."); *Griswold v Connecticut*, 381 US 479, 529–30 (1965) (Stewart dissenting) ("The Ninth Amendment, like its companion the Tenth, [was adopted] to make clear that the adoption of the Bill of Rights did not alter the plan that the Federal Government was to be a government of express and limited powers").

[124] US Const Art I, § 1.

[125] Art II, § 1.

[126] Art III, § 1.

[127] US Const Art II, § 2, cl 1 (emphasis added).

[128] Id.

or a three-branches construction of the Constitution. The Committee of the Whole adopted a resolution on May 30, 1787 stating "that a national government ought to be established consisting of a supreme legislative, judiciary, and executive." This resolution is facially consistent with either a functions or branches construction. We will never know which was intended, for as Gerhard Casper has observed, "this event was the beginning and the end of the consideration of separation of powers *as such* in the Convention."[129] The current language referring to legislative, executive, and judicial "powers" was first added the Committee on Detail on August 9.[130] It does not appear to have generated any discussion at that time, and remained (at least in this respect) unchanged until the final draft was agreed upon.

The ratification materials, on the other hand, provide evidence that at least one important Framer—James Madison—thought of separation of powers in terms closer to what I have called the minimal conception than to either of the rival theories. Many anti-Federalists criticized the Constitution because it contained too many departures from a pure model of separation of powers.[131] Madison set about responding to these concerns in *The Federalist* with two lines of thought. One, which was expressed in No. 37, was to deny that any pure theory of separation of powers was possible:[132]

> Experience has instructed us that no skill in the science of Government has yet been able to discriminate and define, with sufficient certainty, its three great provinces, the Legislative, Executive and Judiciary; . . . Questions daily occur in the course of practice, which prove the obscurity which reigns in these subjects, and which puzzle the greatest adepts in political science.

Obviously, this response does not suggest any understanding that the Constitution incorporated a fixed definition or allocation of governmental functions, such as might be enforced by courts. The other Madisonian response, laid out in Nos. 47–51, was

---

[129] Gerhard Casper, *An Essay in Separation of Powers: Some Early Versions and Practices*, 30 Wm & Mary L Rev 211, 220 (1989).

[130] Farber & Sherry at 423 (cited in note 121).

[131] Herbert J. Storing, *What the Anti-Federalists Were For* 55 (1981).

[132] Federalist 37 (Madison) in Jacob E. Cooke, ed., *The Federalist* 235 (1961).

that even if a strict division of powers was possible, it was not desirable. Here Madison stressed the futility of trying "to mark with precision the boundaries of these departments in the Constitution of the government, and to trust to these parchment barriers against the encroaching spirit of power."[133] Instead, he argued that separation could only be maintained by "so contriving the interior structure of the government, as that its several constituent parts may, by their mutual relations, be the means of keeping each other in their proper places."[134]

In effect, Madison argued that the structure of government established by the Constitution would be preserved through institutional competition—ambition made to counteract ambition[135]—rather than by through any direct enforcement of definitions of powers. This understanding is far more consistent with the minimal understanding than with either formalism or functionalism. The minimal approach would call upon courts to preserve a government of three branches, with all federal offices assigned to one of those branches, and it would do so in part to create the conditions that give rise to institutional competition. In contrast, both formalism and functionalism would have courts enforce the "parchment barriers" that Madison disparaged.

V. Conclusion

The "constitutional principle of separation of powers" could be understood to mean any one of several different things. It could mean, as the formalists argue, that each branch has exclusive power to perform a single designated function, unless the Constitution expressly permits an exception. Or it could mean, as the functionalists believe, that courts should strive to maintain a diffusion of power among the branches. Conceivably, it could mean nothing—the constitutional principle of separation of powers could just be a shorthand reference for the sum of all specific clauses that govern relations among the branches, but add nothing to what these clauses individually require. Each of these interpretations would have serious drawbacks. The exclusive functions construction

---

[133] Federalist 48 (Madison), id at 332–33.

[134] Federalist 51 (Madison), id at 347–48.

[135] Id at 349.

would be too rigid, the diffusion of power understanding too flexible, and neither comports with the full range of Supreme Court decisions defining the structural Constitution. The conclusion that the principle adds nothing to the specific clauses would be more consistent with the pattern of outcomes reached by the Supreme Court, but would be an open invitation to create a Fourth Branch of government that would permit massive evasions of those clauses in the future.

A better strategy would be to interpret the principle as incorporating a minimal requirement that there be only three branches, with every federal office accountable to one of the constitutional branches. Such an understanding would provide substantial continuity with the past: it would be consistent with the text of the Constitution and with Madison's explanation of the mechanism for preserving the constitutional structure, and would not contradict any of the Supreme Court's judgments in major separation-of-powers cases. For the future, it would prevent Congress from circumventing the specific clauses of the Constitution that limit the power of the branches, and would preserve the dynamic tension among the branches that has worked well for over 200 years in maintaining "the liberty and security of the governed."[136]

---

[136] *Washington Airports*, 111 S Ct at 2310.

ABNER S. GREENE

ADJUDICATIVE RETROACTIVITY
IN ADMINISTRATIVE LAW

I. INTRODUCTION

Although decided forty-five years ago, *SEC v Chenery Corp.*
(*Chenery II*)[1] remains the Supreme Court's leading statement on the
issue of retroactivity in administrative adjudication. According to
Chenery II, administrative agencies may give meaning to statutory
terms through adjudication, even if the rules applied in a particular
adjudication have not been previously announced. The Court acknowledged that "announcing and applying a new standard of conduct" in an adjudicative proceeding would have a retroactive effect,
but concluded that the agency's duty to be faithful to the "statutory
design or to legal and equitable principles" may override concerns
about retroactivity.[2]

The Court has since reaffirmed the *Chenery II* principle,[3] but it
has not revisited in detail the issue of adjudicative retroactivity in
the administrative law setting. Lower courts have struggled to
strike a balance between, on the one hand, application of the rule
the adjudicator believes at the time of adjudication to be the correct

* Abner Greene is Assistant Professor of Law, The University of Chicago Law School.

AUTHOR'S NOTE: I thank Albert Alschuler, Anne-Marie Burley, Richard Epstein, Stephen
Gilles, Philip Greene, Elena Kagan, Lawrence Lessig, Michael McConnell, Bernard Meltzer, Geoffrey Miller, Richard Posner, and Cass Sunstein for helpful comments. I am
grateful for financial assistance from the Russell J. Parsons Faculty Research Fund and the
Robert B. Roesing Faculty Fund.

[1] 332 US 194 (1947). This was the second of two identically captioned cases. I discuss
both cases below in Part IIIA.

[2] Id at 203.

[3] *NLRB v Bell Aerospace Co.*, 416 US 267 (1974).

one, and, on the other hand, the harm caused by applying "a new standard of conduct" to antecedent behavior. Based on the authority of the old chestnut *Chenery II*, though, lower courts often defer to agency decisions to proceed by adjudication rather than by rulemaking, even when the agency is announcing a new rule.[4]

A newer chestnut, *Chevron, U.S.A., Inc. v Natural Resources Defense Council, Inc.*,[5] has added another principle of deference to the administrative law lexicon. According to *Chevron*'s two-stage test, if a reviewing court cannot determine congressional intent on a particular issue of statutory construction (stage 1), then the court should defer to a reasonable agency interpretation (stage 2), rather than construct what the court believes would be a generally sound rule of law.

Although *Chevron* might be considered jurisprudentially consistent with *Chenery II* in establishing a rule of deference to administrative agencies, it contains instead the seed of *Chenery II*'s undoing. For one can read *Chevron* as establishing not merely a principle of deference, but also a method for distinguishing between when agencies are following the law laid down by Congress, and when they are, in essence, acting as legislators in their own right. Serving as a clearer, contemporary statement of the lawmaking function of administrative agencies, *Chevron* can help us clarify the connection between that function and the problems caused by an untempered rule of adjudicative retroactivity. Specifically, if agency adjudicators are acting as lawmakers rather than law discerners, then applying adjudicative rules retroactively conflicts with widely accepted principles that disfavor legislative retroactivity.[6] *Chenery II*'s broad deference to administrative adjudicative retroactivity does not fit with deference to agency lawmaking, which is not bound by antecedent congressional intent, and which might occur through adjudication as well as rulemaking.

In Part II, I discuss the connection between values of the rule

---

[4] See note 44.

[5] 467 US 837 (1984).

[6] Although *Chevron* involved informal rulemaking, its logic about the line between congressional and agency lawmaking is applicable to adjudications such as *Chenery II* as well. See *INS v Cardoza-Fonseca*, 480 US 421 (1987) (drawing no distinction between rulemaking and adjudication in applying *Chevron*); *NLRB v United Food & Comml. Workers Union, Local 23*, 484 US 112 (1987) (same); Ronald Levin, *Identifying Questions of Law in Administrative Law*, 74 Georgetown L J 1, 23 (1985).

of law and the concurrent norms of legislative prospectivity and adjudicative retroactivity. In Part III, I argue that adjudicative retroactivity should hold only when the premise that adjudicators are merely applying antecedent rules also holds. Specifically, when an adjudicator can ascertain congressional intent at *Chevron* stage 1, it is appropriate to apply the interpretation retroactively, because the materials to determine congressional intent are available to citizens as well as adjudicators. When sufficient indicia of congressional intent are not available to answer the statutory question, however, then it is inappropriate to apply the adjudicative rule retroactively, because the question has become one of policy for the agency to decide (*Chevron* stage 2), and notice of the agency's policy choice is not available until the agency uses the adjudication to make that choice. In Part IV, I respond to various defenses of *Chenery II*, which acknowledge the possible damage to values of the rule of law done by applying rules retroactively in some adjudications, but which nonetheless contend that the modern administrative state requires such retroactivity. Finally, in Part V, I defend the view that adjudicators may sometimes apply rules prospectively only.

II. ADJUDICATIVE RETROACTIVITY AND THE RULE OF LAW

A. THE VALUES OF THE RULE OF LAW

Three aspects of the rule of law that are sometimes mentioned separately—notice of legal rules, prospective operation of the rules, and the ability to obey the rules[7]—are interconnected in an important way. They focus on citizens' ability to conform their conduct to given rules. Citizens may be sanctioned only for departing from rules that they knew or should have known and to which they could have conformed.

We can reach two conclusions from the centrality of notice to the rule of law. First, the requirement of notice helps limit officials' power; that power can be exercised only in accordance with previ-

---

[7] Professor Fuller listed eight aspects of a properly "legal" regime: rules; notice of the rules; prospectivity of the rules; understandability of the rules; rules that are consistent with each other; rules that are possible to obey; rules that are sufficiently stable that they can be coherently followed; and a congruence between the announced rules and the administration thereof. Lon Fuller, *The Morality of Law* 33–94 (rev ed 1969).

ously established rules.[8] Second, by defining the bounds of governmental power, notice of the laws also helps shape the contours of personal freedom. Knowledge of the laws permits us to foresee the legal consequences of our actions and thus to plan our lives with confidence. By relying on the precept that only extant laws can circumscribe behavior, we can establish a secure arena for free action outside those limits.[9]

The norm of legislative prospectivity follows from the notice principle of the rule of law. Legislation involves the creation of general rules. If such rules were to apply retroactively—that is, if the rules were to "give[ ] to preenactment conduct a different legal effect from that which it would have had without the passage of the statute"[10]—the rule of law values of limiting officials' power and of providing for a safe realm of personal freedom would be undermined.

Conversely, adjudicative retroactivity is generally justified on the ground that adjudicators deciding cases arising under antecedently given rules are applying those rules to particular cases; they are not, on the orthodox view, creating the rules they apply. Thus, because both the adjudicators and the parties are on notice of the antecedent rules—and those are the ones that govern—adjudicative rulings can properly apply to the antecedent conduct that gave rise to the litigation. "Judicial decisions have had retrospective operation for near a thousand years."[11] A similar norm exists in agency adjudication.[12]

In many cases, the adjudicative retroactivity norm is uncontroversial, because the adjudicator is straightforwardly applying preexisting law. But a problem arises in at least two settings. First,

---

[8] See *SEC v Chenery Corp.*, 332 US 194, 209 (1947) (Jackson dissenting); Friedrich Hayek, *The Constitution of Liberty* 131 (1960) (quoting Richard Hooker, 1 *The Laws of Ecclesiastical Polity* 192 (1593)).

[9] See *California v Lo-Vaca Gathering Co.*, 379 US 366, 371 (1965) (Harlan dissenting); Hayek, *Constitution of Liberty* at 21, 133–34, 157 (cited in note 8); John Rawls, *A Theory of Justice* 235–36, 239–41 (1971); Note, *Prospective Overruling and Retroactive Application in the Federal Courts*, 71 Yale L J 907, 910 (1962).

[10] Charles Hochman, *The Supreme Court and the Constitutionality of Retroactive Legislation*, 73 Harv L Rev 692, 692 (1960).

[11] *Kuhn v Fairmont Coal Co.*, 215 US 349, 372 (1910) (Holmes dissenting).

[12] See *SEC v Chenery Corp.*, 332 US 194 (1947); see also *Bowen v Georgetown Univ. Hosp.*, 109 S Ct 468, 478 (1988) (in the adjudicatory setting, "retroactivity is not only permissible but standard") (Scalia concurring); *NLRB v Bell Aerospace Co.*, 416 US 267 (1974).

when adjudicators overrule precedent, they strip the norm of adjudicative retroactivity of its legitimation based in the mere application of antecedent rules. The courts have acknowledged this problem, and have developed balancing tests that account for reliance on the old rule and the absence of notice that the new one would go into effect.[13] Second, both the adjudicator and the citizen may have no good way of choosing between two or more possible readings of the relevant command. The typical case here is the interpretation of a vague statutory term that has not been previously fleshed out through either adjudication or rulemaking. To be sure, the adjudicative retroactivity norm applies more easily here than in the overruling context, for here at least the interpretive question is an open one.[14] But if the question is too open, then binding citizens to one reading over another may be akin to asking them to obey a law of which they could not know.

One can envision an adjudicative spectrum from pure application of law—cases in which there is no reasonable disagreement about what the law means in a particular setting—to pure creation of law—instances in which all would agree that the rule the adjudica-

---

[13] If a party has conformed its conduct to a prior legal regime, adjudicators sometimes forbid retroactive application of a new legal rule. See *Air Transport Assn. v CAB*, 732 F2d 219 (DC Cir 1984); *Patel v INS*, 638 F2d 1199 (9th Cir 1980); *Natural Gas Pipeline Co. v FERC*, 590 F2d 664 (7th Cir 1979); *Drug Package, Inc. v NLRB*, 570 F2d 1340 (8th Cir 1978). Conversely, the absence of conduct based on a prior legal regime will weigh in favor of retroactivity. Thus, if the citizen's response to a changing legal regime is considered inelastic, i.e., if the relevant behavior is not responsive to the legal rules, then new rules will be applied retroactively. See *Ballbe v INS*, 886 F2d 306 (11th Cir 1989), cert denied, 110 S Ct 2166 (1990); *Texaco, Inc. v Department of Energy*, 795 F2d 1021 (Temp Emerg Ct App 1986), cert dismissed, 478 US 1030 (1986); *NLRB v Affiliated Midwest Hosp., Inc.*, 789 F2d 524 (7th Cir 1986); *NLRB v Ensign Elec. Div.*, 767 F2d 1100 (4th Cir 1985), cert denied, 479 US 984 (1986); *NLRB v Niagara Mach. & Tool Works*, 746 F2d 143 (2d Cir 1984). Similarly, if a party is on notice of the strong likelihood of legal change, the argument against retroactivity might run aground. See *NLRB v Wayne Transp.*, 776 F2d 745 (7th Cir 1985); *NLRB v Ensign Elec. Div.*, 767 F2d 1100 (4th Cir 1985), cert denied, 479 US 984 (1986); *Local 900 v NLRB*, 727 F2d 1184 (DC Cir 1984); *California v Simon*, 504 F2d 430 (Temp Emerg Ct App), cert denied, 419 US 1021 (1974).

[14] It is rare to find judicial invalidation of administrative adjudicative retroactivity in a fleshing-out case, which does not involve departure from administrative precedent. For an example, see *J.L. Foti Constr. Co. v OSHRC*, 687 F2d 853 (6th Cir 1982). In the civil judicial setting, courts sometimes treat the "new law" problem of fleshing-out cases with the same caution that they treat overruling cases, but without significant analysis. See *Chevron Oil Co. v Huson*, 404 US 97, 106 (1971) (prospective application if rule announced either by overruling or "by deciding an issue of first impression whose resolution was not clearly foreshadowed"); *Halliday v United States*, 394 US 831, 833 (1969) (Harlan concurring in the result); *Desist v United States*, 394 US 244, 269 (1969) (Fortas dissenting); *Allen v State Bd. of Elections*, 393 US 544, 572 (1969) (questions "involve complex issues of first impression— issues subject to rational disagreement"); *Kuhn v Fairmont Coal Co.*, 215 US 349 (1910).

tor uses to resolve the case has no pedigree in extant sources of law. The legitimacy of adjudicative retroactivity varies directly with the position of a case on this spectrum from law's application to its creation, because the strength of adjudicative constraints, of the sources of law that bind adjudicative decisions, mirrors the strength of notice available to the affected citizens. In the easy cases in which the constraints are strong, the citizens as well as the adjudicators are on notice of how the law must apply in the relevant setting. But if the constraints are weak—the extreme case is the one in which the legislature tells the adjudicator, "make up the law as the cases come before you"—then notice of what the law means is weak as well.

B. POSITIVE SOURCES OF LAW FOR RESTRICTING
ADJUDICATIVE RETROACTIVITY

Much that follows in this article depends upon applying the norm of legislative prospectivity to administrative adjudications that are properly deemed "legislative." Although my argument is based in the general values of the rule of law that undergird the legislative prospectivity norm, for the argument to have force in the American legal system, these values must find a constitutional or statutory anchor. The Constitution expressly addresses retroactive lawmaking in two ways, by prohibiting ex post facto laws[15] and laws impairing the obligation of contracts.[16] But the Supreme Court has held that the Ex Post Facto Clause applies only to criminal laws,[17] and the Contracts Clause is limited in other ways that render it less than a general constitutional prohibition against retroactive lawmaking.[18]

The Due Process Clause[19] could be read to support a general

---

[15] US Const, Art I, § 9, cl 3 & § 10, cl 1.

[16] US Const, Art I, § 10, cl 1.

[17] *Calder v Bull*, 3 Dallas 386 (1798).

[18] For one thing, the Contracts Clause (as well as the Ex Post Facto Clause) applies only to legislative and not to adjudicative action; see *Central Land Co. v Laidley*, 159 US 103 (1895); Thomas Currier, *Time and Change in Judge-Made Law: Prospective Overruling*, 51 Va L Rev 201, 207 (1965) (citing cases); Edward Stimson, *Retroactive Application of Law—A Problem in Constitutional Law*, 38 Mich L Rev 30, 50 (1939); Note, 71 Yale L J at 909 (cited in note 9) (citing cases), so it would be an awkward textual basis for applying the norm of legislative prospectivity to "legislative" adjudications. Moreover, the Contracts Clause textually applies only to the impairment of "contracts," and not to other regulation.

[19] US Const, Amend V & Amend 14, § 1.

constitutional requirement of prospective lawmaking; one of the core due process values is that citizens must be given notice before being deprived of life, liberty, or property.[20] But the Court has been inconsistent in its application of the Due Process Clause to retroactive legislation. On the one hand, the Court requires Congress to state clearly if it intends to alter retroactively the legal status of antecedent conduct; moreover, the Court sometimes strains to read a law as applying merely prospectively. A venerable line of cases supports these propositions.[21]

On the other hand, when Congress has expressly legislated retroactively, the Court has found a variety of ways to uphold the legislation against due process challenge. In at least two settings, the holdings can be at least somewhat reconciled with the values of the rule of law. The Court's approval of laws that alter the tax consequences of prior conduct is based in part in the notion that the tax bar follows pending legislation and can inform its clients of possible legislative changes.[22] In addition, if the Court concludes that the earlier conduct would not have been different had the later, retroactive law then governed, it will uphold the law.[23] But the Court has also upheld expressly retroactive legislation after applying nothing more than a version of the rational basis test. In one case, it approved retroactive compensation for coal miners, essentially on the theory that Congress can choose to redistribute wealth retroactively as well as prospectively.[24] In another case, it upheld a law imposing retroactive liability on employers withdraw-

---

[20] Such a due-process based doctrine could draw on the rule of lenity, fair warning, and vagueness cases, all of which constrain application of vague statutory terms based on the rule of law value of notice. See *Bell v United States*, 349 US 81, 83 (1955); *Bouie v City of Columbia*, 378 US 347, 350–51 (1964); *Papachristou v City of Jacksonville*, 405 US 156, 166–67 (1972); *Marks v United States*, 430 US 188, 191–92 (1977).

[21] See *United States v Heth*, 3 Cranch 399 (1806); *Murray v Gibson*, 15 Howard 421 (1854); *White v United States*, 191 US 545 (1903); *Bowen v Georgetown Univ. Hosp.*, 109 S Ct 468 (1988); see also *Kaiser Alum. & Chem. Corp. v Bonjorno*, 110 S Ct 1570, 1579 (1990) (Scalia concurring).

[22] See *United States v Darusmont*, 449 US 292 (1981); *Welch v Henry*, 305 US 134 (1938). The Court has not extended this reasoning to other areas of law.

[23] See *Bradley v Richmond School Bd.*, 416 US 696 (1974) (later-enacted attorney's fees statute would not have changed school board's prior conduct); *Welch v Henry*, 305 US 134 (1938) (retroactive increase in income tax would not have altered citizen's prior conduct; distinguishes retroactive gift tax on theory that donor's decision whether to give gift might have been altered had tax previously existed).

[24] *Usery v Turner Elkhorn Mining Co.*, 428 US 1 (1976).

ing from multiemployer pension plans, primarily on the ground that such liability was necessary to prevent flight.[25] In short, although the Court applies a clear statement test in construing congressional statutes, the Due Process Clause stands as only a weak barrier when Congress expressly legislates retroactively.[26]

A final possible source of legal restriction on adjudicative retroactivity is the Administrative Procedure Act. The APA arguably forbids agencies to apply regulations retroactively, in large part because the APA states that a "rule," which is made in a rulemaking proceeding, is of "future effect."[27] There is a substantial argument to the contrary,[28] however, and the Court has not resolved the matter.

My argument below could thus be supported in positive law in one of three ways. First: One could argue that Congress must clearly state when it intends to authorize agencies to make law

---

[25] *Pension Benefit Guaranty Corp. v R.A. Gray & Co.*, 467 US 717 (1984); see also *General Motors Corp. v Romein*, 112 S Ct 1105, 1112 (1992) (upholding against due process challenge state legislation that reversed retroactively state supreme court interpretation that had, in turn, adopted unexpected retroactive interpretation of state legislation). In *Gray*, Congress was concerned that employers would flee plans once they learned a bill was under serious consideration, so the initial proposed bill clearly stated that withdrawal liability would begin on the day that bill was introduced. Once Congress was confident that employers were generally heeding the liability date, it advanced that date in the final law to a period five months prior to the law's enactment. Although the Court brushed aside the due process challenge, whether Congress should be permitted to guide business behavior through signaling in a bill that liability will run from the bill's introduction date rather than the date of the law's enactment raises some perplexing separation of powers questions. See *Metropolitan Washington Airports Auth. v Citizens for the Abatement of Aircraft Noise, Inc.*, 111 S Ct 2298 (1991) (Congress may not directly control policymaking other than by a law passed through the Article I, section 7 constitutional process); *Bowsher v Synar*, 478 US 714, 736 (1986) (Stevens concurring in the judgment) (same); *INS v Chadha*, 462 US 919 (1983) (same).

[26] Similarly, although courts have sometimes refused to allow the application of adjudicatively created law of which a citizen could not have known, see *SEC v Chenery Corp.*, 318 US 80 (1943) (*Chenery I*, discussed in Part IIIA); *Gelpcke v City of Dubuque*, 1 Wallace 175 (1864), the Court has at other times indicated, often implicitly, that applying a new rule retroactively does not violate the Due Process Clause. See *Vandenbark v Owens-Illinois Glass Co.*, 311 US 538 (1941); *Great Northern R. Co. v Sunburst Oil & Refining Co.*, 287 US 358 (1932).

[27] 5 USC § 551(4); see *Bowen v Georgetown Univ. Hosp.*, 109 S Ct 468, 475 (1988) (Scalia concurring).

[28] See *Citizens to Save Spencer County v United States EPA*, 600 F2d 844 (DC Cir 1979); William Luneberg, *Retroactivity and Administrative Rulemaking*, 1991 Duke L J 106, 134; Glen Robinson, *The Making of Administrative Policy: Another Look at Rulemaking and Adjudication and Administrative Procedure Reform*, 4 U Pa L Rev 485, 498 (1970); Frederick Schauer, *A Brief Note on the Logic of Rules, with Special Reference to Bowen v Georgetown University Hospital*, 42 Admin L Rev 447 (1990); David Shapiro, *The Choice of Rulemaking or Adjudication in the Development of Administrative Policy*, 78 Harv L Rev 921, 933 (1965).

retroactively, either through rulemaking or through adjudication. This clear statement requirement, already present for reviewing legislation, is needed even more when examining the action of the unelected agencies.[29] Second, one could maintain that the Court's weak review of expressly retroactive laws should be strengthened to accommodate the important values of the rule of law underlying the norm of legislative prospectivity, that the Due Process Clause is an appropriate constitutional source on which to base such heightened review, and that agency adjudication that is truly "legislative" should be reviewed in similarly strict fashion. Third, the APA could be read to require that agency adjudication correctly considered "legislative" must not be applied retroactively.

III. What Administrative Adjudicators Do: From Chenery II to Chevron

A. THE CURRENT LAW OF ADMINISTRATIVE ADJUDICATIVE RETROACTIVITY: THE CHENERY II PRINCIPLE

The *Chenery II* principle resulted from the second of two connected Supreme Court cases, both titled *SEC v Chenery Corp.*[30] The cases arose in the following fashion. During the reorganization of the Federal Water Service Corporation (Federal), corporate management purchased preferred over-the-counter stock, which it then sought to convert into common stock under the reorganization plan. The SEC denied the conversion, requiring instead the surrender of the preferred stock at cost plus accumulated dividends.[31] The SEC acted pursuant to the Public Utility Holding Company Act of 1935, which required it to determine whether the "terms of issuance of the new common stock were 'fair and equitable' or 'detrimental to the interests of investors.'"[32] Although the trades were made at market price and with complete disclosure of the purchasers' identity, the SEC relied on its understanding that common law fiduciary theory barred trustees from trafficking in property held for others.[33]

---

[29] See *Hampton v Mow Sun Wong*, 426 US 88 (1976); *Kent v Dulles*, 357 US 116 (1958).

[30] 318 US 80 (1943) (*Chenery I*); 332 US 194 (1947) (*Chenery II*).

[31] See 318 US at 81–84; 332 US at 197–98.

[32] 318 US at 85.

[33] Id at 85–90.

But as the Court explained in *Chenery I*, management does not hold the stock it owns in trust for the shareholders; furthermore, the SEC misread common law, which did not then impose restrictions against trading by corporate management during reorganization. Although the Act gives the SEC broad power to regulate securities practices, and to do so through adjudication as well as rulemaking, the Court concluded that the SEC must do so through standards of conduct existing and known to exist at the time of the purported infraction. As the Court explained:[34]

> Had the Commission, acting upon its experience and peculiar competence, promulgated a general rule of which its order here was a particular application, the problem for our consideration would be very different. . . . But before transactions otherwise legal can be outlawed or denied their usual business consequences, they must fall under the ban of some standards of conduct prescribed by an agency of government authorized to prescribe such standards—either the courts or Congress or an agency to which Congress has delegated its authority. Congress itself did not proscribe the respondents' purchases of preferred stock in Federal. Established judicial doctrines do not condemn these transactions. Nor has the Commission, acting under the rulemaking powers delegated to it by sec. 11(e), promulgated new general standards of conduct.

Thus, not only had the SEC relied upon an erroneous understanding of the common law of corporate management fiduciary duty, but furthermore, and of importance for the retroactivity problem, the SEC had failed to identify another source of law—agency precedent or regulation, or an appropriate understanding of congressional intent in passing the governing statute—that prohibited the trades that Federal's management had made.

Although the above passage suggests that the *Chenery I* Court intended to require adjudication by standards extant at the time of the antecedent conduct, there is other language in the opinion indicating that the Court might have permitted the SEC to propose a new standard in the case before it and apply that standard retroactively. Thus, the opinion earlier states, "the Commission did not in this case proffer new standards reflecting the experience gained

[34] Id at 92–93.

by it in effectuating the legislative policy."[35] The Court also noted, "The Commission did not rely upon 'its special administrative competence'; it formulated no judgment upon the requirements of the 'public interest or the interest of investors or consumers' in the situation before it."[36] These passages suggest that the Court would have permitted the SEC to flesh out a standard under its statutory authority in the *Chenery* adjudication itself and to apply that standard to conduct predating its announcement. On this reading of *Chenery I*, the Court's primary concern was not the retroactivity problem, but the SEC's failure to announce or apply any standard whatsoever.[37]

But I need not show that *Chenery I* got the retroactivity issue right while *Chenery II* did not. *Chenery I* identified a problem with applying new rules to antecedent conduct. *Chenery II* represents at the very least a reversal in tone and attitude on this issue. As I shall explain below, values of the rule of law require resolving the adjudicative retroactivity problem in a way at odds with the *Chenery II* approach.

It is to *Chenery II* that I now turn. By remanding to the SEC rather than reversing outright, the *Chenery I* Court left the door open for the SEC's next move: Avoiding reliance on common law fiduciary theory, the Commission concluded that management's trades were inconsistent with the "purposes and standards" of the federal statute.[38] Without concluding that the SEC's interpretation was commanded by an appropriate understanding of congressional intent, the Court in *Chenery II* gave great deference to the SEC's statutory construction and sustained its order.[39] Regarding the retroactivity question—could the agency announce an interpretation of the statute neither previously announced nor commanded by congressional intent, and apply it to antecedent conduct?—the Court explained that the Commission had to decide the case before

---

[35] Id at 89.

[36] Id at 92.

[37] In his dissent in *Chenery II*, Justice Jackson similarly focused at times on the retroactivity problem of applying a newly minted standard to antecedent conduct and at other times on the quite different problem of the SEC's failure to apply any standard at all to the case before it, relying instead on an ad hoc judgment. See 332 US at 209–18.

[38] See 332 US at 199.

[39] Id at 207–9.

it under proper standards, "regardless of whether those standards previously had been spelled out in a general rule or regulation." As the Court stated:[40]

> [P]roblems may arise in a case which the administrative agency could not reasonably foresee, problems which must be solved despite the absence of a relevant general rule. Or the agency may not have had sufficient experience with a particular problem to warrant rigidifying its tentative judgment into a hard and fast rule. Or the problem may be so specialized and varying in nature as to be impossible of capture within the boundaries of a general rule. In those situations, the agency must retain power to deal with the problems on a case-to-case basis if the administrative process is to be effective. . . .
>
> Hence we refuse to say that the Commission, which had not previously been confronted with the problem of management trading during reorganization, was forbidden from utilizing this particular proceeding for announcing and applying a new standard of conduct. That such action might have a retroactive effect was not necessarily fatal to its validity. Every case of first impression has a retroactive effect, whether the new principle is announced by a court or by an administrative agency. But such retroactivity must be balanced against the mischief of producing a result which is contrary to a statutory design or to legal and equitable principles. If that mischief is greater than the ill effect of the retroactive application of a new standard, it is not the type of retroactivity which is condemned by law.

As Justice Jackson explained in dissent,[41] this formulation differs significantly from that in *Chenery I*, which had focused at least in part on the rule of law virtues of applying only a rule extant at the time of the governed conduct. The *Chenery II* opinion, by contrast, expressly approves the retroactive application of a rule announced after the fact by the agency. The question is whether the *Chenery II* Court, whose explication of the problem of administrative adjudicative retroactivity stands today, adequately addressed the concerns of the *Chenery I* Court.

In my view, it did not. Three defenses for the *Chenery II* position can be found in the opinion itself.[42] First: Vague statutory standards often cannot be made meaningful until real, specific cases

---

[40] Id at 202–3.

[41] Id at 209.

[42] I respond to other possible defenses in Part IV.

arise. Agencies must be able to deal with problems on a case-by-case basis, for it is not always possible to know in advance what sort of problems might arise under a vague statutory standard. As I will argue in Parts IV and V, however, one can accommodate this need for evolution of standards either through rulemaking or by permitting rules to be developed through adjudication and applied prospectively only.

Second: The failure to apply the newly announced rule to the antecedent conduct would "produc[e] a result which is contrary to a statutory design or to legal and equitable principles."[43] That is, if the agency has determined that the new rule is the proper way of regulating conduct under the statute, but if it is prevented from regulating the conduct in the case before it under such a rule, then that conduct will escape, as it were, the censure it otherwise deserves. But whether the conduct at issue in a particular case should be covered by what the agency considers to be the proper rule of law under the statute is one thing; whether that rule should be applied to conduct predating its announcement is another. *Chenery II* focuses on the first matter, but does not adequately address the second.

Third: *Chenery II* is not blind to the retroactivity problem; it leaves an opening for a balancing test that would consider the harm caused by retroactivity. But the Court did not indicate how such a balance should be struck and has never invalidated an agency balance permitting adjudicative retroactivity. Moreover, the lower courts often grant great deference to an agency's balance.[44]

---

[43] Id at 203.

[44] A leading D.C. Circuit case elucidated the balance suggested in *Chenery II* by focusing on the following factors: (*a*) Is this a case of first impression, or does the party that seeks the application of a new rule to antecedent conduct rely on the efforts of an earlier, rule-changing litigant? (*b*) Does this case overrule a prior case or merely flesh out a statutory provision for the first time? (*c*) Was there reliance on the prior rule? (*d*) What burden would retroactivity impose? (*e*) What is the statutory interest in applying the new rule? *Retail, Wholesale and Dept. Store Union v NLRB*, 466 F2d 380 (DC Cir 1972). Many lower courts have applied the *Retail* test. See *General Am. Transp. Corp. v ICC*, 883 F2d 1029 (DC Cir 1989) (petn. for rehearing), cert denied, 493 US 1069 (1990); *Southwestern Pub. Serv. Co. v FERC*, 842 F2d 1204 (10th Cir 1988); *NLRB v Wayne Transp.*, 776 F2d 745 (7th Cir 1985); *NLRB v Niagara Mach. & Tool Works*, 746 F2d 143 (2d Cir 1984); *J.L. Foti Constr. Co. v OSHRC*, 687 F2d 853 (6th Cir 1982); *Petrolite Corp. v FERC*, 667 F2d 664 (8th Cir 1981); *E.L. Wiegland Div. v NLRB*, 650 F2d 463 (3d Cir 1981), cert denied, 455 US 939 (1982); *Maceren v District Director, INS*, 509 F2d 934 (9th Cir 1974); *California v Simon*, 504 F2d 430 (Temp Emerg Ct App), cert denied, 419 US 1021 (1974).

As a result of a Supreme Court case following *Chenery II*, *NLRB v Bell Aerospace Co.*, 416 US 267 (1974), the D.C. Circuit has recently construed the *Retail* balancing test as requiring

Thus, the *Chenery II* Court did not adequately deal with the fact that law had "stopped" with the "fair and equitable" and "detrimental to the interests" statutory standards, and had begun again when the SEC fleshed out those standards with a categorical rule that had not previously existed. Where law stops with vague statutory standards, there law begins again with the agency's fleshing out of those standards; if the rule against retroactivity properly applies to legislation, it ought to apply to administrative adjudication that is functionally equivalent to legislation as well.

B. A NEW LAW OF ADMINISTRATIVE ADJUDICATIVE RETROACTIVITY: APPLYING THE CHEVRON MODEL

Both the delegation doctrine, as applied, and *Chevron* reveal, unmistakably, the degree to which the Court acknowledges and accepts the broad lawmaking function of administrative agencies. Although the delegation doctrine formally forbids Congress from delegating legislative power, in practice the Court has permitted just such delegation. Although the Court still requires statutes to state an "intelligible principle" for the agency to follow,[45] the Court has approved statutory standards requiring agencies to make rules "in the public interest" or to prohibit "unfair methods of competition."[46] Thus, it is fairly clear that almost any statutory standard, no matter how vague or general, will suffice. To be sure, the Court sometimes construes a delegation of power narrowly,[47] under the theory that Congress would speak more clearly if it truly meant to delegate more broadly, or pursuant to the interpretive canons that

---

a strong presumption of adjudicative retroactivity with an "abuse of discretion" safety valve. *General Am. Transp. Corp. v ICC*, 872 F2d 1048 (D.C. Cir 1989), cert denied, 493 US 1069 (1990); see also Russell Weaver, *Challenging Regulatory Interpretations*, 23 Ariz St L J 109, 146 (1991); Note, *The National Labor Relations Board's Proposed Rules on Health Care Bargaining Units*, 76 Va L Rev 115, 155–56 (1990) ("Since *Bell Aerospace*, both the Supreme Court and the circuit courts have shown continued reluctance to interfere with an administrative agency's choice of rulemaking or adjudication"). Courts sometimes say that "manifest injustice" must be shown to overcome the retroactivity presumption. See *General Am. Transp. Corp. v ICC*, 872 F2d 1048 (DC Cir 1989), cert denied, 493 US 1069 (1990); *Montgomery Ward & Co. v FTC*, 691 F2d 1322 (9th Cir 1982); *Natural Gas Pipeline Co. v FERC*, 590 F2d 664 (7th Cir 1979).

See also notes 13 and 14.

[45] See *Touby v United States*, 111 S Ct 1752, 1756 (1991); see also *J.W. Hampton, Jr., & Co. v United States*, 276 US 394, 409 (1928).

[46] See *New York Central Securities Corp. v United States*, 287 US 12 (1932); *FTC v Gratz*, 253 US 421 (1920).

[47] See *Industrial Union Dept., AFL-CIO v American Petroleum Inst.*, 448 US 607 (1980).

dictate narrow construction to avoid reaching a constitutional question or invalidating a law on constitutional grounds. But for the most part the Court has allowed the practice of delegating to agencies sweeping lawmaking power barely constrained by statutory standards.

Chevron also shows that agencies possess a great swath of judicially sanctioned legislative power. In *Chevron*, the Court approved a two-stage process for evaluating whether an agency has correctly construed a statute. At the first stage, a court reviewing an agency's statutory interpretation must determine, using traditional tools of statutory construction to ascertain congressional intent, whether there is a proper answer to the issue at hand.[48] Here, the agency's interpretation is but one (albeit important) piece of evidence regarding the statute's meaning. At this stage, a court determines how far down the law reaches, as it were; in other words, a court determines the parameters of statutory coverage from the available evidence of congressional intent. At some point, there will be insufficient evidence of congressional intent to reach an understanding of whether the statute covers the case at hand. Then, at the second stage, interpretation of the statute—that is, application of the statute to specific settings as to which the normal sources of interpretation are silent—falls to the agency, whose interpretation the court must accept so long as it is reasonable.[49] At the end of *Chevron*, the

---

[48] 467 US at 842–45 & n 9. The debate on the Court regarding the nature of stage 1 *Chevron* review involves two interrelated issues: (1) If a statute is "susceptible of two meanings," *Young v Community Nutrition Inst.*, 476 US 974, 988 (1986) (Stevens dissenting), may the agency choose between the possible meanings, even if the court thinks one meaning is a better construction of congressional intent? (2) To what extent should the reviewing court look to legislative history and other nontextual sources to ascertain congressional intent? Although more stage 1 answers will lead to more retroactivity under my model, I need not in this article take a position on these questions.

[49] I deliberately avoid the terms "question of law" and "mixed question of law and fact," because one cannot categorize a question as one or the other merely by examining the question itself. See Levin, 74 Georgetown L J at 27–29 (cited in note 6). All questions involving statutory interpretation are initially questions of the following sort: Can we ascertain congressional intent on the question? If we cannot ascertain congressional intent on the question, what we are often left with is the application of a vague statutory term to a particular factual setting. At this point, it is appropriate to defer to the agency's interpretation. But we defer not because the question is one of "law application" rather than a "purely legal question." Rather, we defer because Congress has not answered the question, and because it is better (for reasons I need not discuss here) for an agency than a court to make the ensuing policy choice, i.e., to pronounce what the law shall be (made by the agency) after the law (made by Congress) has stopped. See 467 US at 864–66; see also Henry Monaghan, *Marbury and the Administrative State*, 83 Colum L Rev 1, 29–30 (1983). This is so whether or not Congress actually chose to delegate policymaking authority to the agency. See 467 US at 865.

Court rather candidly explained that when it cannot find an answer to a statutory question according to congressional intent (stage 1), it is appropriate to conclude that the question is one of policy for the agency to decide (stage 2).[50] In short, at stage 1, a court determines the meaning of the law to the extent possible given the standard sources of law, and forbids the agency from acting outside the scope of such meaning. But at stage 2 law has stopped, as it were, and discretion takes over;[51] here, the agency may (and, indeed, must) flesh out the statute on its own, for there is no antecedent source of law prescribing the result.

The underenforced delegation doctrine and the second stage of the *Chevron* interpretive process reveal that the Court has approved agency power to prescribe, in the first instance, the specific commands to which citizens must conform. Insofar as agencies issue such commands through informal (notice and comment) rulemaking procedures, and apply those commands prospectively, there is no rule of law problem. But as we can see from *Chenery II*, the Court has approved the retroactive application of new legal standards, so long as this occurs through adjudication rather than rulemaking. If we are troubled by legislative retroactivity, though, then we ought to be troubled as well by the retroactive application of an agency policy choice unconstrained by congressional intent.

Examining *Chevron* in greater detail reveals the flaw in *Chenery II*. For even though *Chevron* is methodologically part of a line of cases regarding judicial review of agency statutory interpretation that includes *Chenery II*,[52] it clarifies the connection between the absence of interpretive constraints and the fact of agency lawmaking. As I have explained above, *Chevron* requires courts to review agency statutory interpretation by conducting a de novo examination of traditional sources of congressional intent—text, structure, history. When the courts conclude from such a review that the seemingly vague or ambiguous term in fact has a proper meaning, then that is the meaning the agency must follow. It is precisely in these *Chevron* stage 1 cases that we should permit agencies to apply

---

[50] 467 US at 865–66.

[51] See Kenneth Davis, *Discretionary Justice: A Preliminary Inquiry* 21 (1969) ("Where law ends individualized justice begins").

[52] Recall that in *Chenery II* the Court gave great deference to the SEC's "interpretation" of the statute.

adjudicative rules retroactively, for if the courts can discover a proper meaning from an evaluation of traditional sources of congressional intent, then so can the affected citizens.

There are, however, cases in which the courts conclude that there is no proper answer to a question of statutory interpretation, that the legislature left the matter open, either explicitly or implicitly,[53] to be decided by the agency. *Chevron* candidly acknowledges that Congress sometimes leaves to agencies the determination of policy:[54]

> In these cases, the Administrator's interpretation represents a reasonable accommodation of manifestly competing interests and is entitled to deference: the regulatory scheme is technical and complex, the agency considered the matter in a detailed and reasoned fashion, and the decision involves reconciling conflicting policies. Congress intended to accommodate both interests, but did not do so itself on the level of specificity presented by these cases. . . .
> . . . [A]n agency to which Congress has delegated policy-making responsibilities may, within the limits of that delegation, properly rely upon the incumbent administration's views of wise policy to inform its judgments. While agencies are not directly accountable to the people, the Chief Executive is, and it is entirely appropriate for this political branch of the Government to make such policy choices . . . .
> When a challenge to an agency construction of a statutory provision, fairly conceptualized, really centers on the wisdom of the agency's policy, rather than whether it is a reasonable choice within a gap left open by Congress, the challenge must fail.

In *Chevron*, the Court was unable to resolve at stage 1 the statutory interpretation question presented by examining the traditional sources of legislative meaning. So the Court moved on to the second stage of analysis, concluding that Congress had given the agency the responsibility of fleshing out an otherwise unclear statutory term, that the agency, in other words, had become the lawmaker after Congress had started the ball rolling. Although dubbing the agency the "lawmaker" is in tension with the formal view

---

[53] See 467 US at 865. As Judge Breyer has pointed out, "Congress is rarely . . . explicit about delegating the legal power to interpret a statute." Stephen Breyer, *Judicial Review of Questions of Law and Policy*, 38 Admin L Rev 363, 369 (1986).

[54] 467 US at 865–66.

of legislative delegation, it fits with the Court's underenforcement of the delegation doctrine, and helps show how once law stops (a court cannot discover congressional intent regarding a certain type of problem) there law begins again (the next-in-line governmental actor, the agency, may say what the law is).[55] If a question of statutory interpretation is resolvable only at this second stage, as a matter of agency policy choice, of agency lawmaking, then, in keeping with the norm against legislative retroactivity, we should not allow the announced rule to apply retroactively.

The point here is an important one, revealing the link between adjudicative constraints and notice, and thus helping to show how we can adjust the *Chenery II* principle of administrative adjudicative retroactivity to accommodate rule of law values. *Chevron*'s lesson is more than just that Congress sometimes leaves important lawmaking functions to agencies. The further lesson of *Chevron* is that it is appropriate for agencies to be lawmakers only when the available sources for determining congressional intent—for determining what the law is—are inadequate to the task. It is here that we can see the firm connection to the concerns of the rule of law, because the sources that constrain agency adjudicators in determining what the law means are precisely the same sources that give citizens notice of their legal obligations. If an agency adjudicator or court can determine a proper answer to a question of statutory interpretation from an evaluation of traditional sources of congressional intent, then citizens too are on notice of congressional intent regarding the question, for they can evaluate the same sources examined by the agency or the court. However, if the interpretive question is resolvable not from examining sources of congressional intent, but instead only by an agency policy choice made at the time of the adjudication, then citizens are not on notice of the source of law that governs until the agency announces its policy choice.[56]

---

[55] Whether there is congressional "law" to apply or whether an agency may act in a fairly unfettered manner in creating the "law" is a question that arises in a slightly different posture in cases interpreting APA § 701(a)(2), which renders the APA judicial review chapter inapplicable "to the extent that agency action is committed to agency discretion by law." See *Heckler v Chaney*, 470 US 821 (1985); *Citizens to Preserve Overton Park, Inc. v Volpe*, 401 US 402 (1971); see also Cass Sunstein, *Reviewing Agency Inaction After Heckler v Chaney*, 52 U Chi L Rev 653 (1985).

[56] Cf. Harry Wellington, *Common Law Rules and Constitutional Double Standards: Some Notes on Adjudication*, 83 Yale L J 221, 242–43 (1973) (retroactive application of an adjudicative rule may be problematic if the policy of the governing statute "could have been effectuated

Thus, *Chevron* both (*a*) acknowledges that agencies make law, and (*b*) provides a device for determining when administrative adjudicative retroactivity is permissible and when it is not. Rules developed through administrative adjudication will sometimes be properly based in extant sources of law, but will at other times represent a relatively unconstrained choice by the adjudicator. As the *Chevron* two-stage process reveals, we have the means to determine on which side of this line a case falls.[57]

Unfortunately, form often obscures function in our thinking about administrative adjudicative retroactivity; in particular, consider the sharp distinctions often drawn between rulemaking and adjudication in administrative law. Informal rulemaking looks like congressional lawmaking—the notice and comment process is the administrative analogue to congressional hearings, bill mark-ups, and floor debates. Accordingly, restrictions on retroactive rulemaking are strict. Administrative adjudication, on the other hand, looks like a process for applying law to fact, for merely deciding a case; thus, retroactive adjudication is the norm. But this focus on the

---

in a number of ways and . . . there was nothing in prior published decisions or regulations to suggest that a rule extinguishing [a right of one of the parties] was to be the chosen instrument for furthering the policy. This problem of potentially alternative rules (and, therefore, of discretion) available to a decisionmaker is endemic to rules justified by policies").

[57] My discussion here has focused on statutory interpretation by administrative agencies. The *Chevron* model is predicated on the belief that ascertaining congressional intent (or, perhaps, statutory "purpose") is the appropriate task for adjudicators engaged in statutory interpretation. I need not discuss here the question of which constraints are appropriate in common law adjudication. Likewise, I need not now consider the application of the *Chevron* model to the fleshing out of vague constitutional commands, and mention now only a few possible concerns. Whether constitutional interpretation should rest on an originalist premise, of ascertaining the framers' intent, is a difficult and controversial question. Also, in the constitutional setting especially, one might contend that adjudicative retroactivity helps support the proposition that we are a "government of laws, not men," a proposition that perhaps bolsters public support for the judicial system. See Paul Mishkin, *Foreword: The High Court, The Great Writ, and the Due Process of Time and Law*, 79 Harv L Rev 56, 60–70 (1965). This theory is problematic, however, in part because it is not clear that people actually believe we are a government of laws, not men. Cf. Jerome Frank, *Law and the Modern Mind* 36 (1930) (myth that judges don't make law "leads, sooner or later, to a distrust of the judges, a disrespect for their opinions").

There is one other type of case to address: When a court interprets a statute without a prior agency interpretation, the *Chevron* model should still apply (unless Article III of the Constitution requires a different result, see note 97). That is, if the court can determine the correct answer to the interpretive question at the equivalent to stage 1 of *Chevron*, it may apply the resulting rule retroactively. Conversely, if the court itself must make what is the equivalent of a stage 2 *Chevron* policy choice (which it must do absent an agency choice to which it can defer), then the resulting rule should not be applied retroactively.

applying-the-law, deciding-a-case part of adjudication obscures the pure lawmaking that agency adjudicators do.

To understand how the problem of form obscuring function might arise in practice, consider the following variations on *Chevron* and *Chenery II*. In *Chevron*, Congress had permitted a maximum amount of pollution from a "stationary source"; the question was whether this term required each pollution-emitting device in a plant to emit no more than the maximum level of pollution, or whether an entire plant could be considered a "stationary source," thus permitting a company to credit the under-pollution from some devices against the over-pollution from others. The EPA issued a regulation adopting the latter interpretation; after determining that there were insufficient sources of congressional intent to resolve the question, the Court upheld the regulation, concluding that Congress had left the policy choice to the agency.

But what if *Chevron* had arisen in the course of an EPA enforcement proceeding against a polluter for emitting too much pollution from a single device; the polluter had defended by arguing that its entire plant-wide pollution should be considered; and the EPA had rejected that argument, determining instead that "stationary source" refers to each device, and not the entire plant? On *Chevron*'s logic, this interpretation (the opposite of the one the EPA actually chose) should be upheld, because Congress left the lawmaking choice to the agency. Under the *Chenery II* rule permitting adjudicative retroactivity, the polluter could be penalized for a choice that was proscribed after the fact, not before. But this result doesn't seem correct; because *Chevron* approves agency lawmaking, we should be concerned about the retroactivity of such "laws" just as we are concerned about the retroactivity of Congress' laws.

Now consider a variation on *Chenery II*: The SEC announced a new principle through adjudication, namely, that management may not trade in the shares of its own corporation during reorganization. The agency applied this principle to the parties by ordering the stock surrendered to the corporation. Thus, it applied a new principle (a gloss on a vague statutory term) retroactively. But what if the SEC had proceeded by rulemaking instead of adjudication, and had promulgated the same no-trading rule? Under the accepted norm disfavoring retroactive rulemaking, that rule could not be applied retroactively. Why should an agency be permitted to apply new law retroactively in one instance and not in another?

Shifting focus from form to function also raises a tantalizing question about agency rulemaking: We accept the nonretroactivity of informal administrative rulemaking without serious question, in part because of the APA's text,[58] but also because of the legislative form of such rulemaking. But under the *Chevron* model for choosing between retroactivity and nonretroactivity in administrative adjudication, rulemaking rules as well as adjudicative rules should be applied retroactively if they follow from congressional intent as a *Chevron* stage 1 matter. Agency rulemaking is not perfectly analogous to congressional legislation for retroactivity purposes, because while the source of authority for congressional legislation, the Constitution, generally does not compel any particular legislation; statutes sometimes do compel the agency to adopt certain rules. If an agency adjudicator may properly apply an adjudicative rule retroactively because it follows from congressional intent, then perhaps an agency rulemaker should be permitted to apply a rulemaking rule retroactively in similar circumstances.[59]

In the 1990 Term, in an otherwise minor, uncontroversial case, the Court revealed how far the fact of agency lawmaking has penetrated the judicial mind, even as judges strain to retain the formal theory of agency-as-law-applier. In *Martin v Occupational Safety and Health Review Commission*,[60] the Court unanimously held that when the Secretary of Labor and the Commission disagree as to the meaning of a regulatory term, the reviewing court must defer to the Secretary rather than the Commission. The decision turned primarily on the unusual nature of the Commission, which Congress split off from the Department of Labor to ensure an impartial set of administrative law judges who were empowered merely to resolve disputes, leaving to the Secretary the role of fleshing out legislative commands. In the opinion, the Court twice referred to the Secretary's task in fleshing out statutes as "interpretive lawmaking."[61] I have been unable to find any other federal court opinion that has ever used this term. It is a good term, for it nicely describes what agencies do (and are permitted to do) when they make sense

---

[58] See note 27 and accompanying text.

[59] See the debate in *City of Dothan v FERC*, 684 F2d 159, 162–63 n 2 (DC Cir 1982); id at 168–69 n 8 (Mikva dissenting).

[60] 111 S Ct 1171 (1991).

[61] Id at 1176–77.

of vague statutory terms. It is a term that appropriately describes the agency function as (often) legislative. The Court should carry its descriptive accuracy through to a normative conclusion: Whenever an agency acts as an "interpretive lawmaker," either in its rulemaking or adjudicative capacity, it should be subject to the same rule disfavoring retroactivity as the original, "noninterpretive lawmaker," Congress.

IV. THE AFFIRMATIVE DEFENSES OF CHENERY II

I have criticized the permissive *Chenery II* acceptance of administrative adjudicative retroactivity for its failure to recognize the lawmaking role agency adjudicators sometimes play. In doing so, I have not focused on the use of the adjudicative form to develop the law, and the role played by retroactive application in this development. In this part, I shall respond to four such affirmative defenses for *Chenery II*. These defenses acknowledge that agency adjudicators do not always "apply" antecedent law; that is, these defenses do not support *Chenery II* on the formalist ground that adjudicative rules should apply retroactively because adjudicators never make law. Rather, the defenses offer a more sophisticated, "realist" fortification for a strong norm of administrative adjudicative retroactivity.

A. THE NEED FOR REGULATORY FLEXIBILITY

The first defense of *Chenery II* acknowledges that the values of the rule of law might be impaired in some instances by applying adjudicative rules retroactively, but offers countervailing values to offset the damage to the rule of law. On this view, courts and agencies must have the power to develop new rules through adjudication and apply them retroactively because it is the courts and agencies, and not the legislatures, that can respond to specific cases as they arise and to changing societal conditions.[62] If government may operate by prospectively applied legislative or rulemaking rules alone, then situations will arise in the interstices of those

---

[62] See *SEC v Chenery Corp.*, 332 US 194 (1947); Fuller, *Morality of Law* at 56 (cited in note 7) ("If every time doubt arose as to the meaning of a rule, the judge were to declare the existence of a legal vacuum, the efficacy of the whole system of prospective rules would be seriously impaired").

rules that would be ungovernable until the legislature or rulemakers could again assemble and confront the problem. Delay would be harmful in many settings, and in other settings the problems would not be significant enough to warrant legislative or rulemaking response. Only by permitting agencies to fill the gaps through case-by-case development of statutory principles can we respond to the nuanced changes in the social fabric.[63] Put differently, the stringent demands of the rule of law must be moderated for the sake of social order. The best the legislature or rulemakers can do is issue commands of a general nature; as long as the citizens are on notice of those commands and of the reasonable spectrum of interpretation thereunder, they must do their best to conform their behavior to the likely or possible adjudicative outcomes.

The result of accepting such a theory, however, might be that citizens will conform their conduct to a wide array of possible interpretations of the governing law, to avoid penalties, thereby reducing their spectrum of liberty in planning their lives. Beneath each vague statutory standard, there exists a variety of specific rules that might be permissible interpretations of congressional intent. If there is insufficient evidence of congressional intent to answer the statutory question at *Chevron* stage 1, if the agency is empowered to choose which more specific categories are covered and which are not, and if the norm of adjudicative retroactivity applies, then people might conform their conduct to the array of possible administrative "interpretations" rather than wait to see which categories the agency chooses to cover and which not. This overdeterrence is the result of a strong norm of adjudicative retroactivity.[64]

But we can avoid such overdeterrence. For the supposed need to ensure regulatory flexibility through adjudicative retroactivity is overstated. First, substantial regulatory flexibility is afforded by underenforcing the delegation doctrine and permitting what amounts to administrative lawmaking through informal rulemaking procedures. Second, flexibility is advanced by permitting agencies

---

[63] See Davis, *Discretionary Justice* at 28–42 (cited in note 51) (values of administrative adjudicative retroactivity include (*a*) responsiveness to changing conditions, (*b*) better development of rules case by case, (*c*) need to resolve disputes, (*d*) legislative inertia).

[64] See Richard Fallon and Daniel Meltzer, *New Law, Non-Retroactivity, and Constitutional Remedies*, 104 Harv L Rev 1731, 1792 (1991); J. Skelly Wright, *Review: Beyond Discretionary Justice*, 81 Yale L J 575, 589 (1972).

to apply adjudicative rules purely prospectively.[65] Third, I am not advocating that every adjudicative specification of a general statutory standard may not be applied retroactively; there must be a method for distinguishing those adjudicative rules that were fairly ascertainable in advance by the parties and those that were not. I proposed one such method in Part IIIB.

There is an additional problem, as well. The *reductio ad absurdum* of the argument for regulatory flexibility is an autocracy, that is, a government in which one person develops the rules as cases arise. To guarantee pinpoint responses to the variety of situations that arise under a statutory scheme, a government would ideally place all power within the hands of one person, who could coordinate responses to the set of cases, and who could act swiftly to ensure no time gap between rules and governed behavior. To some degree, the framers' choice of a unitary rather than a plural executive reflects these concerns with coordination and efficiency (as well as accountability).[66] But the framers were equally clear about the vices of placing lawmaking powers in the hands of one person; they placed the lawmaking function in the hands of the many rather than the one, and created a cumbersome process for the creation of law.[67] As the Supreme Court has reminded us, unfettered flexibility is not one of the hallmarks of the American constitutional structure.[68]

B. THE COMMON LAW MODEL

The preceding argument—that adjudicative retroactivity ensures regulatory flexibility—treats adjudicative retroactivity as a necessary by-product of the administrative state. But one could focus more directly on the common-law virtues of adjudicative retroactivity. The common law tradition backs the interstitial judicial development of such statutory terms as "reasonable," "fair and equitable," etc. According to supporters of common law methodology, case-by-case development of standards is a good thing, be-

---

[65] See Part V.

[66] See *The Federalist* No 70 (Hamilton).

[67] See US Const, Art I, § 7.

[68] See *INS v Chadha*, 462 US 919 (1983); see also Henry Friendly, *The Federal Administrative Agencies: The Need for a Better Definition of Standards* 20–21 (1962) (flexibility and predictability are inversely related).

cause adjudicators can sometimes develop standards more carefully than can legislators;[69] because adjudicators, faced with real facts, can distinguish cases, and thus develop subcategories of principle as the occasion warrants; and because adjudicative rulings do not have as broad an impact as statutes, and thus the cost of adjudicative mistakes is less. As the Court put it in *Chenery II*, "Not every principle essential to the effective administration of a statute can or should be cast immediately into the mold of a general rule. Some principles must await their own development, while others must be adjusted to meet particular, unforeseen situations."[70] All adjudication is, in a sense, a form of common law development of standards—"rules are a kind of by-product of the adjudicative process"[71]—and adjudicative retroactivity is descriptive of the value of having one's conduct governed in the best possible fashion, by rulings tailored to the equities of the case at hand.[72]

The norm of adjudicative retroactivity might well be a product of our common law tradition. Common law courts combine the adjudicative and legislative functions. They consider both what the law is and what the law will be. The notion of a "developing" body of law captures this confluence. Thus, when a common law court announces a new rule but explains its pedigree in old rules, applying the new rule retroactively makes sense.[73] But when a common law court overrules its own precedent or announces a rule

---

[69] See Davis, *Discretionary Justice* at 20–21 (cited in note 51).

[70] 332 US at 202.

[71] Lon Fuller, *Adjudication and the Rule of Law*, Proc Am Soc of Int'l L 6 (1960).

[72] For example, although advocating generally that "legal newness is best analyzed as a matter of a decision's relative predictability," 104 Harv L Rev at 1794 (cited in note 64), Professors Fallon and Meltzer ultimately adopt a more specific definition of new law, approving new law treatment for claims that were "not 'clearly foreshadowed' by precedent," but "exclud[ing] instances of ordinary legal evolution." Id at 1796; see id at 1817. In other words, "legal rules and principles are new to the extent that, ex ante, their recognition as authoritative would have been viewed as relatively unlikely by competent lawyers." Id at 1763. If an adjudicative rule does not represent a "clear break with the past" (such as an overruling case), such a rule should be denied retroactive application only if it "lacks the kind of foreshadowing that characterizes ordinary legal evolution." Id at 1831. Fallon and Meltzer's definition (although not applied by them to the administrative law setting) would seem to exclude from new law treatment the fleshing out of vague statutory standards, i.e., their definition would consider fleshing-out rules as worthy of normal, retroactive application.

[73] The retroactivity norm of the common law exists in large part because many cases are "easy," i.e., decidable deductively from preexisting law. See Currier, 51 Va L Rev at 241 n 122 (cited in note 18); Lon Fuller, *The Forms and Limits of Adjudication*, 92 Harv L Rev 353, 392 (1978).

that cannot reasonably be said to be an outgrowth of prior rules or of other legal constraints, the norm of adjudicative retroactivity is on shaky ground. Put another way, common law courts do not "make up" the law as legislatures may "make up" the law; it is wrong to view the common law as merely a rolling act of judicial creativity.[74] Rather, judges acting in a common law capacity must seek to fit their rulings with the social understandings of the day, to capture "common" behavior in the "common" law.[75] A common law ruling that surprises people whose behavior it governs would, in departing from the core notion of common law constraints, be untrue to the common law pedigree, especially if applied retroactively.[76]

Thus, we can distinguish three types of case facing administrative adjudicators. First, some statutory standards recognize the difficulty of developing more finely honed rules, and leave to the case-by-case decisionmaking process the application of these standards. For example, adjudication under a statutory standard requiring "reasonable" conduct might, like its common-law cousin, generally fail to foster interstitial rules that would then serve as precedent for later cases.[77] Rather, the standard might itself be recognized as the final statement of law, which is then left for case-by-case application. But we accept such law-applying not because we want or expect the decisionmaker to decide cases in an unconstrained manner. Rather, we expect the decisionmaker applying a standard such as "reasonable" to be guided by accepted behavioral norms of the relevant community.

---

[74] "Over much of its history the common law has been largely engaged in working out the implications of conceptions that were generally held in the society of the time. This large measure of coincidence between moral and legal demands reduced greatly the force of the objection that the rules of the common law were, in contrast with those of a code, difficult of access." Fuller, *Morality of Law* at 50 (cited in note 7).

[75] See Mishkin, 79 Harv L Rev at 60 (cited in note 57); Stephen Munzer, *Retroactive Law*, 6 J Legal Stud 373, 376 (1977); Wellington, 83 Yale L J at 236 (cited in note 56); id at 256 ("changing morality that is there and knowable to the normal adult is filtered through existing common law doctrine"). This is why it makes sense to say that adjudicative precedent "binds" the citizens just as laws do. See *NLRB v Wyman-Gordon Co.*, 394 US 759, 769 n 1 (1969) (Black concurring in the result).

[76] The attempt to constrain adjudication to extant sources of principle is the source of the administrative law requirement that agencies explain consistency with precedent. See *SEC v Chenery Corp.*, 318 US 80 (1943); Richard Berg, *Re-Examining Policy Procedures: The Choice Between Rulemaking and Adjudication*, 38 Admin L Rev 149, 162 (1986).

[77] For exceptions to the generalization, see Stephen Gilles, *Rule-Based Negligence and the Regulation of Activity Levels*, 21 J Legal Stud (Forthcoming) (1992).

In a second type of case, the administrative agency might announce in the adjudication a previously unannounced rule of law developed under a statutory standard that did not spell out the rule. But, acting in similar fashion to the decisionmaker in the first case, the adjudicator in this second case would carefully explain how the announced rule followed from congressional intent, that is, that its choice was not just one among many policy positions, but rather was compelled by a legally constraining norm.[78] Here, then, the announcement and application of a rule in the administrative adjudication, although different from the first case by virtue of being a categorical pronouncement with intended precedential value, is nonetheless similar to the first case by relying on a source of legal constraint.

The third type of case is similar to the second in that the adjudicator announces rules that had been previously unannounced. But unlike both of the prior types of case, in this third type of case the adjudicator derives the rule not from an accepted pool of legal constraints, but rather from the less-constrained world of "policy" preferences. That is, the decision is based on what the adjudicator thinks will lead to a better social outcome. These decisions will not be "unconstrained" in the sense of being arbitrary; they will, that is, be based on familiar arguments about social good. But one agency's theory of the good might differ drastically from another's, often depending upon the administration controlling the White House at the time.[79] The policy choices made in this third type of case will be those sorts of choices that courts leave to agencies at stage 2 of the *Chevron* test. They are not true to the common law form.

C. WHO BEARS THE RISK OF UNCERTAINTY?

One might contend that I have assumed without argument that the party that would gain from a new adjudicative rule must bear

---

[78] I have focused on congressional intent as a source of legal constraint, for that is *Chevron*'s focus. An agency adjudicator might also be constrained by prior agency precedent or regulation, even if the precedential rule or regulation was not itself required by congressional intent as a stage 1 *Chevron* matter. When adjudicative rules should be applied retroactively because of a basis in precedent is a difficult matter that I do not address here. Similarly, I bracket the related issue of an agency's following its own regulations.

[79] See *Chevron, U.S.A., Inc. v Natural Resources Defense Council, Inc.*, 467 US 837, 865–66 (1984).

all the risk that such a rule was uncertain to follow from the statute. Assume both parties to a transaction know they are within the realm of a particular statutory term, and both know that the term is currently vague. They believe that different interpretations of the term are correct, and they order their affairs accordingly. An adjudicator then decides that the vague rule "means" what one party says it means. Under my analysis in Part IIIB, the rule should not apply to the other party's behavior if that party had insufficient reason to know the rule "meant" what the adjudicator later said it meant—that is, if the adjudicator's choice turned out to be a policy choice unconstrained by congressional intent. But this seems to beg the question of which party should bear the risk that its guess as to what the law means is wrong; my analysis always places the risk on the winning party.[80]

My proposal is consciously grounded in a baseline of existing wealth distribution.[81] Taking away someone's wealth is a disruption of the status quo, requiring special justification. The party who argues that a rule of law operates to deprive another party of held wealth bears the burden of showing that the rule was sufficiently knowable in advance of the other party's primary conduct that is in question. In other words, the argument that the party hurt by the new rule should bear (or share) the risk of the uncertain application of the statute ignores the value of the settled expectation of the status quo, which holds unless ruptured by a prospective rule.

It might be easier to see how this position is reached by recalling how the rule of law results in the norm of legislative prospectivity. Consider this situation: I refuse to hire some people merely because of their excessive weight; no law prohibits such refusal to hire. The next day the government enacts such a law and purports to apply it to my antecedent conduct. Now one could say that there was a

---

[80] Cf. *Aliceville Hydro Associates v FERC*, 800 F2d 1147, 1152–53 (DC Cir 1986).

[81] For an argument that the principle against retroactive legislation should be relaxed in the face of "a distribution that does not conform to the pattern prescribed by justice," see Stephen Munzer, *A Theory of Retroactive Legislation*, 61 Tex L Rev 425, 436 (1982); see also William Eskridge, Jr. & Philip Frickey, *Cases and Materials on Legislation: Statutes and the Creation of Public Policy* 263–64 (1988) (statutes sometimes "have great continuity with the pre-existing legal landscape," and "must sometimes be retroactive in order to get at the problems they attack"); Mishkin, 79 Harv L Rev at 70 (cited in note 57) ("if the old law is clearly unjust or immoral by community standards . . . , reliance upon it should not be considered justified, and a court should feel no inhibitions about adopting a new rule"); Rawls, *Theory of Justice* at 242–43 (cited in note 9).

"risk of uncertainty" regarding whether such an ordinance would be enacted. But to say I should bear a portion of that risk by paying for antecedent conduct would make a mockery of the values of the rule of law discussed in Part II.

In other words, we do not require both parties to a redistribution of wealth to bear some of the risk of uncertainty that new laws will be applied retroactively. We accept (and, indeed, admire) the liberty that follows from being able to plan one's conduct under the extant legal regime. One must still, of course, account for and bear the risk of the uncertain application of the legal rules that currently exist. But stage 1 *Chevron* cases involve just such situations: Many laws that are not crystal clear will, nonetheless, properly apply to antecedent conduct, for sufficient constraints will exist for both the adjudicator and the citizen to understand what those laws mean in the relevant situation. Applying the rule of a stage 2 *Chevron* case to antecedent conduct, however, is functionally identical to applying a congressional law retroactively, and should be disfavored for the same reasons we disfavor retroactive legislation. We should not require the party that the new adjudicative rule would harm to share the risk of uncertainty any more than we require a citizen to share the risk of uncertainty that new law will be applied retroactively. We operate under a strong (though not absolute) norm of legislative prospectivity, because although we accept the prospective regulation of the status quo of wealth distribution,[82]

---

[82] Accepting the status quo wealth distribution as a baseline for placing the risk of a retroactive disruption on the advantaged party says nothing about the virtues or vices of laws affecting wealth allocation prospectively. Although such laws may also upset the status quo wealth distribution, they do not impair settled expectations by redefining the legal status of past transactions or conduct as retroactive laws do.

One might object that even prospective wealth redistribution might upset reliance interests based on the prior legal regime; people might not have invested in a certain sort of property, for instance, had they known that the property would be subject in the future to more restrictive zoning regulations. But it may be possible to acknowledge a difference between primary and secondary retroactivity. See *Bowen v Georgetown Univ. Hosp.*, 109 S Ct 468, 477 (1988) (Scalia concurring); Munzer, 61 Tex L Rev at 426 (cited in note 81); but see generally Richard Epstein, *Takings: Private Property and the Power of Eminent Domain* (1985). We could, perhaps, apply a strong rule against primary retroactivity only; i.e., we could ensure that rules do not alter the legal status of prior acts. Were we to forbid secondary retroactivity as well—i.e., any new rule that affected the value of prior investments— legislation would be hard to come by. See Hochman, 73 Harv L Rev at 701 (cited in note 10) (discussing comment of Justice Holmes in *Pennsylvania Coal Co. v Mahon*, 260 US 393, 413 (1922)); Shapiro, 78 Harv L Rev at 934 (cited in note 28). All I mean to do here is apply my analysis to primary retroactivity; I need take no position now regarding whether secondary retroactivity can be successfully distinguished.

retroactive legislation is thought to be in significant tension with values of the rule of law. We should do the same for administrative adjudication that is properly labeled a "policy choice."

We might distinguish three types of situation in which the administrative adjudicative retroactivity problem would arise. First, there are cases in which the government brings an enforcement action against a private party. In these cases, any talk of "sharing the risk of uncertainty" seems out of place. It is awkward to talk of the government as having a reliance interest. Furthermore, in the public law settings with which this article is concerned, the government is parceling out the packages of rights and duties; it is not the recipient. Finally, the singling-out problem that exists in cases with two private parties disappears when the government is acting in its enforcement capacity. In a case with two private parties, the party that is favored by the new adjudicative rule—but that would not receive the benefit of its application under my theory—must bear the cost of the risk of uncertainty. But the government serves as a collective pooler of risk; even in its capacity of protecting public values against the intrusion of certain private interests, the government can spread widely among the citizens the cost of the risk of uncertainty.

Second, there are cases in which two private parties are involved, the statutory term at issue is vague, and the rule the adjudicator thinks best to decide the case is of the *Chevron* stage 2 variety, that is, it is an agency policy choice not mandated by congressional intent. Here, the case is functionally identical to a case of retroactive lawmaking: Forcing the party that would benefit from retroactive application to bear the risk of uncertainty generated by the unclarity of the statutory term is precisely like requiring a party that would benefit from retroactive application of a congressional law to bear the risk of uncertainty that the law would be enacted, a risk we permit without question.

The third set of cases is the hardest for my model: Here, private parties dispute the meaning of a statutory term that, although unclear and without a stage 1 *Chevron* answer, nonetheless admits of only a few, rather than many, possible meanings.[83] Consider again the variation on *Chevron* discussed near the end of Part IIIB. Assume for now that a damages remedy is potentially available to

---

[83] One might consider this a case of ambiguity; the prior type of case, one of vagueness.

plaintiff, NRDC. The dispute is whether the term "stationary source" means a particular pollution-emitting device or an entire plant of such devices. Other interpretations are not available. Thus, unlike the second type of case, in which the agency chooses from a broad range of options under a wide-open standard, when the agency is choosing from options that are few in number and known by both parties to be options, one might contend that each party should bear some of the risk of the uncertainty of how the term would be applied.

But even in this setting, the agency choice between the two options is, as a stage 2 *Chevron* matter, a policy choice not constrained by congressional intent. Consider as an analogy this situation: A set of companies is polluting in an environment currently unregulated by either statute or regulation. Congress is considering two options: (*a*) permitting X level of pollution from each smokestack, or (*b*) permitting Y level of pollution from each plant, or set of smokestacks. The polluters and the environmental litigation groups know that if Congress enacts (*a*), these polluters will have to pay fines if they continue polluting, but that if Congress enacts (*b*), these polluters will be within the legal limits. If Congress enacts (*a*), and seeks to impose fines for past as well as future pollution, we would say that values of the rule of law have been impaired by retroactive legislation, even though the polluters knew that the legislative options were limited and knew that one of the two choices would cover their plants. By analogizing stage 2 *Chevron* cases to the congressional setting, we can again see the flaws with the risk-sharing argument.[84]

D. INCENTIVES TO LITIGATE

Finally, one might object that were adjudicators forbidden from applying new rules retroactively, the development of the law would stultify because plaintiffs[85] seeking the announcement of new law

---

[84] Even if one adopted the risk-sharing argument in the third type of case, one could still adopt my model in the first two types of case, and even in the third case, one could impose only that proportion of retroactive liability that represents the polluters' share of the risk of uncertainty.

[85] Conceivably defendants, once dragged into litigation, might also advocate the fleshing out of vague statutory standards, but because defendants are already party to litigation against their will, there is little reason to believe that adopting my theory of adjudicative retroactivity would deter them from urging new rules in their responsive pleadings.

under vague standards would have no incentive, or a reduced incentive, to bring such litigation, knowing that the adjudicators
would not apply a new rule retroactively.[86] Thus, the application
of new adjudicative rules to antecedent conduct helps ensure that
statutory standards are properly developed.[87]

But there are several reasons why we should not be concerned
that limiting adjudicative retroactivity will excessively deter litigation that seeks to develop new rules. First, many cases that currently result in the announcement of a new rule are not brought
by the plaintiff with that purpose in mind. Plaintiffs might think
they can win at *Chevron* stage 1—that the rule they advocate is the
proper reading of congressional intent, not merely one of a number
of policy choices the agency is permitted to make.[88] Only when
plaintiffs seek rules that they know are not resolvable at stage 1 of
Chevron will the possibility of nonretroactivity create a disincentive
for litigation.

Second, plaintiffs who have an interest not only in recovering
damages or in undoing a past transaction, but in affecting the future
state of affairs as well, will still have a strong incentive to sue, for
a relaxed norm of adjudicative retroactivity might still permit the
adjudicator to apply a new rule prospectively only. This category
of plaintiff includes those seeking injunctive or declaratory relief
as well as institutional plaintiffs who see the same sorts of issues
arise a number of times. In short, any "repeat player" might still
seek legal change through adjudication.[89]

Third, our legal system already includes the qualified immunity
doctrine, which deters suits against government officials that might

---

[86] See, for example, *Mackey v United States*, 401 US 667, 675 (1971) (Harlan concurring
in the judgment); *Stovall v Denno*, 388 US 293 (1967); Albert Alschuler, *"Close Enough for
Government Work": The Exclusionary Rule After Leon*, 1984 Supreme Court Review 309, 340–
41; Fallon and Meltzer, 104 Harv L Rev at 1804 (cited in note 64); Fuller, *Morality of Law*
at 57 (cited in note 7); Mishkin, 79 Harv L Rev at 60–62 (cited in note 57); Note, 71 Yale
L J at 945 n 192 (cited in note 9).

[87] This problem would not exist, of course, when the government is the plaintiff, for it
can always institute a rulemaking proceeding to enunciate a new rule. See *Vermont Yankee
Nuclear Power Corp. v NRDC*, 435 US 519, 528 (1978) (government spots unresolved issue
in adjudication and begins rulemaking to resolve it).

[88] Cf. Currier, 51 Va L Rev at 215 (cited in note 18); Fallon and Meltzer, 104 Harv L
Rev at 1806 (cited in note 64); Mishkin, 79 Harv L Rev at 61 (cited in note 57).

[89] See Currier, 51 Va L Rev at 215 (cited in note 18); Fallon and Meltzer, 104 Harv L
Rev at 1804 (cited in note 64); Fuller, *Morality of Law* at 57 (cited in note 7).

change the law or declare a new principle.[90] Under current qualified immunity principles, individual governmental actors cannot
be held personally liable in damages for acts that might later be
deemed unconstitutional, if a reasonable government official would
have believed that the acts were constitutional.[91] Thus, the system
already has a built-in deterrent to using adjudication to penalize
people acting with the reasonable belief that their conduct was
lawful. Limiting adjudicative retroactivity fits within this system.

Fourth, one need not use agency adjudication to seek a new rule
of law under an unclear statutory standard; rather, one can seek
statutory clarification in Congress or a new rule through the informal agency rulemaking process.[92] These deliberative processes permit the public to enter the debate in a more fully formed way, are
more widely publicized, and by providing a general response rather
than one to a specific set of facts, avoid the dangers of singling
out.[93] Granted, some new rules benefit only a small minority of
citizens who might lack the political clout to achieve new rules
through either legislation or rulemaking.[94] But I am not currently
addressing the development of constitutional rights, which, because often beneficial to a disenfranchised citizen or group of
citizens, might require development through nonpolitical adjudicators. Rather, I am discussing the fleshing out of statutory standards, developed in the first instance by Congress, and developed
further by agencies. Both Congress and agencies are political
actors, and their statutes and rules create rights and obligations
agreed to by a majority of the peoples' representatives.

Fifth, if the foregoing responses do not seem sufficient, we could
adopt a system of modified retroactivity, allowing the plaintiff who
initially sues to create a new rule to benefit from it, but not permitting other similarly situated plaintiffs to benefit.[95] This would im-

---

[90] See Fallon and Meltzer, 104 Harv L Rev at 1805 (cited in note 64).

[91] See *Harlow v Fitzgerald*, 457 US 800 (1982).

[92] See Fuller, *Morality of Law* at 172–76 (cited in note 7); see also *Patel v INS*, 638 F2d
1199 (9th Cir 1980) (virtues of making categorical rule through rulemaking procedure).

[93] See Arthur Bonfield, *State Administrative Policy Formulation and the Choice of Lawmaking
Methodology*, 42 Admin L Rev 121, 122–36 (1990) (various arguments favoring informal
rulemaking over adjudication); Note, 76 Va L Rev at 144–47 (cited in note 44) (same).

[94] Cf. Alschuler, 1984 Supreme Court Review at 341 (cited in note 86).

[95] See *Stovall v Denno*, 388 US 293 (1967); *Clark-Cowlitz Joint Operating Agency v FERC*,
826 F2d 1074 (DC Cir 1987); Fallon and Meltzer, 104 Harv L Rev at 1806 (cited in note
64).

pose a rule of law cost on the defendant in the initial case, but would grant other similarly situated defendants an immunity from the retroactive application of the new rule. The Court has rejected modified retroactivity in both the criminal and civil contexts,[96] however, considering the net damage to the equality norm as greater than the net gain from a system of modified retroactivity. It is difficult to quantify the various factors in this "calculation," but given the various ways discussed in this section of ameliorating the concern with deterring litigation that seeks new rules, and given the cost to cardinal values of the rule of law from imposing retroactive obligations, the Court's rejection of modified retroactivity seems an appropriate outcome.

V. Defending Pure Adjudicative Prospectivity

When an agency chooses a rule that is not derivable from sources of law as a *Chevron* stage 1 matter, but rather represents an agency policy choice as a *Chevron* stage 2 matter, then one might conclude that the agency should announce the rule, but apply it to future conduct only. New rules that flesh out unclear statutes could be developed through agency adjudication, but they would be applied prospectively only.

One might object, though, that despite the problems with adjudicative retroactivity, pure adjudicative prospectivity is not the solution. On this view, while it is wrong for adjudicators to apply new law retroactively, it is also wrong for them to apply new law merely prospectively.[97] Adjudicators must remain in the role of interpreter of another's command, and if that command is too vague to yield an answer constrained by congressional intent, but

---

[96] See *Griffith v Kentucky*, 479 US 314 (1987) (criminal); *James B. Beam Distilling Co. v Georgia*, 111 S Ct 2439 (1991) (civil).

[97] See *NLRB v Wyman-Gordon Co.*, 394 US 759, 783 n 2 (1969) (Harlan dissenting) (if "new rule so departs from prior practices that it cannot fairly be applied retroactively," rulemaking is required because agency may not announce purely prospective adjudicative rules). For Article III courts, the Constitution might compel the retroactive application of adjudicative rules. See *James B. Beam*, 111 S Ct at 2449 (Blackmun concurring in the judgment); id at 2450 (Scalia concurring in the judgment); *Mackey v United States*, 401 US 667, 675 (1971) (Harlan concurring in the judgment); Currier, 51 Va L Rev at 216 (cited in note 18); Fallon and Meltzer, 104 Harv L Rev at 1798 (cited in note 64); but see Note, 71 Yale L J at 929 n 138 (cited in note 9) (quoting from 1 James Moore, Federal Practice 4082–84 (2d ed 1959)). Agency adjudicators are not governed by the strictures of Article III.

rather requires an agency policy choice, then the adjudicators can only point this out and "remand" the matter to the legislature or the rulemaking process.[98] In this Part, I shall explain that the leading Supreme Court case sometimes thought to reject purely prospective adjudicative rules does not in fact do so. I shall also demonstrate the virtue of such rules.

The leading case on whether agencies may announce a rule through adjudication and apply it purely prospectively is *NLRB v Wyman-Gordon Co.*[99] In a prior adjudication, *Excelsior Underwear Inc.*,[100] the NLRB had considered a union challenge to management's refusing to turn over a list of the names and addresses of employees eligible to vote in a union representation election. Rather than resolving the matter through briefs and arguments from the parties, the NLRB did the following three unusual things: (1) It invited various union and management groups to submit amicus briefs and participate in oral argument. (2) It did not apply the resulting rule—that management must provide a list of eligible employees—to the parties in the adjudication. (3) It declared that the rule would apply only to elections held at least thirty days after the date of the ruling. In *Wyman-Gordon*, the NLRB had applied the *Excelsior* rule in a dispute between the International Brotherhood of Boilermakers and the Wyman-Gordon Co.; the questions before the Court were the validity of the *Excelsior* rule itself and whether it was otherwise appropriate for the NLRB to order the Company to submit an eligible employees list to the Union.

In an opinion by Justice Fortas, four Justices concluded that the NLRB had improperly promulgated the *Excelsior* rule. The plurality's principal concern was that the NLRB had deliberately circumvented the APA rulemaking process. The plurality explained that the NLRB had improperly "purported to establish [a] general rule," and that it had "replace[d] the statutory [rulemaking] scheme with a rulemaking procedure of its own invention."[101] The NLRB had not published the final rule in the Federal Register, and it had solicited arguments from certain groups instead of publishing a general notice of proposed rulemaking in the Federal Reg-

---

[98] Cf. Frank Easterbrook, *Statutes' Domains*, 50 U Chi L Rev 533 (1983).

[99] 394 US 759 (1969).

[100] 156 NLRB 1236 (1966).

[101] 394 US at 763–64.

ister. It is in this context — of criticizing the NLRB for using an adjudication to conduct a clandestine rulemaking proceeding—that the plurality noted that the NLRB "did not even apply the rule it made to the parties in the adjudicatory proceeding, the only entities that could properly be subject to the order in that case."[102] But the concern of the plurality was not that in an otherwise normal adjudication, an agency had decided to apply a rule purely prospectively. Rather, the concern was that "the Board [had] purported to make a rule: *i.e.*, to exercise its quasi-legislative power."[103] Thus, although the *Wyman-Gordon* plurality disapproved of a particular purely prospective adjudicatory rule, it did so because of the manner in which the NLRB had sought to promulgate that rule; it did not issue a stark holding that purely prospective adjudicative rules are always improper.[104]

The two separate opinions also disapproving the *Excelsior* rule more clearly rejected the very concept of a purely prospective adjudicative rule.[105] But the reasoning of these opinions is open to challenge. Justice Harlan concluded, "The language of the [APA] does not support the Government's claim that an agency is 'adjudicating' when it announces a rule which it refuses to apply in the dispute before it."[106] He reached this result in the following manner: An agency "adjudicates"[107] only when it formulates an "order," which is defined as what an agency issues in "a matter other than rulemak-

---

[102] Id at 765.

[103] Id; see Cornelius Peck, *A Critique of the National Labor Relations Board's Performance in Policy Formulation: Adjudication and Rule-Making*, 117 U Pa L Rev 254, 266 (1968) (in *Excelsior*, NLRB engaged in "the fiction of adjudication").

[104] Although the plurality rejected the *Excelsior* rule, and although the NLRB had cited *Excelsior* in ordering the Wyman-Gordon Co. to furnish an eligible employee list, the plurality nonetheless upheld the order that the Wyman-Gordon Co. furnish such a list! In apparent disregard of the *Chenery I* tenet that agency action must be justified on the basis the agency cites, the plurality explained that "[t]o remand would be an idle and useless formality" because the NLRB clearly has the substantive power to order such a list. 394 US at 766 n 6. Even though the other two Justices who disapproved of the *Excelsior* rule would have followed *Chenery I* and reversed the NLRB in this case, see id at 775 (Douglas dissenting); id at 780 (Harlan dissenting), the plurality was joined in the result by the other three Justices, who thought the *Excelsior* rule legitimate (but who also indicated they would have remanded pursuant to *Chenery I* if they had disapproved of the *Excelsior* rule). See id at 769 (Black concurring in the result).

[105] Id at 775 (Douglas dissenting); id at 780 (Harlan dissenting).

[106] Id at 780.

[107] 5 USC § 551(7).

ing."[108] A rule made through rulemaking procedures has "future effect" only.[109] Therefore, because the NLRB declared that the *Excelsior* rule would be effective only in the future, that rule had to be issued through a rulemaking proceeding.

This argument is flawed. There is indeed a good argument that the APA requires rulemaking rules to have future effect only.[110] But it does not follow, from either policy or the statutory text, that an adjudicative rule may not, on occasion, also have future effect only. I shall discuss the policy concerns below. As a textual matter, the APA does not require that an adjudicative rule have at least retroactive effect.[111] The APA does not say, as Justice Harlan's logic implies, that all rules having future effect only must be announced through rulemaking proceedings. Requiring the rules that are announced through rulemaking proceedings to have future effect only is not the same thing as forbidding adjudicative rules from having such effect. The APA does the former; it does not do the latter.[112]

Justice Douglas agreed with Justice Harlan that "an agency is not adjudicating when it is making a rule to fit future cases."[113] As Justice Douglas explained, informal rulemaking ensures at least two values that adjudication might thwart. First, by requiring a notice of proposed rulemaking to which any member of the public may respond, the rulemaking procedures ensure a generality of participation that might be lacking in the often bipolar world of adjudication. Second, by publishing the notice of proposed rulemaking and the final rule in a commonly available general source —the Federal Register—rulemaking ensures an openness of debate that might be lost in the less public world of adjudication.

To be sure, these arguments somewhat overstate the differences between rulemaking and adjudication. In important adjudications, members of the affected communities can often enter as intervenors or submit amicus briefs to ensure a wider degree of participation

---

[108] Id at § 551(6).

[109] Id at §§ 551(4)(5).

[110] See note 27 and accompanying text.

[111] See 5 USC §§ 551(6)(7).

[112] Even if Justice Harlan's position were correct, one need not concede the demise of pure adjudicative prospectivity; rather, if persuaded that pure adjudicative prospectivity is a valuable agency tool, Congress could amend the APA to permit it.

[113] 394 US at 777.

in the construction of rules. Also, the availability of adjudicative agency decisions through looseleaf services or computer databases mitigates the "hidden" nature of adjudicative rules. But the rule-making procedures still offer the best mechanism for constructing general rules that respond to, and are available to, the community at large.

Nonetheless, there are good reasons to support the occasional agency announcement of an adjudicative rule applied merely prospectively. First, if an adjudicator has made a policy determination regarding how to flesh out an unclear statutory standard and thus has concluded that rule of law concerns militate against retroactive application, the adjudicator can serve the purposes of both law reform and the rule of law by announcing the rule but applying it merely prospectively.[114] We can forbid agencies from doing what the NLRB did in *Wyman-Gordon*—deliberately use an adjudication, from the outset, to conduct a quasi-rulemaking proceeding—but still endorse a purely prospective adjudicative rule that results from a standard adjudication.[115] Second, in many cases, the parties to the litigation will be affected by the ruling's prospective effects, even if the new rule is not applied to their antecedent conduct. Thus, the ruling will not be purely advisory, and the possibility that the adjudicator will not apply the rule of the case to antecedent conduct will deter only a small amount of litigation.[116]

Third, if an agency may not apply a rule purely prospectively but must also be alert to improper retroactive application, there will be times that an adjudicator will have to dismiss an adjudication after time and energy have been spent on it, because the rule the adjudicator chose could neither be properly applied to the parties nor announced purely prospectively.[117] Fourth, a strict rule against pure adjudicative prospectivity, combined with a healthy regard for the problems of retroactive application of new adjudicative rules, would perhaps force too many issues out of adjudication

---

[114] See id at 773–74 (Black concurring in the result).

[115] As Justice Black pointed out in his *Wyman-Gordon* opinion, even in *Excelsior*, "The Board did not abstractly decide out of the blue to announce a brand new rule of law to govern labor activities in the future, but rather established the procedure as a direct consequence of the proper exercise of its adjudicatory powers." Id at 773 (Black concurring in the result); see also Mishkin, 79 Harv L Rev at 61 (cited in note 57).

[116] See Part IVD.

[117] See 394 US at 774–75 (Black dissenting).

and onto the rulemaking docket. Although rulemaking should be the primary source for the creation of agency policy out of unclear statutes, permitting pure adjudicative prospectivity would ensure agency attention even to those smaller issues that might not make it to the rulemaking docket. Fifth, agencies might sometimes develop better rules by responding to the concrete specifics of adjudicative situations than by considering the more abstract comments submitted during the notice-and-comment rulemaking process. In sum, the advantages of the occasional announcement of a purely prospective adjudicative rule outweigh the disadvantages.[118]

Against these arguments favoring pure adjudicative prospectivity, *Wyman-Gordon* seems a weak precedential barrier. Although one might construe that case as "holding" that agencies lack the power to announce a purely prospective new rule through adjudication,[119] there are reasons to believe the Court would not prevent an agency from doing so in an appropriate case. The Court has long adhered to the fundamental proposition that an agency generally has discretion to choose either rulemaking or adjudication to announce new rules.[120] Although approving significant adjudicative

---

[118] In apparent, although often silent, recognition of these arguments, the Court has, in the judicial context, adopted pure adjudicative prospectivity both for new law that overruled old law, see *Buckley v Valeo*, 424 US 1 (1976); *Chevron Oil Co. v Huson*, 404 US 97 (1971); *Mackey v United States*, 401 US 667 (1971); *Desist v United States*, 394 US 244 (1969); *Stovall v Denno*, 388 US 293 (1967); *Johnson v New Jersey*, 384 US 719 (1966); *Linkletter v Walker*, 381 US 618 (1965); *Reynolds v Sims*, 377 US 533 (1964); *James v United States*, 366 US 213 (1961), and for new law that merely fleshed out vague mandates, see *Allen v State Bd. of Elections*, 393 US 544 (1969); *England v Louisiana State Bd. of Medical Examiners*, 375 US 411 (1964); see also *Chevron Oil Co. v Huson*, 404 US 97, 106 (1971); *Halliday v United States*, 394 US 831, 833 (1969) (Harlan concurring in the judgment). The Court has also held that a party to state-court litigation does not have a federal constitutional right to retroactive application of the rule announced in the adjudication. *Great N. R. Co. v Sunburst Oil & Refining Co.*, 287 US 358 (1932).

[119] See *Bowen v Georgetown Univ. Hosp.*, 109 S Ct 468, 478 (1988) (Scalia concurring); Merton Bernstein, *The NLRB's Adjudication-Rule Making Dilemma Under the Administrative Procedure Act*, 4 Yale L J 571, 610 (1970).

[120] See *NLRB v Bell Aerospace Co.*, 416 US 267 (1974); *SEC v Chenery Corp.*, 332 US 194 (1947). Lower courts have usually followed suit. See note 44. For two departures, see *First Bancorp. v Board of Governors*, 728 F2d 434 (10th Cir 1984) (invalidating a new rule, although applied to the parties, because agency should promulgate new, broad rule through rulemaking procedure); *Ford Motor Co. v FTC*, 673 F2d 1008, 1010 (9th Cir 1981) (setting aside adjudicative order, "because the rule of the case . . . will have general application"), cert denied, 459 US 999 (1982).

The Court has, though, encouraged agencies to use the rulemaking process when they know in advance that they want to announce new categorical rules. See *Morton v Ruiz*, 415 US 199 (1974); *SEC v Chenery Corp.*, 332 US 194, 202 (1947); see also Davis, *Discretionary Justice* at 61–64 (cited in note 51) (suggesting the promulgation of rules phrased as responses to factual hypotheticals).

retroactivity, the Court has left the door open (without significant discussion) for denial of such retroactivity if the equities warrant.[121] The Court has not indicated or implied that in such a case, an agency would be deprived of its usual discretion to choose adjudication over rulemaking. Thus, if an agency may choose adjudication, and if the equities warrant a denial of retroactivity, then the agency would be permitted to announce a new rule through adjudication prospectively only.[122]

In addition, a flat rule against pure adjudicative prospectivity in the agency context is somewhat inconsistent with the Court's applying its own decisions prospectively;[123] *Wyman-Gordon* does not address this line of cases.[124] Finally, some lower courts have, in the face of *Wyman-Gordon*, approved purely prospective adjudicative rulemaking,[125] and the Court might find the views of its appellate colleagues persuasive. Indeed, as discussed above, four of the six *Wyman-Gordon* Justices who voted against pure adjudicative prospectivity in that case seemed more concerned with the NLRB's quasi-notice and comment rulemaking procedure and less concerned with the prospectivity of the rule simpliciter.[126]

VI. CONCLUSION

Although the Court has recently attempted to shape the contours of adjudicative retroactivity in the setting of both criminal[127] and civil[128] constitutional law, its attention has not turned to

---

[121] See *NLRB v Bell Aerospace Co.*, 416 US 267, 294 (1974); *SEC v Chenery Corp.*, 332 US 194, 203 (1947).

[122] See *NLRB v Wyman-Gordon Co.*, 394 US 759, 772 (1969) (Black concurring in the result); Stephen Breyer and Richard Stewart, *Administrative Law and Regulatory Policy* 484 n 76 (2d ed 1985); Robinson, 4 U Pa L Rev at 510 (cited in note 28).

[123] See Robinson, 4 U Pa L Rev at 512–13 (cited in note 28); see note 118.

[124] See *McDonald v Watt*, 653 F2d 1035, 1042 n 17 (5th Cir 1981).

[125] See *Petrolite Corp. v FERC*, 667 F2d 664 (8th Cir 1981); *McDonald v Watt*, 653 F2d 1035 (5th Cir 1981); *Transwestern Pipeline Co. v FERC*, 626 F2d 1266 (5th Cir 1980), cert denied, 451 US 937 (1981); see also *H. & F. Binch Co. v NLRB*, 456 F2d 357, 365 (2d Cir 1972) (Friendly) ("It is indeed surprising that the Board should so consistently have refused . . . to develop techniques of prospective ruling and overruling save in one notable instance where it overdid this. *NLRB v Wyman-Gordon*"); Shapiro, 78 Harv L Rev at 934 (cited in note 28).

[126] See *McDonald v Watt*, 653 F2d 1035, 1042 n 17 (5th Cir 1981).

[127] See *Teague v Lane*, 109 S Ct 1060 (1989); *Griffith v Kentucky*, 479 US 314 (1987). The Court has also held that its decisions should not be applied to a state defendant's federal

the related issue of adjudicative retroactivity in administrative law. Even as it has provided a clearer picture of the lawmaking powers of administrative agencies—powers that are exercised through both rulemaking and adjudication—the Court has not revisited its forty-five-year-old doctrine permitting broad administrative adjudicative retroactivity. But *Chevron*'s insight into agency lawmaking demands a new look at *Chenery II*'s understanding of agency adjudication. *Chevron*'s two-stage test for determining when courts must permit agencies to make law can serve as the model for determining when agencies should be disabled from applying their rules retroactively. For *Chevron* can help us see the connection between interpretive constraints and notice of what the law is. When there is insufficient evidence of congressional intent to bind an agency to a particular regulatory choice, then there is insufficient evidence of congressional intent for the affected citizens to know what the law is, and to conform their behavior accordingly. When a regulatory choice is properly deemed an act of lawmaking, then to the extent that we do not permit laws to apply retroactively, the regulatory choice should also not apply retroactively, whether announced in a rulemaking or in an adjudication.

---

habeas corpus proceeding unless the decisions were "dictated by precedent existing at the time the petitioner's conviction became final." *Butler v McKellar*, 110 S Ct 1212, 1214 (1990). A decision is "dictated by precedent" only if there are no "reasonable, good-faith interpretations" to the contrary. Id at 1217. Although *Butler* erects a steep barrier to adjudicative retroactivity in the habeas corpus setting, and the *Chevron* model also enunciates a stricter rule against adjudicative retroactivity than has been previously applied in the administrative law context, one test should not be confused with the other. There are at least two important distinctions. First, *Butler*'s concern is with the law that existed on the date the defendant's conviction became final. After *Butler*, in the habeas setting a court need not pay attention to which rule existed at the time of the primary conduct at issue (usually that of the defendant or the police). *Butler*'s concern is not with notice and the rule of law; rather, *Butler* focuses on federalism, and whether the state courts made "reasonable, good-faith interpretations of existing precedents." Id. Second, the *Butler* test permitting retroactivity only when a new rule is "dictated by precedent" is more stringent than my test permitting retroactivity when one can ascertain congressional intent on a question of statutory interpretation. The difference between the tests is based at least in part on the difference between the purposes behind the tests, bolstering federalism in *Butler*, adhering to rule of law values, in the *Chevron* model.

[128] See *James B. Beam Distilling Co. v Georgia*, 111 S Ct 2439 (1991); *American Trucking Assns., Inc. v Smith*, 110 S Ct 2323 (1990).

SHELDON M. NOVICK

THE UNREVISED HOLMES
AND FREEDOM OF EXPRESSION

I. INTRODUCTION

Justice Oliver Wendell Holmes's opinions on freedom of speech are the foundation of First Amendment jurisprudence, but there is a puzzle about them that besets our understanding of the First Amendment today. Just after World War I, in a series of brief opinions that began with *Schenck v United States*,[1] Holmes, speaking for the Supreme Court, upheld convictions of political dissidents for expressions that had created a "clear and present danger" of obstructing the draft law.[2] In a second series of apparently similar cases beginning a few months later with *Abrams v United States*,[3]

Sheldon M. Novick is Scholar in Residence, Vermont Law School.

AUTHOR'S NOTE: This article was prepared in the course of editing the memorial edition of Holmes's collected works, to be published by the University of Chicago Press. I am glad to acknowledge and express my thanks for support of this work by the Permanent Committee on the Oliver Wendell Holmes Devise. I am grateful also for the gracious assistance and continuing access to the Holmes papers provided by the librarians and staff of the Harvard Law School Library, who have granted permission for the use I have made of Holmes's unpublished works; and for the very valuable assistance given me by my colleague Karen McLaughlin, Esq., and by Claire Reinhardt, Managing Editor of the collected works project. My thanks also to Judge Richard A. Posner and Professors Albert W. Alschuler and Catherine A. MacKinnon for their thoughtful criticisms of earlier drafts. Responsibility for the views expressed here is of course mine alone.

[1] 249 US 47 (1919); *Frohwerk v United States*, 249 US 204 (1919); *Debs v United States*, 249 US 211 (1919).

[2] *Schenck v United States*, 249 US 47, 52 (1919).

[3] 250 US 616 (1919).

the Court again affirmed convictions for speech obstructing the war effort, but in these cases Holmes dissented.[4]

"The law of free speech we know today grows out of [Holmes's] Supreme Court decisions following World War I,"[5] but judges and scholars have found it difficult to reconcile Holmes's opinions for the Court with his later passionate dissents. In recent years, a revisionist school of commentators has said that Holmes was cynically seeking results that suited him at different times;[6] or, more commonly, that in the summer of 1919 he was persuaded to change his mind.[7]

The argument over the meaning of Holmes's opinions has become part of a larger struggle over constitutional doctrine. His dissent in *Abrams* is cited as precedent for an expansive, rights-based view of the freedom of speech; from this perspective *Schenck* is simply an embarrassment.[8]

Historical evidence has been used selectively in this debate. Viewed as a whole, the evidence shows without much doubt that Holmes's views did not change, and that *Schenck* and *Abrams* were cut from the same bolt.[9] If there were really any doubt about the historical record, an unpublished dissent by Holmes[10] in *Baltzer v United States*,[11] recently discovered by the author, puts it to rest.

---

[4] *Abrams v United States*, 250 US 616, 624 (1919) (Holmes dissenting); *Pierce v United States*, 252 US 239, 253 (1920) (Brandeis and Holmes dissenting); *Schaeffer v United States*, 251 US 466, 482 (1920) (Brandeis and Holmes dissenting); *Gitlow v New York*, 268 US 672, 673 (1925) (Holmes dissenting); *Whitney v California*, 274 US 357, 372 (1927) (Brandeis and Holmes concurring).

[5] Robert Bork, *Neutral Principles and Some First Amendment Problems*, 47 Ind L J 1, 23 (1971). A Lexis search in April, 1991, found 908 federal cases in which the phrase "clear and present danger" appeared, for instance. A best-selling novel at the time was Tom Clancy, *Clear and Present Danger* (1990), which had nothing to do with freedom of speech.

[6] See, e.g., Alan Dershowitz, *Shouting 'Fire!'* The Atlantic Monthly 72 (January 1989).

[7] See, e.g., Fred Ragan, *Justice Oliver Wendell Holmes, Jr., Zechariah Chafee, Jr., and the Clear and Present Danger Test for Free Speech: The First Year, 1919*, 58 J Am Hist 24 (1971); see Section XIII.

[8] See Section XIII.

[9] See Sections X, XI.

[10] *Baltzer v United States* (Holmes dissenting), memorandum distributed to the Justices on December 3, 1918; Oliver Wendell Holmes, Jr., Papers, Harvard Law School Library (cited below as "Holmes Papers"); reprinted Appendix infra. Holmes referred to this dissent in unpublished letters, see Holmes to Mrs. Gray, March 5, 1921, Holmes Papers; see Sheldon Novick, *Honorable Justice: The Life of Oliver Wendell Holmes* (cited below as "*Honorable Justice*") 325, 471 n 63 (Little, Brown, 1989), which was the first published reference to *Baltzer*.

[11] No opinion was ever issued in this case; see Section VIII.

Baltzer was the first of the wartime First Amendment cases to be considered by the Court, months before the decision in *Schenck*, and in it Holmes had written a strong dissent on behalf of free speech. The Court's deliberations in *Baltzer* show that Holmes's role in shaping First Amendment jurisprudence from the beginning was even more important than had been thought, and confirms the common-sense view that Holmes's opinions were stubbornly consistent.

The two sets of Holmes's opinions on freedom of speech expressed different aspects of a single doctrine. Holmes thought the First Amendment required that two things be proven before criminal liability could be imposed for speech or publication: foreseeability of harm of a kind Congress had power to forbid; and a subjective intent to bring about the specific, forbidden harm. Holmes, known to us now as the champion of the external standard of liability, insisted that proof of subjective intent—of improper motive—was needed to defeat a claim of Constitutional right. This doctrine has proven remarkably durable, and the Court regularly returns to it, or something like it, as if to a fixed point of reference.

II. THE COMMON LAW BACKGROUND

To expose the skeletal structure of Holmes's opinions it will be helpful to begin with his work on the common law. Holmes did not join the Supreme Court, and had little experience of federal law, until he was past sixty. His ideas on fundamental questions were shaped by his long study of the common law, his fifteen-year practice at the Massachusetts bar, and his twenty years on the Massachusetts bench.[12]

This was better preparation than it would be now. When Holmes joined the United States Supreme Court in 1902, it viewed itself as a common law court, and its prior decisions had established that the Bill of Rights incorporated principles of the common law.[13] Holmes's unrivaled mastery of the common law therefore gave him unusual influence in some constitutional cases, and during his

---

[12] See *Honorable Justice*, cited in note 10, at 114–237. Although his law practice and judicial experience were primarily in the common law of Massachusetts, Holmes did have extensive experience of admiralty and bankruptcy cases in federal district court. Id.

[13] See Section VII.

thirty years on the Court Holmes managed to write many of his ideas about the common law into constitutional adjudication. To understand Holmes's First Amendment opinions clearly, therefore, we must begin at some distance.

Holmes believed that judge-made law was an expression—limited and shaped by precedent—of public opinion, the "unconscious will" of the dominant forces in society.[14] This will was essentially selfish: "in the last resort, a man rightly prefers his interest to that of his neighbors."[15] To the extent that a dominant class accomplished its selfish purposes (moderated only by "sympathy and all the social feelings"[16]), it would survive. Law, therefore, was both an instrument and a reflection of human evolution. Holmes concluded that the common law was evolving toward greater consciousness of its own purposes—the purposes of the law-making power—and toward a more scientific design of the legal instruments for their accomplishment.[17]

Holmes's principal evidence for his thesis was the gradual evolution of the supposed basis for all liability, civil and criminal, in the common law. The basis of liability, Holmes argued, had changed from primitive vengeance, through intermediate moral stages, to a modern "external" or objective standard of liability. The purpose of modern criminal law, accordingly, was "to induce external conformity to rule," and the standard used to determine whether courts should impose punishment or liability was correspondingly "external."[18] Civil liability for torts, similarly, in the most famous formulation of Holmes's external standard, had come to be imposed only in those cases where the defendant's conduct was such that, in the circumstances, a person of ordinary prudence would have

---

[14] O. Holmes, *The Common Law* (cited below as "*Common Law*") 35–36 (Little, Brown, 1881); Holmes, *Privilege, Malice, and Intent*, 8 Harv L Rev 1 (1894) (cited below as "*Privilege, Malice, and Intent*"); *The Path of the Law*, 10 Harv L Rev 457 (1897), reprinted in Holmes, *Collected Legal Papers* 167, 180–84 (Harcourt, Brace & Howe, 1920); cf. *Gitlow v New York*, 268 US 652, 674 (1925) ("If in the long run the beliefs expressed in proletarian dictatorship are destined to be accepted by the dominant forces of the community, the only meaning of free speech is that they should be given their chance and have their way").

[15] [Holmes], *The Gas Stoker's Strike*, 7 Am L Rev 582, 583 (1873); *Common Law*, cited in note 14, at 44 (in almost the same words).

[16] Id at 44.

[17] *Common Law*, cited in note 14, at 36. See also Holmes, *Law in Science, Science in Law*, 12 Harv L Rev 443 (1899).

[18] *Common Law*, cited in note 14, at 49–50.

foreseen that harm would result.[19] The result of this evolution was that law had come to be a finely crafted instrument, designed to prevent harms with the least concomitant restriction on individual liberty.[20]

Holmes was at pains from the first to explain some apparent exceptions to the external standard. One such was the class of legally recognized privileges to do harm. There were numerous cases in which defendants could have foreseen, and in fact had foreseen, that their conduct would injure someone, and yet were not held liable for the harm that followed. The commonest instance was found in the law of defamation. Slanders and libels by definition were foreseeably damaging, yet often the defendant could avoid liability by claiming that the speech or writing in question was "privileged"; in other words that, in the circumstances, he or she was privileged to cause foreseeable harm. The real substance of the defense of privilege was not that the injury was unforeseen, but that "the law considered the damage to the plaintiff of less importance than the benefit of free speaking."[21]

The Common Law, Holmes's fullest statement of his general theory, was published in 1881, and when Holmes took his seat on the Massachusetts Supreme Judicial Court the following year, his theoretical work was largely complete. In his early years as a judge he tested his ideas in practice and felt assured that they were correct.[22] He had the satisfaction of making the external standard of liability the explicit and general rule in Massachusetts, and through the writings of his friends, especially Sir Frederick Pollock, his opinions were noticed and cited by the English courts. Pollock eventually would complain lugubriously that the "external standard" had begun to appear on students' examination papers.[23] Yet Holmes's work as a judge forced him to consider a number of cases in which the external standard of foreseeable harm did not seem

---

[19] Id at 145–47. For a recent criticism of this view of negligence in the common law, see Kelley, *A Critical Analysis of Holmes's Theory of Torts*, 61 Wash U L Q 681 (1983).

[20] See *Common Law*, cited in note 14, at 95–96.

[21] Id at 139.

[22] Speech, at a dinner given to Chief Justice Holmes by the Bar Association of Boston on March 7, 1900, in Holmes, *Speeches* 82, 84 (Harvard, 1913).

[23] See Frederick Pollock to Holmes, August 31, 1893, 1 *Holmes-Pollock Letters* 46 (Harvard, 1941).

to apply, cases which forced him to broaden his theory to take into account, among other things, the limitations on the privilege accorded to free speech.

III. Privilege, Malice, and Intent

Holmes eventually divided these anomalous cases into two categories.

The first were cases in which some third person had intervened between the defendant's act and the plaintiff's injury. In these cases, foreseeability seemed not to be at issue. In *Elmer v Fessenden*,[24] for instance, a doctor falsely told one of his patients—who worked in a buggy-whip factory—that silk used to make the buggy-whip snaps was contaminated with arsenic. Other employees heard the story and quit work; the factory owner sued Dr. Fessenden. The doctor's defense was that his advice to his patient was privileged, and that the persons who repeated and spread the story, and not he, in any case were the cause of the harm.

It was argued in rebuttal that the slander was bound to be repeated, and that Fessenden was bound to foresee the injury. But Holmes, writing for the court, held that Fessenden could not be held liable for the repetitions: "The general rule, that a man is not liable for a third person's actionable and unauthorized repetition of his slander, is settled."[25] In this, and in a series of tort and contract cases, Holmes followed the long-established doctrine that liability would not be imposed on the defendant if the wrongful acts of a third party intervened between the defendant's conduct and the plaintiff's injury.[26] (This would later prove to be an important line of cases for Holmes's First Amendment jurisprudence, because political dissidents would be prosecuted, not for directly interfering with the war effort, but for inciting others to do so.)

To explain these cases, and to reconcile them with his general scheme, Holmes enlarged upon the idea of "foreseeability." A person was not held by the common law to foresee wrongdoing by others. "[I]f the third person's act was lawful, it stands like the

---

[24] 151 Mass 359 (1890).

[25] Id at 362.

[26] *Graves v Johnson*, 156 Mass 211, 212–13 (1892); *Hayes v Hyde Park*, 153 Mass 514 (1891); *Clifford v Atlantic Cotton Mills*, 146 Mass 47 (1888).

workings of nature, and the question is whether it reasonably was to be anticipated or looked out for."[27] But intervening third-party wrongdoers were by definition unforeseeable, presumably because their behavior was unnatural in some sense.[28] Liability accordingly was limited to cases of foreseeable harms.

This may look arbitrary to a modern eye, but it was not so at the time. Holmes never had any knowledge of probability or statistics, and he did not think in quantitative terms. Furthermore, he was explaining precedents that had been decided in a still earlier age, an age of natural law thinking, when "rational" and "proper" were nearly synonymous.[29] For Holmes, foresight meant extending into the future the lines of orderly and proper behavior. If lawful behavior "stands like the workings of nature," all else is an Act of God—fortuitous and "unforeseeable," even if perfectly unsurprising. It was in this old-fashioned sense that Holmes could say with a perfectly good conscience that one should not be held to "foresee" injuries caused by the independent wrongdoing of others.[30]

A puzzling aspect of these cases, however, was that the defendant's subjective expectations seemed important. The precedents were clear that a defendant could not shelter behind wrongful behavior of a third party that he or she in fact expected;[31] but Holmes accepted this qualification without at first attempting to explain it. With regard to these third-party wrongdoer cases, therefore, Holmes felt his scheme was preserved, although, as Frederick Pollock remarked, his analysis was too finely honed for everyday use.[32]

The second class of cases that had to be reconciled with the "external standard" were those in which a defense of privilege had been raised. Holmes had addressed these briefly in *The Common*

---

[27] Holmes, *Privilege, Malice, and Intent*, 8 Harv L Rev 1 at 11–12.

[28] Note, *Origin of the Modern Standard of Due Care in Negligence*, 1976 Wash U L Q 447 (1977).

[29] Id.

[30] *Privilege, Malice, and Intent*, cited in note 14, at 12 (citation omitted) and cases cited within n 21. Holmes extended the same analysis to cases in which the invalidity of a contract was asserted because on objective grounds it contemplated illegal behavior by third parties, *Graves v Johnson*, 156 Mass 211, 212–13 (1892).

[31] *Common Law*, cited in note 14, at 134.

[32] Pollock to Holmes, March 30, 1898, 1 *Holmes-Pollock Letters* at 84 (cited in note 23). Pollock did not think the House of Lords had adopted Holmes's refined analysis of privilege and intent, but on the contrary had decided competition was a matter of right and so not examinable as to motives. Id.

Law.[33] In such cases, the defendant admittedly could foresee that her conduct would cause injuries, and yet still asked to be excused from liability. A privilege, if properly asserted, could then be defeated only by a showing of actual malice.[34] In one case that interested Holmes, a couple had given advice to a married woman, as a consequence of which she had left her husband. The injured husband sued the interfering couple, but did not succeed, because, despite his foreseeable injury, the advice was privileged. On appeal, the plaintiff took exception to the trial court's having admitted evidence of the defendants' motives. Holmes said evidence of motive was properly admitted at the trial, for the defendants "had a right to show their advice was given honestly, with a view to the welfare of both parties." On such a showing the defendants' advice could have been held to be privileged, and the couple would not be liable.[35] Similarly, Dr. Fessenden's advice to his patient, if honestly given, was privileged.[36] A newspaper report of corruption in office was privileged unless published with actual malice.[37]

It is interesting that in these cases of privilege for expressions, falsity was pleaded and for the most part assumed by the court. Truth was an affirmative defense at common law, but was quite independent of the defense of privilege. If an otherwise privileged statement made in good faith turned out to be false, the privilege nevertheless was good unless the statement was shown to be made with actual malice.

Holmes, in *The Common Law*, had denied that "actual malice" referred to the subjective intentions of the defendant; indeed, he gave this phrase as an example of the persistence of older language implying fault despite the law's having evolved beyond moral standards, based on the defendant's state of mind, to an external standard based on behavior.[38] In *The Common Law*, Holmes had interpreted the modern cases to say that "actual malice" meant no more than that by an external standard the defendant's statement was

---

[33] *Common Law*, cited note 14, at 138–39.

[34] Id.

[35] *Tasker v Stanley*, 153 Mass 148 (1891).

[36] *Elmer v Fessenden*, 151 Mass 359 (1890).

[37] *Burt v Advertiser Newspaper Co.*, 154 Mass 238 (1891); see also *Cowley v Pulsifer*, 137 Mass 392 (1882).

[38] *Common Law*, cited in note 14, at 139.

patently false and likely to cause harm.[39] "The fact that the defendant foresaw and foresaw with pleasure the damage to the plaintiff, is of no . . . importance. . . ."[40] But as a judge, Holmes was obliged to concede that liability depended, not on an external standard alone, but also on evidence of the actual motives of the defendants. This was the same anomaly that had turned up in the third-party wrongdoer cases. Holmes set out to explain it.

The answer he gave was set out in an article, "Privilege, Malice, and Intent," published in 1894.[41] The article began with bravado: "The law of torts as now administered has worked itself into substantial agreement with a general theory." This theory, which Holmes went on to summarize, was his own theory of the external standard, presented in the opening chapters of *The Common Law*, and worked through in his opinions for the Massachusetts Supreme Judicial Court.[42] But this theory was now only the "first part" of a more general synthesis. To complete the synthesis Holmes added his explanation of cases in which subjective intent was relevant to liability.

In every such case, Holmes insisted, one began with a prima facie demonstration of liability based on the external standard. "I assume that we have got past the question which is answered by the test of the external standard. There is no dispute that the manifest tendency of the defendant's act is to inflict temporal damage upon the plaintiff."[43]

Holmes then turned to the defense of privilege that might be offered in response to this prima facie showing of foreseeable harm. Repeating the analysis given in *The Common Law*, Holmes said that privileges were always based on tacit social policy, a judgment that the harms done by free speaking, for instance, were justified by the benefits.[44] So far, the law was still in the realm of the external standard.

When a privilege was absolute—as for statements from the

---

[39] Id.

[40] Id.

[41] *Privilege, Malice, and Intent*, cited in note 14.

[42] Id at 1–2 and notes p 2.

[43] Id at 2.

[44] Id at 3–5.

bench—the analysis went no farther. One was privileged to do harm, regardless of one's motive.[45]

But in the more usual case of free speaking, the privilege was qualified. "Not only the existence but the extent or degree of privilege will vary with the case."[46] A qualified privilege would be defeated if the defendant were shown to have acted on an expectation or a desire that damage would result. Similarly, a defendant who would not otherwise be liable for harm caused through the intervention of third-party wrongdoers would be denied this defense if she had in fact foreseen or intended the wrongdoing.[47]

The reason for this, Holmes said, was based in social policy. Privileges were granted for policy reasons—most generally, as part of the policy in favor of letting people do as they wished. A malicious motive, by increasing the probability that harm would result from otherwise privileged behavior, would tip the balance of advantage the other way.[48]

> There is no general policy in favor of allowing a man to do harm to his neighbor for the sole pleasure of doing harm. . . . If the privilege [extended to some useful behavior] is qualified, the policy in favor of the defendant's freedom generally will be found to be qualified only to the extent of forbidding him to use for the sake of harm what is allowed for the sake of good.

Holmes continued to insist that all liability at common law was based on "foreseeability" of harms that the dominant forces in society wished to prevent. This was still an old-fashioned sort of foreseeability; it was not a matter of mathematical probabilities, but rather a projection into the future of the lines of lawful conduct and the expected course of natural events—"a manifest tendency to inflict temporal damage."[49] Holmes also continued to insist that certain behavior, like free speaking, was privileged as a matter of

---

[45] Id at 3–4.

[46] Id at 4.

[47] Note that we have already gotten past the prima facie case, which in libel included an assertion that the publication was both false and damaging (truth was an affirmative defense). Holmes seems to have assumed that under these circumstances actual knowledge of falsity, or reckless disregard for the truth, were identical to an intention to cause harm. In this form, Holmes's formulation is equivalent to the constitutional standard for libel stated in *New York Times v Sullivan*, 376 US 254 (1964); see Section XVII.

[48] *Privilege, Malice, and Intent*, cited in note 14, at 5–7.

[49] Id at 3.

social policy, despite its manifest tendency to do harm in particular cases, because overall the behavior complained of created benefits that outweighed the harm.

The new element in his theory was simply the recognition that actual intent to cause harm or induce unlawful conduct would defeat a claim of privilege. This new element, Holmes claimed, also was a matter of social policy, to discourage otherwise privileged speech that posed too great a risk of harm.

The doctrine of "clear and present danger" had been born.[50] Another twenty-five years would elapse before Holmes would apply the doctrine in First Amendment cases. In the intervening years, he tested it in his judicial laboratory.

IV. LABOR UNIONS

In the early 1890s, the United States seemed to many to be sliding into class warfare. In 1892, New Orleans had suffered a general strike; in Buffalo, railroads were halted by a switchmen's strike; in Idaho, a copper miners' strike turned violent, and there were shootings and deaths. In the coal fields of east Tennessee, miners went on strike, and in the Monongahela River Valley of western Pennsylvania the Carnegie Steel Company went to war against its union, hiring a private army of Pinkerton guards who fought pitched battles with striking steel workers. More violence was promised to come. In the summer of 1893, the inflated market for railroad bonds collapsed, there was a panic, and the United States plunged into a depression. Labor struggles, already bitter, became desperate.[51]

---

[50] When a lifetime later he was asked about its origin Holmes said, vaguely, his work on the "common law," but his handwriting makes it difficult to say whether he was referring to the book or its subject, and by then he thought of *Privilege, Malice, and Intent* as an extension of the earlier book in any case. Holmes to Z. Chafee, June 12, 1922, Zechariah Chafee, Jr., Papers, Harvard Law School, B14, F12. As he also refers in this letter to his later attempt and conspiracy opinions, he must be taken to have referred to the later, refined statement. Failure to distinguish between the external standard as stated in *The Common Law*, and the later formulation in *Privilege, Malice, and Intent*, has bedeviled revisionist commentators, who take this letter to mean—against all other evidence—that Holmes was mechanically applying an external standard in the early First Amendment cases. See Ragan, *Justice Oliver Wendell Holmes, Jr., Zechariah Chafee, Jr., and the Clear and Present Danger Test for Free Speech: The First Year, 1919*, 58 J Am Hist at 26–27; Rabban, *The Emergence of Modern First Amendment Doctrine*, 50 U Chi L Rev at 1265; Section XIII.

[51] See Novick, *Honorable Justice*, cited in note 10, at 192–206.

The courts were drawn into the conflicts, as factory owners sought injunctions against strikes and boycotts. Striking unions were being treated as criminal conspiracies in England,[52] and in some American courts.[53] The trade union cases that Holmes expected to come before his court would raise the most solemn questions he had encountered since his service in the Civil War.

Holmes prepared himself for such cases carefully. He began a systematic course of reading, beginning with Hobbes's *Leviathan* and continuing with Hegel, Karl Marx, Herbert Spencer, and William Morris on socialism.[54] He did not read Malthus or Darwin, but he had absorbed Malthusian and evolutionary thinking from the atmosphere of his earliest years, and he emerged from these studies a confirmed Malthusian evolutionist. Population, unless controlled, would always press against the limits of the environment; in the struggle for scarce resources the weakest would perish. Human society, like other species, would evolve by natural selection through survival of the fittest.[55]

As part of his program of studies, Holmes quietly called upon a labor leader—apparently Frank Foster, president of the Boston Typographer's Union.[56] Foster, it appeared, shared Holmes's evolutionist philosophy: he hoped for the victory of labor in the struggle for existence, and he argued simply for fair terms in the fight.[57]

Holmes, despite unswerving loyalty to his own class, heard Foster's plea with sympathy. The code of honor that Holmes had absorbed from earliest childhood, the code of a gentleman, required fairness. Chivalry and science, the two great themes of his time, fused in the idea of evolution through fair competition in the market. His own studies had persuaded him that law had evolved into a system of fair, peaceful combat.[58]

Holmes had long argued that privileges to do harm were based

---

[52] *Temperton v Russell* I QB 715 (1893).

[53] See, e.g., *Carew v Rutherford*, 106 Mass 1 (1870).

[54] See *Honorable Justice*, cited in note 10, at 201–2.

[55] Id at 202. I have tried to avoid the term "Social Darwinism," which is vague and pejorative, and was not used by Holmes's contemporaries. The views Holmes held were widely shared among classical economists, and really had very little to do with Charles Darwin.

[56] Id at 198–99.

[57] See The Labor Leader, March 10, 1882, p 2; *Honorable Justice*, cited in note 10, at 199.

[58] *Honorable Justice*, id at 204.

on social policy. The question in labor cases therefore was whether such privileges should be extended to labor unions. The social policy in question was not whether labor unions were desirable— Holmes thought they were socialist humbug[59]—but whether the struggle for life should be carried on peacefully and fairly. This more fundamental principle, he thought, required that labor unions be accorded the same privilege as capital, to organize and to inflict economic injuries on their opponents.[60] But the trade unions' privilege did not go so far as to allow them to do damage simply for the sake of harm; the privilege would be defeated by a showing of malice.[61]

The opportunity to test these ideas came shortly after publication of "Privilege, Malice, and Intent." Sitting as a judge in the equity court in Boston, Holmes heard a petition from a factory owner for an order halting picketing and a boycott by striking factory workers. Holmes declined to enjoin peaceful picketing or a boycott that relied solely on acts of persuasion, on the ground that these were privileged; but he did grant an injunction against acts of violence. His decision, in *Vegelahn v Guntner*, was reversed by the full Supreme Judicial Court, however, and he entered a solitary dissent:[62]

> I have seen the suggestion made that the conflict between employers and employed is not competition. But I venture to assume that none of my brethren would rely on that suggestion. If the policy on which our law is founded is too narrowly expressed in the term free competition, we may substitute free struggle for life. . . .
>
> One of the eternal conflicts out of which life is made up is that between the effort of every man to get the most he can for his services, and that of society, disguised under the name of capital, to get his services for the least possible return. Combination on the one side is patent and powerful. Combination on the other is the necessary and desirable counterpart, if the battle is to be carried on in a fair and equal way.

---

[59] See *Plant v Woods*, 176 Mass 492, 504 (1900) (Holmes dissenting).

[60] *Privilege, Malice, and Intent*, cited in note 14, at 7–9.

[61] Id at 9–10.

[62] *Vegelahn v Guntner*, 167 Mass 92, 107–8 (1896) (Holmes dissenting). See also *Plant v Woods*, 176 Mass at 504 (1900) (Holmes dissenting).

This was Holmes's first application of the theory of "Privilege, Malice, and Intent"; it had taken him another step toward the First Amendment.

V. Conspiracies and Attempts

Holmes continued to serve on the Massachusetts Supreme Judicial Court for six more years in which he continued to address common-law questions, working his ideas out in practice. He applied the ideas of "Privilege, Malice, and Intent" to cases of criminal attempts and conspiracies, where the defendant's state of mind again was relevant; and now he had the pleasure of seeing the majority of his court explicitly adopt his reasoning.

In criminal attempts, the problem for the court was similar to that in cases of privilege: the defendant's acts were not in themselves punishable, but they increased the risk of harm in particular circumstances. A year after his dissent in *Vegeblan*, Holmes spoke for the court in a spectacular case of attempted murder, *Commonwealth v Kennedy*.[63] William Kennedy had taken an interest in the wife of his employer, Alfred T. Learoyd. When Learoyd fired him, Kennedy surreptitiously pasted rat poison under the bar of Learoyd's mustache cup.[64] Kennedy had argued among other things that putting poison under the mustache bar, even if proven, was too uncertain a method to constitute an attempt at murder. Holmes seized the opportunity to deliver a little essay, with copious citations to English and American cases, on the law of attempts, extending the argument of "Privilege, Malice, and Intent" to this new class of cases.[65] "As the aim of the law is not to punish sins, but is to prevent certain external results, the act done must come pretty near to accomplishing that result before the law will notice it. . . . Every question of proximity must be determined

---

[63] 170 Mass 18 (1897). It may be necessary to explain, nowadays, that a "mustache cup" was a teacup with a bar across the top to keep one's mustache dry.

[64] *Commonwealth v Kennedy*, 170 Mass at 19.

[65] In *The Common Law*, cited in note 14, at 66–68, Holmes said that actual intent had to be proven only in cases where further acts of the defendant were necessary to complete the crime. The discussion in Kennedy used some of the language and examples from *The Common Law*, but the analysis was the more refined one of *Privilege, Malice, and Intent*, in which actual intent was to be proven in any case where the overt behavior was privileged or where the eventual harm depended on wrongdoing of the defendant or others.

by its own circumstances. . . ."[66] In determining the degree of "proximity" to the completed crime, Holmes said, the court was to consider both an external standard and the defendant's subjective expectation or intent.[67] In this case, Kennedy expected and intended that Learoyd would drink poisoned tea from the cup and die, the expectation was reasonable in the circumstances, and so Kennedy was properly convicted of attempted murder.[68]

A third category of cases had been added to the list of those in which subjective intent was relevant to liability. In attempted crimes, as in the privilege and intervening-wrongdoer cases, behavior that was not in itself a crime, although dangerous in the circumstances, could not be punished unless a subjective intent to cause the harm could be proven.

In criminal attempt cases, unlike the earlier tort cases, no harm had actually occurred, and proximity of harm was a more difficult question. In attempt cases, the defendant's actual intent to do harm could be used to show that harm was actually more likely to occur than may have appeared by the external standard alone. In the *Kennedy* opinion Holmes delivered an interesting dictum, which like other elements of his analysis would reappear later in First Amendment cases. Where there was an apprehension of truly grave crimes, Holmes said, liability might "begin at a point more remote from the possibility of accomplishing what is expected than might be the case with lighter crimes."[69] This germ of the modern analysis of risk, with separate components of probability and magnitude of harm, eventually was imported into the clear-and-present-danger standard.[70]

Holmes further extended and clarified the Privilege, Malice, and Intent analysis in a well-known case of attempted arson, *Commonwealth v Peaslee*.[71] He repeated his foreseeability analysis in more detail: To prove an attempted crime one first extended into the

---

[66] *Kennedy*, 170 Mass at 20–22.

[67] Id at 21.

[68] Id at 21, 24–25.

[69] Id at 22. Compare *Whitney v California*, 274 US 357, 379 (1927) (Brandeis and Holmes concurring); see Section XV. Although similar language is used in *The Common Law*, cited in note 14, at 68–69, I do not think Holmes in 1881 had yet arrived at just this point.

[70] See notes 302–3 and accompanying text.

[71] *Commonwealth v Peaslee*, 177 Mass 267 (1901).

future lines of proper behavior and the course of natural events. Behavior that in and of itself foreseeably would lead to crime was not privileged, and no further showing was required. But attempts which fell short might still approach dangerously close to forbidden consequences.[72]

> The question on the evidence, more precisely stated, is whether the defendant's acts come near enough to the accomplishment of the substantive offence to be punishable. The statute does not punish every act done toward the commission of a crime, but only such acts done in an attempt to commit it. The most common types of an attempt are either an act which is intended to bring about the substantive crime and which sets in motion natural forces that would bring it about in the expected course of events but for an unforeseen interruption . . . or an act which is intended [by an external standard] to bring about the substantive crime and would bring it about but for a mistake of judgment in a matter of nice estimate or experiment, as when a pistol is fired at a man but misses him, or when one tries to pick a pocket which turns out to be empty. In either case the would-be criminal has done his last act.

Such behavior—like falsely shouting "fire!" in a theater[73]—is plainly punishable in and of itself. But the case is more difficult when future wrongdoing by the defendant or others is required to complete the crime. In such circumstances, the first preparations are privileged unless the further wrongdoing is actually intended; then the combination of hazardous acts and specific intent brings the completed crime dangerously near.[74]

> If the preparation comes very near to the accomplishment of the act, the intent to complete it renders the crime so probable that the act will be a misdemeanor although there is still a locus penitentioe in the need of a further exertion of the will to complete the crime. As was observed in a recent case, the degree of proximity held sufficient may vary with circumstances, including among other things the apprehension which the particular crime is calculated to excite. [Citing *Kennedy v Commonwealth*, supra.]

It is interesting to note that Holmes here again foreshadows, not just the clear-and-present-danger doctrine of *Schenck v United States*,

---

[72] Id at 271.

[73] *Schenck v United States*, 249 US 47 (1919).

[74] *Peaslee*, 177 Mass at 273–74 (citations omitted, including citation to *Kennedy*, 170 Mass 18, see notes 65–69 and accompanying text).

which was held to be a matter of proximity and "degree,"[75] but also the more refined analysis of risk which eventually was incorporated into the clear-and-present-danger standard.[76]

But these developments lay in the future. In *Peaslee*, the defendant had collected the materials for a fire and prepared a candle, but had left without lighting it.[77] This was not enough to support a conviction. Wrongful acts by the defendant or others would have been required to complete the crime, and in such circumstances a wrongful intent to bring about those acts would also have to be shown.[78] For instance, the defendant had solicited one of his employees to put a candle among flammable debris and light it. This was enough to show his actual intent, and if the solicitation had been properly charged in the indictment, the defendant's conviction would have been upheld.[79]

Conspiracy cases offered a modest extension of the same line of thought. Where the conspiracy had not carried out a completed crime, the prosecutor was required to prove an overt act in furtherance of the conspiracy and the defendants' actual intent to carry it through. The overt act need not be in itself criminal, and might be harmless or even privileged behavior. Acts wrongful because of their immediate consequences then would be required to complete the crime for which the conspiracy prepared. The defendant's actual expectation of such unlawful conduct made harm more likely, and therefore would defeat any privilege that otherwise might be accorded.[80]

The Massachusetts Supreme Judicial Court expressly adopted Holmes's reasoning as to conspiracies in 1902, citing "Privilege, Malice, and Intent";[81] and Holmes had the further triumph of seeing his theory of conspiracies in opinions concerning labor unions cited as precedent in the English Court of Appeal.[82]

In 1905, soon after his appointment to the Supreme Court, Holmes wrote the opinion for the Court in *Swift and Co. v United*

---

[75] 249 US at 52. See Chafee, *Freedom of Speech in Wartime*, 32 Harv L Rev 932, 963 (1919).

[76] See Section XVI.

[77] *Peaslee*, 177 Mass at 269.

[78] Id at 273.

[79] Id at 274.

[80] *Privilege, Malice, and Intent*, cited in note 14, at 9.

[81] *Plant*, 176 Mass 492.

[82] *Alan v Flood* (1898) AC 1.

States,[83] upholding an injunction issued against a conspiracy of meat-packers in violation of the Sherman Act. Repeatedly citing his own opinion in *Commonwealth v Peaslee*, Holmes wrote into the federal law of criminal conspiracies and attempts the argument of "Privilege, Malice, and Intent"; where individual acts charged were each lawful, an actual intent to accomplish a crime must be proved.[84]

By the time of his First Amendment opinions, therefore, Holmes had seen the doctrines of "Privilege, Malice, and Intent" tested in practice, thoroughly assimilated into his general theory of the common law, and made a part of the common law of England and the United States. It was Holmes's conviction that in all cases of otherwise privileged behavior, it was a fundamental principle that two things must be proved before liability could be imposed: the foreseeability of harm by an objective standard, and the subjective intent to bring it about.

Eventually, he would find this fundamental principle in the Constitution as well, the principle of proximity of harm that would eventually come to be called the doctrine of the clear and present danger. To a modern eye, accustomed to the legislative-style holdings that the Supreme Court now renders, it is a frustrating principle. It seems to call out for completion, for some quantitative, legislative statement: How close must the harm be to justify suppression of privileged behavior? But Holmes insisted that the line of forbidden proximity be marked out, case by case, rather than drawn in advance.

VI. CONSTRUING THE CONSTITUTION

In his first years of service on the Massachusetts Court, there were comparatively few opportunities to address constitutional questions, and at least until he became Chief Justice, Holmes did not seek the opportunities available. He had little interest in constitutional law as such. One of his brother justices lampooned Holmes's preoccupation with the common law:[85]

---

[83] 196 US 375 (1905).

[84] *Swift and Co. v United States*, 196 US 375, 396 (1905).

[85] This was written by Justice James M. Barker—perhaps scribbled during a conference—and found in his locker when he died. The clerk of the court passed it on to Holmes, and it is now among his papers. Holmes Papers, cited in note 10, at B45 F21.

> When around this table we do sit
> And constitutions are discussed
> And 'tis inquired of what the Fathers writ
> Holmes says, says he, that he'll be cussed
> If for all that he cares a single bit—
>
> But when the topic's trover
> Or replevin as 'tis called
> Then like a bee among the clover
> From ancient flower to flower he flits
> That bloom upon the Year Book's pages
> And swears that here's the wisdom of the ages.

Holmes addressed constitutional questions only when he thought duty required him to do so. In Massachusetts practice, for instance, the legislature requested advisory opinions from the justices of the Supreme Judicial Court on the constitutionality of statutes, and Holmes thought it his duty to give his own opinion.[86] And beginning in 1899, during the incapacity of Chief Justice Waldbridge Field, followed by Holmes's succession to his place, Holmes began his long career as spokesman for his courts on constitutional questions. As Chief Justice of Massachusetts, Holmes found it necessary, simply to clear the docket, to use his talents as an opinion writer in constitutional cases.

In most of those few instances before 1899 in which he was obliged to give an opinion on questions of constitutional law, and many of those afterward, Holmes announced his consistent principle of deference to the legislature.

Holmes's doctrine was that, if the constitutionality of a statute were challenged, the court should uphold it unless reasonable people could not disagree that it violated the constitution.[87] Although he acknowledged the importance of the separation of powers, and the deference due to an equal branch of government, Holmes's reason for deferring to the legislature in this way was more fundamental. As he said in a letter to a friend,[88]

---

[86] See, e.g., Opinions of the Justices, 160 Mass 586, 593 (1894): "If the questions proposed to the justices came before us as a court and I found myself unable to agree with my brethren, I should defer to their opinion without any intimation of dissent. But the understanding always has been that questions like the present are addressed to us as individuals and require an individual answer."

[87] See, e.g., *Coppage v Kansas*, 236 US 1, 28 (1915) (Holmes dissenting); *Adair v US*, 208 US 161, 190 (1908) (Holmes dissenting); *Lochner v New York*, 198 US 45, 74 (1905) (Holmes dissenting); *Perry*, 155 Mass at 123 (Holmes dissenting).

[88] Holmes to James B. Thayer, November 2, 1893, Holmes Papers, cited in note 10. See Opinions of the Justices, 160 Mass 586, 593 (1894) (legislature may create referendum

[A] state legislature has the power of Parliament, i.e. absolute power, except insofar as expressly or by implication it is prohibited by the constitution—that the question always is where do you find the prohibition—not, where do you find the power—I think the contrary view [held by some of his fellow judges] dangerous and wrong.

This was the reasoning of Thomas Cooley's influential book, *Constitutional Limitations*, which Holmes had read, admiringly reviewed, and apparently used as a source for his lectures when teaching an undergraduate course in constitutional law at Harvard College; but it was a line of argument that in any case was consistent with Holmes's common-law jurisprudence.

After his appointment to the Supreme Court, Holmes was rigorously consistent in deferring to the legislatures, especially when substantive rights were concerned. Indeed, a large part of his output for the first twenty years of his tenure on the Supreme Court was as its spokesman in constitutional cases, for the most part upholding challenged government action.

Before 1918, he was rarely obliged to consider constitutional guarantees of free speech. In two Massachusetts cases in which a constitutional right of free speech was claimed, Holmes found that the constitution did not apply and so he had no need to discuss the substance of its provisions. The City of Boston could exclude the public entirely from Boston Common, Holmes held for the Supreme Judicial Court, and therefore the city might exclude preachers from the Common without infringing any right.[89] And the Town of New Bedford could dismiss a policeman for electioneering, Holmes famously decided: "The petitioner may have a constitutional right to talk politics, but he has no constitutional right to be a policeman."[90]

---

process); Opinions of the Justices, 155 Mass 598 (1892) (state may authorize municipal coal yards); *Perry*, 155 Mass at 123 (Holmes dissenting) (state may regulate employers' practice of withholding charges from wages); cf. *Commonwealth v Davis*, 162 Mass 510 (1895) (state has absolute control over its property). Thayer's reasons for deference—separation of powers, and comity—although politely acknowledged in this letter, actually seemed to carry little weight with Holmes. See, e.g., *In re Janvrin*, 174 Mass 514 (1899) (Holmes), upholding in an unusually tortured opinion a statute delegating to a panel of the Supreme Judicial Court the duty to set water rates by legislative-style rules; *Frank v Mangum*, 237 US 309 (1915) (Holmes dissenting) (comity plays no role in habeas corpus challenge to fairness of state trial).

[89] *Davis*, 162 Mass 510.

[90] *McAuliffe v Mayor of New Bedford*, 155 Mass 216 (1892).

Even after Holmes's appointment to the Supreme Court of the United States in 1902, he rarely encountered First Amendment claims—and came up against no claims on behalf of political speech—until *Schenck* was decided seventeen years later. There were as yet few federal regulatory statutes. The great constitutional questions of those years arose under the Fourteenth Amendment, and to the extent Holmes concerned himself with the constitutional limits on free speech it was in that setting.

It is worth noting, before discussing such cases, that in the early years of the twentieth century the Court had little control over its docket, and the bar had generally come to take for granted a last appeal to the Supreme Court in large numbers of cases that the Court would now decline to hear.[91] Furthermore, the justices had no clerks or chambers. The Court met in the old Senate chamber in the capitol, the justices worked at home, and each had only a stenographer and a messenger to help him. Holmes hired a law clerk (then called a "secretary") in place of the stenographer, and wrote out his opinions by hand, but the clerk's principal duties were to summarize petitions for certiorari, to balance Holmes's checkbook, and to keep Mrs. Holmes company.[92] Like the other justices, Holmes rarely asked a clerk to do research. The justices relied heavily on oral arguments and briefs, and their opinions were rarely burdened with a large apparatus of citations.

This mode of work affected their handling of constitutional cases. Each term they received dozens of writs of error and appeals asserting claims under the Fourteenth Amendment. Most of these were frivolous or dilatory, but the Court heard oral argument in nearly every case and then decided each with a written opinion.[93] The inevitable result was that some of the opinions were ill-considered, even off-hand, to modern eyes. Holmes became the most frequent spokesman of the Court in Constitutional cases for almost twenty years partly because of his skill in turning off such cases quickly and persuasively. His usual method was to reserve constitutional principles for truly fundamental questions; he and

---

[91] See Felix Frankfurter and James Landis, *The Business of the Supreme Court: A Study in the Federal Judicial System* (Macmillan, 1927).

[92] See *Honorable Justice*, cited in note 10, at 245–46, 288–89.

[93] Id at 249; Alexander Bickel and Benno Schmidt, *The Judiciary and Responsible Government, 1910–1921*, at 201, 305–11 (Macmillan, 1984).

the Court would refuse to extend Constitutional rights to their logical extremes in minor questions. "Some play must be allowed for the joints of the machine,"[94] Holmes declared, dismissing yet another claim that a penalty violated the Fourteenth Amendment's requirement of due process and equal protection of the laws.

Holmes's early encounters with the First Amendment were plainly affected by this casual method of disposition. In *Patterson v Colorado*,[95] a newspaper editor had been convicted of criminal contempt for ridiculing the state's supreme court. The First Amendment did not apply, but the defendant had argued that the Fourteenth Amendment's guarantee of due process of law forbade prosecutions for truthful publications. Holmes, writing for the Court, and unfamiliar with constitutional jurisprudence, rather awkwardly avoided the Fourteenth Amendment question by saying off-handedly that the First Amendment only prohibited prior restraints, and the Fourteenth Amendment would not require more.[96] In a similar case, the Court upheld without much deliberation the conviction under a state statute of the author of a newspaper article advocating public nudity, in violation of a state statute prohibiting incitement to crime, where the state court seemed to limit prosecutions to situations in which actual violations of the law were likely.[97] In another case, he decided copyright questions, where the First Amendment had not even been invoked.[98] These cases all seemed to confirm that speech might be regulated in various ways, the First Amendment notwithstanding, but in none were the limits of regulation clearly addressed.[99]

If Holmes at first did not contribute anything to the Court's thinking on freedom of speech, he did become the architect of substantive due process, which in turn became the route by which his theory of the common law entered constitutional jurisprudence.

---

[94] *Missouri, Kansas and Texas R Co v May*, 194 US 267 (1904).

[95] 205 US 454 (1907). In a similar case as late as 1918, Holmes did not mention the First Amendment (but did say he would have reversed on common-law criminal contempt principles). *Toledo Newspaper Co v United States*, 247 US 402, 422 (1918) (Holmes dissenting).

[96] *Patterson*, 205 US at 462.

[97] *Fox v Washington*, 236 US 273, 277 (1915).

[98] *Bleistein v Donaldson Lithographing Co.*, 188 US 239 (1903).

[99] See David Currie, *The Constitution in the Supreme Court: The Second Century, 1888–1986*, at 115–17 (U Chicago, 1990).

VII. Substantive Due Process and the Bill of Rights

The Court in those years looked for the content of constitutional provisions in principles thought to underlie the common law. In 1884, in *Hurtado v California*,[100] one of its first important interpretations of the Fourteenth Amendment's requirement of due process of law, the Court set the foundation of this approach. The Court upheld a conviction for murder under a state statute that allowed trial on information rather than indictment (as the common law would have required). The due process clauses of the Fifth and Fourteenth Amendments, the Court held, did set substantive limits on legislation, but these were broad and were intended only to secure the individual from the arbitrary exercise of government power. Their content was defined by principles of natural justice, as expressed in the common law.[101]

> It is more consonant to the true philosophy of our historical legal institutions to say that the spirit of personal liberty and individual right, which they embodied, was preserved and developed by a progressive growth and wise adaptation to new circumstances and situations of the forms and processes found fit to give, from time to time, new expression and greater effect to modern ideas of self-government. This flexibility and capacity for growth and adaptation is the peculiar boast and excellence of the common law.

This view of what we now call substantive due process was widely accepted.[102] Even Ernst Freund, a severe contemporary critic of the state courts' tendency to identify liberty with property rights, accepted the view that the Due Process Clause set substantive limits on legislation.[103]

---

[100] 110 US 516 (1884).

[101] Id at 530. See Albert Alschuler, *Preventive Pretrial Detention and the Failure of Interest-Balancing Approaches to Due Process*, 85 Mich L Rev 510, 520–25 (1986). In an interesting opinion for the Massachusetts Supreme Judicial Court, *Tyler v Judges of the Court of Registration*, 175 Mass 71 (1900) (Holmes, CJ), upholding a land title registration statute, Holmes cited *Hurtado* for the proposition that due process of law was a balance of government convenience against the "substantial justice" to which holders of titles that might be cut off were entitled, 175 Mass at 74. He immediately went on to say that he himself differed from the majority of his court and would have rested the decision solely on the common law, which allowed actions in rem without actual notice to affected individuals. Id at 75.

[102] See, e.g., Hough, *Due Process of Law Today*, 32 Harv L Rev 218 (1919).

[103] See Ernst Freund, *Standards of American Legislation: An Estimate of Restrictive and Constructive Factors* 207 (U Chicago, 1917).

Beginning with his first opinion for the Court, Holmes solidified and made more rigorous the Court's reliance on fundamental principles of justice, identifying them solely with the common law. Cutting away the language of natural rights, Holmes sought these principles within the law itself. In *Otis v Parker*, written less than a month after his appointment, Holmes announced the method he would employ for thirty years thereafter: The broad guarantees of the Fourteenth Amendment did have substantive as well as procedural content, Holmes wrote, but they contained only "relatively fundamental principles of right" that could be discovered in the common law.[104]

Soon afterward, Holmes wrote the opinion for the majority in *Aikens v Wisconsin*.[105] A group of newspaper publishers had been convicted under a Wisconsin malicious-mischief statute, for conspiring to injure a competitor. The defendants challenged the statute under the Fourteenth Amendment, but Holmes declared that due process did not require more than the common law afforded, and at common law, the privilege to do competitive harm was defeated by a showing of actual malice.[106] The Wisconsin statute therefore could punish such malice without contravening the Constitution.[107]

In *Gompers v United States*[108] Holmes gave a famous statement of his method of construing the Constitution:[109]

> [T]he provisions of the Constitution are not mathematical formulas having their essence in form; they are organic living institutions transplanted from English soil. Their significance is vital not formal; it is to be gathered not simply by taking the words and a dictionary, but by considering their origin and the line of their growth.

In these phrases Holmes managed to compress his view that constitutional restrictions were limited to the fundamental principles of the common law, and that even these were not to be taken

---

[104] *Otis v Parker*, 187 US 606 (1903).

[105] 195 US 194 (1904).

[106] Id at 206.

[107] Id.

[108] 233 US 604 (1914).

[109] Id at 610.

to logical extremes, with his view that common-law principles themselves were evolving. It was a paraphrase of the famous opening sentence of *The Common Law:* "The life of the law has not been logic, it has been experience." But fundamental principles were few, and in dozens of opinions for the Court, Holmes recited the homily of substantive due process, while upholding most state statutes against constitutional challenge.

In a parallel line of cases, the Court had held the Bill of Rights generally to be merely declaratory of the common law. This again was a view taken by Thomas Cooley in *Constitutional Limitations*, cited approvingly by the Supreme Court in *Hurtado*.[110] Cooley argued that the First Amendment, for instance, although it abolished the English law of seditious libel, otherwise protected only existing rights at common law:[111]

> [W]e understand liberty of speech and of the press to imply not only liberty to publish [free of prior restraints], but complete immunity for the publication, so long as it is not harmful in its character, when tested by such standards as the law affords. For these standards we must look to the common-law rules which were in force when the constitutional guarantees were established.

This approach was adopted by the Supreme Court in *Robertson v Baldwin*,[112] holding that the Bill of Rights was subject to traditional common-law limitations:[113]

> The law is perfectly well settled that the . . . Bill of Rights [was] not intended to lay down any novel principles of government, but simply to embody certain guaranties and immunities which we had inherited from our English ancestors, and which had from time immemorial been subject to certain well-recognized exceptions arising from the necessities of the case.

This is an attitude more familiar now in English constitutional law than American:[114]

---

[110] *Hurtado*, 110 US at 525.

[111] Thomas Cooley, *Constitutional Limitations* 422 (Little, Brown, 1868).

[112] 165 US 275 (1897).

[113] Id at 281; cited as authority for limitations on the First Amendment in *Frohwerk v United States*, 249 US 204, 206 (1919) (Holmes, J).

[114] Casey, *Mankind in Conversation: The Philosophy of Michael Oakeshott and Its Misunderstandings*, The Times Literary Supplement, March 29, 1991, p 3, col 1.

> When English statesmen have talked . . . of freedom, they
> have not been invoking a purely abstract idea, but have been
> appealing to specific traditions, which are enshrined in English
> history and in the Common Law tradition. Even the American
> Founding Fathers, in formulating their Bill of Rights, were
> unconsciously guided by what was intimated by the habits of
> behavior they had inherited from the English political tradition.

When Holmes served on the Court, it was close enough to this
tradition that it usually understood the broad guarantees of liberty
in the constitution to mean fundamental principles found in the
common law, subject to traditional limitations.[115]

Holmes followed this approach through his whole career as a
judge. In his Massachusetts opinions on constitutional law, he regularly referred to the common law for a standard; on the federal
bench, his landmark opinions on the First Amendment were based
on his common-law jurisprudence.

VIII. Holmes's Unpublished Dissent

In 1914, the United States, still being settled by immigrants, mirrored many of the conflicts which broke into war in
Europe. In a still predominantly British population, immigration
from Germany, Italy, and the Austro-Hungarian Empire was then
running at more than one million per year. From 1900 to 1914,
when war cut off the flow, about two million new immigrants also
came to the United States from Eastern Europe, most of them
Russian and Polish Jews fleeing persecution.[116]

At the outbreak of the Great War, the United States therefore
was divided on lines of class and national origin that to some extent
coincided with the battle lines in Europe. The American middle
and upper class, the Republican Party, government, and business
leaders tended to favor the British and French in the European
war; the working class, the Democratic Party, trade unions, and
left-wing political movements were less sympathetic to the Allied

---

[115] This is the meaning of Holmes's puzzling remark, that there may be "exceptions" to
the sweeping command of the First Amendment, *Abrams v United States*, 250 US 616, 631
(1919); see Currie, *The Constitution in the Supreme Court, The Second Century* at 123 n 206
(cited in note 99).

[116] See, Bureau of the Census, *Historical Statistics of the United States, 1789–1945*, at 16–38
(1949).

cause and favored neutrality or outright support of Germany. When the United States government began to mobilize for eventual entry into the war on the British side there was widespread opposition. Conflicts over "preparedness" broke out. Eugene Debs, Socialist Party candidate for President, opposed entry into the war; unions conducted a nationwide strike of the railroads, and even a general strike was threatened. Labor leaders were prosecuted for bombings.[117] To Holmes and others of his class it seemed that the chronic conflict between nationalities and classes had entered a new and more violent stage: "I don't know but that it is getting time to find out what is/who are the governing power in this country."[118]

Early in 1917, Germany began unrestricted submarine warfare against American shipping. On April 17, the United States declared war. The federal government moved swiftly to conscript an army, to mobilize industry and shipping, and to suppress dissent. The Justice Department and local police agencies cooperated to enforce the new draft law. Eventually, they conducted "sweeps" of major cities, arresting tens of thousands of draft-age men. The Postmaster General revoked second-class mailing privileges of newspapers and magazines opposed to the war, effectively shutting them down.[119]

To assist the Justice Department in enforcing the new draft law, in June, 1917, Congress passed the Espionage Act of 1917 making it a crime, among other things, to attempt by speech or otherwise to obstruct recruitment.[120] The Justice Department and local police forces then brought hundreds of successful prosecutions against opponents of the draft.[121]

Suppression of dissent took on a more marked political tinge within months: in October, 1917, the Russian government was overthrown by Bolsheviks, then little known in the United States, who promptly after seizing power withdrew Russia from the war. German armies, immobilized until then on the eastern front,

---

[117] See, e.g., *Honorable Justice*, cited in note 10, at 321–22.

[118] Letter, Holmes to Felix Frankfurter, March 27, 1917, Holmes Papers, cited in note 10; quoted *Honorable Justice* cited in note 10, at 322.

[119] See *Milwaukee Social Democratic Pub. Co. v Burleson*, 255 US 407 (1921).

[120] The Espionage Act of June 15, 1917, c. 30 Title I, Sec 3.

[121] For a discussion of these cases, see Z. Chafee, *Freedom of Speech* 56 (Harcourt, Brace & Howe, 1920).

wheeled about and flung themselves against the western trenches. The long stalemate of the war was broken and the German army began to advance toward Paris.

In the United States, there was widespread fear that American troops would not reach the battlefields quickly enough to help stem the German offensive. Mobilization efforts were redoubled, and the repression of dissent took on an even more decidedly political tone. There was a general feeling that the Bolsheviks were simply German agents, and their foreign-born supporters in the United States were treated as disloyal. In response to public sentiment, the Wilson Administration sent some troops into Russia. The purpose of this effort was never very clearly stated but it was widely believed to be an effort to reverse the Russian Revolution.

On the home front, the American political left, which generally sympathized with the new Soviet government, was now openly viewed as disloyal. The Administration asked for and got new amendments to the Espionage Act, sometimes called the Sedition Act of 1918, prohibiting among other things criticism of the American form of government.[122] The Justice Department brought hundreds of new prosecutions for such crimes as having written to a newspaper saying, "I am for the people and the government is for the profiteers."[123] Federal district courts handed out sentences of up to twenty years in these cases. "Some of the lower judges got rather hysterical," Holmes complained privately.[124]

American troops did arrive in Europe in time to help stem the German offensive, and the Great War ended abruptly in the fall. But the campaign against foreign subversion continued after the war was over. The Justice Department used the machinery set up during the war to arrest and deport immigrants with radical views. Young friends of Holmes's—immigrants Harold Laski and Felix Frankfurter, who were teaching at Harvard—became targets of the hysteria, and efforts were made to have them removed from the Harvard faculty. Laski was obliged to resign.[125] All together, two

---

[122] See Richard Polenberg, *Fighting Faiths: The Abrams Case, the Supreme Court, and Free Speech* 31–35 (1980).

[123] Chafee, *Freedom of Speech* 52 (cited in note 121).

[124] Holmes to Alice S. Green, March 26, 1919, Holmes Papers, cited in note 10, at B43 F13.

[125] See *Honorable Justice*, cited in note 10, at 329.

thousand convictions were obtained under the Espionage Act during the war, and by the October, 1918 term, appeals from some of these cases were reaching the Supreme Court.

The first case to be argued and voted on by the Court was *Baltzer v United States*, one of a half-dozen cases of obstructing the draft which had been brought to the Court. Because the Government confessed error at the eleventh hour the Court never issued a decision in *Baltzer*, and Holmes's dissenting opinion remained among his papers, unseen by anyone outside the Court for the next seventy years. It is reproduced in the Appendix, below.

Baltzer was argued in late November, 1918, and the other draft obstruction cases were scheduled for argument in January, 1919. In personal letters at this time, Holmes expressed chagrin that the Wilson Administration did not abandon the sedition prosecutions, now that the war was over.[126] But the Court had no choice except to hear the appeals.

In *Baltzer*, a group of German-Americans in South Dakota, members of the Socialist Party, had been convicted of efforts to obstruct the draft by writing to the Governor and other state officials, demanding reforms in the selective service procedure, and demanding that the war debt be repudiated. The authors of the letters threatened to vote the Governor out of office if the demands were not met. These letters, which had not been published, were the principal evidence that the defendants had willfully obstructed the recruiting and enlistment service, and conspired to prevent the Governor from discharging his duties.[127]

The Court apparently voted 7–2 to uphold these convictions. The only votes for reversal seem to have been Holmes's and Brandeis's.[128]

After the Court's conference at which the vote was taken (probably Saturday, November 30), Holmes set to work drafting a dissenting opinion that he sent off to the printer on the following Monday, and as usual he distributed his draft to the other justices, probably on the following Tuesday, December third.

---

[126] See, e.g., Holmes to Alice S. Green, March 26, 1919, Holmes Papers, cited in note 10, at B43 F13.

[127] See Appendix infra.

[128] Returns from other justices that Holmes kept among his papers show only Brandeis would have joined in this dissent, which would have been consistent with the later decisions of the Court in which the votes are known.

The dissent was brief—it filled just two pages in proof:[129]

> It seems to me that this petition to an official by ignorant persons who suppose him to possess power of revision and change that he does not, and demand of him as the price of votes, of course assumed to be sufficient to turn the next election, that he make those changes, was nothing in the world but the foolish exercise of a right. . . .
>
> Real obstructions of the law, giving real aid and comfort to the enemy, I should have been glad to see punished more summarily and more severely than they sometimes were. But I think that our intention to put all our powers in aid of success in war should not hurry us into intolerance of opinions and speech that could not be imagined to do harm, although opposed to our own. It is better for those who have unquestioned and almost unlimited power in their hands to err on the side of freedom. We have enjoyed so much freedom for so long that perhaps we are in danger of forgetting that the bill of rights which cost so much blood to establish still is worth fighting for, and that no tittle of it should be abridged.

This was Holmes at his best, and the draft dissent had an immediate effect. Chief Justice White, plainly very concerned to secure a unanimous Court in the first of these important cases, sent back a brief note: "Please stall."[130] Apparently a strategy of delay had been discussed, perhaps at the conference, for Justice Brandeis also urged delay: "I gladly join you," Brandeis's return reads. "As I said, I think in decency—this case should be held until the many involving the same and similar positions—advanced for January— are heard."[131]

The only other return that remains in Holmes's papers is a brief note from Justice Mahlon Pitney: "I submit with great respect, that this reads as if it proceeded from the heart rather than the head—Pitney. P.S. A good fault perhaps, but still a fault. P."[132]

A delay may have been agreed upon in the Court's conference December 7. In the following week, the Justice Department seems

---

[129] *Baltzer v United States* (Holmes dissenting) (distributed to the Justices December 3, 1918); see Appendix infra.

[130] Note on back sheet of return in Holmes Papers, cited in note 10. The second word is not entirely clear.

[131] Id.

[132] Id.

to have been warned of the damaging dissent Holmes planned to read. In any event, the government filed a motion asking that the Baltzer case be restored to the docket. On Monday morning, December 16, when the Court routinely heard motions, the matter was finished. Holmes made a note with evident satisfaction: "After opinion written by me—but before delivery Govt. asked to restore to docket and on Dec. 16 US confessed error."[133]

The Chief Justice thereupon wrote a brief per curiam opinion: "Judgement reversed, upon confession of error; and cause remanded for further proceedings in accordance with law."[134]

These extraordinary events put Holmes at the center of the Court's deliberations on freedom of speech.

IX. BALTZER AND SCHENCK

Holmes's dissent in *Baltzer* requires hardly a word of explication. The powerful statement of facts leads ineluctably to the conclusion, and the passionate address at the end is all the more forceful for the opinion having been put on such narrow grounds. Holmes relied, not on the freedom of speech, but on the First Amendment's very specific guarantee of "the right of the people . . . to petition the government for a redress of grievances."[135] The great authorities of Holmes's youth, Chancellor James Kent[136] and Judge Thomas Cooley,[137] had each emphasized the great historic importance of the right of petition in English law, and Kent had asserted an absolute privilege for such petitions.[138] Holmes himself evi-

---

[133] Note in Holmes's index of his opinions for the term, Holmes Papers, cited in note 10.

[134] *Baltzer v United States*, 248 US 593 (1918).

[135] The leading commentaries familiar to Holmes and his generation were far more strongly worded when they came to the right of petition than they were concerning the right of free speech more generally. Chancellor Kent, who thought the English doctrine of seditious libel was in effect in the United States, nevertheless asserted an absolute immunity for petitions to the government. 2 James Kent, *Commentaries on American Law* at 16 (Holmes ed., 12th ed, 1873). Thomas Cooley, although more progressive than Kent on free speech, was eloquent only when he addressed the right of petition. Cooley, *Constitutional Limitations* at 349 (cited in note 111).

[136] 2 Kent, *Commentaries on American Law* at 16 (cited in note 135).

[137] *Constitutional Limitations*, cited in note 135, at 349.

[138] Kent, *Commentaries on American Law*, cited in note 135. Holmes's view of the privilege has been adopted. See *Monitor Patriot Co. v Roy*, 401 US 265 (1971) (privilege defeated by actual malice).

dently did not go quite so far, because repeatedly in his draft dissent he emphasized the defendants' state of mind: that they honestly if ignorantly supposed the Governor had power to act on their petition was important, presumably because an improper motive would have defeated the qualified privilege. The case, as stated by Holmes, was otherwise so squarely within the right of petition that no argument seemed needed, and he gave no citation of authority—not even the First Amendment was needed to reject this affront to fundamental principle.

The remaining cases concerning obstruction of the draft were argued in January, 1919. *Schenck* was argued January 9 and 10; in a similar case, *Sugarman v United States*,[139] oral argument was waived and the case submitted for decision on the briefs January 9.[140] The remaining two cases, *Frohwerk* and *Debs*,[141] were argued on January 27 and January 28. The opinions of the Court were not issued until March, however. Holmes, to whom the opinions had been assigned, usually liked to circulate an opinion in two or three days. While these were three opinions close together, the records were not extensive and the delay of several weeks in issuing the opinions is surprising, and suggests that the members of the Court had some difficulty in coming to unanimous agreement.

The January, 1919 cases were apparently considered as a group. Sugarman would be dismissed for want of jurisdiction, and the opinion was assigned to Brandeis, the other justice who had joined Holmes's dissent in *Baltzer*.[142] The justices agreed that the principal opinion on constitutional issues would be given in *Schenck v United States*. The Chief Justice took the critical first step by assigning the opinion to Holmes, thereby ensuring that the restrictive position the majority had been willing to adopt in *Baltzer* would not become law.

---

[139] 249 US 182 (1919).

[140] Id at 182.

[141] *Frohwerk*, 249 US 204 (1919); *Debs v United States*, 249 US 211 (1919).

[142] *Sugarman*, 249 US at 185. Brandeis's brief opinion for a unanimous Court held that no substantial constitutional question was presented by a jury instruction: "A man has a right to honestly discuss a measure or a law, and to honestly criticize it. But no man may advise another to disobey the law, or to obstruct its execution, without making himself liable to be called to account therefor." Id at 185. This was substantially the rule Holmes had derived from the common law. It emphasized the importance of motive or intent as a constitutional standard, but the Court was not required to say whether this element of the instruction was required, only that the instruction as a whole posed no significant question.

Holmes's published opinion for the Court in *Schenck* was as opaque as his dissent in *Baltzer* was cogently lucid. Considering the importance of the subject, both to him and to the Court, this is surprising. But the opinion did seem to have been more clear to its immediate audience, the other members of the Court, than it does now when torn out of context. Holmes destroyed most of the returns he received on his opinions, and among his papers there are only three uninformative concurrences in *Schenck* that praise the opinion's clarity.[143] There may have been an earlier, more contentious, draft, and responses may have been given in conference, or as marginal corrections on a draft that Holmes did not keep, or both. The Court had begun deeply divided and ended unanimous; it seems unlikely this could have been accomplished with so little back-and-forth among the justices. The extreme brevity of Holmes's opinion is suggestive of a process Holmes often went through in securing a majority; when he had difficulty it was often because of objections to his blunt statements of principle, and he would prune the opinion to remove offending material. Each successive draft accordingly was often shorter and more obscure, or indirect, than its predecessor.[144] Whatever the cause, Holmes's final opinion in *Schenck* was terse, and obscure on what later proved to be the point of difference between him and the majority of the Court: whether the constitution required proof of actual intent to cause a criminal result.

X. SCHENCK

Charles T. Schenck was general secretary of the Socialist Party of Philadelphia. Shortly after conscription began in August, 1917, the Party arranged to print and mail 15,000 leaflets asserting

---

[143] In accordance with his usual practice, Holmes kept only the backing page of the returns, with the justice's remarks and concurrence. For *Schenck* the returns are these: Day—"Yea, verily." McKenna—"Suggestion p. 3 [not preserved]. Direct as you usually are and as strong as direct—Concur." White—"Yes.—EDW. *Admirably well put.* I have been quite unfit and am going away for a day or so." There are no returns at all among Holmes's papers in the Frohwerk case. In *Debs*, there are these returns: McReynolds (savage as always)—"I agree & may he enjoy many days." Van Devanter—"Yes I think you have happily disposed of a bunch of unattractive cases." Day—"Right again." Holmes Papers, cited in note 10.

[144] Compare, for instance, the draft and final opinions in *Georgia v Tenn. Copper Co.*, 206 US 230 (1907), in *Holmes's First Draft*, Vt L Rev (forthcoming).

that the Selective Service law was unconstitutional and urging the reader to "wake up" and "assert your rights." The leaflets were to be mailed only to young men who had already been selected for induction by their draft boards. Schenck had personally joined in the decisions to print and mail the leaflets, and to send them only to draftees. Schenck and another alleged officer, Elizabeth Baer, were convicted of violating the Espionage Act and sentenced to six months in jail. The Government had charged Schenck and Baer "in substance . . . with attempting to induce young men subject to the draft law to disobey the requirements of that law."[145] There was no evidence that the attempt had succeeded or that anyone who read the leaflet was moved to resist induction. In an earlier round of appeals, *Goldman v United States* (The Selective Service Cases),[146] the Court had upheld prosecutions under the Selective Service Act for conspiracies and unsuccessful attempts to violate the draft laws. In *Schenck*, in briefs and argument, both sides assumed that the statute required proof of specific intent to obstruct the draft. This was the federal law of conspiracies and attempts, as established by Holmes's opinion in *Swift*[147] and the Court's recent decision in *Goldman*.[148] The government treated the question of specific intent to obstruct the draft as the only seriously disputed question of fact in *Schenck*. The government's case on this point was simple: "The defendants chose as the recipients of the circulars young men who had been accepted by the draft boards and were simply awaiting the orders to report for duty. This in itself is sufficient to support the verdict of the jury that the intent of the defendants was to influence the conduct of persons subject to the draft . . . ."[149] The government argued that this showing of specific intent, in itself, was sufficient to defeat a claim of privilege under the First Amendment.[150] The defendants insisted, however, that the evidence showed the leaflets were no more than an "expres-

---

[145] Government's brief at 12, in 18 *Landmark Briefs and Arguments of the Supreme Court*, 1021, 1037 (Univ Pubns of America, Kurland and Casper eds 1975) (cited below as "*Landmark Briefs*").

[146] *Goldman v United States*, 245 US 474 (1918).

[147] *Swift and Co. v United States*, 196 US 375 (1905); see Section V.

[148] *Goldman*, 245 US 474.

[149] Government's Brief at 12–13, in 18 *Landmark Briefs*, cited in note 145, at 1037–38.

[150] Id.

sion . . . made with sincere purpose to communicate honest opinion or belief" protected by the First Amendment, apparently conceding that the convictions would stand if this seemingly innocent speech "mask[ed] a primary intent to incite to forbidden action. . . ."[151]

Arguing in the alternative, however, the defendants claimed that even if specific intent were proven, the statute itself was unconstitutional to the extent it punished speech. This amounted to a claim for an absolute privilege for speech: "[T]he right of free speech, if it is allowed fully, gives the right to persuade another to violate a law. . . ."[152]

On March 3, 1919, Holmes announced the decision of the Court.[153] The first portion of his opinion was a recital of the charges in the indictment. Holmes quickly disposed of objections taken to evidence at trial and then summarized the admitted evidence that seemed crucial—the text of the leaflet, and the fact that it was to be mailed only to draftees. To Holmes and to the Court, these facts were sufficient to establish the elements of a crime:[154]

> Of course the document would not have been sent unless it had been intended to have some effect, and we do not see what effect it could be expected to have upon persons subject to the draft except to influence them to obstruct the carrying of it out. The defendants do not deny that the jury might find against them on this point.

With the elements of a criminal conspiracy and an attempt to commit a crime—overt acts and specific intent—proven, defendants had only their constitutional claim, the claim of privilege under the First Amendment, remaining.

Holmes began (as he had in *Baltzer*)[155] by correcting his earlier misstatement in *Patterson v Colorado*:[156] The First Amendment did prohibit some punishments after the fact, as well as prior restraints on publication. Under other circumstances than these, the First

---

[151] Defendants' brief at 14, in 18 *Landmark Briefs*, cited in note 145, at 989, 1002.

[152] Id at 7; 18 *Landmark Briefs*, cited in note 145, at 985.

[153] *Schenck v United States*, 249 US 47 (1919).

[154] 249 US at 51.

[155] See Appendix infra.

[156] 205 US 454 (1907).

Amendment might have prevented prosecution for the defendants' leaflets.[157]

In the circumstances of this case, however, the First Amendment provided no protection. Holmes began his discussion with the defendants' claim of absolute privilege, which he disposed of quickly. There was no absolute privilege for speech in general: "The most stringent protection of free speech would not protect a man in falsely shouting fire in a theater and causing a panic. It [the First Amendment] does not even protect a man from an injunction against uttering words that may have all the effect of force."[158] Speech was accorded only a qualified privilege. Words may have all the effect of force by the very impact of their meaning and so they may be regulated as other acts are regulated, whenever they stand sufficiently close to the forbidden effect:[159]

> The question in every case is whether the words used are used in such circumstances and are of such a nature as to create a clear and present danger that they will bring about the substantive evils that Congress has a right to prevent. It is a question of proximity and degree.

This was simply another restatement of Holmes's general principle of liability at the common law, as applied to conspiracies and attempts. In other words, since the First Amendment did not extend an absolute privilege, Congress could in some cases provide for the punishment of speech that would have forbidden consequences. But the First Amendment did contain a qualified privilege: Congress could not go beyond the liability imposed by the common law. It could only authorize punishment for expressions when they lay sufficiently close to a forbidden result to pose a "clear and present danger."

The next question was whether these proven attempts to obstruct the draft posed such a danger. Congress plainly could outlaw

---

[157] *Schenck*, 249 US at 52.

[158] Id, citing *Gompers v Bucks Stove & Range Co.*, 221 US 418, 439 (1911) (upholding an injunction to enforce a consent decree). This is one of the most famous passages in the law, and is often and misleadingly cited, and as often attacked. Professor Dershowitz has devoted a whole brief article to debunking the "shouting fire" image, in *Shouting "Fire!*," The Atlantic Monthly (January 1989) at p 72 (cited in note 6). His attack, like most criticism, rests on the assumption that Holmes was stating the reason for his holding in the case. But Holmes was just ticking off a subsidiary point in the argument—that the First Amendment does not protect all speech. See *Texas v Johnson*, 491 US 397, 430 (1989) (Rehnquist dissenting).

[159] *Schenck*, 249 US at 52.

speech that actually obstructed the draft: "When a nation is at war many things that might be said in time of peace are such a hindrance to its effort that their utterance will not be endured so long as men fight and that no Court could regard them as protected by any constitutional right."[160]

If Congress had the right to punish otherwise privileged expressions that actually obstructed the war effort, then it only remained to be decided whether it might also forbid unsuccessful conspiracies and attempts by way of speech or publication. The Court had already held, in *Goldman*,[161] that the Espionage Act applied to unsuccessful conspiracies and attempts.[162]

> [T]hat case [*Goldman*] might be said to dispose of the present contention [that the First Amendment prohibits prosecution for attempts by speech] if the precedent covers all *media concludendi*. But as the right to free speech was not referred to specifically [in *Goldman*], we have thought fit to add a few words.

Holmes then summarized the constitutional limits on legislation in an unusually terse formula: In attempts by speech, as in other criminal attempts, the government was required to prove, first, an overt act, which had a forbidden tendency; and second, that the defendant had the specific intent to bring about the forbidden result. "If the act, (speaking, or circulating a paper,) its tendency and the intent with which it is done are the same, we perceive no ground for saying that success alone warrants making the act a crime."[163]

In this brief passage Holmes said that when the alleged criminal act was speech, the Constitution required that both an objective standard of foreseeability, and the specific intent to bring about the forbidden result, be proven. This was, of course, the common-law requirement for overcoming a privilege as well as for proving an attempt, as Holmes had stated it in "Privilege, Malice, and Intent," and then imported into the Constitution as a fundamental principle of right.

What is not clear in this opinion is whether the "specific intent" required by the Constitution was an actual subjective intent—a

---

[160] Id.

[161] *Goldman*, 245 US 474.

[162] *Schenck*, 249 US at 52.

[163] Id (emphasis added).

conscious desire to bring about the result forbidden by Congress—or was simply an intent imputed from the manifest tendency to do harm, judged by an external standard. Holmes hinted, but did not plainly say, that the required intent was subjective. (If it were not, referring both to the tendency of the act and the intent with which it was done would have been redundant.) Whether Holmes's brethren entirely agreed on this last point in *Schenck* was not clear.

Even without his hint of a need for proof of motive, Holmes's opinion was taken as a victory for freedom of speech. Some lower courts and perhaps the majority of the Supreme Court itself in *Baltzer* had been treating the Espionage Act of 1917 as if it created a category of forbidden expression—words of opposition to the war effort.[164] Holmes's accomplishment was to shift the focus of the Court's attention away from the proscribed category of expression, to the narrower question of whether in the circumstances of the case the defendant's language posed a real threat.

XI. ABRAMS

Before the close of its term in June, 1919, the still-unanimous Court delivered two more opinions affirming convictions for attempts to obstruct the draft. Holmes wrote both opinions. In them he mentioned constitutional questions only in passing and to say that such questions had been decided in *Schenck*.

The more difficult to decide of the two was the case of Jacob Frohwerk,[165] who had written a series of anti-war articles for the *Missouri Staats Zeitung* in the summer of 1917. Frohwerk had failed to obtain a bill of exceptions from the trial court, and his appeal came on without an adequate record. As Holmes noted, it was not clear what evidence had been introduced on the critical question of intent, and the Court accordingly felt "more anxiety than if [the case had] presented only the constitutional question"—validity of the statute—strenuously argued by Frohwerk's counsel.[166] As to the validity of the Espionage Act under the First Amendment,

---

[164] See generally Chafee, *Freedom of Speech in Wartime*, 32 Harv L Rev 932 (1919).

[165] *Frohwerk*, 249 US 204.

[166] Id at 206.

Holmes simply expanded the statement given in *Schenck*. The First Amendment did not grant an absolute immunity.[167]

> [T]he First Amendment while prohibiting legislation against free speech as such cannot have been, and obviously was not, intended to give immunity for every possible use of language. . . . We venture to believe that neither Hamilton nor Madison, nor any other competent person then or later, ever supposed that to make criminal the counselling of a murder within the jurisdiction of Congress would be an unconstitutional interference with free speech.

The Court had just held in *Schenck* that Congress could make attempts to obstruct the draft by speech a crime. It remained only to consider the evidence concerning Frohwerk's intent, which the Court did with some care, concluding that the language of the newspaper articles themselves was sufficient to sustain the jury verdict; but expressing concern that other facts relevant to actual intent which might have been in the record were not available for review.[168]

The second of these distasteful cases concerned Eugene Debs, one of the founders of the Socialist Party of America and its candidate for President in every campaign since 1900. Debs would run for President again in 1920, from prison, and poll nearly a million votes. He had been convicted for giving a public address in Canton, Ohio, in which he criticized the war and the draft, praised men and women who had been convicted of criminally obstructing the draft, and strongly hinted that his listeners should emulate them.[169] In the climate of the time it might have been supposed that such a speech would cause resistance to the draft. A sentence of ten years' imprisonment was imposed. The harsh sentence, and the Administration's insistence on continuing to prosecute a political figure even after the war had been won, distasteful in themselves, also made Holmes fear from the outset that if the conviction were upheld it would seem to be because of Debs's politics rather than his alleged efforts to obstruct the draft.[170]

---

[167] Id, reference to *Robertson v Baldwin*, 165 US 275, 281 (1897) (guarantees of bill of rights subject to exceptions in common law), see Section VI.

[168] *Frohwerk*, 249 US at 208–9.

[169] *Debs v United States*, 249 US 211 (1919).

[170] Holmes to Harold Laski, March 16, 1919, 1 *Holmes-Laski Letters* 189, 190 (Harvard, 1953).

The principal question on appeal was adequacy of the government's evidence of specific intent. The Court again upheld the conviction, and Holmes again wrote the opinion. He carefully noted that the jury had been properly instructed that for a guilty verdict they must find both the "natural tendency, and reasonable, probable effect" of Debs's speech to have been "to obstruct the recruiting service," and further, that the defendant also "had the specific intent to do so in his mind." Holmes reviewed the evidence of Debs's statements and held them sufficient to support a jury verdict. He had no doubt about the law, but he was sorry to have to affirm the verdict and privately expressed hopes that President Wilson would pardon Debs; but the President on October 2, 1919, suffered a stroke from which he would never recover, and the prosecutions of dissidents ground on.

Holmes's opinions in the *Frohwerk* and *Debs* cases were approved by all the Justices, and the Court recessed for the summer. Holmes, his opinions completed before the recess, enjoyed two months of leisure at his summer home in Beverly Farms, Massachusetts—his first carefree summer since war had broken out in 1914.

When he returned to Washington for the beginning of the October term, there was a new, and to Holmes still more distasteful, round of cases to be decided under the Espionage Act. These cases arose under the 1918 amendments known as the Sedition Act, which among other things prohibited speech critical of the American form of government during wartime.[171]

The first of these cases to be decided was *Abrams v United States*.[172] Jacob Abrams was one of a group of recent Jewish immigrants from Russia, anarchists living in Manhattan. In the summer of 1918, the group met to plan protests against the sending of American troops into the Soviet Union. Soon afterward, one of them threw copies of two leaflets from a window on lower Broadway. One leaflet was in English and the other in Yiddish. Each denounced the sending of troops to Russia and the "hypocritical" statements of the President on this subject. The Yiddish leaflet called for a general strike of all American workers. A puzzled passerby turned the Yiddish leaflet in at a police station and within

---

[171] Espionage Act of 1918, 40 Stat 553.
[172] 250 US 616 (1919).

days, Abrams and four of his colleagues, three men and a woman, all in their twenties, were in custody. Tried in federal district court for violations of the Sedition Act, Abrams and the others were convicted and given brutal sentences of up to twenty years' imprisonment.[173]

When the defendants' appeals reached the Supreme Court, the government's brief emphasized strongly, even passionately, the inherent right of any government to protect itself from violent dissolution,[174] seeming thereby to acknowledge that the defendants had been prosecuted, not for any perceived threat they may have posed to the war effort, but for fear of their threat to the system of government of the United States.

A majority of the Court evidently accepted the prosecutors' view of the case and of the condition of the country. The eventual majority opinion by Justice Clarke held simply that it was a jury question whether these leaflets, on objective grounds, posed a clear and present danger of obstructing the war effort. A call for a general strike to halt the intervention in Russia would be understood by any reasonable person to result in an obstruction of the war effort as well. By an external standard the specific intent required for an attempt therefore was proven and the convictions sustained.[175]

After the case had been discussed in conference, Holmes circulated a memorandum that would be a dissent if the convictions were upheld.[176] The majority were deeply disturbed. In what may be a unique instance, a delegation of three justices called on Holmes at his home and pleaded with him not to publish his dissenting opinion, apparently on the ground that unanimity of the justices was as important during the Red Scare as it had been in wartime. Holmes's wife, Fanny, joined in the plea.[177]

Holmes was not persuaded, and published his dissent.[178]

He began, as usual, by reciting the charges of the indictment and reviewing the evidence as to each. The principal evidence was

---

[173] *Abrams*, 250 US at 629 (Holmes dissenting).

[174] *Landmark Briefs*, cited in note 145, at 1021.

[175] *Abrams*, 250 US at 621.

[176] Holmes to Frederick Pollock, November 6, 1919, 2 *Holmes-Pollock Letters* 29 (cited in note 23).

[177] Dean Acheson, *Morning and Noon* 119 (Houghton, Mifflin, 1965).

[178] *Abrams*, 250 US 616, 624 (1919) (Holmes dissenting).

the two leaflets themselves, which the defendants did not deny printing and distributing. Of the four counts of the indictment, Holmes focused on the fourth, a charge that the defendants had advocated curtailing production of war materiel, with intent to hinder prosecution of the war. This count alone charged a completed crime, rather than an unsuccessful attempt. The evidence of advocacy was principally in the second leaflet, which called (in Yiddish) for a general strike of American workers. The majority found that this pamphlet did "urge curtailment of production of things necessary to the prosecution of the war." But even assuming that this pathetic leaflet might have had some tendency in that direction, the statute also required proof of "intent . . . to cripple or hinder the United States in the prosecution of the war."

Holmes delivered a brief lecture on the subject of intent. Intent in a free speech case must be understood "in a strict and accurate sense," as encompassing both the external standard, so familiar from Holmes's own writings, and the subjective intent or motive to produce just those results forbidden by Congress. Holmes gave a brief example to show that unless specific intent in the sense of motive were part of the statute's requirement, it might be applied to honest criticism of the government's policies.[179]

> A patriot might think that we were wasting money on aeroplanes, or making more cannon of a certain kind than we needed, and might advocate curtailment with success, yet even if it turned out that the curtailment hindered and was thought by other minds to have been obviously likely to hinder the United States in the prosecution of the war, no one would hold such conduct a crime.

As to completed crimes, therefore, as well as under the law of criminal attempts as Holmes had stated it in previous opinions, the specific, subjective intent to bring about the harms that Congress had a right to forbid must be proven in every case involving freedom of speech.[180]

---

[179] Id at 627. It is characteristic and perhaps amusing that Holmes turns to the First Amendment only after laying out these broad principles of freedom of speech.

[180] Id at 628. At least where private rights are not concerned. Holmes plainly means to limit the clear-and-present-danger standard to cases of attempted crime, but it does not then follow that all other speech is afforded a higher degree of protection, as Professor Currie suggests. Currie, *The Constitution in the Supreme Court* at 123 (cited in note 99). Evidently a different standard is to be applied where private rights are concerned, but Holmes probably just meant that the First Amendment did not disturb the common law of defamation; see Section XVII.

The difference between Holmes and the Court was now plainly stated. As Professor Corwin observed, the majority had applied a purely external standard to determine intent.[181] Holmes believed that the constitution required an added showing of actual malice or subjective intent.[182] And in *Abrams*, evidence of specific, subjective intent was wholly absent. Holmes thought the only evidence was the publications themselves, and their words related solely to the intervention in Russia.[183]

> I do not see how anyone can find the intent required by the statute in any of the defendants' words. The second leaflet [in Yiddish] is the only one that affords even a foundation for the charge and . . . it is evident from the beginning to the end that the only object of the paper is to help Russia and stop American intervention there against the popular government—not to impede the United States in the war that it was carrying on.

Specific intent had not been proven, and Holmes thought conviction on the fourth count of the indictment should have been reversed. On the same reasoning, and with even more force, the other counts (charging attempts) should have been dismissed.

Holmes went on to make a final point. Even if there had been sufficient evidence of intent and the jury had been properly instructed—"Even if I am technically wrong and enough can be squeezed from these poor and puny anonymities to turn the color of legal litmus paper"—Holmes's outrage at the twenty-year sentences imposed could not be restrained. The brutal sentences and the government's insistence on pursuing the case were proof to Holmes that the prosecution had nothing to do with the war effort. "[T]he most nominal punishment seems to me all that possibly could be inflicted, unless the defendants are to be made to suffer

---

[181] Edward Corwin, *Freedom of Speech and Press under the First Amendment*, 30 Yale L J 48 (1920).

[182] There arguably was an "obscurity" in the opinion, however, as to whether the specific intent and the external standard of risk "were alternative bases of criminal liability, or rather that both elements had to be shown." Lawrence Tribe, *American Constitutional Law* 843 n 16 (Foundation Press, 1988). I think the opinion is clear enough that, as to completed acts of advocacy, specific intent is an additional element; but Holmes suggests that for attempts, the intent may make up for a lack of objective risk in the overt acts alone. Here the ambiguity was in the law of attempts, which imposed criminal liability for some acts that could not in themselves lead to harm unless part of a larger plan or because of circumstances known only to the defendant.

[183] 250 US at 628–29.

not for what the indictment alleges but for the creed that they
avow. . . ."[184]

In *Baltzer*, Holmes had remarked that it was better for those
who held unquestioned and almost unlimited power to err on the
side of freedom. Now, plainly moved by genuine feeling, he went
on to explain more fully why the government should refrain from
prosecuting people for expressing their political beliefs, even when
there might be nominal evidence of a crime:

> Persecution for the expression of opinion seems to me perfectly
> logical . . . . But when men have realized that time has upset
> many fighting faiths, they may come to believe even more than
> they believe in the very foundations of their own conduct that
> the ultimate good desired is better reached by free trade in
> ideas—that the best test of truth is the power of the thought
> to get itself accepted in the competition of the market, and that
> truth is the only ground upon which their wishes safely can be
> carried out. That at any rate is the theory of our Constitution.
> It is an experiment, as all life is an experiment. Every year if
> not every day we have to wager our salvation upon some proph-
> ecy based upon imperfect knowledge. While that experiment
> is part of our system I think that we should be eternally vigilant
> against attempts to check the expression of opinions that we
> loathe and believe to be fraught with death, unless they so
> imminently threaten immediate interference with the lawful
> and pressing purposes of the law that an immediate check is
> required to save the country. . . . Of course I am speaking only
> of expressions of opinion and exhortations, which were all that
> were uttered here, but I regret that I cannot put into more
> impressive words my belief that in their conviction upon this
> indictment the defendants were deprived of their rights under
> the Constitution of the United States.[185]

This was the fullest statement Holmes ever made of the social
policy behind the privilege accorded to speech and the press at the
common law, and inscribed in the Constitution. Life was made up
of conflicts, but it was the duty of the government to see that the
struggle for life was carried out peacefully, in the marketplace
rather than on the battlefield, and that it was conducted fairly in
the sense that the government, with its monopoly of violent force,
should not interpose on behalf of one party or another. The First

---

[184] Id at 629.

[185] Id at 630–31.

Amendment accordingly, as Holmes had noted in *Frohwerk*, forbade legislation against the expression of ideas or opinions, as such. Speech used in such a way, and intended, to threaten harm might be punished, but opinion in and of itself could not be suppressed.

Disbelieving in absolutes, however, Holmes immediately qualified this principle: even an honest expression of opinion, uttered with no intent to do harm, might be suppressed under extraordinary circumstances—perhaps in some desperate war for national survival—if it interfered with pressing business and an "immediate check [was] required to save the country."[186] In other less desperate circumstances only those statements intended to cause violations of law could be punished.

XII. THE RATIONALE FOR FREEDOM OF SPEECH

Stripped of its poetry and restated in logical order, Holmes's argument was this. The "theory of our Constitution"[187] was that "truth" was the only ground on which the desires of men "safely" could be carried out. This "truth" that ensured safely, according to the Constitution, was to be determined by victory of ideas in peaceful competition, which Holmes said was to be preferred to "persecution" as a method of determining truth.

The premise, on which all the rest depended, was that the desires of men (expressed in laws) could only be carried out "safely" if they were based on "truth." What could "safely" mean in this context? One interpretation of this passage might be that the Framers feared violent revolution, and tried to forestall it by allowing free expression of ideas. This is part of the answer.[188] Yet Holmes's dissent in *Abrams* shows the deepest contempt for the government's

---

[186] Misled by the conviction that Holmes's dissent in *Abrams* stated a different doctrine than his opinion for the Court in *Schenck*, some commentators have speculated that the phrase "an immediate check is required to save the country" was meant as a gloss on "clear and present danger." See note 195. But this is a misreading; the "save the country" phrase would not make sense as a general standard, and if that were not clear from the context, Holmes immediately went on to say, "Of course I am speaking only of expressions of opinion and exhortations, which were all that were uttered here."

[187] Not, evidently, Holmes's own theory. He often said he was not sure he believed in freedom of speech, although he hoped that he would be willing to die for it. See, e.g., Holmes to Harold Laski, October 26, 1915, 1 *Holmes-Laski Letters* 217 (1953). He apparently meant that he was loyal to the peaceful rule of law, but had doubts whether it would prevail over regimes more frankly committed to the use of force.

[188] See *Whitney v California*, 274 US 352, 372 (1927) (Brandeis and Holmes concurring).

fear of revolution, and this interpretation does not quite match Holmes's always careful and precise syntax. Another interpretation, more in accord with the words and with Holmes's general ideas, is that "safely" means "with assurance of success." In Holmes's writings, the purpose of law is to achieve the desires of the dominant class. To the extent the lawmaker understands his own self interest well, and designs his laws properly, his own survival and the survival of the system he has made will be ensured. The prevention of rebellion is only one of the prudent considerations that go into designing a legal system to ensure survival.[189]

Peaceful competition evidently is to be preferred to violent persecution as a method of ascertaining truth in this limited and pragmatic sense. The marketplace of politics and the markets of commerce may show whether the legal system is well designed for survival—at least that is the theory the Constitution requires to be tested by experiment. We are to test in the laboratory of experience—and ultimately in war—whether governments based on peaceful discourse are better equipped to survive than governments that rule by violence.[190] Thus:[191]

> There are two grounds on which freedom of speech is generally considered an inherent part of democratic living. One is that there can be no dignity in the individual life without it. The other is that it gives survival value to a government. It is the second to which Holmes gives expression here.

It is fundamental to Holmes's view of freedom of speech, that ideas attacking the very basis of government be allowed to flourish and to prevail, if they can, by peaceful discourse. Only in this way could the viability of government be tested. Holmes repeatedly returned to this point. In 1919, the same year in which the Court affirmed Jacob Abrams's conviction, Benjamin Gitlow was tried in a New York courtroom and found guilty of criminal anarchism for publishing a Communist "manifesto." When the case reached his

---

[189] See, e.g., *Law in Science—Science in Law*, 12 Harv L Rev 443 (1899), reprinted in Holmes, *Collected Legal Papers* at 210 (cited in note 14).

[190] Compare Holmes's frequently quoted opinion that the Constitution allows experiments in social policy to be carried out "in the insulated chambers afforded by several of the states." *Truax v Corrigan*, 257 US 312, 344 (1921).

[191] Max Lerner, *The Mind and Faith of Justice Holmes* 306 (Little, Brown, 1944; reissued, 1990). See also Rabban, *The Emergence of First Amendment Doctrine*, 50 U Chi L Rev at 1310–11 (cited in note 50).

Court and the conviction was affirmed, Holmes dissented, saying, "If in the long run the beliefs expressed in proletarian dictatorship are destined to be accepted by the dominant forces of the community, the only meaning of free speech is that they should be given their chance and have their way."[192] In 1928, he said, dissenting from the Court's decision that a pacifist, Rosika Schwimmer, because of her beliefs could not become a citizen of the United States:[193]

> Some of her answers might excite popular prejudice, but if there is any principle of the Constitution that more imperatively calls for attachment than any other it is the principle of free thought—not free thought for those who agree with us but freedom for the thought that we hate.

This was the lesson Holmes had learned in a lifetime of warfare and study, crystallized in his article "Privilege, Malice, and Intent." The rule of law meant that the struggle for survival was to be carried on fairly and peacefully. The judge's duty was to ensure free and peaceful competition among political ideas, even if—especially if—his own survival, or the survival of the social order that held everything of value for him, was at stake. Peaceful government under law ultimately rested not upon the rights of the governed but upon the honor and sense of fairness of the judges, upon their paradoxical willingness to risk everything, even survival itself, to see that fairness was preserved.

What is striking and unique in Holmes's doctrine is that this whole system of open discourse rests on the principle that speech may not be punished unless it has both an objectively harmful tendency and is subjectively intended to cause specific harms that the legislature has power to forbid. Motive, the touchstone of a morality that the young Holmes said was stripped from the law by relentless natural selection, now reappeared as a principle so fundamental as to be incorporated into an otherwise spare Constitution.

Holmes never explained why he had come to feel motive was so important a factor in cases of Constitutional privilege. At common law, actual malice undoubtedly was an answer to the defense of

---

[192] *Gitlow v New York*, 268 US 652, 673 (1925).

[193] *United States v Schwimmer*, 279 US 644, 654–55 (1929).

privilege, but Holmes never pointed to anything in the case law to support his insistence that this point was fundamental. I will return to this question in the concluding section; for the moment, I want to emphasize only that Holmes's insistence on proof of subjective intent or motive was what separated him from the majority of his court.

XIII. THE REVISIONIST VIEW

I have taken the trouble to parse Holmes's arguments closely and to turn his poetry into prose because, with the passage of time and the accretion of commentary, Holmes's opinions as he and his colleagues on the Court understood them have become nearly inaccessible. In recent years a reading at variance with the one given here has gained wide support.

Holmes's ideas about the First Amendment now may seem cool to the First Freedom. Holmes insisted that there was no fundamental difference between speech and other forms of activity, and that both might be regulated on the same ground—to prevent foreseeable harms that Congress had a right to prevent.[194] In *Abrams*, Holmes repeated his view that there was no absolute immunity for political speech; and even the modest protection afforded by the clear-and-present-danger doctrine applied only to speech on public questions that Congress sought to punish criminally. As we have seen, Holmes conceded that under some circumstances even the expression of honest opinion on public matters, as such, might be suppressed when it "so imminently threaten[s] immediate interference with the lawful and pressing purposes of the law that an immediate check is required to save the country."[195]

---

[194] Holmes to Harold Laski, July 7, 1918, 1 *Holmes-Laski Letters* 160, 161 (cited in note 170): "we should deal with the act of speech as we deal with any other overt act that we don't like." Holmes was speaking here of the abstract power of the sovereign, absolutely sure of its premises, not of the proper way of proceeding under the United States Constitution, but he clearly saw no intrinsic difference between speech and other acts.

[195] *Abrams*, 250 US at 630–31. The revisionists have hinted that this represents a rephrasing of the clear-and-present-danger standard, rather than an entirely new standard applicable to expressions of honest opinion, see, e.g., Rabban, 50 U Chi L Rev at 1307–8 (cited in note 50); and so great is the hydraulic pressure exerted by the revisionist attack that Professor Currie, although correctly describing the "save the country" passage as an independent standard for punishing even expressions of opinion, nevertheless allows himself to suggest

Holmes's ideas are quite at variance with an important modern school of thought, which holds that the First Amendment draws a sharp line between "expression" and "action," and extends absolute protection to all forms of expression.[196] Not surprisingly, commentators writing from this perspective in recent years have criticized Holmes for his lack of sensitivity to First Amendment freedoms. The objective of at least some of the criticism—Alan Dershowitz is engagingly frank about this—is simply to discredit *Schenck*, whose forceful language is constantly and often inappropriately cited by prosecutors.[197]

Assaults on Holmes really began after 1951, when the Supreme Court decided *Dennis v United States*,[198] and relied on *Schenck* to uphold criminal convictions of the leaders of the Communist Party. This decision, declaring what was nominally a political party to be a criminal conspiracy, and coming as it did at the height of a new post-war Red Scare, deeply distressed many people in the academic community, and for many years thereafter "clear and present danger" was under the anathema of the law professors.[199]

In earlier years, Holmes's dissents had been celebrated and he himself had been considered a liberal, but Holmes's liberal credentials were officially withdrawn, as it were, by Samuel Konefsky, in an influential book, *The Legacy of Holmes and Brandeis*, published in 1956. Konefsky argued that Holmes had no real ideas of his own, only unreflective prejudices—"clear and present danger" was just a casual remark, a rationalization to uphold criminal convictions, that did not become a rationale for protecting freedom of speech until Justice Brandeis lent his "powerful support."[200] There was a heavy air of suggestion about the study, a suggestion that

---

that it represents a liberalization of Holmes's views. Currie, *The Constitution in the Supreme Court* at 123–24 (cited in note 99).

[196] See, e.g., Thomas Emerson, *The System of Freedom of Expression* (Random House, 1970).

[197] Dershowitz, *Shouting 'Fire!'*, The Atlantic Monthly (January 1989) p 72 (cited in note 6).

[198] 341 US 494 (1951); see Section XVI.

[199] See Frank Strong, *Fifty Years of "Clear and Present Danger": From Schenck to Brandenburg—and Beyond*, 1969 Supreme Court Review 41 and sources cited there; Hans Linde, *"Clear and Present Danger" Reexamined: Dissonance in the Brandenburg Concerto*, 22 Stan L Rev 1163 (1970). Strong, citing the onslaught of academic criticism, wrote a sort of premature obituary for Holmes's version of the doctrine. See Section XVI.

[200] Samuel Konefsky, *The Legacy of Holmes and Brandeis* at 201 (Macmillan, 1956).

Brandeis was the true source of the supposedly liberal ideas and the dissents for which Holmes was admired.[201]

Judge Learned Hand, who gave the Holmes Lectures at Harvard in 1958,[202] devoted part of one lecture to an attack on the clear-and-present-danger doctrine, comparing it unfavorably with his own objective test of incitement.[203] Justice William O. Douglas, concurring in *Brandenburg v Ohio*,[204] approvingly cited Hand's book as authority for the violent attack on Holmes's standard that has continued to this day.[205]

The attack on Holmes continued in the 1960s, in a book-length study by Yosal Rogat,[206] in which among other things Rogat traced the doctrine of *Schenck* to the external standard of *The Common Law*.[207] This was an understandable misreading of an obscurely written opinion. The criticism has since taken an odd turn, however. Holmes's dissents in *Abrams*, *Gitlow*, and *Schwimmer*, are among the most eloquent statements in our legal literature on behalf of free speech; the *Abrams* dissent was said to be "the greatest utterance on intellectual freedom by an American, ranking in the English tongue with Milton and Mill."[208] On the strength of *Abrams*

---

[201] David Rabban has amplified this suggestion into a fully developed theory that a cabal of liberal law professors manipulated Holmes and consciously misrepresented his ideas and their own, in order to achieve a compromised doctrine of the First Amendment that was nevertheless more liberal than Holmes first intended, an effort that Rabban calls "heroic but often disingenuous." In this theory, Brandeis became converted to the effort to put a spin on Holmes's opinions in the 1920s, when his dissents and concurrences added a libertarian gloss to Holmes's unreflective aphorisms. Rabban, *The Emergence of First Amendment Doctrine*, 50 U Chi L Rev at 1210–11 (cited in note 50).

[202] Published as *Learned Hand, The Bill of Rights* (Harvard, 1958).

[203] Id at 57–59. There is a certain irony here—the *Dennis* Court had relied on Hand's own formulation of the clear-and-present-danger standard to affirm the convictions of the Communist leaders. 341 US at 510.

[204] *Brandenburg v Ohio*, 395 US 444 (1969).

[205] Id at 454 (Douglas concurring).

[206] Yosal Rogat, *Mr. Justice Holmes: A Dissenting Opinion* I, 15 Stan L Rev 3 (1962); II, id at 254 (1963); *The Judge as Spectator*, 31 U Chi L Rev 213 (1964); Rogat and James O'Fallon, *Mr. Justice Holmes: A Dissenting Opinion—the Speech Cases*, 36 Stan L Rev 1349 (1984).

[207] See Rogat, *The Judge as Spectator*, 31 U Chi L Rev at 215–18; Rogat and O'Fallon, *Mr. Justice Holmes: A Dissenting Opinion—The Speech Cases*, 36 Stan L Rev at 1368–78. James M. O'Fallon completed the manuscript written in the 1960s by Rogat and left unfinished at his death.

[208] Lerner, *The Mind and Faith of Justice Holmes*, at 306 (cited in note 191).

even Holmes's critics treat him as the father of modern First Amendment jurisprudence.[209]

The problem for the critics therefore has been to distinguish the Holmes of *Schenck* from the Holmes of *Abrams*. An effort has been made to do this. The argument is that when he wrote the *Schenck* opinion, Holmes was not especially concerned about protecting free speech, but that sharp criticism of *Schenck* stung him into changing his position. In *Abrams*, the argument goes, he gave the *Schenck* doctrine a gloss which made it more protective of free speech than it had been originally.

This argument, separating the Holmes of *Abrams* from the Holmes of *Schenck*, was first sketched by Fred Ragan in 1971,[210] and then considerably amplified and strengthened by Learned Hand's biographer, Gerald Gunther (who gave Hand most of the credit for the change).[211]

The Ragan-Gunther argument was given its most effective presentation by David Rabban in 1983, who called it the "revisionist" view.[212] Rabban carefully excavated the earliest common-law origins of Holmes's opinion in *Schenck*, but like Rogat, Rabban mistakenly concluded that Holmes had never moved past the external standard of *The Common Law*, and that the Holmes of *Schenck* therefore propounded a meager view of the First Amendment based on an external standard of foreseeable harm.[213] This, as we have seen, exactly reverses Holmes's position. Rabban seemed not to notice that even in his own account, when Learned Hand and Ernst Freund argued with Holmes, it was Hand and Freund who put forward an external standard, and Holmes who stubbornly clung to his doctrine of subjective intent.[214]

---

[209] David Rabban, for instance, whose influential revisionist article on Holmes's opinions was titled simply, *The Emergence of Modern First Amendment Doctrine* (cited in note 50).

[210] Ragan, *Justice Oliver Wendell Holmes, Jr., Zechariah Chafee, Jr., and the Clear and Present Danger Test for Free Speech: The First Year, 1919*, 58 J Am Hist 24 (1971).

[211] Gerald Gunther, *Learned Hand and the Origins of Modern First Amendment Doctrine: Some Fragments of History*, 27 Stan L Rev 719 (1975).

[212] Rabban, *The Emergence of Modern First Amendment Doctrine*, 50 U Chi L Rev at 1208 (cited in note 50).

[213] Id at 1271–78.

[214] Id at 1281–83.

In 1988, Laurence Tribe approvingly cited Gunther's version of the revisionist argument in his authoritative treatise,[215] and David Currie presented the Gunther-Rabban theory in his history of constitutional law in the Supreme Court.[216] It seemed on its way to becoming not the revisionist but the established view.

On this theory, Holmes simply changed his mind about freedom of speech during the summer of 1919. In Gunther's formulation: ". . . The *Schenck* standard was not truly speech-protective; and . . . it was not until the fall of 1919, with his famous dissent in [*Abrams*], that Holmes put some teeth into the clear and present danger formula. . . ."[217]

Such a turnabout in Holmes's thinking on a fundamental question, when he was seventy-eight years old, had been a judge for thirty-six years, and had already written three opinions on the question for a unanimous Supreme Court, calls for an explanation.

Ragan had suggested that criticism of *Schenck* by Holmes's young friends had prodded him into the change.[218] Not much in the way of "probing criticism" has ever come to light, however. An article by Ernst Freund in *The New Republic* in the summer of 1919 did criticize Holmes,[219] and he wrote a letter of reply that showed he was stung;[220] but Ernst Freund was not a friend nor a man whose opinion Holmes particularly respected. Holmes was annoyed, but it was characteristic irritation at being misunderstood.[221] He called the Freund article "poor stuff."[222]

Professor Gunther emphasized criticism by Judge Learned Hand, who was not a close friend, but who was in a circle that included Holmes's friends Harold Laski and Felix Frankfurter.

---

[215] Tribe, *American Constitutional Law* at 842 n 8 (cited in note 182).

[216] Currie, *The Constitution in the Supreme Court*, at 122–24 (cited in note 99); Currie had earlier expressed more doubt, see Currie, *The Constitution in the Supreme Court: 1910–1921*, 1985 Duke L J 1111 (1985).

[217] Gunther, *Learned Hand and the Origins of Modern First Amendment Doctrine: Some Fragments of History*, 27 Stan L Rev at 720 (cited in note 211).

[218] Ragan, cited in note 7, at 37–45.

[219] Ernst Freund, *The Debs Case and Freedom of Speech*, 19 New Republic 13 (1919).

[220] The letter was addressed to one of the editors of The New Republic, Herbert Croly. Holmes sent it instead to Harold Laski, March 13, 1919, 1 *Holmes-Laski Letters* at 202 (cited in note 170).

[221] Bogen, *The Free Speech Metamorphosis of Mr. Justice Holmes*, 11 Hofstra L Rev 97 (1982).

[222] Holmes to Harold J. Laski, May 13, 1919, 1 *Holmes-Laski Letters* at 202 (cited in note 170).

Hand had a conversation with Holmes in a railway car in June, 1918, when they were both on their way to summer homes in New England. Holmes apparently opened the conversation with one of his standard gambits about the power of a sovereign to punish speech, or anything else, unless for reasons of prudence it chose not to—a gambit he had used on Justice White as early as 1906, and with which he opened his discussion of the policy behind the First Amendment in Abrams in 1919.[223]

Holmes's gambit was not about freedom of speech, which he used only as an example (to show that nothing was sacred), but about the basis of sovereignty. Holmes believed that government represented the dominant power and unless overthrown was not restrained by anything except prudence. Hand accepted this, but wrote a letter afterward adding that as a matter of prudent self-interest the sovereign ought to allow free speech.[224] Holmes agreed, as he told Laski, for in most cases the sovereign couldn't be sure of being right.[225]

As to the desirable limits of free speech, however, in March, 1919, as the Red Scare was gathering momentum, Hand wrote to Holmes, "I haven't a doubt that Debs was guilty under any rule conceivably applicable."[226] He praised the result in Schenck, Frohwerk, and Debs, but also very delicately hinted that Holmes, in his statement of doctrine, might have gone a little farther in the direction pointed by Hand's own opinion of two years earlier, Masses Publishing Co. v Patten.[227] In that case, Hand had suggested an external standard of "direct incitement" which he put forward as a way of controlling the discretion of the lower court judges.[228] As Gunther acknowledges, Holmes did not remember the details of Hand's opinion and so did not understand the hint, and did not

---

[223] *Abrams*, 250 US at 630 (Holmes dissenting). See the exchange of letters among Holmes, Hand, and Harold Laski just after this meeting, 1 *Holmes-Laski Letters* at 158–61 (cited in note 170).

[224] Hand to Holmes, June 2, 1918, id at 159

[225] Holmes to Laski, June 25, 1918, id at 158.

[226] Hand to Holmes, undated, but apparently shortly after the *Debs* decision, Holmes Papers, cited in note 10, B43 F30; reprinted in Gunther, 27 Stan L Rev at 758–59 (cited in note 211).

[227] 244 F 535 (SDNY), reversed, 246 F 24 (2d Cir 1917).

[228] Id.

quite see where Hand disagreed.[229] If Hand was trying to influence Holmes's views on the First Amendment, there is not one word in any of his letters or papers to suggest Holmes was aware of it. Nor did Holmes's later opinions show any sign of his adopting a purely external standard as Hand recomended; just the contrary.

According to Rabban's more elaborate account, Holmes was influenced by other young friends in the circle drawn about him by Felix Frankfurter. But Holmes was forty years their senior, and they always used his title when addressing him. Zechariah Chafee alone seems to have made any effort to influence Holmes. Chafee, a Harvard law professor, was an admirer of Holmes's jurisprudence, and wrote understandingly about the *Schenck*, *Frohwerk*, and *Debs* opinions shortly after they appeared.[230] Chafee praised the clear-and-present-danger standard announced in *Schenck*, but he did have two complaints about Holmes's opinions. He felt that Holmes's case-specific decision in *Schenck* did not provide enough guidance to restrain the lower courts,[231] and he felt that there was not enough evidence to go to the jury in *Debs*.[232] Chafee tackled Holmes on this second point, at a tea party arranged by Laski that summer, but came away persuaded that he had made no impression.[233] Holmes had responded that while as a juror he might have voted to acquit Debs, he had no warrant to reverse the actual jury's verdict.[234]

But as Rabban was obliged to concede, despite Chafee's reservations about the result in *Debs*, Chafee never wavered from his support of the clear-and-present-danger standard, arguing for it even in private letters.[235]

---

[229] See Gunther, 27 Stan L Rev at 736 (cited in note 211).

[230] Chafee, *Freedom of Speech in Wartime*, 32 Harv L Rev 932 (1919).

[231] Id at 944.

[232] Id at 967–68.

[233] See Chafee to Judge Charles F. Amidon, September 30, 1919, Zechariah Chafee, Jr. Papers, Harvard Law School Library, B4 F1, quoted in Rabban, *The Emergence of Modern First Amendment Doctrine*, 50 U Chi L Rev at 1315 (cited in note 50).

[234] Id. Rabban affects to see a contradiction between Holmes's belief there was evidence to go to the jury, and his assertion that he himself would have voted to acquit. Id at 1280, and letters cited there.

[235] Id at 1289–1303. Far from trying to sway Holmes to adopt Learned Hand's Masses test, Chafee (like Holmes) did not see where they differed, and thought Hand's test the same as Holmes's. Rabban tried to get around all this by calling Chafee dishonest. Id.

The other young men's letters to Holmes had a uniform tone of praise. Frankfurter—a strong supporter of the war and of the Wilson Administration—did not criticize the *Schenck* line of opinions; his letters to Holmes that summer do not mention *Schenck, Frohwerk,* or *Debs.*[236]

Harold Laski, who was closest to Holmes, praised the opinions. Shortly after they were delivered, Laski—who was not shy about disagreeing openly with Holmes—wrote:[237]

> I read your three opinions [*Schenck, Frohwerk,* and *Debs*] with great care, and though I say it with deep regret they are very convincing. . . . I think you would agree that none of the accused ought to have been prosecuted; but since they have been and the statute is there, the only remedy lies in the field of pardon. Your analogy of a cry of fire in a crowded theater is, I think, excellent. . . .

Holmes was supposed to have been swayed as well by fear of losing favor at *The New Republic,* which had consistently praised him in the past, and whose praise he is said to have coveted.[238] Felix Frankfurter had introduced *The New Republic*'s editors to Holmes and they were occasional callers at his house in Washington. Like Frankfurter, they supported both the war and the Wilson Administration, were deferential to Holmes, and praised his opinions. The only editorial on this subject in *The New Republic* appeared after the *Debs* opinion and said, "Eugene Debs has gone to the West Virginia Penitentiary to begin his ten-year sentence. There is no doubt about the legality of his conviction. His Canton Speech clearly violated the Espionage Act."[239]

In short, Holmes's young radical friends praised Holmes's opinions in *Schenck, Frohwerk,* and *Debs,* and—except for Chafee's reservation about the evidence in *Debs*—approved the results. The

---

[236] In November, after the *Abrams* dissent, Frankfurter wrote, "You speak there as you have always spoken—of course." Frankfurter to Holmes, November 12, 1919, Holmes Papers, cited in note 10, B30 F3.

[237] Harold Laski to Holmes, March 18, 1919, 1 *Holmes-Laski Letters* at 191 (cited in note 170).

[238] See Kelley, *Book Review: Honorable Justice, The Life of Oliver Wendell Holmes,* 68 Wash U L Q 429, 480–81 (1990).

[239] Editorial, The New Republic (April 19, 1919), p. 362. The editors went on to urge the President to pardon Debs.

"probing criticism" did not happen in the summer of 1919 or at any other time.[240]

But the premise of the whole revisionist argument in all its permutations is wrong anyway. Even if there had been a campaign, it did not work—Holmes did not change his position. The *Abrams* dissent was not different in substance from the opinion in *Schenck*, and it propounded the same doctrine that Holmes had cloven to for twenty-five years, since the publication of "Privilege, Malice, and Intent."

As if to prove his consistency, after delivering his dissent in *Abrams*, Holmes voted with the majority to uphold the conviction in *Gilbert v Minnesota*[241] of an official of an antiwar organization who had been charged with obstructing recruitment by making a speech. A Minnesota statute, as construed in that case, made it a misdemeanor to speak or publish "against enlistment" while a war was in progress and an army was being raised. Joseph Gilbert, an officer of the Nonpartisan League, gave a speech at a public meeting of the League, during the war while men were subject to the draft, and was convicted of violating the statute. His speech was similar to that for which Debs had been convicted. While he did

---

[240] A recent round of revisionist arguments would have it that the Frankfurter circle were too clever to criticize Holmes directly, and instead seduced him by flattery and praise into imagining that *Schenck* could be given the gloss which he then put on it in *Abrams*. Of course, this contradicts other versions of the revisionist thesis. The germ of the argument was suggested by Gerald Gunther, who speculated that Zechariah Chafee's articles praising *Schenck* were disingenuous—Chafee "secretly" preferred Hand's view, but subtly pretended to admire Holmes's. The other young men then flattered Holmes into thinking that Hand's ideas were really his own. Rabban built up this hint into a full-blown account in which Chafee purposely misconstrued Holmes's opinions, "sacrifice[d] scholarly accuracy to libertarian ideology," and consciously presented "inaccurate and misleading" accounts of history simply to create "propaganda" with which to influence Holmes. Rabban, 50 U Chi L Rev at 1289–1303 (cited in note 50). Chafee has always been known as an honest and courageous man; the only justification offered for this torrent of abuse is Rabban's apparent certainty that no one could honestly praise the doctrine of *Schenck*. Another difficulty with this argument is that Chafee, even in private letters, consistently defended the clear-and-present-danger doctrine, but Rabban simply treats these views with contempt. Id.

Polenberg and Kelley give more temperate versions of this story, but they all rely on an extraordinary degree of intellectual dishonesty on Chafee's part, which is wildly improbable, and a degree of vanity and gullibility on Holmes's part that is equally incredible. See Polenberg, *Fighting Faiths* at 218–28 (cited in note 122); Kelley, *Book Review* at 480–81 (cited in note 238). This latest twist of the argument resembles nothing so much as the gossip of Holmes's day, that he was the dupe of Brandeis's wiles. One believes this sort of thing or one doesn't.

[241] 254 US 325 (1921).

not expressly advocate disobedience of the law, the speech might have been understood as encouraging disobedience.[242]

When Gilbert's appeal reached the Supreme Court, all of the justices agreed that his conviction would have been upheld under the federal Espionage Act, under the doctrine of *Schenck*, *Frohwerk*, and *Debs*. The only question seriously argued was whether states had the power to punish speech that threatened to interfere with the draft, or whether the field was preempted by federal legislation.[243] In a diffuse opinion, Justice McKenna, writing for a majority, held that the states were not preempted, and that whatever guarantees of free speech may have applied to the states under the federal constitution, state legislatures were not more limited in this regard than Congress had been by the First Amendment.

Holmes concurred in the result, without joining McKenna's rambling opinion. Except that prosecution had been under a state statute, the case was on all fours with *Debs*, and Holmes's concurrence showed he had not changed his mind: the Holmes of *Schenck* was very much in evidence long after *Abrams*.[244]

If there were any doubt, Holmes's dissent in the *Baltzer* case

---

[242] Gilbert was charged with saying, among other things, "We are going over to Europe to make the world safe for democracy, but I tell you we had better make America safe for democracy first. . . . If this is such a great democracy, for Heaven's sake why should we not vote on conscription of men. . . . . I tell you if they conscripted wealth like they have conscripted men, this war would not last over forty-eight hours. . . ." *Gilbert*, 254 US at 327.

[243] Chief Justice White and Justice Brandeis would have held that the field was preempted by federal law, and both dissented. Brandeis wrote a dissenting opinion, 254 US at 334, which no other justice joined, in which he argued that the states were forbidden to abridge freedom of speech because it was one of the privileges and immunities of national citizenship guaranteed by the Fourteenth Amendment. Therefore Congress alone, subject to the restraints of the First Amendment, could limit freedom of speech. Brandeis argued further that *Schenck*, *Frohwerk*, and *Debs* were based on the federal War Power. To the extent the state statute drew on this authority, it was preempted by the federal government, and to the extent it went beyond this power it was invalid under the privileges and immunities clause. White, who supported the preemption branch of this analysis, retired from the Court the following year, and Brandeis thereafter abandoned this single excursion away from Holmes's protective aegis, and in later opinions returned to the clear and present danger doctrine.

[244] *Gilbert*, 245 US at 334. The cases were on all fours as to facts. The Minnesota statute did not expressly require proof of intent as the Espionage Act did, see *State v Gilbert*, 141 Minn 263, 265 (1918), but evidence of intent was presented to the jury and the verdict may have rested on that ground. It is not clear whether Holmes concurred because there was evidence to take the case to the jury, even under federal standards, or because as he suggested later the states had more latitude, as they were not bound by the strict language of the First Amendment. See *Gitlow v New York*, 268 US 652, 673 (1925) (Holmes dissenting).

should now put it to rest. The Holmes of *Abrams* was also in evidence—but not on display—long before *Schenck*. In *Baltzer* as in *Abrams*, Holmes said the First Amendment was based on the government's duty of self-restraint, adding: "We have enjoyed so much freedom for so long that perhaps we are in danger of forgetting that the bill of rights which cost so much blood to establish still is worth fighting for, and that no tittle of it should be abridged."[245] The old man, supposedly so eager to curry favor with his young admirers, put that dissent in a drawer and never so much as hinted to them of its existence.

What then shall we make of the revisionist argument? It appears to begin with the general proposition that *Schenck* and *Abrams* cannot be reconciled. Historical evidence is then selectively enlisted in support of one or another explanation of the supposed change in Holmes's views. And so there are several different accounts with a single conclusion.

The fundamental objection to *Schenck* seems to be that Holmes treated speech as a form of activity that had practical consequences, and so at least with regard to its intended effects speech was not entitled to protection greater than that afforded to other types of behavior. It was only to honest expressions of ideas, considered as such, that Holmes believed the Constitution extended near-absolute guarantees.

The late Harry Kalven, a leading revisionist, complained that Holmes washed out the political element of speech entirely: he put the speech of Eugene Debs, a national party candidate for president, on the same footing as a cry of "fire!" in a theater.[246] One encounters the same difficulty, if it is one, in many of Holmes's opinions. He resolutely refused to consider the political context. That refusal seemed to Ernst Freund, Harry Kalven, and other revisionists to require an explanation. It seemed remarkable to them that Holmes should insist on treating Eugene Debs as if he had counseled robbery rather than draft resistance, just as it had seemed incredible to other critics that Holmes would insist on treating the Northern Securities Company as if it were a small

---

[245] Appendix infra.

[246] See Harry Kalven, *A Worthy Tradition* (1988); Kalven, *Professor Ernst Freund and Debs v United States*, 40 U Chi L Rev 235 (1973).

exporting grocer.[247] But that detachment is what Holmes deeply believed his duty as a judge required of him.

XIV. THE IMPORTANCE OF MOTIVE

At least some contemporary commentators saw well enough that the point of difference between Holmes and the majority of his Court was on a narrow question, the precise intent required to be shown before speech could be punished. Zechariah Chafee, in his articles at the time praising Holmes, and Day Kimball, a young critic who was about to begin his clerkship with Holmes, saw that *Schenck* was an extension of the common law of attempts; Chafee even noticed the similarity in language and holding to Holmes's opinion in the Massachusetts attempted arson case, *Commonwealth v Peaslee*.[248] Each saw that a showing of intent was required by Holmes's opinion for the Court in *Schenck*, and that the outcome in *Abrams*, where Holmes dissented, depended on the question, not clearly resolved in *Schenck*, whether the First Amendment allowed reliance on intent proven by an external standard, or whether it also required the government to prove that the defendants acted on a motive to bring about wrongdoing or harm of the kind specifically and lawfully prohibited by Congress.

In *Abrams*, the majority opinion by Justice Clarke made it plain what issue divided them. According to Clarke, while there was evidence of the motive that Holmes demanded, the defendants might have been convicted on the external standard alone. The Espionage Act required that it be shown the defendants intended to injure the war effort; but by an external standard, as Holmes himself had once insisted, this "intent" did not refer to the defendants' actual state of mind, it was only a shorthand term for the general doctrine that one might be held liable for any harms that an ordinary person would have foreseen:[249]

---

[247] *Northern Securities Co. v United States*, 193 US 197, 401 (1904) (Holmes dissenting).

[248] Chafee, *Freedom of Speech in Wartime*, 32 Harv L Rev 932, 963 (1919). Not everyone agreed; see Corwin, *Constitutional Law in 1919–1920*, 14 Am Pol Sci Rev 635, 637 (1920) (clear and present danger "made up out of whole cloth").

[249] *Abrams*, 250 US 616, 621 (1919). In Day Kimball's note, defending the position of the majority of the Court, he argued that the common law of attempts met the constitutional standard established in *Schenck*, and that this required no more than a showing of intent by an external standard. Note, *The Espionage Act and the Limits of Legal Toleration*, 33 Harv L Rev 442, 444–45 (1920).

> It will not do to say, as is now argued [in Holmes's dissent], that the only intent of these defendants was to prevent injury to the Russian cause. Men must be held to have intended, and to be accountable for, the effects which their acts were likely to produce.

Clarke might have been quoting *The Common Law*. But Holmes, as we have seen, had broadened his perspective in the 1890s, and had come to think that, in addition to the external standard, the defendant's state of mind should be considered in cases of privilege, to determine whether a privilege to do foreseeable harm had been overcome by malice. He accordingly dissented in *Abrams*, and said that the Constitution required that a specific, subjective intent to bring about a forbidden result must be shown, before a conviction could be sustained under the doctrine of *Schenck*.[250]

To see why this seemingly narrow question should have had such significance, it will help to follow the later cases in some detail. Three more cases of wartime dissent were decided after *Abrams*, the first two under the federal Espionage Act,[251] and the third under a Minnesota statute.[252] Justice Brandeis wrote dissents in the Espionage Act cases, asserting that the government's evidence was not adequate under the clear and present danger standard; and Holmes joined in these dissents.[253]

In *Schaeffer v United States*,[254] newspaper articles were found by a jury to be false statements published with intent to obstruct the draft, in violation of the Espionage Act. The Supreme Court upheld the convictions, and Brandeis dissented on the ground there was no evidence that the articles objectively posed a clear and present danger of obstructing recruitment. Defendants' intent was not at issue.

In the second of the federal cases, *Pierce v United States*,[255] how-

---

[250] 250 US at 627–28; Chafee, *A Contemporary State Trial: The United States versus Jacob Abrams, et al.*, 33 Harv L Rev 747, 751–54 (1920). Chafee noted pointedly that Learned Hand was cited approvingly by the majority in favor of their strict liability standard, id at 752 n 7. Chafee's first article, on the *Schenck* case (32 Harv L Rev 932 (1919)), was approvingly cited shortly thereafter, in Justice Brandeis's dissent in which Holmes concurred, in *Schaeffer v United States*, 251 US 466, 486 (1920).

[251] *Pierce v United States*, 252 US 239 (1920); *Schaeffer v United States*, 251 US 466 (1920).

[252] *Gilbert v Minnesota*, 254 US 325 (1921).

[253] 252 US at 253; 251 US at 482.

[254] 251 US 466 (1920).

[255] 252 US 239 (1920).

ever, evidence of intent was critical. Defendants were officers of a
branch of the Socialist Party in Albany, New York, and were
charged with distributing a pamphlet, "The Price We Pay," with
intent to obstruct the draft and the war effort. The defendants'
intent was hotly disputed. The pamphlet was described as recruiting literature for the Socialist Party, intended to draw people to
socialism by showing that the war was a product of capitalism, and
that a socialist government would have kept the peace. The pamphlet itself was the principal evidence of intent, and the Court held
that while the pamphlet might aid the Socialist Party, it would
thereby also hinder the war effort. Mahlon Pitney, for the majority, stated the external standard once more: the government was
required to prove only that the language of an anti-war pamphlet
"itself furnished a ground for attributing to [the defendants] an
intent to bring about . . . such consequences as reasonably might
be anticipated from its distribution."[256]

Brandeis, with Holmes joining, argued in dissent that the standard established in *Schenck* required proof of actual, specific intent
to hinder the war effort as such, proof that was lacking in this case.
Brandeis and Holmes expressly compared the *Schenck* standard to
the actual malice required to defeat a claim of privilege in a libel
action.[257]

In the third case, *Gilbert v Minnesota*,[258] discussed above, intent
was not the issue, and prosecution had been under a state statute.
The majority affirmed the conviction, and Holmes concurred in
the result;[259] Brandeis dissented alone.[260]

In the whole line of cases from *Schenck* through *Gilbert*, Holmes's
position remained stubbornly fixed. Because he rested his dissents

---

[256] Id at 249.

[257] Id 269–72.

[258] 254 US 325 (1921).

[259] 254 US at 334.

[260] Id at 341. See note 243. Brandeis argued for a more stringent limitation on state action
in peacetime—based on the privileges and immunities of United Sates citizens, which
Brandeis suggested for the first time created a zone of "privacy" into which no government
could intrude in peacetime—than the Court had established in *Schenck* for the federal government at war. Brandeis abandoned this line of argument after this dissent, and returned to
Holmes's clear and present danger standard for state as well as federal law, but advanced a
similar privacy notion based on the Fourth and Fifth Amendments in *Olmstead v United
States*, 277 US 438, 470 (1928) (Holmes dissenting), where Holmes again declined to accept
Brandeis's expansive doctrine.

on the narrowest available ground, his difference with the majority usually could be expressed in a single point of doctrine: the question of motive.

But the underlying difference between Holmes and the Court lay deeper. Proof of subjective intent would have required attention to the unique defendants and the particular circumstances of individual cases. In Holmes's view, stated in all the criminal attempt and conspiracy cases from *Kennedy* to *Schenck*, it was only these particular circumstances that the Court had a right to consider in determining whether there had been a clear and present danger of harm.

The majority of the Court avoided such particularized deliberation by applying an external standard, based on the defendants' words cut free from their immediate context. This allowed the majority to turn its attention to broader, quasi-legislative questions of policy.

In the realm of policy, there was no real dispute that civil unrest and dissent, if unchecked, might have hindered the war effort. Holmes himself was incensed by railroad strikes and threats of a general strike.[261] Holmes and the majority probably also agreed, although it is more difficult to be sure about this point, that the radical political movement that generally opposed the war, and of which Abrams and his fellow defendants were a small part, posed a threat—even a clear and present danger—of obstructing the war effort. Holmes in any case would have deferred to the factual determination of a judge or legislature on such a question.

In *Schenck* and *Pierce*, the pamphlets distributed by the defendants were copies of literature being distributed in large numbers by national organizations. In *Abrams*, the leaflets were filled with familiar, stereotyped harangues, and the defendants plainly considered themselves part of a larger revolutionary movement. By looking at the language of the pamphlets alone in these cases, cut free from motives and circumstances in each, the Court majority allowed itself to consider the danger posed by the political movement as a whole. It treated the stereotyped vocabulary of the political

---

[261] Holmes to Lewis Einstein, October 12, 1914, *Holmes-Einstein Letters* 100 (Peabody ed. St. Martin's Press, 1964); Holmes to Felix Frankfurter, March 27, 1917, Holmes Papers (cited in note 10).

left as a forbidden category or form of expression, and held the defendants strictly liable for using it.

Justice Clarke, speaking for the *Abrams* Court, for instance, quoted liberally from articles found in the defendants' possession but written by others. These articles may have been relevant to the defendants' intent, but by quoting from them at length, Clarke seemed to treat the defendants as representatives of a movement, and to affirm their guilt simply for using the movement's language. To the majority it did not seem that the defendants had been held guilty for expressing ideas, but only for lending their support, however small, to a criminal enterprise. In contrast to Clarke's method, Holmes's insistence on proof of both the defendants' subjective intent to cause wrongdoing or harm, and proof that on objective grounds the forbidden result was dangerously near in the circumstances of the case, would have required the Court to focus on the liberty of the individual defendants, rather than on a form or manner of expression.

Holmes's doctrine was not always very protective of freedom of expression, as the results in *Schenck*, *Frohwerk*, and *Debs* amply attest. But by insisting on attention to the particular circumstances and motives of the defendant, Holmes refused to sacrifice the liberties of the individual, such as they were, to the administrative convenience of the state.

XV. SANFORD AND BRANDEIS

Within a year after *Pierce*, *Schaeffer*, and *Gilbert*, there had been a profound change in the makeup of the Court, but the fundamental division on First Amendment cases remained.

Former President William Howard Taft was appointed Chief Justice in 1921, and he energetically assisted the President in filling seats on the Court that quickly became vacant. Peirce Butler, George Sutherland, and Edward T. Sanford joined him, and Willis Van DeVanter—whom Taft himself had appointed—made a comfortable majority of like-minded, able men. They were an unusually powerful group, including as they did both a former President and a former chairman of the Senate judiciary committee. Taft masterfully managed their dealings with Congress and the executive branch, and by 1925 the Chief Justice was at the head of a unified federal judiciary.[262] The Court was in control of its docket through the newly authorized expansion of the writ of certiorari, and could choose the questions of policy on which it would focus. Through Taft's efforts, the Court soon would have a new building, and the justices each would have offices and a staff; the Court would be in practice as well as theory an equal branch of government.[263]

The prosecution of dissidents continued through the 1920s. Twenty states adopted peacetime statutes prohibiting sedition, criminal anarchy, or "syndicalism," a radical creed identified with the Industrial Workers of the World.[264] The first appeals from peacetime prosecutions under these statutes came to the Supreme Court in 1925, when Taft's new majority was securely in place. The Taft Court quickly put the categorization approach to sedition cases on a firmer footing than their predecessors had succeeded in doing.

Benjamin Gitlow, an officer of the tiny, nascent Communist party was convicted of advocating criminal anarchism in violation of a New York statute. The violation consisted in the publication of a "Left Wing Manifesto" and other documents that in plain, if turgid, Leninist language called for overthrow of the United States government by force.

Justice Sanford, writing for the seven members of the Court who had voted to affirm Gitlow's conviction, now made powerfully explicit what had lain submerged in *Abrams*. Gitlow had been convicted, not because he himself had been shown to threaten or even to desire an immediate insurrection, but because the New York legislature had determined that the forms of language he had used posed a danger to the state. Assuming that freedom of speech was protected against state action by the Due Process Clause of the Fourteenth Amendment, as it was protected against federal action by the First, the Court nevertheless upheld the constitutionality of the convictions.[265]

Justice Sanford emphasized that the New York statute was not construed to prohibit the expression of ideas or opinions as such,

---

[262] Frankfurter and Landis, *The Business of the Supreme Court* (cited in note 91).

[263] A. T. Mason, *William Howard Taft, Chief Justice* (Simon & Schuster, 1965).

[264] See *Brandenburg v Ohio*, 395 US 444, 447 (1969).

[265] *Gitlow*, 268 US at 670.

but was directed only against "advocacy," which the Court took to be equivalent to incitement of crime.[266] By an external standard, the language of the "Left Wing Manifesto" was shown to contain language of "direct incitement,"[267] and both the statute and the prosecution under it would pass muster under the First Amendment, even if it were made applicable to the states by the Fourteenth. Justice Sanford wrote for the majority:[268]

> That utterances inciting to the overthrow of organized government by unlawful means, present a sufficient danger of substantive evil to bring their punishment within the range of legislative discretion, is clear. Such utterances, by their very nature, involve danger to the public peace and to the security of the State. They threaten breaches of the peace and ultimate revolution. And the immediate danger is none the less real and substantial, because the effect of a given utterance cannot be accurately foreseen. The State cannot reasonably be required to measure the danger from every such utterance in the nice balance of a jeweler's scale. A single revolutionary spark may kindle a fire that, smoldering for a time, may burst into a sweeping and destructive conflagration. It cannot be said that the State is acting arbitrarily or unreasonably when in the exercise of its judgment as to the measures necessary to protect the public peace and safety, it seeks to extinguish the spark without waiting until it has enkindled the flame or blazed into the conflagration.
>
>   . . . . And the general statement in the *Schenck Case* that the "question in every case is whether the words are used in such circumstances and are of such a nature as to create a clear and present danger" . . . has no application to [cases] like the present, where the legislative body itself has previously determined the danger of substantive evil arising from utterances of a specified character.

When *Gitlow* was decided in 1925, Holmes was eighty-four years old. More than forty years before, he himself had called attention to the fundamentally legislative character of privileges, and had repeatedly counseled deference to the legislature on such questions of policy. He agreed that the fundamental principles of free speech taken from the evolving common law were incorporated in both

---

[266] Id at 664–65.

[267] Id at 665.

[268] Id at 669 (emphasis added).

the First Amendment and the Due Process Clause of the Fourteenth. He dissented from the majority's conclusion as to what
those principles required, but he had no adequate response to Sanford's argument, and was reduced to reiterating—in moving, mem-
orable language to be sure—his doctrine of the clear and present
danger.[269]

As to the external standard submitted to the jury in this case,
which allowed them to find that the language of the publication
considered alone was an "incitement," Holmes had only his famous
but unhelpful dictum, "every idea is an incitement."[270] But surely
some forms of expressions were greater incitements than others,
and Holmes was a lifelong enemy of the argument, "Where will
you draw the line?"[271] He insisted without explanation that the
only permissible way of distinguishing true incitements to crime
from other expressions of ideas was to consider the circumstances
of the particular case in isolation. "[W]hatever may be thought of
the redundant discourse before us it had no chance of starting a
present conflagration."[272] If the whole category of expression was
dangerous—well, that was the sort of danger the First Amendment
required us to tolerate: "If in the long run the beliefs expressed in
proletarian dictatorship are destined to be accepted by the dominant forces of the community, the only meaning of free speech is
that they should be given their chance and have their way."[273] This
was nobly and memorably said. But, Holmes neither addressed
nor answered the argument that the legislature had the power to
identify categories of peculiarly hazardous forms of speech that
threatened to cause, not peaceful political change, but crime.

Two years later, in *Whitney v California*,[274] Justice Brandeis attempted a different form of reply to Sanford. Whitney had been
convicted of violating the California Criminal Syndicalism Act,
which was closely similar to New York's Criminal Anarchy statute.

---

[269] Id at 673 (Holmes dissenting).

[270] Id.

[271] See, e.g., Holmes to Herbert J. Croly, May 12, 1919, 1 *Holmes-Laski Letters* 202, 203
(cited in note 170): "for thirty years I have made my brethren smile by insisting [the law]
to be everywhere a matter of degree."

[272] *Gitlow*, 268 US at 673.

[273] Id.

[274] 274 US 357 (1927).

The opinion for the majority upholding the conviction was again written by Justice Sanford. He repeated the argument that speech that fell within a reasonable legislative category could be punished in and of itself, with no showing of clear and present danger in the circumstances.[275]

There had been evidence, on which the conviction might have rested, that activities of the Communist Labor Party posed a danger of violence, and Whitney failed to argue that her own activities in themselves did not pose a clear and present danger.[276] Holmes and Brandeis both concurred in upholding the conviction, but Justice Brandeis wrote a concurring opinion, in which Holmes joined, to answer Sanford's argument and to insist on the application of the *Schenck* doctrine:[277]

> It is said to be the function of the legislature to determine whether at a particular time and under the particular circumstances the formation of, or assembly with, a society organized to advocate criminal syndicalism constitutes a clear and present danger of substantive evil; and that by enacting the law here in question the legislature of California determined that question in the affirmative. Compare Gitlow v New York . . . .

Brandeis said that the Court alone should determine whether the danger *in the circumstances* would justify the curtailment of the defendant's right of free speech. The basis of his argument was that freedom of expression had a fundamental value which had not yet been mentioned in the opinions of the Court. True, the contest of ideas was a method for shaping practical legislation, but this was not the only value of free expression:[278]

> Those who won our independence believed that the final end of the State was to make men free to develop their faculties . . . . They valued liberty both as an end and as a means. They believed liberty to be the secret of happiness and courage to be the secret of liberty. They believed that freedom to think as

---

[275] Id at 371–72.

[276] Holmes would not go on disputing a point of law once it had been settled by repeated decisions of the Court. The logic of Brandeis's opinion seems to point toward a dissent (surely it is the prosecutor's responsibility to offer evidence of a clear and present danger, not the defendant's responsibility to deny it) but Holmes was probably unwilling to join a dissent at such a late date and Brandeis may have concurred in order to gain his support.

[277] *Whitney*, 274 US at 374 (Brandeis concurring).

[278] Id at 375 (Brandeis concurring).

you will and to speak as you think are means indispensable to
the discovery and spread of political truth . . . [but also] that
the greatest menace to freedom is an inert people; that public
discussion is a political duty; and that this should be a fundamental principle of the American government.

Freedom of speech therefore was not only a means, it was an end
in itself: it was a form of the self-realization that was a fundamental
purpose of the American state. This freedom could not be restricted simply on ordinary legislative grounds; it could only be
restricted in a particular case after weighing the individual liberty
it was designed to protect.[279] This argument touched for the first
time on the fundamental importance of the individualized nature
of the clear-and-present-danger standard, and Holmes joined in
Brandeis's opinion—which he did not do lightly, even at this late
stage in his career.[280] But I do not think that Brandeis's answer was
entirely Holmes's.

The question had come up between them before. Holmes had
relentlessly ridiculed the antitrust statutes as both foolish and futile; the Sherman Act, Holmes remarked, commanded everyone to
fight but forbade anyone to be victorious.[281]

Brandeis's answer had always been that the antitrust laws (which
he had in part written) were not solely economic measures; they
were also political measures designed to preserve the freedom and
autonomy of a modern yeomanry—artisans, union members, and
small business people—against the power of the trusts. Brandeis
thought it was a part of the task of government to foster the virtues

---

[279] The last link in Brandeis's argument—the reason why his rationale for free speech
requires individualized adjudication and forbids Justice Sanford's strict liability—is not
explicitly made, and I have interpolated what seems to me implicit. Brandeis's dissents in
Gilbert and *Olmstead* seem to support this reading, but Brandeis plainly was still uncomfortable with clear and present danger and I suppose would have preferred a more straightforward approach to a right of privacy or self-realization, if he had been able to secure Holmes's
support. Professor, later Judge, Bork denied on related grounds that Brandeis had given
any adequate answer to Sanford; Bork denied that speech had any special role, more than
other forms of behavior, in self-realization. See Bork, *Neutral Principles and Some First Amendment Problems*, 47 Ind L J 1, 25 (1971).

[280] Holmes did not join Brandeis's dissenting opinions in *Gilbert v Minnesota*, 254 US 325
(1920) or *Olmstead v United States*, 277 US 438 (1928), in both of which Brandeis argued for
a right of personal freedom or "privacy" that was not anchored in specific provisions of the
constitution.

[281] Quoted by Holmes's former law clerk Francis Biddle. F. Biddle, *Justice Holmes, Natural
Law, and the Supreme Court* 9 (Macmillan, 1961).

of citizens of the Republic, a class of independent freeholders who might be poor but would stand up against the swollen institutions of big government and big business.[282]

Holmes thought Brandeis's vision of small-scale republican institutions attractive, but he did not agree that the Constitution had in it any program of social reform.[283] So I do not think Holmes entirely accepted Brandeis's argument in Whitney. But Brandeis had at last touched the core of Holmes's decisions, the protection of individual liberty against the administrative state that had been born in the First World War.

XVI. The Vitality of "Clear and Present Danger"

That was the end of Holmes's part of the story, and perhaps we should stop there. After joining in Brandeis's concurring opinion in *Whitney*, Holmes did not add anything of significance to the doctrine of the clear and present danger. A few earlier opinions perhaps do cast side-lights on his thinking. In 1921, Holmes said in dissent that the First Amendment forbade the Postmaster General from withholding a newspaper's second class privileges because of the paper's anticipated content;[284] but in this dissent there was no need to say anything more than that the First Amendment prohibited prior restraints on expression. Holmes's famous dissent on behalf of Rosika Schwimmer's right to be admitted to citizenship ("not free thought for those who agree with us but freedom for the thought that we hate"),[285] as I have already noted, gave particularly vivid expression to the principle of freedom for dissenting thought, but the First Amendment was not involved.

In another well-know line of dissents, Holmes suggested limits on judges' summary contempt power, in terms similar to "clear and present danger"—summary punishment of contempts of court was warranted only to prevent an "imminent possibility of obstruc-

---

[282] See Holmes to Harold J. Laski, January 1, 1923, 1 *Holmes-Laski Letters* 469 (cited in note 170) (quoting Brandeis); see T. McCraw, *Prophets of Regulation* 103–42 (1984).

[283] See Paul Freund, *Holmes and Brandeis in Retrospect*, Boston Bar J at 7, Sept.-Oct. 1984.

[284] *Milwaukee Social Democrat Pub. Co. v Burleson*, 255 US 407, 436 (1921) (Holmes dissenting) (tacitly abandoning the license-privilege distinction of *McAuliffe v Mayor of New Bedford*, 155 Mass 216 (1892)).

[285] *United States v Schwimmer*, 279 US 644, 655 (1929).

tion" of justice.[286] At issue in these cases was the defendant's right to procedural due process, but Holmes's view of the summary contempt power was eventually adopted by the Court,[287] and when reaffirming the clear-and-present-danger standard in *Dennis v United States*,[288] the Court cited the modern summary contempt cases among precedents favoring Holmes's view of the First Amendment.[289]

Holmes's views fell into neglect for a time. In 1932, he retired from the Court. Taft's majority was gone by 1937, but their New Deal replacements gratefully inherited the strong, policy-oriented institution Taft had built. In opinions on the First Amendment, the Court continued to use Sanford's categorization approach, and sometimes used it affirmatively to protect at least some favored categories of speech. By 1942, with *Chaplinsky v New Hampshire*,[290] the Court had erected an explicit scheme of categorization. Certain "well-defined and narrowly limited classes of speech" including "the lewd and obscene, the profane, the libelous, and the insulting or 'fighting' words'" fell outside the protection of the First Amendment, and so were within the legislative power of the states.[291] Advocacy of sedition, of course, also fell into an unprotected category.[292]

Chaplinsky was also quickly understood to mean, on the other hand, that political speech and other expressions of opinion and ideas that were not direct incitements to wrongdoing fell into a specially protected category.[293] The rule was thereafter said to be that a rarely surmounted standard of "compelling state interest" must be met before punishment could be authorized for speech that fell within a protected category—apparently without regard for the danger posed in particular circumstances.[294]

---

[286] See, e.g., *Toledo Newspaper Co. v United States*, 247 US 402, 422 (1918) (Holmes dissenting).

[287] *Nye v United States*, 313 US 33 (1941).

[288] 341 US 494, 508–11 (1951).

[289] Id at 507 n 5.

[290] 315 US 568 (1942).

[291] Id at 571–72.

[292] *Whitney v California*, 274 US 352 (1927).

[293] See, e.g., *West Virginia Board of Education v Barnette*, 319 US 624 (1943); *Terminiello v Chicago*, 337 US 1, 4–5 (1949).

[294] See *Elrod v Burns*, 427 US 347 (1976); *Buckley v Valeo*, 424 US 1 (1976); John Ely, *Democracy and Distrust* 113–15, 233–34 n 27 (Harvard, 1980); Lawrence Tribe, *American*

The categories of expression that the Court established were based on external standards applied to the words or forms of expression themselves, and left little room for consideration of particular circumstances in each case. Congress and the state legislatures appeared to be free to apply strict liability for any use of expressions in the prohibited categories. In upholding a statute that punished fighting words in *Chaplinsky*, for instance, the category consisted of words that would have an inflammatory effect on "men of common intelligence."[295] No evidence was required that the words were intended to cause a disturbance or that in the circumstances of the case they were likely to do so. When it came to define "obscenity," the Court adopted an external standard based on community values.[296] Once again, no evidence of risk of harm was required in the circumstances. In *Bellotti*, the Court separated the speech from the speaker entirely, and concluded that political speech—apparently any speech in connection with the governmental process—was protected in and of itself.[297]

Yet the Court occasionally returned to a version of clear and present danger. The most spectacular and controversial revival of Holmes's doctrine occurred in 1951, in *Dennis v United States*,[298] affirming the conviction of the leaders of the American Communist Party for violations of the Smith Act,[299] a federal statute, patterned after the state laws in *Whitney* and *Gilbert*, which forbade advocacy, or organizing a conspiracy to advocate, revolution.

Although no opinion commanded a majority of the Court, all the justices except Frankfurter and Black assumed that the outcome depended upon whether the defendants' conduct in the circumstances posed a clear and present danger of some harm that Congress had power to prohibit. Chief Justice Vinson, with whom

---

Constitutional Law 829–36 (Foundation Press, 2d ed 1988). Tribe treats clear and present danger as if the Court in each case determined whether expressions of the kind at issue posed a threat, making it a special, ad hoc, category of speech.

[295] 315 US 568, 573 (1942). Cf. *Terminiello v City of Chicago*, 337 US 1 (1949), where a statute was held invalid on its face because it incorrectly defined the category of fighting words.

[296] See *Paris Adult Theater v Slaton*, 413 US 49 (1973); *Roth v United States*, 354 US 476, 485 (1957, rejecting a clear-and-present-danger analysis offered in the court below, 237 F2d 796, 801–2 (2d Cir 1956) (Frank concurring); see Tribe, *American Constitutional Law* at 908 (2d ed, cited in note 294).

[297] 435 US at 777.

[298] 341 US 494 (1951).

[299] 54 Stat 671 (1940).

three other justices joined, said that the convictions could be affirmed on Holmes's original understanding of the standard in *Schenck*.[300]

Specific intent was taken as proved, since the defendants were the leaders of the Communist Party and their actual intent to carry out its expressed purposes by organizing the party and advocating its aims was not seriously at issue. The difficulty in the case concerned the external branch of the standard—there was no evidence in the trial record that the violent revolution which the Communist leaders advocated and presumably desired was at all likely to occur.[301]

In addressing this point the Chief Justice adopted reasoning that had first turned up in Holmes's Massachusetts attempt cases:[302] The serious nature of the harm that was feared outweighed the small chance that it would occur in the near future. In cases where violent insurrection was threatened, Vinson held, the government was not required to wait until the event was upon it, but could act as soon as a significant risk—in the form of a well-organized and active conspiracy—was clear and present.[303]

There was little evidence in the trial record of immediate danger posed by the Communist Party's activities; the government, however, had proven to a jury's satisfaction that the Party was a well-organized conspiracy whose plan was to act when the circumstances should be propitious, and that it therefore posed an unacceptable risk of grave harm.[304]

---

[300] 341 US at 505–10.

[301] Id at 588 (Douglas dissenting).

[302] This risk analysis had been applied to freedom of speech cases by both Sanford and Brandeis, see *Whitney*, 274 US at 372 (Brandeis and Holmes concurring), and adopted by Learned Hand in the court below in *United States v Dennis*, 183 F2d 201, 212 (2d Cir 1950) (Hand, J).

[303] 341 US at 510. Risk analysis is now a generalized method of approaching government regulation that Holmes to some degree anticipated. See *Toledo Newspaper Co. v United States*, 247 US 402 (1918); cf. *Commonwealth v Peaslee*, 177 Mass 267 (1901) (Holmes, J), and *Commonwealth v Kennedy*, 170 Mass 18 (1897) (Holmes, J) (the degree of risk that will justify a conviction for criminal attempts is a function of factors such as the defendant's intent and the gravity of the crime). See notes 64–69 and accompanying text.

[304] 342 US at 510–11. Justice Jackson, concurring in the result, appears to have accepted this reasoning but rejected the language of "clear and present danger." Jackson, fresh from the prosecution at Nuremburg, had no difficulty accepting that a political party might in fact be a criminal conspiracy. He would simply have held that organizing the conspiracy, and not the advocacy, was a crime. Id at 561. With his vote, a majority appeared to approve the reasoning, if not the label attached to it, in Vinson's opinion. Justice Douglas, dissenting,

It would seem, therefore, that in *Dennis* the Court returned to Holmes's doctrine, requiring proof of a clear and present danger posed by the particular acts of the defendants, and the specific intent to cause the harm that was threatened. The plurality added the gloss that the magnitude of the harm might be used to balance the probability of its coming to pass.[305]

Six years later, the Court reaffirmed these aspects of the reasoning of *Dennis*, in *Yates v United States*,[306] reversing the convictions of lower-echelon Communist Party functionaries. In *Yates*, the charge of organizing a conspiracy was barred by the statute of limitations,[307] and the Court was obliged to deal with the purported crime of advocacy alone. Justice Harlan's opinion for the Court took specific intent as proven, and the only remaining question was whether the defendants themselves had contributed culpably to the risk posed by the Party. The jury had been instructed to find only that the defendants advocated revolution, not that their advocacy had added to the risk of resulting wrongdoing. The Court accordingly reversed the convictions, relying in part on *Schenck*,[308] and said that it must be proven that the individual defendants had advocated action in a manner that might have brought it about, and had not merely advocated belief in a doctrine.[309] The Court, expressly reaffirming *Schenck* and *Dennis*, required the lower courts

---

also assumed that *Schenck* would govern the result, but declined to accept the plurality's view that an imminent risk of distant future harm met the *Schenck* standard, even in cases of very great potential harm. Id at 581. Only Justices Frankfurter and Black, from their different perspectives, argued over the power of Congress to prohibit a category of speech—advocacy of revolution—on legislative grounds. Justice Frankfurter concurred in the result, but relied on the majority opinions in *Gitlow* and *Whitney* and rejected Holmes's clear-and-present-danger standard, id at 542–46; Justice Black dissented, insisting that advocacy of revolt fell within the category of protected speech, id at 579.

[305] There was some commentary to the effect that clear and present danger had displaced Sanford's categorization method. As Professor Currie noted, "clear and present danger had become the test of convictions even under statutes specifically directed to subversive speech." Currie, *The Constitution in the Supreme Court* at 354 (cited in note 99). And as Yosal Rogat pointed out, by "modifying" the standard of clear and present danger in accordance with Learned Hand's opinion below, the Court had "reconstituted its original elements." Rogat, *The Judge as Spectator*, 31 U Chi L Rev 213, 215 n 11 (1964). Rogat was not claiming Holmes had been vindicated, he was heaping the coals of *Dennis* on Holmes's head. See, to the same effect, Bork, *Neutral Principles and Some First Amendment Problems*, 47 Ind L J at 23 ("The great Smith Act cases of the 1950's . . . mark the triumph of Holmes and Brandeis").

[306] 354 US 298 (1957).

[307] Id at 312.

[308] Id at 318.

[309] Id at 318–19.

to consider the danger posed in the circumstance by the defendants' overt acts in furtherance of the conspiracy.[310]

The Supreme Court confirmed this approach again in 1969, in *Brandenburg v Ohio*.[311] In *Brandenburg*, the Court restated the rule of *Dennis* and *Yates*, which to an innocent eye was also the rule of *Schenck*, Holmes's dissent in *Abrams*, and Brandeis's concurrence in *Whitney*:[312]

> [T]he constitutional guarantees of free speech and free press do not permit a State to forbid or proscribe advocacy of the use of force or of law violation except where such advocacy is directed to inciting or producing imminent lawless action and is likely to produce such action.

That is, a state may not proscribe a category of speech as such, but may punish speech of a particular kind only where it is intended to and does pose a specific threat. The words "directed to" clearly seem in this context to mean "aimed at" or "actually intended," and so understood this is the standard announced by Holmes in 1919.[313]

---

[310] Id at 319–27, 334. Justice Harlan spoke of the need to find incitement to action in particular words used by the defendants, and Professor Harry Kalven therefore argued that in *Yates* the Court had implicitly rejected the clear-and-present-danger standard in favor of Hand's categorization scheme—Kalven apparently assuming that only words of "direct incitement" would show the kind of advocacy called for by the Court—and thereby worked a sort of revolution in First Amendment jurisprudence. Harry Kalven, *A Worthy Tradition*, 211–22 (Harper & Row, 1988). With the greatest deference and respect to the late Professor Kalven, this view does not seem tenable. The Court, although never doctrinaire, certainly seemed to act in *Yates* as if it had adopted the Holmes-Brandeis standard, remanding some of the defendants for new trials to determine whether in the circumstances their advocacy was an incitement to crime or only exhortation to belief, which hardly sounds like a per se standard based on the words alone. 354 US at 331–33.

[311] 395 US 444 (1969) (per curiam).

[312] 395 US at 447. By this time, of course, the Court had applied the language of the First Amendment to the states through the due process clause of the Fourteenth Amendment.

[313] Professor Gunther insists, however, that under *Brandenburg*, a class of language, the language of "direct incitement," may be prohibited so long as an external threat in the circumstances is shown. In other words, Gunther argues, the Court had at last adopted Learned Hand's external standard, coupling it with a version of *Schenck*. Gunther, *Learned Hand and the Origins of Modern First Amendment Doctrine*, 27 Stan L Rev at 722, 754 (cited in note 217). For the life of me, I cannot see why the Court's phrase, "directed to inciting," should be taken to mean "words literally demanding the performance of a crime." The only natural interpretation of this phrase seems to be that it refers to the defendant's intent. Ely disagrees with Gunther, and argues that Brandenburg created a more general category of incitements, not tied to specific forms of words. Ely, *Democracy and Distrust* at 110. He doesn't explain how one can decide whether a particular expression is an incitement to wrongdoing.

In *New York Times v Sullivan*,[314] decided in 1964, the newspaper had carried an ad complaining of a police "wave of terror" against students who were conducting civil rights protests in Montgomery, Alabama. The county commissioner responsible for supervising the police sued for libel. The ad contained a number of admitted false statements, and an Alabama court awarded general and punitive damages.[315]

The Supreme Court reversed. Justice Brennan's opinion for the Court in some respects parallelled Holmes's opinions in *Abrams* and *Schenck*, but also cited the gloss put on them by Justice Brandeis in *Whitney v California*.[316]

Brennan's premise was that the people, not the government, were sovereign. The purpose of the First Amendment (made applicable to Alabama by the Fourteenth) was to ensure free and open criticism by the people of the government and its officials.[317] This was a new rationale for the First Amendment. Holmes had imagined a battlefield or a marketplace, and Brandeis a solitary freeholder, master in his own house; Brennan's vision was of a community of equals: a town meeting.[318]

Yet the substance of the doctrine was the same. The protection afforded by the First Amendment was not absolute, Brennan continued; there were many well recognized exceptions. But the state could not take a case out of the protection of the Constitution just by putting a label on it and placing it in a disfavored category. State charges of "libel" were no more insulated from constitutional restraint than claims of "insurrection," advocacy of unlawful acts, or contempts of court. Drawing the now-familiar analogy between liability for criticism of public officials and contempts of court that had originated in Holmes's opinions in contempt cases, Brennan said that "such repression can be justified, if at all, only by a clear and present danger" in the circumstances of the case itself.[319]

---

[314] 376 US 254 (1964).

[315] Id at 256.

[316] Id at 270.

[317] Id at 269–70.

[318] Id; see also, William Brennan, *Address*, 32 Rutgers L Rev 173 (1979).

[319] 376 US at 273. It is worth noting that Brennan at about this time began dissenting from the Court's categorization approach to obscenity. See *Paris Adult Theater v Slaton*, 413 US 49, 97 (1973) (Brennan dissenting).

A critical question in setting constitutional limits was the defendant's state of mind. Even false statements about public figures were privileged unless made with actual malice—knowledge of falsity, or reckless disregard for the truth.[320]

The similarity to the clear-and-present-danger standard was striking. Indeed, as we have seen, Brandeis and Holmes, dissenting in *Pierce*, had drawn precisely this comparison forty years before. Holmes would have accepted Brennan's formulation as consistent with the common law: Falsity alone would not defeat the privilege accorded to the press at common law, so long as a publication was made in good faith; but actual malice—in the sense of a falsehood uttered knowingly or with reckless disregard of the truth—would overcome the privilege.[321]

Justice Brennan did not explicitly rest the requirement of actual malice on the common law; but he did cite the general trend of state libel law, without explaining why this was relevant.[322] Later, it is true, he sharply distinguished the constitutional requirement of "actual malice" from a supposed common-law "malice," equivalent to mere spite or ill will.[323] But however the common law may have been understood, in some jurisdictions in Brennan's day, his doctrine was substantially the same as Holmes's common law.

Which is not to suggest that Holmes necessarily anticipated the holding of *New York Times v Sullivan*, or that Justice Brennan was simply following Holmes's reasoning. But it is striking that the two justices, beginning from such different places, should have arrived at results that differed so little.

A final more recent example is provided by the flag-burning cases. In *Texas v Johnson*,[324] protestors had burned an American flag and had been convicted of violating a Texas statute that prohibited

[320] 376 US at 279–83.

[321] See id at 279; *Monitor Patriot Co. v Roy*, 401 US 265 (1971) (First Amendment privilege for petitions to government defeated by showing of actual malice).

[322] 376 US at 279–80. Justice Brennan believed that the Due Process Clause of the Fourteenth Amendment incorporated the Bill of Rights, as such, rather than any fundamental common-law principles underlying the amendments, and so it is not at all clear why tort law should have any relevance here except on pure policy grounds. See id at 295–96 (Black concurring), arguing that the Fourteenth Amendment contains the literal terms of First, without any common-law limitations.

[323] See *Rosenbloom v Metromedia, Inc.*, 403 US 29, 52 n 18 (1971) (Brennan plurality opinion).

[324] 491 US 397 (1989).

desecration of a "venerated object."[325] The protest occurred during the Republican National Convention in 1984. Republican television advertising had relied heavily on images of the flag. The protestors, by publicly burning a flag, forcefully expressed their dislike for the message of the Republican campaign, the Reagan Administration, and its supposed corporate backers, and secured extensive free television coverage for their counter-message.

Writing for a bare majority, and without referring expressly to that case, Brennan applied the *Schenck* analysis. Flag burning, although a form of expression, was not necessarily protected under the Fourteenth and First Amendments. In some circumstances Texas might punish flag burning—if the burning threatened to trigger "imminent" disorder, for instance.[326] No such harms were threatened in this case, however, and the prosecution could not be sustained. Rather, Justice Brennan concluded, the facts were very like the situation in *Abrams:* the protestors, whatever their intent, could not have achieved the kind of harm that the government had a right to forbid.[327]

XVII. The Meaning of "Clear and Present Danger"

The few examples that we have considered—*Dennis, Sullivan,* and the flag-burning case *Texas v Johnson*—show that the Court sometimes still turns to an analysis like Holmes's. This is striking, especially when we think that clear and present danger was very deeply rooted in Holmes's own history, in a common-law analysis and a Malthusian rationale that would be rejected now if they had not been forgotten. First Amendment jurisprudence has grown and ramified in other directions, and has developed its own language and its own themes.

It might be possible to show that Holmes's and Sanford's ideas still move and clash beneath the highly technical forms of modern First Amendment jurisprudence, but this is not the place for such a demonstration. For the present, *Dennis, Sullivan,* and *Johnson* sim-

---

[325] Id at 400.

[326] Id at 409.

[327] Id at 418–19. Because of the lack of evidence of any specific threat, Brennan had no need to discuss the defendant's intent.

ply mark points at which the Court has turned to something like Holmes's doctrine, reinventing clear and present danger.

This process of reinventing it in new circumstances helps us to see what the doctrine, fundamentally, means. I would therefore like to consider two much humbler examples—cases from lower courts that may already have been superceded when these words are published, but which nicely show how Holmes's approach differed from Sanford's, and what that difference meant.

In the first example, *In re the Welfare of R.A.V.*,[328] the Supreme Court of Minnesota upheld St. Paul's hate-crime ordinance, which forbade among other things public display of burning crosses and "Nazi swastikas." The court held that the St. Paul ordinance did not violate the First Amendment because it was to be applied only in circumstances such that, if the symbols are displayed, "one knows or should know [they] will create anger, alarm or resentment based on racial, ethnic, gender or religious bias."[329] The prohibited displays, construed in this way, fell within an unprotected category of expressions.[330] The second branch of this holding adds a gloss of categorization language, but a *Schenck* test must be met first—the defendant's acts must have posed a clear and present danger *in the circumstances*.

The second example, which concerns pornography, is a marked contrast. "Pornography" in this sense is defined as words or pictures that are used to dominate women, and to sexualize the domination.[331] Like the burning cross and swastika, pornography is part of a sometimes violent system of oppression.

A leading proponent of laws to punish damaging pornography has been Catherine A. MacKinnon, who relies on the system of categorization for her argument. To MacKinnon, the case for regulating pornography is far stronger than that for regulating obscenity, traditionally held to be outside the protection of the First Amendment.[332]

---

[328] *In re the Welfare of R.A.V.*, 464 NW2d 507, 510 (1991), certiorari granted, 111 S Ct 2795 (1991).

[329] Id. Citing *Texas v Johnson*, 491 US 397 (1989) rather than *Schenck*.

[330] 464 NW2d at 507, citing *Brandenburg v Ohio*, 395 US 444 (1969). The case has been argued but not decided by the Supreme Court at this writing.

[331] Andrea Dworkin, *Pornography: Men Possessing Women* (1981); see also Catherine MacKinnon, *Pornography, Civil Rights, and Speech*, 20 Harv CR-CL L Rev 1 (1985).

[332] MacKinnon, id at 21–22.

> Obscenity . . . is a moral idea; an idea about judgments of good and bad. Pornography, by contrast, is a political practice, a practice of power and powerlessness. . . . Nudity, excess of candor, arousal or excitement, prurient appeal, illegality of the acts depicted, and unnaturalness or perversion are all qualities that bother obscenity law when sex is depicted or portrayed. Sex forced on real women so that it can be sold at a profit to be forced on other real women; women's bodies trussed and maimed and raped and made into things to be hurt and obtained and accessed and this presented as the nature of women in a way that is acted on and acted out over and over; the coercion that is visible and the coercion that has become invisible—this and more bothers feminists about pornography. Obscenity as such probably does little harm. Pornography is integral to attitudes and behaviors of violence and discrimination which define treatment and status of half the population.

Andrea Dworkin and MacKinnon have drafted a municipal ordinance which gives women injured by sex discrimination (or other persons injured as women are) a cause of action against those who make or traffic in any pornography that contributes to the injury, or that in itself constitutes an act of sexual subordination. Such an ordinance was adopted by the city of Indianapolis, and struck down as unconstitutional by the Seventh Circuit Court of Appeals.[333]

At first glance, the Indianapolis ordinance seems more narrowly drawn than St. Paul's. Pornography by definition is part of actual, continuing oppression, and not like a swastika, a reminder of distant horrors. The pornography ordinance applies only in cases where the plaintiff has been injured and where there is evidence that the pornography caused or contributed to the injury. It would seem a prime candidate for approval under the same analysis with which the Supreme Court of Minnesota upheld St. Paul's hate-crime ordinance, or the *Schenck*-type analysis of *Texas v Johnson*.

But *Schenck* is not the ground on which such ordinances are defended. MacKinnon relies on the categorization argument, perhaps because of the enforcement scheme she favors. MacKinnon argues that state antipornography laws are authorized by the Fourteenth Amendment's guarantee of equal protection of the laws; she would

---

[333] *American Booksellers Assoc. v Hudnut*, 771 F2d 323 (7th Cir 1985).

treat pornography and rape as cases of sex discrimination,[334] and the Indianapolis ordinance has an administrative enforcement system, similar to that widely used to process claims of racial discrimination.

The reason that pornography has been placed within the category of protected speech, according to MacKinnon, rather than beyond the pale like obscenity, is that our legal system does not recognize sexual subordination as an injury. The law itself is part of the system of subordination of women.[335] Judge Easterbrook, writing for a unanimous panel of the Seventh Circuit, to some degree accepted this analysis. Pornography, he agreed, was part of the system of subordination of women. As such, it was a form of political speech and afforded near-absolute protection.[336] In Easterbrook's view, categories of unprotected speech like obscenity and sedition were neutral as to the content of particular works. A prohibition of pornography would not be neutral in this sense, apparently because it defines sexual oppression as an injury: "Indianapolis has created an approved point of view and so loses the support of these cases [establishing disfavored categories of expression]."[337]

Holmes's doctrine, while equally a product of a male-dominated system of law,[338] is more at ease with the punishment of pornographers. In upholding St. Paul's hate-crime ordinance under a version of the *Schenck* doctrine, for instance, the Minnesota Supreme Court seemed to recognize that the effect of race hatred was a harm the legislature had power to prevent. Liability, accordingly, might be imposed for expressive acts, notwithstanding their political content, when they caused or imminently threatened such harm.

Yet neither the Indianapolis pornography ordinance nor the St. Paul hate-crimes law quite met Holmes's test, unless altered by construction. The difficulty, once again, was that each created a

---

[334] See MacKinnon, *The Palm Beach Hanging*, The New York Times, December 15, 1991, E15; "Pornography as Defamations and Discrimination," 71 Bos U L Rev 793 (1991).

[335] C. MacKinnon, *Toward a Feminist Theory of the State*, 167–70, 195–214 (1989).

[336] *American Bookseller Assoc. v Hudnut*, 771 F2d at 331–32.

[337] Id at 332.

[338] MacKinnon points out, and I imagine Holmes would have agreed, that the vocabulary of neutral objectivity and causation-of-harm, the whole fabric of tort law on which Holmes's jurisprudence is based, is a product of a male-dominated system. Holmes had no problem with this, however. Compare MacKinnon, *Toward a Feminist Theory of the State* at 195–214 with Novick, *Holmes's Philosophy*, 1992 Wash U L Q (forthcoming).

category of expression punishable without regard to actual intent. Under the doctrine of *Schenck*, however, a prosecutor would be obliged to prove in every case, not only that the defendant made or trafficked in pornography that was present at the scene of the crime, but that he *intentionally* had created a clear and present danger.[339] Construed in this way, prohibitions of pornography or racial epithets would be difficult to enforce, except in egregious cases; but they would pose little danger of repressive censorship— suppressing serious works of art, for instance.

These cases cast retrospective light on the differences between Holmes's doctrine of the clear and present danger, and Sanford's categorization method. Holmes's doctrine was not necessarily more protective of freedom of expression. His doctrine did, however, resist the sacrifice of individual liberty to the needs of the administrative state, whether radical or liberal, feminist or paternalistic. From Holmes's perspective, freedom of speech was a limited and specific liberty; but such as it was, it took precedence over any of the other forms of government.

XVIII. CONCLUSION

Recall there were two strands of Holmes's thought. First, there was Holmes's theory of the social policy on which he believed the privilege accorded to free speech was based. Second, there was the justification Holmes gave for restraints on the privilege.

As to the first, Holmes's theory of the First Amendment was that among the "relatively fundamental" principles of the common law, embedded in the evolving Constitution, were freedom of speech and of the press. It was Holmes's conviction that legal protection for such individual freedoms was not based upon supralegal Rights of Man, but was logically and historically derived from the self-restraint of the governing power. Self-restraint, Holmes believed, could be based only on self-interest; the relentless operation of natural selection would extinguish any other motive.

But on grounds of self-interest alone, the governing power ought not to allow experiments with ideas and laws designed and in-

---

[339] Assuming, that is (as Holmes did not), that the First Amendment applies in literal terms to local as well as federal law.

tended to ensure its destruction. From the perspective of the governing power's self-interest, there should never be freedom for the thought we hate, for the opinion that is fraught with death. Government is not a chess game, that one resigns without playing out the final moves. Holmes believed that peaceful competition would prepare the nation for international conflict, but this was not a reason for the government to capitulate without a violent struggle.

This, indeed, has always been the difficult question about free speech. Holmes's contemporaries on the Court, more consistent evolutionists than he, accepted the government's argument in *Abrams*, that the state had a right—even a duty—to ensure its own survival by repressing dangerous ideas.

Holmes, as we have seen, was perfectly aware of the difficulty. He felt that his own sense of duty, and the duties of his class, often called for self-sacrifice. His definition of a gentleman was someone who would die for a point of honor;[340] or for a feather.[341] The willingness of the soldier to die, and of the scholar, scientist, or judge to sacrifice themselves to truth, Holmes believed, must have an evolutionary basis. He compared these instincts with the behavior of the grub, that prepared a chamber for the winged thing that it was to be.[342] Evolution, Holmes came to believe, had purposes beyond the merely human, and the instinct of self-sacrifice somehow played its part in the larger design of the cosmos; but a soldier's duty was to do and die, without understanding the plan of battle.[343] This philosophy Holmes called "mystical materialism." To an observer who does not share his faith, Holmes's mysticism looks to be just his recognition of a dilemma in his thought and an expression of trust that the logical difficulty didn't matter.

There is a similar problem in the second strand of Holmes's thinking, his explanation for the limitations placed on free speech and all other rights. In *The Common Law*, Holmes had argued that

---

[340] Endlessly repeated in letters and speeches: e.g., "But if . . . the gentleman and the soldier is a survival, still it is a joy to some of us to see embodied in a lively picture man's most peculiar power—the power to deny the actual and to perish." Paul Bourget, Remarks at a Tavern Club Dinner, December 4, 1893, in Mark Howe, *Occasional Speeches of Justice Holmes*, 69, 70 (Harvard, 1962).

[341] ". . . a bit of red ribbon that a man would die to win. . . ." Harvard College in the War, Holmes, *Speeches*, 13, 14 (1913).

[342] Law and the Court, id at 98.

[343] See, e.g., The Soldier's Faith and Memorial Day, id.

privileges to do harm were extended for the sake of the social benefit of the behavior that was thereby encouraged. Competition in the marketplace was privileged even when it was carried on maliciously and for the sake of causing damage. (In a zero-sum world, as we would say now, the injury to the loser was as much the object of competition as the benefit to the winner.) Later in life, however, he changed his mind about this, and after a decade as a judge began to accept the reality behind the language of "actual malice:" A privilege would be withdrawn if it were used for a malicious motive.

Holmes was careful to find an instrumental rather than a moral justification for this concern with subjective motive, and so preserved the overall framework of his philosophy. He said the common law had judged the risk of harm from malicious motives to tip the balance of social advantage back against the privilege. "It seems to me hard," Holmes said, "for the law to recognize a privilege to induce unlawful conduct." Hard, indeed, but was the difficulty really a practical one? Judges often held that even lives might be sacrificed in the competition of the marketplace.[344] Indeed, tort law in Holmes's day seemed to be built around just this principle.[345] Why then should not the law accept the added increment of harm, if such there was, that came with more fierce competition, or even a malicious pleasure in victory? Were the judges' unconscious judgments of empirical advantage really so finely drawn?

Holmes's insistence that actual intent or malice would always defeat a privilege separated him from his own court. It was at the heart, as we have seen, of what was distinctive in his approach; and once again we find difficulties as we approach the heart of Holmes's theory.

It seems to me that the difficulties on both lines of Holmes's thought were related, that he answered them in the same way, and it is this reply that begins to explain the durability of his views. Holmes's answer was given in the Massachusetts labor cases and in his other writings on the judge's role: The true justification for the freedom accorded to ideas lay in the judge's duty to deal fairly

---

[344] As Holmes liked to repeat, a ship's officer was justified in closing a hatch to contain a fire, although a carpenter in the hold was smothered as a result. *Pierce v Cunard Steamship Co.*, 151 Mass 87 (1891).

[345] See *United Zinc & Chem. Co. v Britt*, 258 US 268 (1922) (Holmes, J).

with the parties before him. Freedom of speech was judge-made law. There were no statutes encouraging attacks on the government, no executive agencies devoted to protecting unpopular ideas. And Holmes was a judge above all. When the freedom of speech cases were decided he had been on the bench for nearly forty years. He had spent those years subordinating himself to his task. The judge's devotion to fairness was something fundamental to Holmes, an instinct to be accepted like the other data of natural history. Whatever he might have thought or said about the legislative policy that lay behind the common law, in the end he could do no other than to perform his fundamental function as a judge, to decide each case fairly—without regard to his own interests—whatever the ultimate consequences might be.

If freedom of speech rested on the duty of the judge to deal fairly, then it was easier to see why the privilege was particularly important in cases where the defendant's beliefs were freighted with death. It was especially then that the judge's sense of honor and duty was called upon. Frank Foster's plea for fair treatment for the trade unions counted most with Holmes, counted more than all the Spencers and Darwins in the world. This is why Holmes's words are so powerful; we see looming behind them, overshadowing all calculations of self-interest, a man who was prepared to die for freedom of speech, not because of its practical importance, but because that was his duty.

One can see, if freedom of speech is based on fairness, why the privilege would be destroyed by bad intent. The malicious party had sacrificed his claim to fair treatment; he came with unclean hands. And one can see why Holmes insisted on attention to the particular circumstances of the defendant's behavior. Twenty years as a judge in Massachusetts had taught him that fairness was not a question to be decided by abstract forms, but only in the concrete circumstances of particular cases. Legislative categories in themselves necessarily disregarded fairness in some individual cases,[346]

---

[346] See *Smith v Mayor and Alderman of Worcester*, 182 Mass 232 (1902); *Sears v Street Commissioners*, 180 Mass 274 (1902); *Lincoln v Board of Street Commissioners*, 176 Mass 210 (1900); *Carson v Sewerage Commissions of Boston*, 175 Mass 242 (1900). In these cases, the constitutional question was whether a street or sewer assessment was reasonably related to the benefits conferred, and hence not a taking of private property without compensation. Holmes's

and the question was where the constitution required one to drawn the line. "Clear and present danger" was just one of many shorthand expressions for this central idea, the point at which individual liberty was set aside by the importance of government interest.

Holmes insisted, not only that trials be conducted fairly, but that politics be conducted fairly, in the sense that the power of the state to do violence should not intrude on peaceful debate. The government must not sweep the pieces from the board and decide public questions by force. This notion of fairness was expressed in a particular doctrine, that an individual should be allowed to have his or her say unless, by seeking to subvert the system of peaceful discourse itself, by intending not persuasion but crime, he or she sacrificed all claim to fair treatment.

This was a position to which the Court has regularly if tacitly returned, and it shows that Holmes's greatness was also in a sense a judge's narrowness, his unwillingness to adopt exclusively legislative considerations, or to adopt the attitude of the executive.[347] To Holmes, law was what judges decided, and the rule of law meant a system of peaceful debate to which all individuals were admitted so long as they followed the rules, no matter how dangerous were their ideas, as such.

Anyone who violated the rules of honest discourse for the purpose of doing harm could be punished as a lawbreaker; but the expression of ideas as such could not be punished, except in the most extraordinary circumstances.

This may not be the only correct view of freedom of speech. But it is a uniquely judicial view; it reflects the long tradition of the common law in a practical way. The question Holmes asked was not whether a particular form of speech should be permitted, but whether a particular person should be punished for speaking; and that is what made all the difference.

---

general rule was that legislative categories necessarily created some disproportion of costs and benefits in particular cases, but that these were acceptable so long as the disproportion was not too great. The parallel to free speech cases seems clear—the government may set up legislative categories to regulate speech, so long as the limitation on rights in particular cases is not too severe, and bears some relation to the defendant's merits.

[347] This is Hans Linde's criticism of clear and present danger, see Linde, "*Clear and Present Danger*" Reexamined: Dissonance in the Brandenburg Concerto, 22 Stan L Rev 1163, 1175 (1970).

APPENDIX: BALTZER V UNITED STATES
             (HOLMES J., DISSENTING)

SUPREME COURT OF THE UNITED STATES.

No. 320.—OCTOBER TERM, 1918.

Emanuel Baltzer, Gottfried Baltzer,
   Fritrich Leneschmidt, *et al.*,
   Plaintiffs in Error,
           vs.
   The United States of America.

In Error to the District
Court of the United
States for the District
of South Dakota.

[   ]
Mr. Justice HOLMES dissenting.

The only evidence against the plaintiffs in error is that the petition set forth in the indictment was signed and sent by them to the Governor of the State, and to two other officials probably supposed to have power. It was not circulated publicly. The signing and sending of it is taken to amount to wilfully obstructing the recruitment and enlistment service of the United States. Uniting to sign and send it is supposed to amount to a conspiracy to do the same thing and also to a conspiracy to prevent the Governor by intimidation from discharging his duties as an officer of the United States in determining the quota of men to be furnished for the draft by the local board. I can see none of these things in the document. It assumes that the draft is to take place and complains that volunteers have been counted with the result that counties have been exempted. It demands that the Governor should stand for a referendum on the draft and advocates the notion that no more expense should be incurred for the war than could be paid for in cash and that war debts should be repudiated. It demands an answer and action or resignation on penalty of defeat at the polls of himself and "your little nation J. P. Morgan." The later phrase was explained by the writer to mean J. P. Morgan's class, as I think it obviously does without explanation. The class is supposed to stand behind the Governor and to be destined to defeat with him if he does not do as he is asked.

It seems to me that this petition to an official by ignorant persons who suppose him to possess power of revision and change that he does not, and demand of him as the price of votes, of course assumed to be sufficient to turn the next election, that he make these changes, was nothing in the world but the foolish exercise of a right. I cannot see how asking a change in the mode of administering the draft so as to make it accord with what is supposed to be required by law can be said to obstruct it. I cannot see how combining to do it is conspiracy to do anything that citizens have not a perfect right to do. It is apparent on the face of the paper that it assumes the power to be in the person addressed. I should have supposed that an article in a newspaper advocating these same things would have left untouched the sensibilities even of those most afraid of free speech. As to the repudiation of the war debt that obviously was a statement of policy not something contemplated as happening forthwith by the fiat of the Governor. From beginning to end the changes advocated are changes by law, not in resistance to it, the only threat being that which every citizen may utter, that if his wishes are not followed his vote will be lost.

The petition purported to come from members of the Socialist party all bearing German names. But those facts were not of themselves evidence of an attempt to obstruct. On the other hand they gave notice of probable bias on the part of the writers that would be likely to be appreciated by the world at large. I do not see that the case can be strengthened by argument if the statement of the facts does not convince by itself.

Real obstructions of the law, giving real aid and comfort to the enemy, I should have been glad to see punished more summarily and severely than they sometimes were. But I think that our intention to put out all our powers in aid of success in war should not hurry us into intolerance of opinions and speech that could not be imagined to do harm, although opposed to our own. It is better for those who have unquestioned and almost unlimited power in their hands to err on the side of freedom. We have enjoyed so much freedom for so long that perhaps we are in danger of forgetting that the bill of rights which cost so much blood to establish still is worth fighting for, and that no tittle of it should be abridged. I agree that freedom of speech is not abridged unconstitutionally in those cases of subsequent punishment with which this court has had to deal from time to time. But the emergency would have to be very great before I could be persuaded that an appeal for political action through legal channels, addressed to those supposed to have power to take such action was an act that the Constitution did not protect as well after as before.